W9-ABI-901

SAS® Programming I: Essentials

Course Notes

http://support.sas.com/onlinedoc/913/docMainpage.jsp

SAS® Programming I: Essentials Course Notes was developed by Michelle Buchecker, Sarah Calhoun, and Larry Stewart. Additional contributions were made by Randall Cates, Lise Cragen, Ted Durie, Susan Farmer, Natalie Murray, Kathy Passarella, and Andy Ravenna. Editing and production support was provided by the Curriculum Development and Support Department.

SAS and all other SAS Institute Inc. product or service names are registered trademarks or trademarks of SAS Institute Inc. in the USA and other countries. ® indicates USA registration. Other brand and product names are trademarks of their respective companies.

SAS® Programming I: Essentials Course Notes

Copyright © 2007 SAS Institute Inc. Cary, NC, USA. All rights reserved. Printed in the United States of America. No part of this publication may be reproduced, stored in a retrieval system, or transmitted, in any form or by any means, electronic, mechanical, photocopying, or otherwise, without the prior written permission of the publisher, SAS Institute Inc.

Book code E70306, course code PROG1, prepared date 18Apr2007.   PROG1_006

ISBN 978-1-59994-460-9

Table of Contents

Course Description

This foundation course focuses on the following key areas: reading raw data files and SAS data sets; investigating and summarizing data by generating frequency tables and descriptive statistics; creating SAS variables and recoding data values; subsetting data; combining multiple SAS files; creating listing, summary, HTML, and graph reports. If you do not plan to write SAS programs and prefer a menu-driven, point-and-click approach, you should consider taking the *Querying and Reporting Using SAS® Enterprise Guide®* course.

To learn more...

A full curriculum of general and statistical instructor-based training is available at any of the Institute's training facilities. Institute instructors can also provide on-site training.

For information on other courses in the curriculum, contact the SAS Education Division at 1-800-333-7660, or send e-mail to training@sas.com. You can also find this information on the Web at support.sas.com/training/ as well as in the Training Course Catalog.

For a list of other SAS books that relate to the topics covered in this Course Notes, USA customers can contact our SAS Publishing Department at 1-800-727-3228 or send e-mail to sasbook@sas.com. Customers outside the USA, please contact your local SAS office.

Also, see the Publications Catalog on the Web at support.sas.com/pubs for a complete list of books and a convenient order form.

Prerequisites

Before attending this course, you should have completed the *Introduction to Programming Concepts Using SAS® Software* course or have at least six months of programming experience. Specifically, you should be able to

- understand file structures and system commands on your operating systems

- write system commands to create and access system files

- understand programming logic.

If you do not feel comfortable with the prerequisites or are new to programming and think that the pace of this course might be too demanding, you can take the *Introduction to Programming Concepts Using SAS® Software* course before attending this course. *Introduction to Programming Concepts Using SAS® Software* is designed to introduce you to computer programming and presents a portion of the *SAS® Programming I: Essentials* material at a slower pace.

Chapter 1   Introduction

1.1   An Overview of the SAS System

Objectives
- Describe the structure and design of the SAS System.
- Outline the course scenario.

2

Components of the SAS System

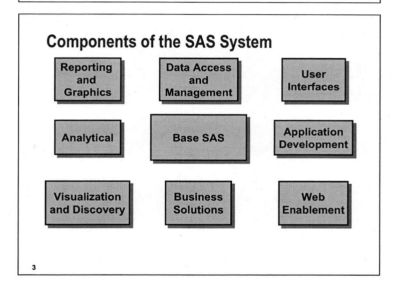

3

Data-Driven Tasks

The functionality of SAS is built around the four
data-driven tasks common to virtually any application:

- data access
- data management
- data analysis
- data presentation

4

---

data access   addresses the data required by the application.

data management   shapes data into a form required by the application.

data analysis   summarizes, reduces, or otherwise transforms raw data into meaningful
                       and useful information.

data presentation   communicates information in ways that clearly demonstrate its significance.

Turning Data into Information

The process of delivering meaningful information
is typically distributed as follows:

- 80% data-related
  - access
  - scrub
  - transform
  - manage
  - store and retrieve
- 20% analysis

5

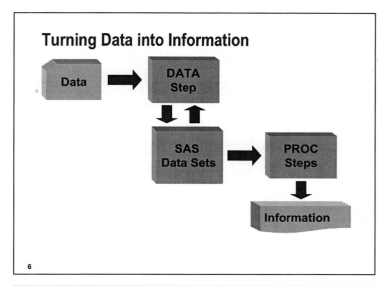

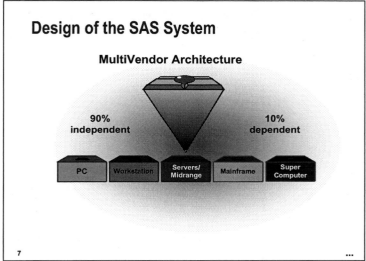

The term MultiVendor Architecture is used to reflect the layered structure of the SAS System. Much of the functionality of the SAS System is contained in a portable component, while the host component provides the required interfaces to the operating system and computer hardware. This enables you to run the same application in all your computing environments and take advantage of cooperative processing.

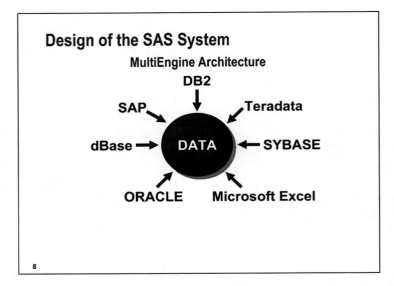

In order to access databases such as ORACLE, the SAS/ACCESS product for your given Database Management System (DBMS) must be licensed in addition to Base SAS software.

Course Scenario

In this course, you work with business data from International Airlines (IA). The various kinds of data that IA maintains are listed below:

- flight data
- passenger data
- cargo data
- employee data
- revenue data

Course Scenario

The following are some tasks that you will perform:

- importing data
- creating a list of employees
- producing a frequency table of job codes
- summarizing data
- creating a report of salary information

10

Chapter 2   Getting Started with SAS

2.1 Introduction to SAS Programs

Objectives

- List the components of a SAS program.
- State the modes in which you can run a SAS program.

3

SAS Programs

A *SAS program* is a sequence of steps that the user submits for execution.

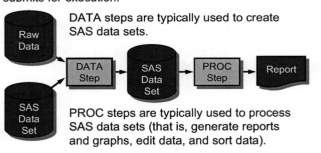

DATA steps are typically used to create SAS data sets.

PROC steps are typically used to process SAS data sets (that is, generate reports and graphs, edit data, and sort data).

4

SAS Programs

```
data work.staff;
    infile 'raw-data-file';
    input LastName $ 1-20 FirstName $ 21-30
          JobTitle $ 36-43 Salary 54-59;
run;

proc print data=work.staff;
run;

proc means data=work.staff;
    class JobTitle;
    var Salary;
run;
```

DATA Step

PROC Steps

5

Examples of raw data filenames:

z/OS[1] (OS/390)	userid.prog1.rawdata(emplist)
Windows	c:\workshop\winsas\prog1\emplist.dat
UNIX	/users/userid/emplist.dat

The DATA step creates a temporary SAS data set named **work.staff** by reading the four variables described in the INPUT statement from the raw data file.

The PROC PRINT step creates a listing report of the **work.staff** data set.

The PROC MEANS step creates a report with summary statistics for the variable **Salary** for each value of **JobTitle**.

---

[1] Any reference to z/OS applies to OS/390, unless otherwise noted.

Step Boundaries

SAS steps begin with either of the following:

- DATA statement
- PROC statement

SAS detects the end of a step when it encounters one of the following:

- a RUN statement (for most steps)
- a QUIT statement (for some procedures)
- the beginning of another step (DATA statement or PROC statement)

6

🖉　　A SAS program executed in batch or noninteractive mode can contain RUN statements, but does not require any RUN statements to execute successfully because the entire program is executed by default. The presence of the RUN statement depends on the programmer's preference.

Step Boundaries

```
data work.staff;
    infile 'raw-data-file';
    input LastName $ 1-20 FirstName $ 21-30
          JobTitle $ 36-43 Salary 54-59;
run;

proc print data=work.staff;

proc means data=work.staff;
    class JobTitle;
    var Salary;
run;
```

7

Examples of raw data filenames:

z/OS (OS/390)	userid.prog1.rawdata(emplist)
Windows	c:\workshop\winsas\prog1\emplist.dat
UNIX	/users/userid/emplist.dat

Running a SAS Program

You can invoke SAS in the following ways:

- interactive windowing mode (SAS windowing environment)
- interactive menu-driven mode (SAS Enterprise Guide, SAS/ASSIST, SAS/AF, or SAS/EIS software)
- batch mode
- noninteractive mode

8

SAS Windowing Environment

Interactive windows enable you to interface with SAS.

9

z/OS (OS/390) Batch Execution

Place the JCL appropriate for your location before your SAS statements.

```
//jobname JOB accounting info,name ...
// EXEC SAS
//SYSIN DD *
data work.staff;
   infile 'raw-data-file';
   input LastName $ 1-20 FirstName $ 21-30
         JobTitle $ 36-43 Salary 54-59;
run;

proc print data=work.staff;
run;

proc means data=work.staff;
   class JobTitle;
   var Salary;
run;
```

10

Noninteractive Execution (Optional)

To execute a SAS program in noninteractive mode,
do the following:

- Use an editor to store the program in a file.
  (Directory-based users should use a filetype
  or extension of SAS.)
- Identify the file when you invoke SAS.

Directory-based:

> **SAS** *filename*

z/OS (OS/390):

> **SAS INPUT**(*filename*)

11

The command for invoking SAS at your site might be different from the default shown
above. Ask your SAS administrator for the command to invoke SAS at your site.

2.2 Running SAS Programs

Objectives
- Invoke the SAS System and include a SAS program into your session.
- Submit a program and browse the results.
- Navigate the SAS windowing environment.

13

Submitting a SAS Program

When you execute a SAS program, the output generated by SAS is divided into two major parts:

SAS log   contains information about the processing of the SAS program, including any warning and error messages.

SAS output   contains reports generated by SAS procedures and DATA steps.

14

SAS Log

```
1     data work.staff;
2         infile 'raw-data-file';
3         input LastName $ 1-20 FirstName $ 21-30
4               JobTitle $ 36-43 Salary 54-59;
5     run;
NOTE: The infile 'raw-data-file' is:
      File Name= 'raw-data-file',
      RECFM=V,LRECL=256
NOTE: 18 records were read from the infile 'raw-data-file'.
      The minimum record length was 59.
      The maximum record length was 59.
NOTE: The data set WORK.STAFF has 18 observations and 4 variables.

6     proc print data=work.staff;
7     run;
NOTE: There were 18 observations read from the dataset WORK.STAFF.

8     proc means data=work.staff;
9         class JobTitle;
10        var Salary;
11    run;
NOTE: There were 18 observations read from the dataset WORK.STAFF.
```

15

Examples of raw data filenames:

z/OS (OS/390)	userid.prog1.rawdata(emplist)
Windows	c:\workshop\winsas\prog1\emplist.dat
UNIX	/users/userid/emplist.dat

PROC PRINT Output

```
                          The SAS System
                       First
        Obs   LastName   Name       JobTitle   Salary
         1    TORRES     JAN        Pilot       50000
         2    LANGKAMM   SARAH      Mechanic    80000
         3    SMITH      MICHAEL    Mechanic    40000
         4    LEISTNER   COLIN      Mechanic    36000
         5    WADE       KIRSTEN    Pilot       85000
         6    TOMAS      HARALD     Pilot      105000
         7    WAUGH      TIM        Pilot       70000
         8    LEHMANN    DAGMAR     Mechanic    64000
         9    TRETTHAHN  MICHAEL    Pilot      100000
        10    TIETZ      OTTO       Pilot       45000
        11    O'DONOGHUE ART        Mechanic    52000
        12    WALKER     THOMAS     Pilot       95000
        13    NOROVIITA  JOACHIM    Mechanic    78000
        14    OESTERBERG ANJA       Mechanic    80000
        15    LAUFFER    CRAIG      Mechanic    40000
        16    TORR       JUGDISH    Pilot       45000
        17    WAGSCHAL   NADJA      Pilot       77500
        18    TOERMOEN   JOCHEN     Pilot       65000
```

16

PROC MEANS Output

```
                    The SAS System
                  The MEANS Procedure
               Analysis Variable : Salary

              N
JobTitle     Obs    N      Mean      Std Dev     Minimum

Mechanic      8     8    58750.00    19151.65    36000.00

Pilot        10    10    73750.00    22523.14    45000.00


               Analysis Variable : Salary
                         N
           JobTitle     Obs      Maximum

           Mechanic      8      80000.00

           Pilot        10     105000.00
```

17

Running a SAS Program – Windows

c02s2d1.sas

- Start a SAS session.
- Include and submit a program.
- Browse the results.

Starting a SAS Session

1. Double-click the SAS icon to start your SAS session.

   🖉 The method that you use to invoke SAS varies by your operating environment and any customizations in effect at your site.

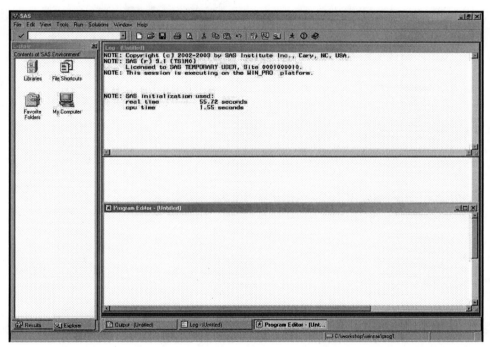

All operating environments support the Program Editor. The Microsoft Windows operating environment supports an additional editor, the Enhanced Editor. Because the Program Editor is available on all operating environments, it is used throughout class.

   🖉 Microsoft Windows users close the Enhanced Editor by selecting ☒. To open the Program Editor, select **View** ⇨ **Program Editor**.

   Refer to the end of this chapter for a discussion about the Enhanced Editor.

   The Results window and the Explorer window have slightly different functionalities in different operating environments. Refer to the end of this chapter for a discussion about these windows.

Including and Submitting a SAS Program

1. To open a SAS program into your SAS session, select **File** ⇨ **Open Program** or click  and then select the file that you want to include. To open a program, your Program Editor must be active.

    You can also issue the INCLUDE command to open (include) a program into your SAS session.

    a. With the Program Editor active, on the command bar type **include** and the name of the file containing the program.

    b. Press ENTER.

    ```
    SAS
    File  Edit  View  Tools  Run  Solutions  Window  Help
    ✓  include 'c02s2d1.sas'
    ```

    The program is included in the Program Editor window.

    ```
    Program Editor - c02s2d1.sas
    data work.staff;
        infile 'emplist.dat';
        input LastName $ 1-20 FirstName $ 21-30
              JobTitle $ 36-43 Salary 54-59;
    run;

    proc print data=work.staff;
    run;

    proc means data=work.staff;
        class Jobtitle;
        var Salary;
    run;
    ```

    You can use the Program Editor window to do the following:
    -   access and edit existing SAS programs
    -   write new SAS programs
    -   submit SAS programs
    -   save SAS programs to a file

    Within the Program Editor, the syntax in your program is color-coded to show these items:
    -   step boundaries
    -   keywords
    -   variable and data set names

2. To submit the program for execution, issue the SUBMIT command or click 🏃 or select **Run** ⇨ **Submit**. The output from the program is displayed in the Output window.

Examining Your Program Results

The Output window

- is one of the primary windows and is open by default.
- becomes the active window each time that it receives output.
- automatically accumulates output in the order in which it is generated. You can issue the CLEAR command or select **Edit** ⇨ **Clear All** to clear the contents of the window, or you can click on the NEW icon 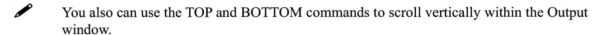 .

To scroll horizontally within the Output window, use the horizontal scrollbar or issue the RIGHT and LEFT commands.

In the Windows environment, the Output window displays the last page of output generated by the program submitted.

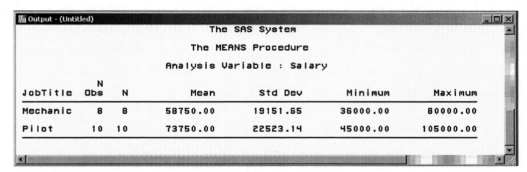

To scroll vertically within the Output window, use the vertical scrollbar or issue the FORWARD and BACKWARD commands or use the PAGE UP or PAGE DOWN keys on the keyboard.

✎   You also can use the TOP and BOTTOM commands to scroll vertically within the Output window.

1.   Scroll to the top to view the output from the PRINT procedure.

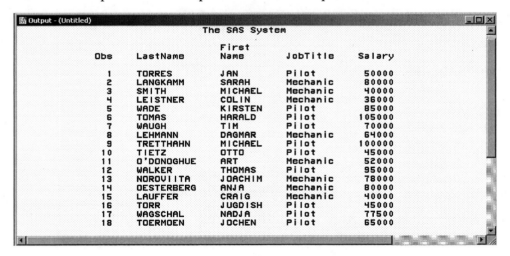

2. To open the Log window and browse the messages that the program generated, issue the LOG command or select **Window** ⇨ **Log** or click on the log.

    The Log window
    - is one of the primary windows and is open by default
    - acts as an audit trail of your SAS session; messages are written to the log in the order in which they are generated by the program.

3. To clear the contents of the window, issue the CLEAR command or select **Edit** ⇨ **Clear All**, or you

    can click on the NEW icon ⬜ .

    Partial Log

```
 Log - (Untitled)                                                      _ □ ×
1     data work.staff;
2         infile 'emplist.dat';
3         input LastName $ 1-20 FirstName $ 21-30
4             JobTitle $ 36-43 Salary 54-59;
5     run;

NOTE: The infile 'emplist.dat' is:
      File Name=C:\workshop\winsas\prog1\emplist.dat,
      RECFM=V,LRECL=256

NOTE: 18 records were read from the infile 'emplist.dat'.
      The minimum record length was 59.
      The maximum record length was 59.
NOTE: The data set WORK.STAFF has 18 observations and 4 variables.
NOTE: DATA statement used:
      real time            0.03 seconds
      cpu time             0.03 seconds


6
7     proc print data=work.staff;
8     run;

NOTE: There were 18 observations read from the data set WORK.STAFF.
NOTE: PROCEDURE PRINT used:
      real time            0.02 seconds
      cpu time             0.02 seconds


9
10    proc means data=work.staff;
11        class Jobtitle;
12        var Salary;
13    run;

NOTE: There were 18 observations read from the data set WORK.STAFF.
NOTE: PROCEDURE MEANS used:
      real time            0.02 seconds
```

The Log window contains the programming statements that are submitted, as well as notes about the following:
- any files that were read
- the records that were read
- the program execution and results

In this example, the Log window contains no warning or error messages. If the program contains errors, relevant warning and error messages are also written to the SAS log.

4. Issue the END command or select **Window** ⇨ **Program Editor** to return to the Program Editor window.

Running a SAS Program – UNIX (Optional)

c02s2d1.sas

- Start a SAS session.
- Include and submit a program.
- Browse the results.

Starting a SAS Session

1. In your UNIX session, type the appropriate command to start a SAS session.

    ✐   The method that you use to invoke SAS varies by your operating environment and any
          customizations in effect at your site.

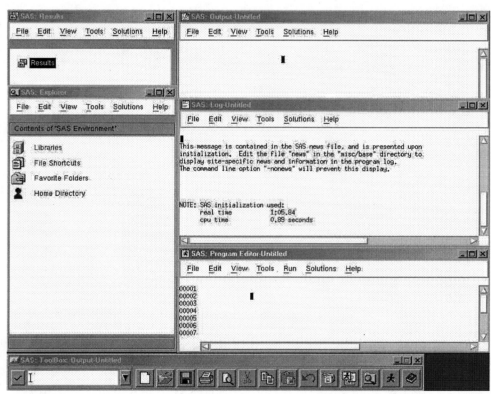

The Results window and the Explorer window have slightly different functionalities in different
operating environments. Refer to the end of this chapter for a discussion about these windows.

Including and Submitting a SAS Program

1. To open (include) a SAS program into your SAS session, select **File** ⇨ **Open** or click  and then select the file that you want to include.

    You can also issue the INCLUDE command to open (include) a SAS program.

    a. Type **include** and the name of the file containing your program on the command bar.

    b. Press ENTER.

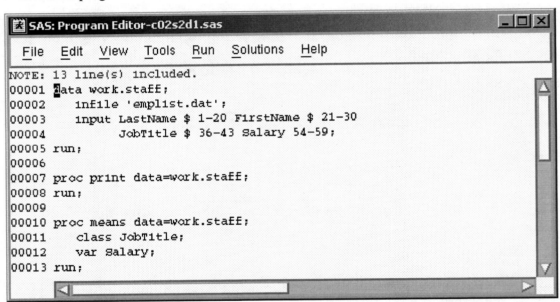

    You can use the Program Editor window to do the following:

    *   access and edit existing SAS programs

    *   write new SAS programs

    *   submit SAS programs

    *   save SAS programs to a file

> ✏️ The program contains three steps: a DATA step and two PROC steps.

2. To submit your program for execution, click 🏃 or select **Run** ⇨ **Submit** or issue the SUBMIT command. The output from your program is displayed in the Output window.

Examining Your Program Results

The Output window
- is one of the primary windows and is open by default.
- becomes the active window each time it receives output.
- automatically accumulates output in the order in which it is generated. To clear the contents of the window, issue the CLEAR command or select **Edit** ⇨ **Clear All** or click [ ].

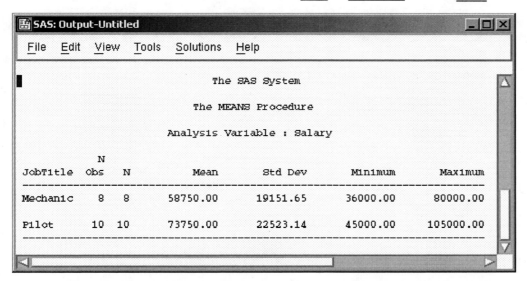

To scroll horizontally within the Output window, use the horizontal scrollbar or issue the RIGHT and LEFT commands.

To scroll vertically within the Output window, use the vertical scrollbar or issue the FORWARD and BACKWARD commands.

     You also can use the TOP and BOTTOM commands to scroll vertically within the Output window.

1. Scroll to the top to view the output from the PRINT procedure.

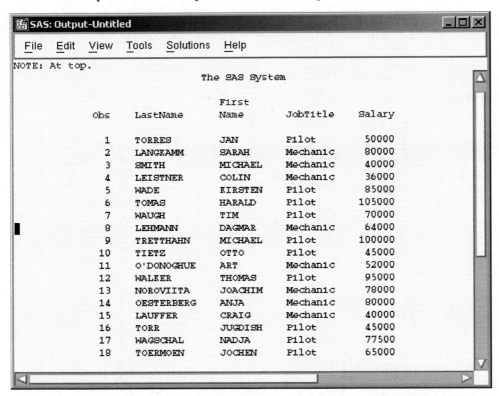

2. To open the Log window and browse the messages that the program generated, issue the LOG
    command or select **View** ⇨ **Log**.

    The Log window
    - is one of the primary windows and is open by default
    - acts as a record of your SAS session; messages are written to the log in the order in which they are
      generated by the program.

3. To clear the contents of the window, issue the CLEAR command or select **Edit** ⇨ **Clear All** or click
    [icon].

Partial Log

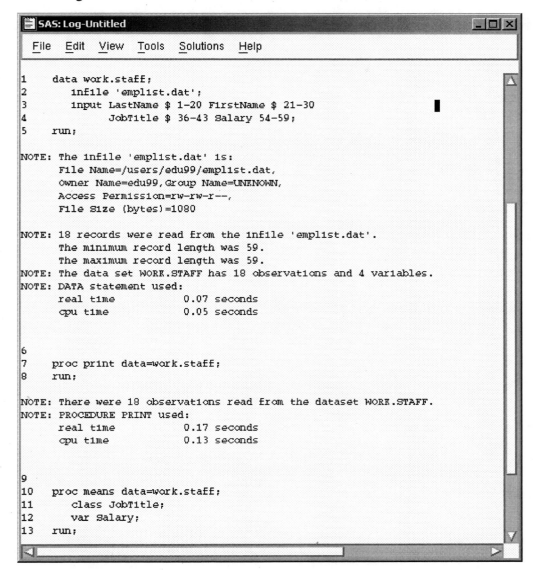

The Log window contains the programming statements that were most recently submitted, as well as notes about the following:

- any files that were read
- the records that were read
- the program execution and results

In this example, the Log window contains no warning or error messages. If your program contains errors, relevant warning and error messages are also written to the SAS log.

4. Issue the END command or select **View** ⇨ **Program Editor** to return to the Program Editor window.

Running a SAS Program – z/OS (OS/390) (Optional)

userid.prog1.sascode(c02s2d1)

- Start a SAS session.
- Include and submit a program.
- Browse the results.

Starting a SAS Session

Type the appropriate command to start your SAS session.

✎   The method that you use to invoke SAS varies by your operating environment and any customizations in effect at your site.

```
┌Log─────────────────────────────────────────────────────────────────────┐
│ Command ===>                                                             │
│                                                                          │
│ NOTE: This session is executing on the z/OS    V01R04M00 platform.       │
│                                                                          │
│ NOTE: Running on IBM Model 2066 Serial Number 023A7A,                    │
│                  IBM Model 2066 Serial Number 123A7A.                    │
│                                                                          │
│                                                                          │
│   Welcome to the SAS Information Delivery System,                        │
│                                                                          │
│         999       000     Release 9.0!  Installed 12Feb2003.             │
│         9  9     0   0                                                   │
│         9  9     0   0     Problems with this version?  Report in DEFECT  │
│          9999     0   0     as Release 9, level TSOM0, platform OS/390    │
│   v   v   99     0   0                                                   │
│    v v    99   0  0  0     Questions or problems?                        │
│     v     99     0   000   Contact Carol Angeli x15088 or Ron Burt x16324 │
└──────────────────────────────────────────────────────────────────────────┘
┌Program Editor────────────────────────────────────────────────────────────┐
│ Command ===> █                                                            │
│                                                                          │
│ 00001                                                                    │
│ 00002                                                                    │
│ 00003                                                                    │
│ 00004                                                                    │
│ 00005                                                                    │
│ 00006                                                                    │
│ 00007                                                                    │
│ 00008                                                                    │
│ 00009                                                                    │
└──────────────────────────────────────────────────────────────────────────┘
```

Including and Submitting a SAS Program

1. To include (copy) a SAS program into your SAS session, issue the INCLUDE command.

   a. Type **include** and the name of the file containing your program on the command line of the Program Editor.

   b. Press ENTER.

```
┌Program Editor──────────────────────────────────────────────────────────────
  Command ===> include '.prog1.sascode(c02s2d1)'█

  00001
  00002
  00003
  00004
  00005
  00006
  00007
  00008
  00009
```

The program is included in the Program Editor window.

You can use the Program Editor window to do the following:

- access and edit existing SAS programs
- write new SAS programs
- submit SAS programs
- save programming statements in a file

The program contains three steps: a DATA step and two PROC steps.

Issue the SUBMIT command to execute your program.

```
┌Program Editor──────────────────────────────────────────────────────────────
  Command ===> submit█

  00001 data work.staff;
  00002    infile '.prog1.rawdata(emplist)';
  00003    input LastName $ 1-20 FirstName $ 21-30
  00004          JobTitle $ 36-43 Salary 54-59;
  00005 run;
  00006
  00007 proc print data=work.staff;
  00008 run;
  00009
  00010 proc means data=work.staff;
  00011    class JobTitle;
  00012    var Salary;
  00013 run;
```

2. The first page of the output from your program is displayed in the Output window.

```
┌─Output─────────────────────────────────────────────PROC PRINT suspended─┐
│ Command ===> █                                                           │
│ NOTE: Procedure PRINT created 1 page(s) of output.                       │
│                         The SAS System                                   │
│                                                                          │
│                          First                                           │
│            Obs    LastName     Name       JobTitle     Salary            │
│                                                                          │
│             1     TORRES       JAN        Pilot         50000            │
│             2     LANGKAMM     SARAH      Mechanic      80000            │
│             3     SMITH        MICHAEL    Mechanic      40000            │
│             4     LEISTNER     COLIN      Mechanic      36000            │
│             5     WADE         KIRSTEN    Pilot         85000            │
│             6     TOMAS        HARALD     Pilot        105000            │
│             7     WAUGH        TIM        Pilot         70000            │
│             8     LEHMANN      DAGMAR     Mechanic      64000            │
│             9     TRETTHAHN    MICHAEL    Pilot        100000            │
│            10     TIETZ        OTTO       Pilot         45000            │
│            11     O'DONOGHUE   ART        Mechanic      52000            │
│            12     WALKER       THOMAS     Pilot         95000            │
│            13     NOROVIITA    JOACHIM    Mechanic      78000            │
│            14     OESTERBERG   ANJA       Mechanic      80000            │
│            15     LAUFFER      CRAIG      Mechanic      40000            │
│            16     TORR         JUGDISH    Pilot         45000            │
│            17     WAGSCHAL     NADJA      Pilot         77500            │
│            18     TOERMOEN     JOCHEN     Pilot         65000            │
│                                                                          │
│                                                                          │
│                                                                          │
└──────────────────────────────────────────────────────────────────────────┘
```

Examining Your Program Results

The Output window

- is one of the primary windows and is open by default.
- becomes the active window each time that it receives output.
- automatically accumulates output in the order in which it is generated. You can issue the CLEAR command or select **Edit** ⇨ **Clear All** to clear the contents of the window.

To scroll horizontally within the Output window, issue the RIGHT and LEFT commands.

To scroll vertically within the Output window, issue the FORWARD and BACKWARD commands.

    You also can use the TOP and BOTTOM commands to scroll vertically within the Output window.

1. Issue the END command. If the PRINT procedure produces more than one page of output, you
    are taken to the last page of output. If the PRINT procedure produces only one page of output,
    the END command enables the MEANS procedure to execute and produce its output.

```
┌Output────────────────────────────────────────────────────────────────────────┐
│ Command ===> █                                                                 │
│ NOTE: Procedure MEANS created 1 page(s) of output.                             │
│                            The SAS System                                      │
│                                                                                │
│                          The MEANS Procedure                                   │
│                                                                                │
│                     Analysis Variable : Salary                                 │
│                                                                                │
│                 N                                                              │
│ JobTitle  Obs   N         Mean        Std Dev        Minimum        Maximum    │
│ --------------------------------------------------------------------------     │
│ Mechanic    8   8      58750.00      19151.65       36000.00       80000.00    │
│                                                                                │
│ Pilot      10  10      73750.00      22523.14       45000.00      105000.00    │
│ --------------------------------------------------------------------------     │
│                                                                                │
│                                                                                │
│                                                                                │
│                                                                                │
│                                                                                │
│                                                                                │
│                                                                                │
│                                                                                │
│                                                                                │
│                                                                                │
│                                                                                │
└────────────────────────────────────────────────────────────────────────────────┘
```

✎   You can issue an AUTOSCROLL 0 command on the command line of the Output window to
    have all of your SAS output from one submission placed in the Output window at one time.
    This eliminates the need to issue an END command to run each step separately.

    The AUTOSCROLL command is in effect for the duration of your SAS session. If you want
    this every time that you invoke SAS, you can save this setting by typing **autoscroll 0;**
    wsave on the command line of the Output window.

2. Issue the END command to return to the Program Editor window.

    After the program executes, you can view messages in the Log window.

    Partial Log

```
┌Log─────────────────────────────────────────────────────────────────┐
│ Command ===> █                                                       │
│                                                                      │
│  1    data work.staff;                                               │
│  2        infile '.prog1.rawdata(emplist)';                          │
│  3        input LastName $ 1-20 FirstName $ 21-30                     │
│  4              JobTitle $ 36-43 Salary 54-59;                        │
│  5    run;                                                           │
│                                                                      │
│  NOTE: The infile '.prog1.rawdata(emplist)' is:                      │
│        Dsname=EDU403.PROG1.RAWDATA(EMPLIST),                         │
│        Unit=3380,Volume=PUB802,Disp=SHR,Blksize=23440,               │
│        Lrecl=80,Recfm=FB                                             │
│                                                                      │
│  NOTE: 18 records were read from the infile '.prog1.rawdata(emplist)'.│
│  NOTE: The data set WORK.STAFF has 18 observations and 4 variables.  │
│  NOTE: The DATA statement used 0.06 CPU seconds and 3158K.           │
│                                                                      │
│  6                                                                   │
│  7    proc print data=work.staff;                                    │
│  8    run;                                                           │
│                                                                      │
│  NOTE: There were 18 observations read from the data set WORK.STAFF. │
│  NOTE: The PROCEDURE PRINT used 0.05 CPU seconds and 3368K.          │
│                                                                      │
│  9                                                                   │
│  10   proc means data=work.staff;                                    │
│  11       class JobTitle;                                            │
│  12       var Salary;                                                │
│  13   run;                                                           │
└──────────────────────────────────────────────────────────────────────┘
```

The Log window

- is one of the primary windows and is open by default.
- acts as a record of your SAS session; messages are written to the log in the order in which they are generated by the program. You can issue the CLEAR command to clear the contents of the window.

The Log window contains the programming statements that were recently submitted, as well as notes about the following:

- any files that were read
- the records that were read
- the program execution and results

In this example, the Log window contains no warning or error messages. If your program contains errors, relevant warning and error messages are also written to the SAS log.

Issue the END command to return to the Program Editor window.

Running a SAS Program – z/OS (OS/390) Batch (Optional)

userid.prog1.sascode(batch)

- Submit a program.
- Browse the results.

Submitting a SAS Program

1. To submit a SAS program, perform the following tasks:

   a. Use an editor to create a file containing the necessary JCL and your SAS program.

   b. Issue a SUBMIT command or perform the steps necessary to submit your program for execution.

```
EDIT         EDU403.PROG1.SASCODE(BATCH) - 01.00        Columns 00001 00072
Command ===> submit█                                    Scroll ===> CSR
****** *************************** Top of Data ****************************
000001 //SASCLASS JOB (,STUDENT),'CARY',TIME=(,5),MSGCLASS=H
000002 /*JOBPARM FETCH
000003 // EXEC SAS9
000004 //SYSIN DD *
000005 data work.staff;
000006    infile '.prog1.rawdata(emplist)';
000007    input LastName $ 1-20 FirstName $ 21-30
000008          JobTitle $ 36-43 Salary 54-59;
000009 run;
000010
000011 proc print data=work.staff;
000012 run;
000013
000014 proc means data=work.staff;
000015    class Jobtitle;
000016    var Salary;
000017 run;
****** *************************** Bottom of Data ****************************
```

The program contains three steps: a DATA step and two PROC steps.

Examining Your Program Results

1. Use a utility (for example, IOF) to view the results of your batch job. You can view the output of your program by selecting **SASLIST**.

```
------------------------------ IOF Job Summary ------------------------------
COMMAND ===>                                             SCROLL ===> SCREEN
--JOBNAME--JOBID----STATUS---RAN/RECEIVED------DAY-------DEST----------------
  SASCLASS J028513  OUTPUT   12:28  12/02/2003 TODAY     KHPLJ2
--RC--PGM---------STEP-----PRSTEP---PROC-----COMMENTS------------------------
   0  SAS          SAS               SAS9
--------DDNAME---STEP-----STAT-ACT-C-GRP-D-SIZE-U-DEST--------------UCS-------
  _   1 LOG       *        HELD      H  1 H    17 L KHPLJ2
  _   2 JCL       *        HELD      H  1 H    50 L KHPLJ2
  _   3 MESSAGES  *        HELD      H  1 H    90 L KHPLJ2
  _   4 SASLOG    SAS      HELD      H  1 H    83 L KHPLJ2
  _   5 SASCLOG   SAS      DONE      H
  s   6 SASLIST   SAS      HELD SEL  H  1 H    36 L KHPLJ2
  _   7 SYSUDUMP  SAS      DONE      H
```

2. The first page of output is displayed.

```
BROWSE - SASLIST          SAS       - Page  1    Line  1      Cols 18-97
COMMAND ===>                                           SCROLL ===> SCREEN
******************************* Top of Data *******************************
                              The SAS System

                                  First
                  Obs   LastName    Name      JobTitle    Salary

                    1   TORRES      JAN       Pilot        50000
                    2   LANGKAMM    SARAH     Mechanic     80000
                    3   SMITH       MICHAEL   Mechanic     40000
                    4   LEISTNER    COLIN     Mechanic     36000
                    5   WADE        KIRSTEN   Pilot        85000
                    6   TOMAS       HARALD    Pilot       105000
                    7   WAUGH       TIM       Pilot        70000
                    8   LEHMANN     DAGMAR    Mechanic     64000
                    9   TRETTHAHN   MICHAEL   Pilot       100000
                   10   TIETZ       OTTO      Pilot        45000
                   11   O'DONOGHUE  ART       Mechanic     52000
                   12   WALKER      THOMAS    Pilot        95000
                   13   NOROVIITA   JOACHIM   Mechanic     78000
                   14   OESTERBERG  ANJA      Mechanic     80000
                   15   LAUFFER     CRAIG     Mechanic     40000
                   16   TORR        JUGDISH   Pilot        45000
                   17   WAGSCHAL    NADJA     Pilot        77500
                   18   TOERMOEN    JOCHEN    Pilot        65000
```

3. Because both the PRINT procedure and the MEANS procedure created output, the SASLIST window
    contains several reports. Use scrolling commands to see the other pages of output.

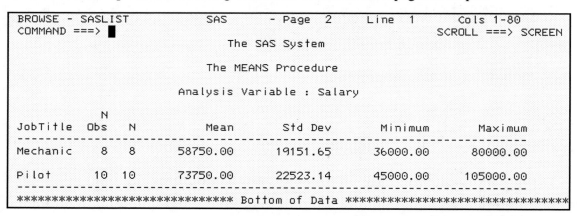

```
BROWSE - SASLIST          SAS        - Page  2    Line  1        Cols 1-80
COMMAND ===> █                                          SCROLL ===> SCREEN
                              The SAS System

                             The MEANS Procedure

                        Analysis Variable : Salary

                N
JobTitle  Obs   N       Mean       Std Dev      Minimum       Maximum
----------------------------------------------------------------------
Mechanic    8   8    58750.00     19151.65     36000.00      80000.00

Pilot      10  10    73750.00     22523.14     45000.00     105000.00
----------------------------------------------------------------------
***************************** Bottom of Data ****************************
```

4. Return to the main job results screen and select **SASLOG** to see a record of your SAS session. Messages are written to the log in the order in which they are generated by the program.

```
------------------------------- IOF Job Summary -----------------------------------
COMMAND ===>                                                    SCROLL ===> SCREEN
--JOBNAME---JOBID--STATUS---RAN/RECEIVED------DAY--------DEST----------------
   SASCLASS J26669  OUTPUT    9:28  7/25/2001 TODAY       SDCMVS
--RC--PGM-------STEP-----PRSTEP---PROC-----COMMENTS-------------------------
    0  SASXALV    SAS                  SAS8
-------DDNAME---STEP-----STAT-ACT-C-GRP-D-SIZE-U--DEST--------------UCS------
  _   1  LOG       *       HELD       Z   1 H   17 L   SDCMVS
  _   2  JCL       *       HELD       Z   1 H   81 L   SDCMVS
  _   3  MESSAGES  *       HELD       Z   1 H  108 L   SDCMVS
  s   4  SASLOG    SAS     HELD       Z   1 H   71 L   SDCMVS
  _   5  SASCLOG   SAS     DONE       Z
  _   6  SASLIST   SAS     HELD SEL   Z   1 H   36 L   SDCMVS
  _   7  SYSUDUMP  SAS     DONE       D
  _   8  SASSNAP   SAS     DONE       D
```

```
BROWSE - SASLOG          SAS      - Page 1    Line  36     Cols 1-80
COMMAND ===> █                                      SCROLL ===> SCREEN
1          data work.staff;
2              infile 'edu403.prog1.rawdata(emplist)';
3              input LastName $ 1-20 FirstName $ 21-30
4                 JobTitle $ 36-43 Salary 54-59;
5          run;

NOTE: The infile 'edu403.prog1.rawdata(emplist)' is:
      Dsname=EDU403.PROG1.RAWDATA(EMPLIST),
      Unit=3380,Volume=PUB802,Disp=SHR,Blksize=23440,
      Lrecl=80,Recfm=FB

NOTE: 18 records were read from the infile 'edu403.prog1.rawdata(emplist)'.
NOTE: The data set WORK.STAFF has 18 observations and 4 variables.
NOTE: The DATA statement used 0.06 CPU seconds and 2537K.

7          proc print data=work.staff;
8          run;

NOTE: There were 18 observations read from the data set WORK.STAFF.
NOTE: The PROCEDURE PRINT printed page 1.
NOTE: The PROCEDURE PRINT used 0.04 CPU seconds and 2619K.

10         proc means data=work.staff;
11             class JobTitle;
12             var Salary;
```

The SASLOG contains the programming statements that were submitted, as well as notes about the following:

- any files that were read
- the records that were read
- the program execution and results

In this example, the SASLOG contains no warning or error messages. If your program contains errors, relevant warning and error messages are also written to the SASLOG.

 **Exercises**

1. **Submitting a Program**

   a. With the Program Editor window active, include a SAS program.

      - Windows and UNIX: Select **File** ⇨ **Open Program** and select the program **c02ex1.sas** or issue the **include 'c02ex1.sas'** command.

      - z/OS (OS/390): Issue the **include '.prog1.sascode(c02ex1)'** command.

   b. Submit the program for execution. Based on the report in the Output window, how many observations and variables are in the **work.airports** data set?   *15 , 3*

   c. Examine the Log window. Based on the log notes, how many observations and variables are in the **work.airports** data set?

   d. Clear the Log and Output windows.

2. **Issuing the KEYS Command (Optional)**

   The KEYS window is

   - a secondary window
   - used to browse or change function key definitions
   - closed by issuing the END command (Windows, UNIX, z/OS) or by clicking on ☒ (Windows, UNIX).

   a. Issue the KEYS command. Browse the contents of the window by scrolling vertically.

   b. Close the KEYS window.

2.3 Mastering Fundamental Concepts

Objectives
- Define the components of a SAS data set.
- Define a SAS variable.
- Identify a missing value and a SAS date value.
- State the naming conventions for SAS data sets and variables.
- Explain SAS syntax rules.
- Investigate a SAS data set using the CONTENTS and PRINT procedures.

21

SAS Data Sets

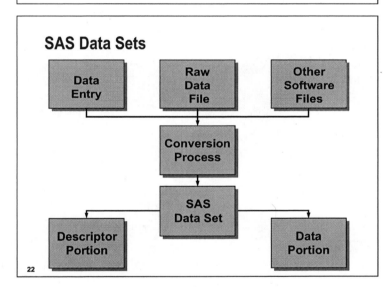

22

Data must be in the form of a SAS data set to be processed by many SAS procedures and some DATA step statements.

A *SAS program* is a file that contains SAS code.

A *SAS data set* is a specially structured file that contains data values.

SAS Data Sets

SAS data sets have a descriptor portion and a data portion.

Descriptor Portion

```
General data set information
* data set name      * data set label
* date/time created  * storage information
* number of observations

Information for each variable
* Name    * Type      * Length  * Position
* Format * Informat  * Label
```

Data Portion

23

Browsing the Descriptor Portion

The *descriptor portion* of a SAS data set contains the following:

- general information about the SAS data set (such as data set name and number of observations)
- variable attributes (name, type, length, position, informat, format, label)

The CONTENTS procedure displays the descriptor portion of a SAS data set.

24

Browsing the Descriptor Portion

General form of the CONTENTS procedure:

```
PROC CONTENTS DATA=SAS-data-set;
RUN;
```

Example:

```
proc contents data=work.staff;
run;
```

c02s3d1

25

Partial PROC CONTENTS Output

```
                        The SAS System

                     The CONTENTS Procedure

Data Set Name: WORK.STAFF              Observations:        18
Member Type:   DATA                    Variables:           4
Engine         V9                      Indexes              0
Created        Monday, December 01,    Observation Length   48
               2003 10:36:59 AM
Last Modified  Monday, December 01,    Deleted Observations 0
               2003 10:36:59 AM
Protection:                            Compressed:          NO
Data Set Type:                         Sorted:              NO
Label:

          Alphabetic List of Variables and Attributes

               #    Variable    Type    Len

               2    FirstName   Char     10
               3    JobTitle    Char      8
               1    LastName    Char     20
               4    Salary      Num       8
```

26

This is a partial view of the default PROC CONTENTS output. PROC CONTENTS output also contains information about the physical location of the file and other data set information.

The descriptor portion contains the metadata of the data set.

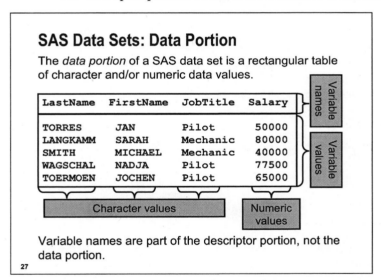

SAS Data Sets: Data Portion

The *data portion* of a SAS data set is a rectangular table of character and/or numeric data values.

LastName	FirstName	JobTitle	Salary
TORRES	JAN	Pilot	50000
LANGKAMM	SARAH	Mechanic	80000
SMITH	MICHAEL	Mechanic	40000
WAGSCHAL	NADJA	Pilot	77500
TOERMOEN	JOCHEN	Pilot	65000

Variable names

Variable values

Character values   Numeric values

Variable names are part of the descriptor portion, not the data portion.

27

The *variables (columns)* in the table correspond to fields of data, and each data column is named.

The *observations (rows)* in the table correspond to records or data lines.

SAS Variable Values

There are two types of variables:

character   contain any value: letters, numbers, special characters, and blanks. Character values are stored with a length of 1 to 32,767 bytes. One byte equals one character.

numeric   stored as floating point numbers in 8 bytes of storage by default. Eight bytes of floating point storage provide space for 16 or 17 significant digits. You are not restricted to 8 digits.

28

In SAS 6 and earlier, character values are stored with a length of 1 to 200 bytes.

SAS Data Set and Variable Names

SAS names have these characteristics:

- can be 32 characters long.
- can be uppercase, lowercase, or mixed-case.
- are not case sensitive.
- must start with a letter or underscore. Subsequent characters can be letters, underscores, or numerals.

29

In SAS 6 and earlier, data set and variable names can only be a maximum of eight characters long. Starting in SAS 8, special characters can be used in data set and variable names if you put the name in quotation marks followed immediately by the letter N.

Example: `class 'Flight#'n;`

In order to use special characters in variable names, the VALIDVARNAME option must be set to ANY. (Example: `options validvarname=any;`)

Valid SAS Names

Select the valid default SAS names.

☐ `data5mon`

☐ `5monthsdata`

☐ `data#5`

☐ `five months data`

☐ `fivemonthsdata`

☐ `FiveMonthsData`

42   ...

SAS Date Values

SAS stores date values as numeric values.

A SAS date value is stored as the number of days between January 1, 1960, and a specific date.

```
←— 01JAN1959 ——— 01JAN1960 ——— 01JAN1961 —→
         │        store      │              │
←——— -365 ——————————— 0 ——————————— 366 ———→
         │       display     │              │
←— 01/01/1959 — 01/01/1960 — 01/01/1961 —→
```

45   ...

Missing Data Values

A value must exist for every variable for each observation. Missing values are valid values.

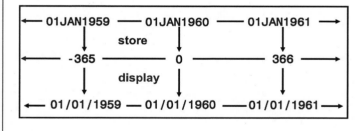

LastName	FirstName	JobTitle	Salary
TORRES	JAN	Pilot	50000
LANGKAMM	SARAH	Mechanic	80000
SMITH	MICHAEL	Mechanic	.
WAGSCHAL	NADJA	Pilot	77500
TOERMOEN	JOCHEN		65000

A character missing value is displayed as a blank.

A numeric missing value is displayed as a period.

46

Browsing the Data Portion

The PRINT procedure displays the data portion
of a SAS data set.

By default, PROC PRINT displays the following:

- all observations
- all variables
- an Obs column on the left side

47

Browsing the Data Portion

General form of the PRINT procedure:

```
PROC PRINT DATA=SAS-data-set;
RUN;
```

Example:

```
proc print data=work.staff;
run;
```

c02s3d1

48

PROC PRINT Output

```
                        The SAS System
                      First
      Obs    LastName  Name       JobTitle    Salary
       1     TORRES     JAN        Pilot        50000
       2     LANGKAMM   SARAH      Mechanic     80000
       3     SMITH      MICHAEL    Mechanic     40000
       4     LEISTNER   COLIN      Mechanic     36000
       5     WADE       KIRSTEN    Pilot        85000
       6     TOMAS      HARALD     Pilot       105000
       7     WAUGH      TIM        Pilot        70000
       8     LEHMANN    DAGMAR     Mechanic     64000
       9     TRETTHAHN  MICHAEL    Pilot       100000
      10     TIETZ      OTTO       Pilot        45000
      11     O'DONOGHUE ART        Mechanic     52000
      12     WALKER     THOMAS     Pilot        95000
      13     NOROVIITA  JOACHIM    Mechanic     78000
      14     OESTERBERG ANJA       Mechanic     80000
      15     LAUFFER    CRAIG      Mechanic     40000
      16     TORR       JUGDISH    Pilot        45000
      17     WAGSCHAL   NADJA      Pilot        77500
      18     TOERMOEN   JOCHEN     Pilot        65000
```

49

SAS Data Set Terminology

SAS documentation and text in the SAS windowing environment use the following terms interchangeably:

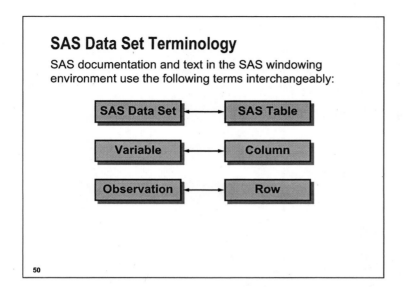

50

SAS Syntax Rules

SAS statements have these characteristics:

- usually begin with an identifying keyword
- always end with a semicolon

```
data work.staff;
   infile 'raw-data-file';
   input LastName $ 1-20 FirstName $ 21-30
         JobTitle $ 36-43 Salary 54-59;
run;

proc print data=work.staff;
run;

proc means data=work.staff;
   class JobTitle;
   var Salary;
run;
```

51

Examples of raw data filenames:

z/OS (OS/390)	*userid*.prog1.rawdata(emplist)
Windows	c:\workshop\winsas\prog1\emplist.dat
UNIX	/users/*userid*/emplist.dat

✎   In most situations, text in quotation marks is case sensitive.

2-36 Chapter 2 Getting Started with SAS

SAS Syntax Rules

- SAS statements are free-format.
- One or more blanks or special characters can be used to separate words.
- They can begin and end in any column.
- A single statement can span multiple lines.
- Several statements can be on the same line.

Unconventional Spacing

```
data work.staff;
infile 'raw-data-file';
input LastName $ 1-20 FirstName $ 21-30
JobTitle $ 36-43 Salary 54-59;
run;
    proc means data=work.staff;
class JobTitle;    var Salary;run;
```

53

SAS Syntax Rules

Good spacing makes the program easier to read.

Conventional Spacing

```
data work.staff;
    infile 'raw-data-file';
    input LastName $ 1-20 FirstName $ 21-30
          JobTitle $ 36-43 Salary 54-59;
run;

proc print data=work.staff;
run;

proc means data=work.staff;
    class JobTitle;
    var Salary;
run;
```

58

SAS programming statements are easier to read if you begin DATA, PROC, and RUN statements in column one and indent the other statements.

SAS Comments

- Type **/*** to begin a comment.
- Type your comment text.
- Type ***/** to end the comment.

```
/* Create work.staff data set */
data work.staff;
   infile 'raw-data-file';
   input LastName $ 1-20 FirstName $ 21-30
         JobTitle $ 36-43 Salary 54-59;
run;

/* Produce listing report of work.staff */
proc print data=work.staff;
run;
```

59   c02s3d2

✎   Avoid placing the /* comment symbols in columns 1 and 2. On some operating environments, SAS might interpret these symbols as a request to end the SAS job or session.

An additional method used for commenting one line of code is to use the asterisk at the beginning of the comment. Everything that is between the asterisk and the semicolon is a comment.

Example: ***infile 'emplist.dat';**

SAS views the entire INFILE statement as a comment in this example.

 **Exercises**

3. **Filling in the Blanks**

   a. SAS statements usually begin with a(n) ___key word___.

   b. Every SAS statement ends with a(n) ___;___.

   c. Character variable values can be up to ___32 767___ characters long and use ___1___ byte(s) of storage per character.

   d. A SAS variable name has ___1___ to ___32___ characters and begins with a ___letter___ or an _____.

   e. By default, numeric variables are stored in ___8___ bytes of storage.

   f. The internally stored SAS date value for January 1, 1960, is ___0___.

   g. A missing character value is displayed as a ___" "___.

   h. A missing numeric value is displayed as a ___.___.

4. **Naming the Pairs**

   a. What are the two kinds of steps? ___Data Proc___

   b. What are the two portions of every SAS data set? ___Desc Data___

   c. What are the two types of variables? ___Char numeric___

   d. What are the two major parts of SAS output? ___Logs output window___

5. **Identifying as True or False**

   a. If a SAS program produces output, then the program ran correctly and there is no need to check the SAS log. ___False___

   b. Omitting a semicolon never causes errors. ___False___

6. **Correcting the Syntax of the SAS Program**

```
data europeflight;
   infile 'testdata.dat';
   input @1 Flt-Num $3. @18 Destination $3.;
proc print data=europe ;
run;
```

2.4 Diagnosing and Correcting Syntax Errors

Objectives

- Identify SAS syntax errors.
- Debug and edit a program with errors.
- Resubmit the corrected program.
- Save the corrected program.

62

Syntax Errors

Syntax errors include the following:

- misspelled keywords
- missing or invalid punctuation
- invalid options

```
daat work.staff;
    infile 'raw-data-file';
    input LastName $ 1-20 FirstName $ 21-30
          JobTitle $ 36-43 Salary 54-59;
run;

proc print data=work.staff
run;

proc means data=work.staff average max;
    class JobTitle;
    var Salary;
run;
```

63

When SAS encounters a syntax error, SAS underlines the error and the following information is written to the SAS log:

- the word ERROR or WARNING
- the location of the error
- an explanation of the error

Examples of raw data filenames:

z/OS (OS/390)	*userid*.prog1.rawdata(emplist)
Windows	c:\workshop\winsas\prog1\emplist.dat
UNIX	/users/*userid*/emplist.dat

Debugging a SAS Program

c02s4d1.sas
userid.prog1.sascode(c02s4d1)

- Submit a SAS program that contains errors.
- Diagnose the errors.
- Correct the program.
- Submit the corrected SAS program.
- Save the corrected program.

Submit a SAS Program with Errors

```
daat work.staff;
    infile 'raw-data-file';
    input LastName $ 1-20 FirstName $ 21-30
          JobTitle $ 36-43 Salary 54-59;
run;

proc print data=work.staff
run;

proc means data=work.staff average max;
    class JobTitle;
    var Salary;
run;
```

The SAS log contains error messages and warnings.

```
1     daat work.staff;
      ----
      14
WARNING 14-169: Assuming the symbol DATA was misspelled as daat.

2         infile 'raw-data-file';
3         input LastName $ 1-20 FirstName $ 21-30
4               JobTitle $ 36-43 Salary 54-59;
5     run;

NOTE: The infile 'raw-data-file' is:
      File Name='raw-data-file',
      RECFM=V,LRECL=256

NOTE: 18 records were read from the infile 'raw-data-file'.
      The minimum record length was 59.
      The maximum record length was 59.
NOTE: The data set WORK.STAFF has 18 observations and 4
      variables.
NOTE: DATA statement used (Total process time):
      real time           0.08 seconds
      cpu time            0.07 seconds
```

(Continued on the next page.)

```
6
7    proc print data=work.staff
8    run;
     ---
     22
       -
        200
ERROR 22-322: Syntax error, expecting one of the following: ;,
              (, DATA, DOUBLE, HEADING, LABEL, N, NOOBS, OBS,
              ROUND, ROWS, SPLIT, STYLE, UNIFORM, WIDTH.
ERROR 200-322: The symbol is not recognized and will be ignored.
9

NOTE: The SAS System stopped processing this step because of
      errors.
NOTE: PROCEDURE PRINT used (Total process time):
      real time           0.06 seconds
      cpu time            0.06 seconds


10   proc means data=work.staff average max;
                               ------- ---
                               22      202
ERROR 22-322: Syntax error, expecting one of the following: ;,
              (, ALPHA, CHARTYPE, CLASSDATA, CLM,
              COMPLETETYPES, CSS, CV, DATA, DESCEND,
              DESCENDING, DESCENDTYPES, EXCLNPWGT, EXCLNPWGTS,
              EXCLUSIVE, FW, IDMIN, KURTOSIS, LCLM, MAX,
              MAXDEC, MEAN, MEDIAN, MIN, MISSING, N, NDEC,
              NMISS, NONOBS, NOPRINT, NOTHREADS, NOTRAP, NWAY,
              ORDER, P1, P10, P25, P5, P50, P75, P90, P95, P99,
              PCTLDEF, PRINT, PRINTALL, PRINTALLTYPES, PRINTIDS,
              PRINTIDVARS, PROBT, Q1, Q3, QMARKERS, QMETHOD,
              QNTLDEF, QRANGE, RANGE, SKEWNESS, STDDEV,
              STDERR, SUM, SUMSIZE, SUMWGT, T, THREADS, UCLM,
              USS, VAR, VARDEF.
ERROR 202-322: The option or parameter is not recognized and
               will be ignored.
11       class JobTitle;
12       var Salary;
13   run;

NOTE: The SAS System stopped processing this step because of
      errors.
NOTE: PROCEDURE MEANS used (Total process time):
      real time           0.05 seconds
      cpu time            0.05 seconds
```

Debugging Your Program

The log indicates that SAS

- assumed the keyword DATA was misspelled and executed the DATA step
- interpreted the word RUN as an option in the PROC PRINT statement (because there was a missing semicolon), so PROC PRINT was not executed
- did not recognize the word AVERAGE as a valid option in the PROC MEANS statement, so the PROC MEANS step was not executed.

1. If you are using the Enhanced Editor, the program remains in the editor.

    However, if you use the Program Editor, the code disappears with each submission. Use the RECALL command or select **Run** ⇨ **Recall Last Submit** to recall the program that you submitted back to the Program Editor. The original program is copied into the Program Editor.

2. Edit the program.

    a. Correct the spelling of DATA.

    b. Put a semicolon at the end of the PROC PRINT statement.

    c. Change the word AVERAGE to MEAN in the PROC MEANS statement.

```
data work.staff;
   infile 'raw-data-file';
   input LastName $ 1-20 FirstName $ 21-30
         JobTitle $ 36-43 Salary 54-59;
run;

proc print data=work.staff;
run;

proc means data=work.staff mean max;
   class JobTitle;
   var Salary;
run;
```

3. Submit the program. It runs successfully without errors and generates output.

Saving Your Program

You can use the FILE command to save your program to a file. The program must be in the Enhanced Editor or Program Editor before you issue the FILE command. If the code is not in the Program Editor, recall your program before saving the program.

z/OS (OS/390):   `file '.prog1.sascode(myprog)'`

Windows or UNIX: `file 'myprog.sas'`

You can also select **File** ⇨ **Save As**.

A note appears that indicates that the statements are saved to the file.

Submitting a SAS Program That Contains Unbalanced Quotation Marks

c02s4d2.sas
userid.prog1.sascode(c02s4d2)

The closing quotation mark for the INFILE statement is missing.

```
data work.staff;
   infile 'raw-data-file;
   input LastName $ 1-20 FirstName $ 21-30
         JobTitle $ 36-43 Salary 54-59;
run;

proc print data=work.staff;
run;

proc means data=work.staff mean max;
   class JobTitle;
   var Salary;
run;
```

Submit the program and browse the SAS log.

```
Log - (Untitled)  DATA STEP running                                    _ □ ×
1      data work.staff;
2         infile 'emplist.dat;
3         input LastName $ 1-20 FirstName $ 21-30
4               JobTitle $ 36-43 Salary 54-59;
5      run;
6
7      proc print data=work.staff;
8      run;
9
10     proc means data=work.staff mean max;
11        class JobTitle;
12        var Salary;
13     run;
```

There are no notes in the SAS log because all of the SAS statements after the INFILE statement became part of the quoted string.

```
Log - (Untitled)  DATA STEP running                                    _ □ ×
```

    The banner on the window indicates that the DATA step is still running because the RUN statement was not recognized.

Correcting Unbalanced Quotation Marks Programmatically

You can correct the unbalanced quotation marks programmatically by adding the following code before your previous statements:

```
*';*";run;
```

If the quotation mark counter within SAS has an uneven number of quotation marks as seen in the above program, SAS reads the quotation mark in the comment above as the matching quotation mark in the quotation mark counter. SAS then has an even number of quotation marks in the quotation mark counter and runs successfully, assuming no other errors occur. Both single quotation marks and double quotation marks are used in case you submitted double quotation marks instead of single quotation marks.

Point-and-Click Approaches to Balancing Quotation Marks

Windows

1. To correct the problem in the Windows environment, click the break icon or press the CTRL and Break keys.

2. Select **1. Cancel Submitted Statements** in the Tasking Manager window and select **OK**.

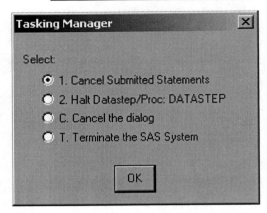

3. Select **Y to cancel submitted statements,** ⇨ **OK**.

UNIX

1. To correct the problem in the UNIX operating environment, open the SAS: Session Management window and select **Interrupt**.

2. Select **1** in the SAS: Tasking Manager window.

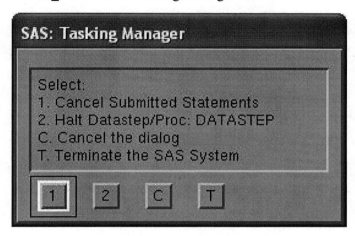

3. Select **Y**.

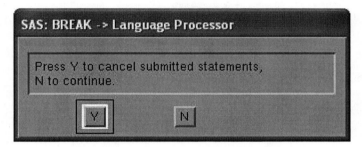

z/OS (OS/390)

1. To correct the problem in the z/OS (OS/390) operating environment, press the Attention key or issue the ATTENTION command.

2. Type **1** to select **1. Cancel Submitted Statements** and press the ENTER key.

```
┌Tasking Manager──────────────────────────────────────────────────
  Select:
  1 █. Cancel Submitted Statements
    2. Halt Datastep/Proc: DATASTEP
    C. Cancel the dialog
    T. Terminate the SAS System
└
```

3. Type **Y** and press ENTER.

```
┌BREAK -> Language Processor──────────────────────────────────────
  Press Y to cancel submitted statements, N to continue.  y █
└
```

Resubmitting the Program

1. Recall the program into the Program Editor window.

2. Add a closing quotation mark to the file reference in the INFILE statement.

3. Resubmit the program.

Partial SAS Log

```
27    data work.staff;
28       infile 'raw-data-file';
29       input LastName $ 1-20 FirstName $ 21-30
30             JobTitle $ 36-43 Salary 54-59;
31    run;

NOTE: 18 records were read from the infile 'raw-data-file'.
      The minimum record length was 59.
      The maximum record length was 59.
NOTE: The data set WORK.STAFF has 18 observations and 4 variables.
32
33    proc print data=work.staff;
34    run;

NOTE: There were 18 observations read from the dataset WORK.STAFF.
35
36    proc means data=work.staff mean max;
37       class JobTitle;
38       var Salary;
39    run;

NOTE: There were 18 observations read from the dataset WORK.STAFF.
```

Recall a Submitted Program

Program statements accumulate in a recall buffer
each time you issue a SUBMIT command.

```
daat work.staff;
   infile 'raw-data-file';
   input LastName $ 1-20 FirstName $ 21-30
         JobTitle $ 36-43 Salary 54-59;
run;
proc print data=work.staff
run;
proc means data=work.staff average max;
   class JobTitle;
   var Salary;
run;
```
Submit
Number 1

```
data work.staff;
   infile 'raw-data-file';
   input LastName $ 1-20 FirstName $ 21-30
         JobTitle $ 36-43 Salary 54-59;
run;
proc print data=work.staff;
run;
proc means data=work.staff mean max;
   class Jobtitle;
   var Salary;
run;
```
Submit
Number 2

65

Recall a Submitted Program

Issue the RECALL command once to recall the most
recently submitted program.

Submit
Number 1

Issue RECALL
once.

Submit
Number 2

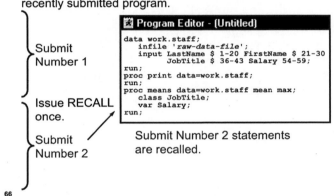

Program Editor - (Untitled)
```
data work.staff;
   infile 'raw-data-file';
   input LastName $ 1-20 FirstName $ 21-30
         JobTitle $ 36-43 Salary 54-59;
run;
proc print data=work.staff;
run;
proc means data=work.staff mean max;
   class JobTitle;
   var Salary;
run;
```

Submit Number 2 statements
are recalled.

66

Recall a Submitted Program

Issue the RECALL command again to recall Submit
Number 1 statements.

Submit
Number 1

Issue RECALL
again.

Submit
Number 2

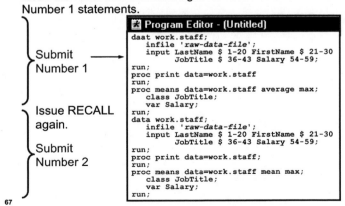

Program Editor - (Untitled)
```
daat work.staff;
   infile 'raw-data-file';
   input LastName $ 1-20 FirstName $ 21-30
         JobTitle $ 36-43 Salary 54-59;
run;
proc print data=work.staff
run;
proc means data=work.staff average max;
   class JobTitle;
   var Salary;
run;
data work.staff;
   infile 'raw-data-file';
   input LastName $ 1-20 FirstName $ 21-30
         JobTitle $ 36-43 Salary 54-59;
run;
proc print data=work.staff;
run;
proc means data=work.staff mean max;
   class JobTitle;
   var Salary;
run;
```

67

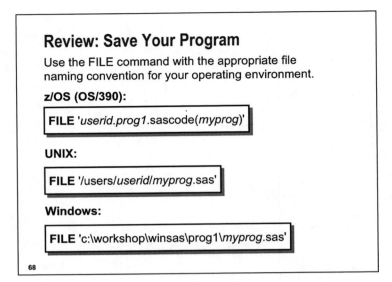

Review: Save Your Program

Use the FILE command with the appropriate file
naming convention for your operating environment.

z/OS (OS/390):

FILE '*userid*.prog1.sascode(*myprog*)'

UNIX:

FILE '/users/*userid*/*myprog*.sas'

Windows:

FILE 'c:\workshop\winsas\prog1*myprog*.sas'

68

z/OS (OS/390):	A file reference of ' . PROG1 . SASCODE (MYPROG) ' assumes that *userid* is the first level of the filename.
Windows and UNIX:	A file reference of 'myprog.sas' assumes that the file will be stored in the current working folder.

When you make changes to the program in the Enhanced Editor and have not saved the new
version of the program, the window bar and the top border of the window reflect that you
changed the program without saving it by putting an asterisk (*) beside the window name.
When you save the program, the * disappears.

 **Exercises**

7. **Correcting Errors**

   a. With the Program Editor window active, include the SAS program **c02ex7**.

      - Windows and UNIX: Select <u>**File**</u> ⇨ <u>**Open Program**</u> and select the program <u>**c02ex7.sas**</u> or issue the **include 'c02ex7.sas'** command.

      - z/OS (OS/390): Issue the **include '.prog1.sascode(c02ex7)'** command.
      In the Program Editor window, edit the program to use the appropriate INFILE statement for z/OS. (Add an asterisk to the beginning of the first INFILE statement and remove the asterisk from the second INFILE statement.)

   b. Submit the program.

   c. Use the SAS log notes to identify the error, correct the error, and resubmit the program.

2.5   Exploring Your SAS Environment (Self-Study)

Exploring Your SAS Environment in Microsoft Windows

c02s5d1.sas

Enhanced Editor

The Enhanced Editor (the default editor in Microsoft Windows) provides many helpful features, including color coding and automatically retaining the program after each submit, which eliminates the need to recall your program.

In the Enhanced Editor, each program that you open will open a new Enhanced Editor. You can have numerous Enhanced Editors open at one time. However, if you are using the Program Editor, you can have only one Program Editor open at a time.

✎   The Enhanced Editor is available only on Windows.

```
c02s5d1.sas
data work.staff;
    infile 'emplist.dat';
    input LastName $ 1-20 FirstName $ 21-30
          JobTitle $ 36-43 Salary 54-59;
run;

proc print data=work.staff;
run;

proc means data=work.staff;
    class Jobtitle;
    var Salary;
run;
```

✎   The program contains three steps: a DATA step and two PROC steps.

When you browse the program, notice the following:

- The syntax is color-coded to show these items:
  - step boundaries
  - keywords
  - variable and data set names
- A section boundary line separates each step.

With the Enhanced Editor, you have the ability to minimize and maximize each DATA or PROC step. A minus sign ⊟ next to DATA or PROC indicates that the code is expanded. To minimize the DATA or PROC step, click on the minus sign. After the step is minimized, the minus sign changes into a plus sign ⊞. To maximize the step after it is minimized, click on the plus sign.

You can customize the appearance and functionality of the Enhanced Editor by selecting **Tools** ⇨ **Options** ⇨ **Enhanced Editor**.

To submit the program for execution, issue the SUBMIT command or click 🏃 or select **Run** ⇨ **Submit**. The output from the program is displayed in the Output window.

You can submit the code when it is collapsed. This is helpful if you want to highlight a portion of the program and submit only that portion. You can highlight the entire line that is visible for a step and submit it. To highlight the entire line, click to the left of the plus sign ⊞.

Navigating in Your SAS Session

1. Open the file **c02s5d1.sas** by selecting **File** ⇨ **Open** or issuing the INCLUDE command or clicking 📂.

2. Submit the program in the Enhanced Editor by issuing the SUBMIT command or selecting **Run** ⇨ **Submit** or clicking 🏃.

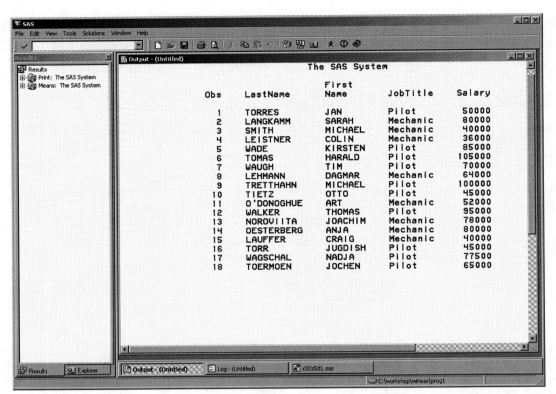

- The Results and Output windows are displayed when you submit a program that generates output.

- You can use the CTRL and Tab keys to navigate between windows.

- You can use the SAS window bar at the bottom of the workspace to navigate between all of the windows in the SAS windowing environment or to minimize and maximize windows.

- Each window in the workspace has its own menu selections that reflect the actions you can perform when that window is active. This applies to all menus.

- The Results window lists all of the reports that appear in the Output window. You can double-click and drill down on each procedure in the Results window, which enables you to go to that report in the Output window.

- Starting in SAS 8, you can also use the Results window to erase particular reports from the Output window. You can delete each individual report by either right-clicking on the output name and selecting **Delete** or by clicking ✕ on the toolbar.

3. Return to the Enhanced Editor by selecting [c02s5d1.sas] from the SAS window bar.

    Unlike the Program Editor, the code is not cleared from the Enhanced Editor after a submission, so you do not need to use a RECALL command.

Exploring SAS Libraries and Files

1. Select the ![Explorer] tab on the SAS window bar to open the Explorer window.

The functionality of the SAS Explorer is similar to explorers for Windows-based systems. In addition to the single-pane view of folders and files that opens by default, you can specify a tree view.

2. You can also select **View** ⇨ **Explorer**.

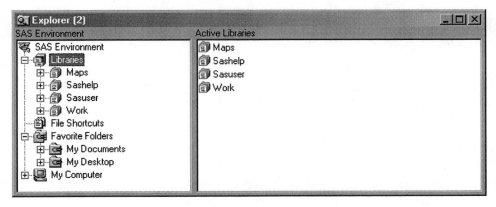

You can change the size of the windows by positioning the cursor on the window divider so that the cursor becomes a double-arrow. Drag the window to the size that you prefer.

3. Expand and collapse directories on the left. Drill down and open specific files on the right.

4. Toggle this view off by selecting **View** ⇨ **Show Tree**.

In addition to the tree view, you can view directories and files in these layouts:

- as large and small icons
- in a list format
- by their detail information

5. Double-click on the **Work** library to show all members of that library.

6. Right-click on the **Staff** data set and select **Properties**.

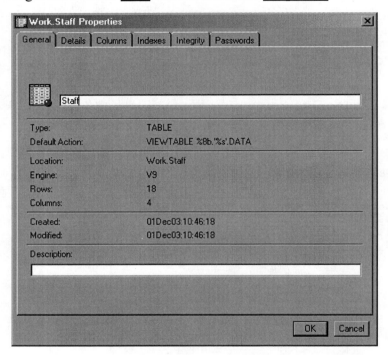

This default view provides general information about the data set, such as the library in which it is stored, the type of information it contains, its creation date, the number of observations and variables, and so on. You can request specific information about the columns in the data table by selecting the **Columns** tab at the top of the Properties window.

7. Select ☒ to close the Properties window.

8.   You can view the data portion of a data set by double-clicking on the file or right-clicking on the file
     and selecting **Open**. This opens the data set in a VIEWTABLE window. A view of **work.staff** is
     shown below.

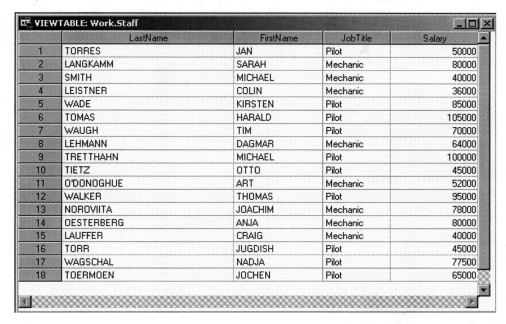

	LastName	FirstName	JobTitle	Salary
1	TORRES	JAN	Pilot	50000
2	LANGKAMM	SARAH	Mechanic	80000
3	SMITH	MICHAEL	Mechanic	40000
4	LEISTNER	COLIN	Mechanic	36000
5	WADE	KIRSTEN	Pilot	85000
6	TOMAS	HARALD	Pilot	105000
7	WAUGH	TIM	Pilot	70000
8	LEHMANN	DAGMAR	Mechanic	64000
9	TRETTHAHN	MICHAEL	Pilot	100000
10	TIETZ	OTTO	Pilot	45000
11	O'DONOGHUE	ART	Mechanic	52000
12	WALKER	THOMAS	Pilot	95000
13	NOROVIITA	JOACHIM	Mechanic	78000
14	OESTERBERG	ANJA	Mechanic	80000
15	LAUFFER	CRAIG	Mechanic	40000
16	TORR	JUGDISH	Pilot	45000
17	WAGSCHAL	NADJA	Pilot	77500
18	TOERMOEN	JOCHEN	Pilot	65000

     In addition to browsing SAS data sets, you can use the VIEWTABLE window to edit data sets,
     create data sets, and customize your view of a SAS data set. For example, you can do the following:

     •   sort your data

     •   change the color and fonts of variables

     •   display variable labels versus variable names

     •   remove and add variables

     Variable labels are displayed by default. Display variable names instead of variable labels
     by selecting **View** ⇨ **Column Names**.

9.   Select ❌ to close the VIEWTABLE window.

Exploring Your SAS Environment under UNIX

c02s5d1.sas

Exploring SAS Libraries and Files

1. When you start your SAS session, the Explorer window is displayed in a single-pane view.

    If the Explorer window is not displayed, you can open it by selecting  in the SAS Toolbox or by selecting **View** ⇨ **Explorer**.

2. Select **View** ⇨ **Show Tree**. This selection toggles the tree view on or off.

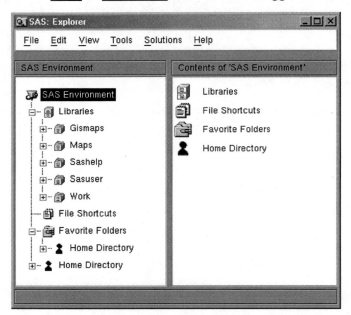

    The functionality of the SAS Explorer is similar to explorers for GUI-based systems. You can choose to use a tree view or a single-pane view of folders and files. The window above shows the tree view.

3. You can change the size of the windows by positioning the cursor on the window divider so that the cursor becomes a double arrow. Drag the window to the size you prefer.

4. You can expand and collapse directories on the left, and drill down and open specific files on the right.

   In addition to the tree view, you can view directories and files in any of the following layouts:
   - as large and small icons
   - in a list format
   - by their detail information

5. Select **Libraries** in the left panel to display the active libraries.

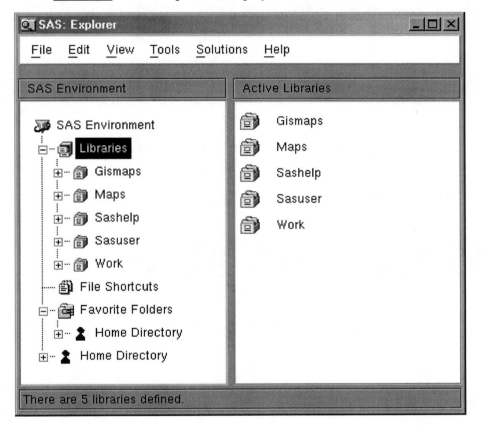

6.   Right-click on the **Work** library and select **Open** to show all members of the library.

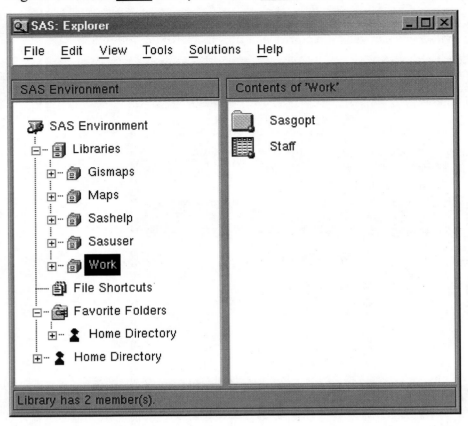

7. Right-click on the **Staff** data set and select **Properties**.

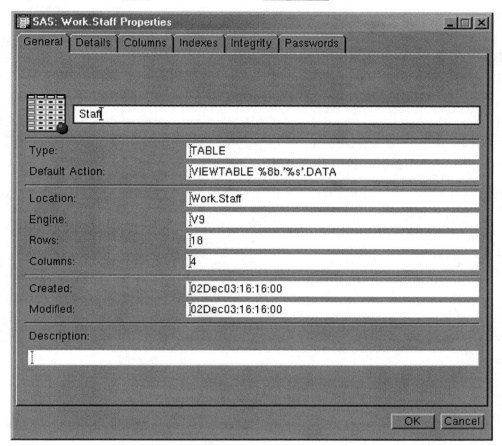

This default view provides general information about the data set, such as the library in which it is stored, the type of information it contains, its creation date, the number of observations and variables, and so on. You can request specific information about the columns in the data table by selecting the **Columns** tab at the top of the Properties window.

8. Select 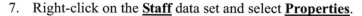 to close the Properties window.

9. View the data portion of a data set by double-clicking on the file or by right-clicking on the file and selecting **Open**. This opens the data set in a VIEWTABLE window. A view of **work.staff** is shown below.

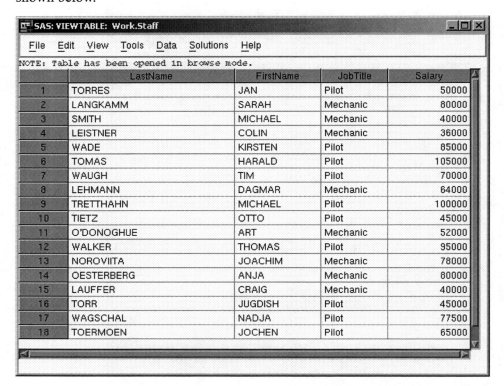

In addition to browsing SAS data sets, you can use the VIEWTABLE window to edit data sets, create data sets, and customize your view of a SAS data set. For example, you can do the following:

- sort your data
- change the color and fonts of variables
- display variable labels versus variable names
- remove and add variables

10. Select **File** ⇨ **Close** to close the VIEWTABLE window.

Exploring Your SAS Environment under z/OS (OS/390)

userid.prog1.sascode(c02s5d1)

Navigating Your SAS Session

To perform tasks in your interactive SAS session, you can type commands on the command line or you can use the following:

- menus
- function keys

1. Type **pmenu** on a command line to turn on the menus.

```
┌─Program Editor────────────────────────────────────────────┐
│ Command ===> pmenu█                                        │
│                                                            │
│ 00001                                                      │
│ 00002                                                      │
└────────────────────────────────────────────────────────────┘

┌─Program Editor────────────────────────────────────────────┐
│ File Edit View Tools Run Solutions Help                    │
│                                                            │
│ 00001                                                      │
│ 00002                                                      │
└────────────────────────────────────────────────────────────┘
```

   If you have a mouse to control the cursor, you can click on a word to see the available actions for each menu item. Click on a word to select an item or click outside the menu area to **not** select an action.

   You can also use your tab or arrow keys to move through the menu and action items. Press the ENTER key when the cursor is positioned on the item that you want. Move your cursor away from the items and press ENTER to **not** select an action.

2. Select **Tools** ⇨ **Options** ⇨ **Turn All Menus Off** to turn off the menus and return to a command line.

Exploring SAS Libraries and Files

1. Open the Explorer window by typing **explorer** on the command line and pressing ENTER or by selecting **View** ⇨ **Explorer**.

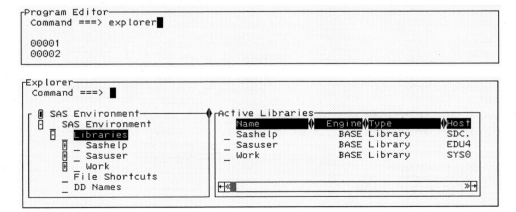

   You can specify a tree view or a single-pane view of folders and files. The window above shows the tree view.

2. Issue the TREE command, or select **View** ⇨ **Show Tree** and press ENTER. This selection toggles the tree view on or off.

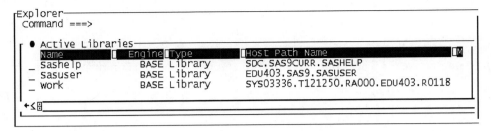

The window above shows the single-pane view.

3. If necessary, toggle the view to show the single-pane view.

4. Type **S** next to the Work library and press ENTER to show all members of that library.

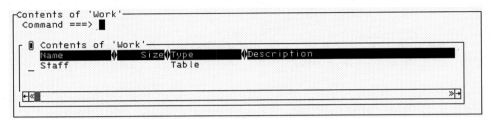

5. Type **?** next to the **staff** data set and press ENTER. Select **Properties** and press ENTER. You can also type **p** next to **staff** and press ENTER.

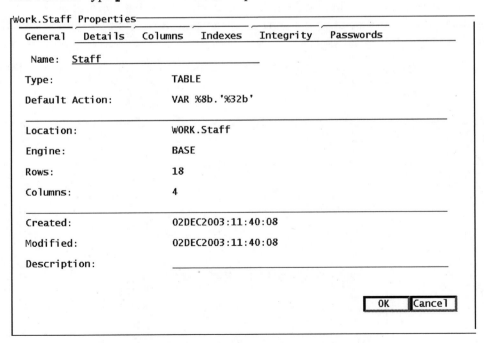

This default view provides general information about the data set, such as the library in which it is stored, the type of information it contains, its creation date, the number of observations and variables, and so on. You can also request specific information about the variables in the data set by selecting the **Columns** tab or by typing **V** next to **staff** and pressing ENTER.

6. Select ▌ OK   to close the Properties window.

7. To view the data portion of a data set, type **?** next to the filename, press ENTER, and select **Open**. This opens the data set in an FSVIEW window. A view of **work.staff** is shown below.

```
┌FSVIEW:    WORK.STAFF (B)─────────────────────────────────────────
│ Command ===>
│
│   Obs       LastName              FirstName    JobTitle       Salary
│
│     1       TORRES                JAN          Pilot          50000
│     2       LANGKAMM              SARAH        Mechanic       80000
│     3       SMITH                 MICHAEL      Mechanic       40000
│     4       LEISTNER              COLIN        Mechanic       36000
│     5       WADE                  KIRSTEN      Pilot          85000
│     6       TOMAS                 HARALD       Pilot         105000
│     7       WAUGH                 TIM          Pilot          70000
│     8       LEHMANN               DAGMAR       Mechanic       64000
│     9       TRETTHAHN             MICHAEL      Pilot         100000
│    10       TIETZ                 OTTO         Pilot          45000
│    11       O'DONOGHUE            ART          Mechanic       52000
│    12       WALKER                THOMAS       Pilot          95000
│    13       NOROVIITA             JOACHIM      Mechanic       78000
│    14       OESTERBERG            ANJA         Mechanic       80000
│    15       LAUFFER               CRAIG        Mechanic       40000
│    16       TORR                  JUGDISH      Pilot          45000
│    17       WAGSCHAL              NADJA        Pilot          77500
│    18       TOERMOEN              JOCHEN       Pilot          65000
│
│                              ■
```

In addition to browsing SAS data sets, you can use the FSVIEW window to edit data sets, create data sets, and customize your view of a SAS data set.

8. Close the FSVIEW window by issuing the END command or by selecting **File** ➪ **Close** and pressing ENTER.

2.6 Solutions to Exercises

1. **Submitting a Program**

   a. Activate the Program Editor window. Issue the appropriate INCLUDE command or select
       File ⇨ **Open** to select the appropriate file.

       ```
       Command ===> include 'operating-system-filename'
       ```

   b. To submit your program for execution, select ⏃ , issue the SUBMIT command, or select
       Run ⇨ **Submit**. Based on the report in the Output window, the **work.airports** data set
       has 15 observations and three variables.

   c. To activate the Log window, issue the LOG command or select **Window** ⇨ **Log**. The log
       notes report that the **work.airports** data set has 15 observations and three variables.

   d. To clear the Log window, issue the CLEAR command or select **Edit** ⇨ **Clear All**. To activate
       and clear the Output window, issue the OUTPUT command or select **Window** ⇨ **Output**. Then
       issue the CLEAR command or select **Edit** ⇨ **Clear All**.

2. **Issuing the KEYS Command (Optional)**

   a. Type **keys** on the command line or command box or select **Tools** ⇨ **Options** ⇨ **Keys**. The
       KEYS window opens and you can view all function keys.

   b. Close the KEYS window by issuing the END command or selecting ⊠ .

3. **Filling in the Blanks**

   a. SAS statements usually begin with an **identifying keyword**.

   b. Every SAS statement ends with a **semicolon**.

   c. Character variable values can be up to **32,767** characters long and use **1** byte(s) of storage
       per character.

   d. A SAS variable name has **1** to **32** characters and begins with a **letter** or an **underscore**.

   e. By default, numeric variables are stored in **8** bytes of storage.

   f. The internally stored SAS date value for January 1, 1960, is **0**.

   g. A missing character value is displayed as a **blank**.

   h. A missing numeric value is displayed as a **period**.

4. **Naming the Pairs**

   a. What are the two kinds of steps? **DATA and PROC**

   b. What are the two portions of every SAS data set? **Descriptor and Data**

   c. What are the two types of variables? **Character and Numeric**

   d. What are the two major parts of SAS output? **SAS Log and Output**

5. **Identifying as True or False**

   a. If a SAS program produces output, then the program ran correctly and there is no need to check the SAS log. **<u>False</u>**

   b. Omitting a semicolon never causes errors. **<u>False</u>**

6. **Correcting the Syntax of the SAS Program**

```
data europeflight;
   infile 'testdata.dat';
   input @1 Flt_Num $3. @18 Destination $3.;
run;
proc print data=europeflight;
run;
```

7. **Correcting Errors**

   a. Activate the Program Editor window by issuing the PGM command or selecting **<u>Window</u>** ⇨ **<u>Program Editor</u>**. Then issue the appropriate INCLUDE command or select **<u>File</u>** ⇨ **<u>Open</u>** to select the appropriate file.

      Command ===> include 'operating-system-filename'

   b. To submit the program for execution, issue the SUBMIT command or select **<u>Run</u>** ⇨ **<u>Submit</u>**.

   c. Activate the Log window by issuing the LOG command or selecting **<u>Window</u>** ⇨ **<u>Log</u>**. Scroll vertically to examine the SAS log notes. These notes confirm that the **work.airports** data set was created. However, an error occurred in the PROC step. The name of the procedure is misspelled.

      To recall the program into the Program Editor window, activate the Program Editor window by issuing the PGM command or selecting **<u>Window</u>** ⇨ **<u>Program Editor</u>**. Then issue the RECALL command or select **<u>Run</u>** ⇨ **<u>Recall Last Submit</u>**.

      Edit the program to correct the spelling of the PRINT procedure.

      Resubmit your program by issuing the SUBMIT command, selecting 🏃 , or selecting **<u>Run</u>** ⇨ **<u>Submit</u>**.

      If you do not see a report in the Output window, re-examine the SAS log notes, recall the program, correct the error, and resubmit the program.

Chapter 3   Getting Familiar with SAS Data Sets

3.1 SAS Data Libraries

Objectives

- Explain the concept of a SAS data library.
- State the difference between a permanent library and a temporary library.
- Use the CONTENTS procedure to investigate a SAS data library.

2

SAS Data Libraries

A *SAS data library* is a collection of SAS files that are recognized as a unit by SAS.

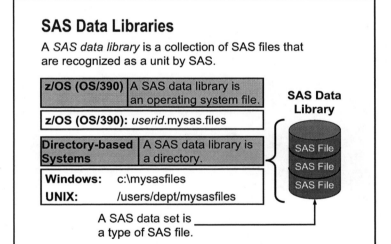

z/OS (OS/390)	A SAS data library is an operating system file.

z/OS (OS/390): *userid*.mysas.files

Directory-based Systems	A SAS data library is a directory.

| **Windows:** | c:\mysasfiles |
| **UNIX:** | /users/dept/mysasfiles |

A SAS data set is a type of SAS file.

3

SAS Data Libraries

You can think of a SAS data library as a drawer
in a filing cabinet and a SAS data set as one of the
file folders in the drawer.

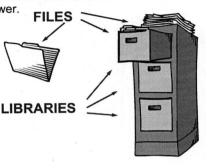

4

Assigning a Libref

Regardless of which host operating system you
use, you identify SAS data libraries by assigning
a library reference name (libref) to each library.

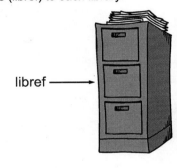

libref

5

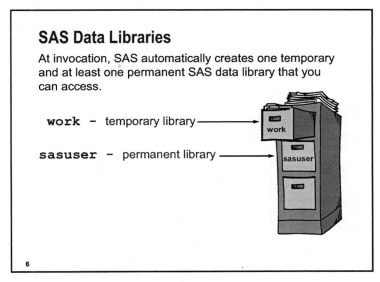

SAS Data Libraries

At invocation, SAS automatically creates one temporary and at least one permanent SAS data library that you can access.

work - temporary library

sasuser - permanent library

6

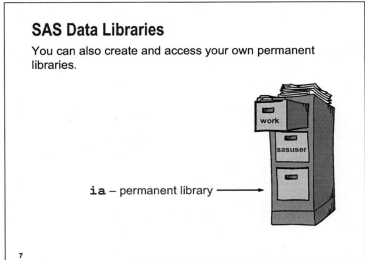

SAS Data Libraries

You can also create and access your own permanent libraries.

ia – permanent library

7

The work library and its SAS data files are deleted after your SAS session ends.

SAS data sets in permanent libraries, such as the **ia** library, are saved after your SAS session ends.

Assigning a Libref

You can use the LIBNAME statement to assign
a libref to a SAS data library.

General form of the LIBNAME statement:

> **LIBNAME** *libref 'SAS-data-library' <options>;*

The rules for naming a libref are as follows:

- must be 8 or fewer characters
- must begin with a letter or underscore
- remaining characters are letters, numbers, or underscores

8

✎ z/OS (OS/390) users can use a DD statement or TSO ALLOCATE command instead
of issuing a LIBNAME statement.

Assigning a Libref

Examples:

Windows

```
libname ia 'c:\workshop\winsas\prog1';
```

UNIX

```
libname ia '/users/userid';
```

z/OS (OS/390)

```
libname ia 'userid.prog1.sasdata' disp=shr;
```

9

✎ DISP=OLD|SHR specifies the disposition of the file. The default is OLD, which enables
both Read and Write access. SHR enables Read-only access.

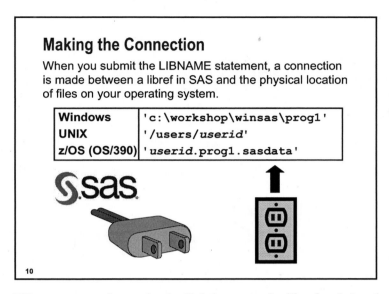

Making the Connection

When you submit the LIBNAME statement, a connection is made between a libref in SAS and the physical location of files on your operating system.

Windows	`'c:\workshop\winsas\prog1'`
UNIX	`'/users/userid'`
z/OS (OS/390)	`'userid.prog1.sasdata'`

10

When your session ends, the link between the libref and the physical location of your files is broken.

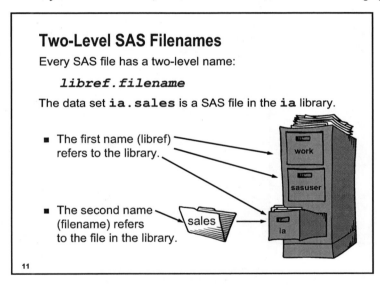

Two-Level SAS Filenames

Every SAS file has a two-level name:

libref.filename

The data set **ia.sales** is a SAS file in the **ia** library.

- The first name (libref) refers to the library.

- The second name (filename) refers to the file in the library.

11

Temporary SAS Filename

The libref **work** can be omitted when you refer to a file in the **work** library. The default libref is **work** if the libref is omitted.

`work.employee` ⬌ `employee`

12

Browsing a SAS Data Library

During an interactive SAS session, the EXPLORER window enables you to manage your files in the windowing environment.

In the EXPLORER window, you can do the following:
- view a list of all the libraries available during your current SAS session
- drill down to see all members of a specific library
- display the descriptor portion of a SAS data set

13

The SAS windowing environment opens the Explorer window by default on many hosts. You can issue the EXPLORER command to invoke this window if it does not appear by default.

The SAS Explorer can be opened by selecting

- **View** ⇨ **Contents Only**

  or

- **View** ⇨ **Explorer**.

In the Contents Only view, the Explorer is a single-paned window that contains the contents of your SAS environment. As you open folders, the folder contents replace the previous contents in the same window.

In the Explorer view of the Explorer window, folders appear in the tree view on the left and folder contents appear in the list view on the right.

Explorer Window: Windows

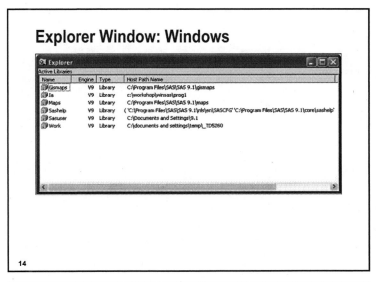

14

Explorer Window: UNIX

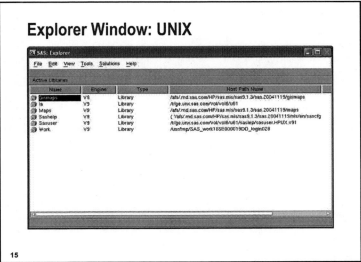

15

Explorer Window: z/OS (OS/390)

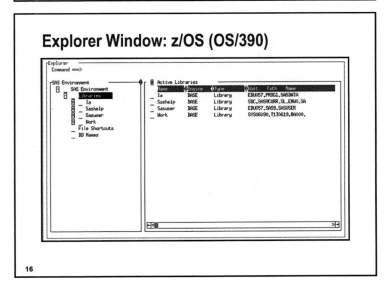

16

Browsing a SAS Data Library

Use the _ALL_ keyword to list all the SAS files in the library and the NODS option to suppress the descriptor portions of the data sets.

General form of the NODS option:

```
PROC CONTENTS DATA=libref._ALL_ NODS;
RUN;
```

NODS can only be used in conjunction with the keyword _ALL_.

```
proc contents data=ia._all_ nods;
run;
```

c03s1d1

17

If you are using a noninteractive or batch SAS session, the CONTENTS procedure is an alternative to the EXPLORER command.

PROC CONTENTS Output

Partial Output

```
                    The SAS System

                  The CONTENTS Procedure

                       Directory

             Libref          IA
             Engine          V9
             Physical Name   C:\workshop\winsas\prog1
             File Name       C:\workshop\winsas\prog1

                     Member    File
       #  Name       Type      Size   Last Modified

       1  ALLGOALS   DATA      5120   31Jul01:08:52:34
       2  ALLGOALS2  DATA      5120   31Jul01:08:52:38
       3  ALLSALES   DATA      5120   31Jul01:08:53:28
       4  ALLSALES2  DATA      5120   31Jul01:08:53:46
       5  APRTARGET  DATA     17408   13Aug01:08:41:42
       6  CHICAGO    DATA     17408   31Jul01:08:54:38
       7  CREW       DATA     13312   31Jul01:08:54:44
       8  DELAY      DATA     66560   31Jul01:08:54:46
```

18

Browsing a SAS Data Library

To explore the descriptor portion of a SAS data set,
specify the data set name in the DATA= option.

```
PROC CONTENTS DATA=libref.SAS-data-set-name;
RUN;
```

```
proc contents data=ia.crew;
run;
```

19   c03s1d1

PROC CONTENTS Output – Part 1

```
                    The SAS System

                The CONTENTS Procedure

Data Set Name        IA.CREW          Observations          69
Member Type          DATA             Variables             8
Engine               V9               Indexes               0
Created              Friday, June 29, Observation Length    120
                     2001 03:15:27 PM
Last Modified        Friday, June 29, Deleted Observations  0
                     2001 03:41:07 PM
Protection                            Compressed            NO
Data Set Type                         Sorted                NO
Label
Data Representation  WINDOWS_32
Encoding             Default
```

20

PROC CONTENTS Output – Part 2

```
              Engine/Host Dependent Information

Data Set Page Size           12288
Number of Data Set Pages     1
First Data Page              1
Max Obs per Page             102
Obs in First Data Page       69
Number of Data Set Repairs   0
File Name                    C:\workshop\winsas\
                             prog1\crew.sas7bdat
Release Created              8.0202M0
Host Created                 WIN_PRO
```

21

PROC CONTENTS Output – Part 3

```
        Alphabetic List of Variables and Attributes

     #    Variable     Type    Len    Format    Informat

     6    EmpID        Char     6
     3    FirstName    Char    32
     1    HireDate     Num      8     DATE9.    DATE9.
     7    JobCode      Char     6
     2    LastName     Char    32
     4    Location     Char    16
     5    Phone        Char     8
     8    Salary       Num      8
```

22

 **Exercises**

1. **Assigning a Permanent SAS Data Library**

   a. Submit the LIBNAME statement to provide access to a permanent SAS data library.

      `libname ia '_____';`

   b. Check the log to confirm that the SAS data library was assigned.

2. **Investigating a SAS Library Interactively**

   a. Windows and UNIX: Double-click on the Libraries icon in the Explorer window to see the available SAS data libraries. Then double-click on the **IA** library. Select **View** ⇨ **Details**.

   b. z/OS (OS/390): Issue the Explorer command to open the Explorer window. Type **s** beside the Ia library in the Active Libraries window and press ENTER.

      A partial listing in the Windows environment is shown below.

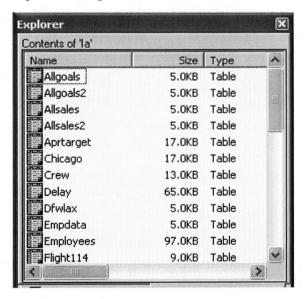

   c. For Windows and UNIX, navigate back to the Active Libraries view in the Explorer window. For z/OS (OS/390), close the Explorer window.

3. Investigating a SAS Data Set with PROC CONTENTS

a. Submit a PROC CONTENTS step to list all the SAS data sets in the **IA** library. Do not display the descriptor portions of the individual data sets.

```
                               The SAS System

                            The CONTENTS Procedure

                                 Directory

                    Libref          IA
                    Engine          V9
                    Physical Name   C:\workshop\winsas\prog1
                    File Name       C:\workshop\winsas\prog1

                            Member      File
               #  Name      Type        Size   Last Modified

               1  ALLGOALS    DATA        5120   31Jul01:08:52:34
               2  ALLGOALS2   DATA        5120   31Jul01:08:52:38
               3  ALLSALES    DATA        5120   31Jul01:08:53:28
               4  ALLSALES2   DATA        5120   31Jul01:08:53:46
               5  APRTARGET   DATA       17408   13Aug01:08:41:42
               6  CHICAGO     DATA       17408   31Jul01:08:54:38
               7  CREW        DATA       13312   31Jul01:08:54:44
               8  DELAY       DATA       66560   31Jul01:08:54:46
               9  DFWLAX      DATA        5120   09Aug01:16:47:56
              10  EMPDATA     DATA        5120   31Jul01:08:54:56
              11  EMPLOYEES   DATA       99328   31Jul01:08:55:28
              12  FLIGHT114   DATA        9216   31Jul01:08:55:32
              13  FLTAT       DATA       13312   31Jul01:08:55:38
              14  FLTATTND    DATA       13312   31Jul01:08:55:44
              15  FRANKFRT    DATA        5120   07Aug01:19:11:32
              16  GERCREW     DATA        5120   31Jul01:08:57:14
              17  GERSCHED    DATA        5120   31Jul01:08:57:34
              18  GOALS       DATA        5120   31Jul01:08:57:38
              19  JUNTARGET   DATA       17408   13Aug01:08:41:18
              20  MAYTARGET   DATA        9216   13Aug01:08:41:30
              21  MECHANICS   DATA        9216   13Aug01:11:22:32
              22  MIAMIEMP    DATA        5120   31Jul01:08:58:58
              23  NEWMECHS    DATA        9216   31Jul01:08:59:18
              24  PARISEMP    DATA        5120   31Jul01:08:59:22
              25  PASSNGRS    DATA        5120   31Jul01:08:59:24
              26  PERFORMANCE DATA        5120   31Jul01:08:59:40
              27  PERSONL     DATA       25600   31Jul01:08:59:44
              28  PILOTS      DATA        9216   10Sep01:10:52:56
              29  ROMEEMP     DATA        5120   31Jul01:08:59:56
              30  SALES121999 DATA      115712   31Jul01:09:01:16
              31  SANFRAN     DATA       13312   31Jul01:09:01:24
              32  TARGET121999 DATA     115712   09Aug01:18:38:22
              33  WEEKREV     DATA        5120   31Jul01:09:01:28
```

b. Modify the PROC CONTENTS step submitted above so that only the descriptor portion
of the data set **IA.pilots** is displayed.

```
                          The SAS System

                        The CONTENTS Procedure

Data Set Name       IA.PILOTS              Observations        20
Member Type         DATA                   Variables           11
Engine              V9                     Indexes             0
Created             Monday, September 10,  Observation Length  96
                    2001 10:52:54 AM
Last Modified       Monday, September 10,  Deleted Observations 0
                    2001 10:52:54 AM
Protection                                 Compressed          NO
Data Set Type                              Sorted              NO
Label
Data Representation WINDOWS_32
Encoding            Default


                   Engine/Host Dependent Information

   Data Set Page Size          8192
   Number of Data Set Pages    1
   First Data Page             1
   Max Obs per Page            84
   Obs in First Data Page      20
   Number of Data Set Repairs  0
   File Name                   C:\workshop\winsas\prog1\pilots.sas7bdat
   Release Created             8.0202M0
   Host Created                WIN_PRO


              Alphabetic List of Variables and Attributes

        #    Variable   Type   Len   Format    Informat

        9    Birth      Num     8    DATE7.    DATE.
        4    City       Char   15
        3    FName      Char   15
        6    Gender     Char    1
       11    HPhone     Char   12
       10    Hired      Num     8    DATE7.    DATE.
        1    IDNum      Char    4
        7    JobCode    Char    3
        2    LName      Char   15
        8    Salary     Num     8
        5    State      Char    2
```

3.2 Solutions to Exercises

1. **Assigning a Permanent SAS Data Library**

    ```
    libname ia 'SAS-data-library';
    ```

2. **Investigating a SAS Library Interactively**

    a. Windows and UNIX: Double-click on the Libraries icon in the Explorer window to see the available SAS data libraries. Then double-click on the **Ia** library. Select **View** ⇨ **Details**.

    b. z/OS (OS/390): Issue the Explorer command to open the Explorer window. Type **s** beside the IA library and press ENTER.

    c. For Windows and UNIX, select **View** ⇨ 📁 **Up One Level** to navigate up to the Active Libraries view in the Explorer window. For z/OS (OS/390), issue the END command or click **X** to close the Explorer window.

2. **Investigating a SAS Data Set with PROC CONTENTS**

    a.
    ```
    proc contents data=ia._all_ nods;
    run;
    ```

    b.
    ```
    proc contents data=ia.pilots;
    run;
    ```

Chapter 4 Producing List Reports

4.1   Getting Started with the PRINT Procedure

Objectives

- Generate simple list reports using the PRINT procedure.
- Display selected variables (columns) in a list report.
- Display selected observations (rows) in a list report.
- Display a list report with column totals.

3

Overview of the PRINT Procedure

List reports are typically generated with PROC PRINT.

```
                          The SAS System

            Emp                              Job
    Obs     ID      LastName    FirstName    Code     Salary

     1     0031   GOLDENBERG     DESIREE     PILOT    50221.62
     2     0040   WILLIAMS       ARLENE M.   FLTAT    23666.12
     3     0071   PERRY          ROBERT A.   FLTAT    21957.71
     4     0082   MCGWIER-WATTS  CHRISTINA   PILOT    96387.39
     5     0091   SCOTT          HARVEY F.   FLTAT    32278.40
     6     0106   THACKER        DAVID S.    FLTAT    24161.14
     7     0355   BELL           THOMAS B.   PILOT    59803.16
     8     0366   GLENN          MARTHA S.   PILOT   120202.38
```

continued...

4

Overview of the PRINT Procedure

You can display the following:

- titles and footnotes
- descriptive column headings
- formatted data values

```
                        Salary Report

        Emp                            Job      Annual
Obs      ID    LastName     FirstName   Code     Salary

  1     0031   GOLDENBERG    DESIREE    PILOT   $50,221.62
  2     0040   WILLIAMS      ARLENE M.  FLTAT   $23,666.12
  3     0071   PERRY         ROBERT A.  FLTAT   $21,957.71
  4     0082   MCGWIER-WATTS CHRISTINA  PILOT   $96,387.39
  5     0091   SCOTT         HARVEY F.  FLTAT   $32,278.40
  6     0106   THACKER       DAVID S.   FLTAT   $24,161.14
  7     0355   BELL          THOMAS B.  PILOT   $59,803.16
  8     0366   GLENN         MARTHA S.  PILOT  $120,202.38
```

continued...

5

Overview of the PRINT Procedure

You can display the following:

- column totals
- column subtotals
- page breaks for each subgroup

```
                    The SAS System

---------------------- JobCode=FLTAT ----------------------

        Emp
Obs      ID    LastName     FirstName     Salary

  1     0040   WILLIAMS      ARLENE M.    23666.12
  2     0071   PERRY         ROBERT A.    21957.71
  3     0091   SCOTT         HARVEY F.    32278.40
  4     0106   THACKER       DAVID S.     24161.14
-------                                   ---------
JobCode                                  102063.37
```

continued...

6

Overview of the PRINT Procedure

```
                    The SAS System

---------------------- JobCode=PILOT ----------------------

        Emp
Obs      ID    LastName      FirstName     Salary

  5     0031   GOLDENBERG     DESIREE     50221.62
  6     0082   MCGWIER-WATTS  CHRISTINA   96387.39
  7     0355   BELL           THOMAS B.   59803.16
  8     0366   GLENN          MARTHA S.  120202.38
-------                                   ---------
JobCode                                  326614.55
                                         =========
                                         428677.92
```

7

Creating a Default List Report

General form of the PRINT procedure:

```
PROC PRINT DATA=SAS-data-set;
RUN;
```

Example:

```
libname ia 'SAS-data-library';
proc print data=ia.empdata;
run;
```

c04s1d1

Creating a Default List Report

ia.empdata

EmpID	LastName	FirstName	JobCode	Salary
0031	GOLDENBERG	DESIREE	PILOT	50221.62
0040	WILLIAMS	ARLENE M.	FLTAT	23666.12
0071	PERRY	ROBERT A.	FLTAT	21957.71

PROC Step

Print all variables.

```
libname ia 'SAS-data-library';
proc print data=ia.empdata;
run;
```

```
                         The SAS System

        Emp                                    Job
Obs     ID      LastName        FirstName       Code    Salary

 1     0031     GOLDENBERG      DESIREE         PILOT   50221.62
 2     0040     WILLIAMS        ARLENE M.       FLTAT   23666.12
 3     0071     PERRY           ROBERT A.       FLTAT   21957.71
```

Printing Selected Variables

The VAR statement enables you to do the following:

- select variables to include in the report
- define the order of the variables in the report

General form of the VAR statement:

```
VAR variable(s);
```

Printing Selected Variables

`ia.empdata`

EmpID	LastName	FirstName	JobCode	Salary
0031	GOLDENBERG	DESIREE	PILOT	50221.62
0040	WILLIAMS	ARLENE M.	FLTAT	23666.12
0071	PERRY	ROBERT A.	FLTAT	21957.71

PROC Step

Select and order variables to print.

```
proc print data=ia.empdata;
   var JobCode EmpID Salary;
run;
```

```
                        The SAS System

                     Job      Emp
              Obs     Code     ID       Salary

               1     PILOT    0031     50221.62
               2     FLTAT    0040     23666.12
               3     FLTAT    0071     21957.71
```

c04s1d2

11

Suppressing the Obs Column

The NOOBS option suppresses the observation numbers on the left side of the report.

General form of the NOOBS option:

PROC PRINT DATA=*SAS-data-set* **NOOBS;**
RUN;

12

Suppressing the Obs Column

`ia.empdata`

EmpID	LastName	FirstName	JobCode	Salary
0031	GOLDENBERG	DESIREE	PILOT	50221.62
0040	WILLIAMS	ARLENE M.	FLTAT	23666.12
0071	PERRY	ROBERT A.	FLTAT	21957.71

PROC Step

Suppress the Obs column.

```
proc print data=ia.empdata noobs;
   var JobCode EmpID Salary;
run;
```

```
                        The SAS System

                     Job      Emp
                     Code     ID       Salary

                    PILOT    0031     50221.62
                    FLTAT    0040     23666.12
                    FLTAT    0071     21957.71
```

c04s1d3

13

Subsetting Data: WHERE Statement

Produce a listing report that displays information for pilots only.

The WHERE statement
- enables you to select observations that meet a certain condition
- can be used with most SAS procedures.

14

Subsetting Data: WHERE Statement

General form of the WHERE statement:

> **WHERE** *where-expression*;

where-expression is a sequence of operands and operators.

Operands include the following:
- variables
- constants

15

Subsetting Data: WHERE Statement

Operators include the following:
- comparison operators
- logical operators
- special operators
- functions

16

Comparison Operators

Mnemonic	Symbol	Definition
EQ	=	equal to
NE	^=	not equal to
	¬=	
	~=	
GT	>	greater than
LT	<	less than
GE	>=	greater than or equal to
LE	<=	less than or equal to
IN		equal to one of a list

17

Comparison Operators

Examples:

```
where Salary>25000;

where EmpID='0082';

where Salary=.;

where LastName=' ';

where JobCode in('PILOT','FLTAT');

where JobCode in('PILOT' 'FLTAT');
```

Character comparisons are case sensitive.
The IN operator allows commas or blanks
to separate values.

18

Logical Operators

Logical operators include the following:

AND &	If both expressions are true, then the compound expression is true.

```
where JobCode='FLTAT' and Salary>50000;
```

OR |	If either expression is true, then the compound expression is true.

```
where JobCode='PILOT' or JobCode='FLTAT';
```

NOT ^	can be combined with other operators to reverse the logic of a comparison.

```
where JobCode not in('PILOT','FLTAT');
```

19

Special Operators

Special operators include the following:

| BETWEEN-AND | selects observations in which the value of the variable falls within a range of values, inclusively. |

```
where Salary between 50000 and 70000;
```

| CONTAINS
? | selects observations that include the specified substring. |

```
where LastName ? 'LAM';
```

(LAMBERT, BELLAMY, and ELAM are selected.)

20

Printing Selected Observations

Use the WHERE statement to control which observations are processed.

EmpID	LastName	FirstName	JobCode	Salary
0031	GOLDENBERG	DESIREE	PILOT	50221.62
0040	WILLIAMS	ARLENE M.	FLTAT	23666.12
0071	PERRY	ROBERT A.	FLTAT	21957.71

ia.empdata

PROC Step

Select rows to print.
```
proc print data=ia.empdata noobs;
   var JobCode EmpID Salary;
   where JobCode='PILOT';
run;
```

```
                 The SAS System
         Job      Emp
         Code      ID         Salary
         PILOT    0031      50221.62
         PILOT    0082      96387.39
         PILOT    0355      59803.16
         PILOT    0366     120202.38
```

21   c04s1d4

Requesting Column Totals

The SUM statement produces column totals.

General form of the SUM statement:

SUM *variable(s);*

The SUM statement also produces subtotals if you print the data in groups.

22

Requesting Column Totals

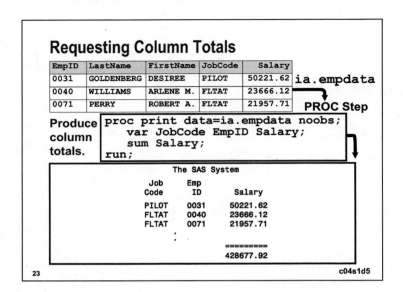

EmpID	LastName	FirstName	JobCode	Salary
0031	GOLDENBERG	DESIREE	PILOT	50221.62
0040	WILLIAMS	ARLENE M.	FLTAT	23666.12
0071	PERRY	ROBERT A.	FLTAT	21957.71

ia.empdata

PROC Step

Produce column totals.

```
proc print data=ia.empdata noobs;
    var JobCode EmpID Salary;
    sum Salary;
run;
```

```
                 The SAS System

            Job     Emp
            Code     ID      Salary

            PILOT   0031    50221.62
            FLTAT   0040    23666.12
            FLTAT   0071    21957.71
                 .
                 .

                        =========
                         428677.92
```

23   c04s1d5

 **Exercises**

For these exercises, use SAS data sets stored in a permanent SAS data library.

Fill in the blank with the location of your SAS data library. Submit the LIBNAME statement to assign the libref **ia** to the SAS data library.

```
libname ia '_____';
```

1. **Printing All Variables and Observations**

   Produce a list report that displays all the variables and observations in the **ia.passngrs** data set. Show column totals for the **FClass**, **BClass**, and **EClass** variables.

   Partial SAS Output

```
                                    The SAS System

            Flight
   Obs        ID       Dest    Depart    FClass    BClass    EClass

    1       IA01802     SEA     15101       10         9       132
    2       IA01804     SEA     15101       11        12       111
    3       IA02901     HNL     15101       13        24       138
    4       IA03100     ANC     15101       13        22       150
    5       IA03101     ANC     15101       14         .       133
    6       IA01802     SEA     15102       12        11       126
    7       IA01804     SEA     15102       12         8       119
    8       IA02901     HNL     15102       14        25       132
    9       IA03100     ANC     15102       16        26       143
   10       IA01802     SEA     15103       12        13       115
   11       IA01804     SEA     15103       12        12       136
   12       IA02901     HNL     15103       12        21       155
   13       IA03100     ANC     15103       14        18       137
    .
    .
    .
   20       IA01804     SEA     15105       11        18       104
   21       IA02901     HNL     15105       13        14       145
   22       IA03100     ANC     15105       15        22        99
   23       IA01802     SEA     15106       12        15       106
   24       IA01804     SEA     15106       10        15       111
   25       IA02901     HNL     15106       13        24       137
   26       IA03100     ANC     15106       15        16       137
   27       IA01802     SEA     15107       12        17       131
   28       IA01804     SEA     15107       10        13       113
   29       IA02901     HNL     15107       13        19       144
   30       IA03100     ANC     15107       15        23       105
                                          ======    ======    ======
                                           376       485       3859
```

2. Selecting Variables and Observations

a. Use the `ia.passngrs` data set to produce a list report that displays only flights to Seattle (`Dest='SEA'`).

SAS Output

Obs	Flight ID	Dest	Depart	FClass	BClass	EClass
			The SAS System			
1	IA01802	SEA	15101	10	9	132
2	IA01804	SEA	15101	11	12	111
6	IA01802	SEA	15102	12	11	126
7	IA01804	SEA	15102	12	8	119
10	IA01802	SEA	15103	12	13	115
11	IA01804	SEA	15103	12	12	136
14	IA01802	SEA	15104	10	18	128
15	IA01804	SEA	15104	11	17	105
19	IA01802	SEA	15105	11	14	131
20	IA01804	SEA	15105	11	18	104
23	IA01802	SEA	15106	12	15	106
24	IA01804	SEA	15106	10	15	111
27	IA01802	SEA	15107	12	17	131
28	IA01804	SEA	15107	10	13	113

b. Alter the program so that only the variables `FlightID`, `Depart`, `FClass`, `BClass`, and `EClass` are displayed. Suppress the observation number.

SAS Output

Flight ID	Depart	FClass	BClass	EClass
	The SAS System			
IA01802	15101	10	9	132
IA01804	15101	11	12	111
IA01802	15102	12	11	126
IA01804	15102	12	8	119
IA01802	15103	12	13	115
IA01804	15103	12	12	136
IA01802	15104	10	18	128
IA01804	15104	11	17	105
IA01802	15105	11	14	131
IA01804	15105	11	18	104
IA01802	15106	12	15	106
IA01804	15106	10	15	111
IA01802	15107	12	17	131
IA01804	15107	10	13	113

c. Alter the program so that only the flights to Seattle with at least 120 **EClass** passengers, but fewer than 15 **BClass** passengers, are displayed.

SAS Output

```
                              The SAS System

            Flight
              ID      Depart    FClass    BClass    EClass

            IA01802    15101      10         9        132
            IA01802    15102      12        11        126
            IA01804    15103      12        12        136
            IA01802    15105      11        14        131
```

3. Selecting Variables and Observations (Optional)

Write a PROC PRINT step for **ia.employees**.

- Suppress the observation column.
- Limit variables to **EmpID**, **Country**, **Division**, **JobCode**, and **Salary**.
- Add the N option to the PROC PRINT statement. The N option prints the number of output observations at the bottom of the report.
- Limit the output to employees from Canada.
- Generate a grand total for **Salary**.

Partial SAS Output

```
                              The SAS System

                                                   Job
      EmpID      Country      Division             Code      Salary

      E00008     CANADA       CORPORATE OPERATIONS OFFMGR    $85,000
      E00039     CANADA       HUMAN RESOURCES      FACCLK    $38,000
      E00041     CANADA       SALES & MARKETING    MKTCLK    $45,000
      E00056     CANADA       AIRPORT OPERATIONS   GRCREW    $29,000
      E00079     CANADA       AIRPORT OPERATIONS   GRCREW    $41,000
      E00122     CANADA       HUMAN RESOURCES      RESMGR    $24,000
      E00164     CANADA       AIRPORT OPERATIONS   GRCREW    $36,000
      E00190     CANADA       HUMAN RESOURCES      RECEPT    $22,000
      E00341     CANADA       SALES & MARKETING    MKTMGR    $38,000
      E00359     CANADA       FLIGHT OPERATIONS    MECHO3    $16,000
      E00392     CANADA       AIRPORT OPERATIONS   BAGCLK    $31,000
      E00430     CANADA       FLIGHT OPERATIONS    MECHO3    $20,000
                                                            ==========
                                                            $425,000

                              N = 12
```

4.2   Sequencing and Grouping Observations

Objectives

- Sequence (sort) observations in a SAS data set.
- Group observations in a list report.
- Print column subtotals in a list report.
- Control page breaks for subgroups.

26

Sorting a SAS Data Set

To request subgroup totals in PROC PRINT, the observations in the data set must be grouped.

The SORT procedure

- rearranges the observations in a SAS data set
- can create a new SAS data set containing the rearranged observations
- can sort on multiple variables
- can sort in ascending (default) or descending order
- does not generate printed output
- treats missing values as the smallest possible value.

27

Sorting a SAS Data Set

General form of the PROC SORT step:

```
PROC SORT DATA=input-SAS-data-set
          <OUT=output-SAS-data-set>;
    BY <DESCENDING> by-variable(s);
RUN;
```

Examples:

```
proc sort data=ia.empdata;
   by Salary;
run;
```

```
proc sort data=ia.empdata out=work.jobsal;
   by JobCode descending Salary;
run;
```

28

Sorting a SAS Data Set

`ia.empdata`

EmpID	LastName	FirstName	JobCode	Salary
0031	GOLDENBERG	DESIREE	PILOT	50221.62
0040	WILLIAMS	ARLENE M.	FLTAT	23666.12
0071	PERRY	ROBERT A.	FLTAT	21957.71

PROC Step

```
proc sort data=ia.empdata out=work.empdata;
   by JobCode;
run;
```

`work.empdata`

EmpID	LastName	FirstName	JobCode	Salary
0040	WILLIAMS	ARLENE M.	FLTAT	23666.12
0071	PERRY	ROBERT A.	FLTAT	21957.71
0031	GOLDENBERG	DESIREE	PILOT	50221.62

29

Printing Subtotals and Grand Totals

Print the data set grouped by **JobCode** with a subtotal
for the **Salary** column for each **JobCode**.

```
proc sort data=ia.empdata out=work.empdata;
   by JobCode;
run;
proc print data=work.empdata;
   by JobCode;
   sum Salary;
run;
```

Using a BY statement and a SUM statement together in
a PROC PRINT step produces subtotals and grand totals.

c04s2d1

30

Data must be indexed or in sorted order to use a BY statement in a PROC PRINT step.

Printing Subtotals and Grand Totals

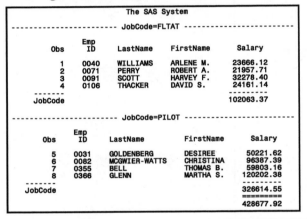

```
                         The SAS System
------------------------ JobCode=FLTAT ------------------------

           Emp
    Obs     ID      LastName       FirstName      Salary

     1     0040     WILLIAMS       ARLENE M.     23666.12
     2     0071     PERRY          ROBERT A.     21957.71
     3     0091     SCOTT          HARVEY F.     32278.40
     4     0106     THACKER        DAVID S.      24161.14
-------                                         ---------
JobCode                                         102063.37

------------------------ JobCode=PILOT ------------------------

           Emp
    Obs     ID      LastName       FirstName      Salary

     5     0031     GOLDENBERG     DESIREE        50221.62
     6     0082     MCGWIER-WATTS  CHRISTINA      96387.39
     7     0355     BELL           THOMAS B.      59803.16
     8     0366     GLENN          MARTHA S.     120202.38
-------                                         ---------
JobCode                                         326614.55
                                                =========
                                                428677.92
```

31

Page Breaks

Use the PAGEBY statement with the BY statement to put each subgroup on a separate page.

General form of the PAGEBY statement:

PAGEBY *by-variable;*

```
proc print data=work.empdata;
   by JobCode;
   pageby JobCode;
   sum Salary;
run;
```

The PAGEBY statement must name a variable that appears in a BY statement.

32   c04s2d2

 The variable in the PAGEBY statement must appear in the BY statement.

Page Breaks

First Page

```
                      The SAS System                        1

------------------- JobCode=FLTAT -------------------------

          Emp
    Obs   ID      LastName    FirstName     Salary

     1    0040    WILLIAMS    ARLENE M.    23666.12
     2    0071    PERRY       ROBERT A.    21957.71
     3    0091    SCOTT       HARVEY F.    32278.40
     4    0106    THACKER     DAVID S.     24161.14
    -------                              ---------
    JobCode                              102063.37
```

33   continued...

Page Breaks

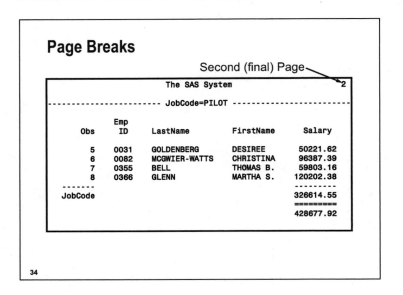

Second (final) Page

```
                        The SAS System                  2
----------------------- JobCode=PILOT -----------------------

         Emp
  Obs    ID    LastName        FirstName      Salary

    5   0031   GOLDENBERG      DESIREE        50221.62
    6   0082   MCGWIER-WATTS   CHRISTINA      96387.39
    7   0355   BELL            THOMAS B.      59803.16
    8   0366   GLENN           MARTHA S.     120202.38
-------                                      ---------
JobCode                                     326614.55
                                            =========
                                            428677.92
```

34

 **Exercises**

For these exercises, use SAS data sets stored in a permanent SAS data library.

> Fill in the blank with the location of your SAS data library. **If you started a new SAS session since the previous lab**, submit the LIBNAME statement to assign the libref **ia** to the SAS data library.
>
> `libname ia '_____';`

4. **Printing Reports with Page Breaks**

   Create the listing described below using the **ia.passngrs** data set.
   - Sequence the report in ascending order by destination (**Dest**) and place the listing for each destination on a separate page.
   - Print only the variables **Depart**, **FClass**, **BClass**, and **EClass**.
   - Display column totals and subtotals for the variables **FClass**, **BClass**, and **EClass**.

   SAS Output

```
                            The SAS System                                    1

----------------------------- Dest=ANC -----------------------------------

        Obs    Depart    FClass    BClass    EClass

         1     15101       13        22        150
         2     15101       14         .        133
         3     15102       16        26        143
         4     15103       14        18        137
         5     15104       14        17        144
         6     15104       13         .        142
         7     15105       15        22         99
         8     15106       15        16        137
         9     15107       15        23        105
        ----              ------    ------    ------
        Dest               129       144       1190
```

   (Continued on the next page.)

```
                            The SAS System                                    2

         ------------------------------ Dest=HNL ------------------------------

              Obs     Depart     FClass     BClass     EClass

               10     15101        13         24         138
               11     15102        14         25         132
               12     15103        12         21         155
               13     15104        13         22         150
               14     15105        13         14         145
               15     15106        13         24         137
               16     15107        13         19         144
              ----               ------     ------     ------
              Dest                  91        149        1001
```

```
                            The SAS System                                    3

         ------------------------------ Dest=SEA ------------------------------

              Obs     Depart     FClass     BClass     EClass

               17     15101        10          9         132
               18     15101        11         12         111
               19     15102        12         11         126
               20     15102        12          8         119
               21     15103        12         13         115
               22     15103        12         12         136
               23     15104        10         18         128
               24     15104        11         17         105
               25     15105        11         14         131
               26     15105        11         18         104
               27     15106        12         15         106
               28     15106        10         15         111
               29     15107        12         17         131
               30     15107        10         13         113
              ----               ------     ------     ------
              Dest                 156        192        1668
                                 ======     ======     ======
                                   376        485        3859
```

5. **Producing List Reports (Optional)**

Create the listing described below using the **ia.person1** data set. (Note that the last character in the data set name is the lowercase letter l not the numeral 1.)

- Sequence the report in ascending order by **Gender** and last name (**LName**) in ascending order within **Gender**.
- Only print observations (rows) for flight attendants (**JobCode** values **'FA1'**, **'FA2'**, **'FA3'**) who live in New York (**State** value **'NY'**).
- Only print the variables **LName**, **FName**, **Gender**, and **Salary**.
- Suppress the observation number.

SAS Output

```
                             The SAS System

              LName        FName       Gender    Salary

              ARTHUR       BARBARA        F       32886
              DEAN         SHARON         F       33419
              DUNLAP       DONNA          F       28888
              EATON        ALICIA         F       27787
              FIELDS       DIANA          F       23177
              JONES        LESLIE         F       22367
              MCDANIEL     RONDA          F       23738
              MURPHY       ALICE          F       32699
              PATTERSON    RENEE          F       28978
              PEARCE       CAROL          F       22413
              RICHARDS     CASEY          F       22862
              VEGA         ANNA           F       27321
              WALTERS      DIANE          F       27896
              WOOD         DEBORAH        F       23916
              YOUNG        JOANN          F       27956
              CAHILL       MARSHALL       M       28572
              COOPER       ANTHONY        M       32217
              SMART        JONATHAN       M       27761
              VEGA         FRANKLIN       M       28278
```

4.3   Identifying Observations (Self-Study)

Objectives

- Use the ID statement to identify observations.
- Combine the BY and ID statements to produce special formatting.

37

Identifying Observations

The ID statement enables you to do the following:

- suppress the Obs column in the report
- specify which variable(s) should replace the Obs column

General form of the ID statement:

> **ID** *variable(s)*;

38

Creating a Default List Report

`ia.empdata`

EmpID	LastName	FirstName	JobCode	Salary
0031	GOLDENBERG	DESIREE	PILOT	50221.62
0040	WILLIAMS	ARLENE M.	FLTAT	23666.12
0071	PERRY	ROBERT A.	FLTAT	21957.71

PROC Step

Replace the Obs column.

```
proc print data=ia.empdata;
     id JobCode;
     var EmpID Salary;
run;
```

```
              The SAS System

         Job      Emp
         Code      ID       Salary

         PILOT    0031      50221.62
         FLTAT    0040      23666.12
         FLTAT    0071      21957.71
```

39   c04s3d1

Special BY-Group Formatting

When the ID and BY statements specify the same variable, the following events occur:

- The Obs column is suppressed.
- The BY line is suppressed.
- The ID/BY variable prints in the leftmost column.
- Each ID/BY value only prints at the start of each BY group (and on the subtotal line, if a SUM statement is used).

40

Special BY-Group Formatting

Specify **JobCode** in the BY and ID statements to change the report format.

```
proc sort data=ia.empdata out=work.empdata;
   by JobCode;
run;
proc print data=work.empdata;
   by JobCode;
   id JobCode;
   sum Salary;
run;
```

41   c04s3d2

Special BY-Group Formatting

```
                      The SAS System

   Job     Emp
   Code    ID     LastName        FirstName      Salary

   FLTAT   0040   WILLIAMS        ARLENE M.     23666.12
           0071   PERRY           ROBERT A.     21957.71
           0091   SCOTT           HARVEY F.     32278.40
           0106   THACKER         DAVID S.      24161.14
   -----                                        ----------
   FLTAT                                        102063.37

   PILOT   0031   GOLDENBERG      DESIREE       50221.62
           0082   MCGWIER-WATTS   CHRISTINA     96387.39
           0355   BELL            THOMAS B.     59803.16
           0366   GLENN           MARTHA S.     120202.38
   -----                                        ----------
   PILOT                                        326614.55
                                                ==========
                                                428677.92
```

42

 **Exercises**

For these exercises, use SAS data sets stored in a permanent SAS data library.

> Fill in the blank with the location of your SAS data library. **If you started a new SAS session since the previous lab**, submit the LIBNAME statement to assign the libref **ia** to the SAS data library.
>
> ```
> libname ia '_____';
> ```

6. **Identifying Observations and Using Page Breaks**

   Create the listing described below using the **ia.passngrs** data set.

   - Sequence the report in ascending order by destination (**Dest**) and place the listing for each destination on a separate page.
   - Print only the variables **Dest**, **Depart**, **FClass**, **BClass**, and **EClass**. Display **Dest** in the left column, suppress the observation number, and suppress redundant values of the **Dest** variable.
   - Display column totals and subtotals for the variables **FClass**, **BClass**, and **EClass**.

   SAS Output

		The SAS System			1
Dest	Depart	FClass	BClass	EClass	
ANC	15101	13	22	150	
	15101	14	.	133	
	15102	16	26	143	
	15103	14	18	137	
	15104	14	17	144	
	15104	13	.	142	
	15105	15	22	99	
	15106	15	16	137	
	15107	15	23	105	
----		------	------	------	
ANC		129	144	1190	

(Continued on the next page.)

```
                      The SAS System                                2

           Dest    Depart    FClass    BClass    EClass

           HNL     15101       13        24        138
                   15102       14        25        132
                   15103       12        21        155
                   15104       13        22        150
                   15105       13        14        145
                   15106       13        24        137
                   15107       13        19        144
           ----              ------    ------    ------
           HNL                 91       149       1001
```

```
                      The SAS System                                3

           Dest    Depart    FClass    BClass    EClass

           SEA     15101       10         9        132
                   15101       11        12        111
                   15102       12        11        126
                   15102       12         8        119
                   15103       12        13        115
                   15103       12        12        136
                   15104       10        18        128
                   15104       11        17        105
                   15105       11        14        131
                   15105       11        18        104
                   15106       12        15        106
                   15106       10        15        111
                   15107       12        17        131
                   15107       10        13        113
           ----              ------    ------    ------
           SEA                156       192       1668
                             ======    ======    ======
                              376       485       3859
```

7. Grouping Observations (Optional)

Write a PROC PRINT step for **ia.delay**.

- Observations should appear in ascending order by **Dest** and in descending order by **Mail**. However, the report should be grouped only by **Dest**.

- Print only the variables **Flight**, **Date**, **Dest**, and **Mail**. Display **Dest** in the left column, suppress the observation numbers, and suppress redundant values of **Dest**.

- Create subtotals for **Mail**.

- Add a WHERE statement that prevents rows from printing if the value of **Dest** is missing.

Partial SAS Output – First BY Group

```
                              The SAS System

                  Dest    Flight       Date      Mail

                  CPH       387      19MAR95       578
                            387      07MAR95       546
                             .
                             .
                             .
                            387      24MAR95       301
                            387      28MAR95       271
                            387      30MAR95         .
                  - - - -                        - - - - - -
                  CPH                             10436
```

Partial SAS Output – Last BY Group

```
                  Dest    Flight       Date      Mail

                  YYZ       132      03MAR95       288
                            132      11MAR95       281
                            132      17MAR95       260
                            132      13MAR95       251
                            132      15MAR95       213
                  - - - -                        - - - - - -
                  YYZ                             24218
                                                 ======
                                                241309
```

4.4 Special WHERE Statement Operators (Self-Study)

Objectives

- Use special operators in the WHERE statement to subset data.

45

Special Operators

Additional special operators supported by the WHERE statement are shown below:

- LIKE
- sounds-like
- IS MISSING (or IS NULL)

continued...

46

Special Operators

The following are special operators:

- LIKE selects observations by comparing character values to specified patterns.

  A percent sign (%) replaces any number of characters.

  An underscore (_) replaces one character.

```
where Code like 'E_U%';
```

The code above selects observations where the value of **Code** begins with an E, followed by a single character, followed by a U, followed by any number of characters.

47

Special Operators

- The sounds-like (=*) operator selects observations that contain spelling variations of the word or words specified.

```
where Name=*'SMITH';
```

  The code above selects names such as SMYTHE and SMITT.

- IS NULL or IS MISSING selects observations in which the value of the variable is missing.

```
where Flight is missing;

where Flight is null;
```

48

 **Exercises**

For these exercises, use SAS data sets stored in a permanent SAS data library.

Fill in the blank with the location of your SAS data library. **If you started a new SAS session since the previous lab,** submit the LIBNAME statement to assign the libref **ia** to the SAS data library.

```
libname ia '_____';
```

8. **Using Special WHERE Statement Operators**

Create the listing described below. Use the **ia.person1** data set. (Note that the last character in the data set name is the lowercase letter l not the numeral 1.)

- Print only the variables **LName** and **FName**.

- Display only the observations where the value of **LName** begins with **BR**.

SAS Output

```
                          The SAS System

                Obs      LName      FName

                 13      BRADLEY    JEREMY
                 14      BRADY      CHRISTINE
                 15      BROWN      JASON
                 16      BRYANT     LEONARD
```

4.5 Solutions to Exercises

1. **Printing All Variables and Observations**

```
libname ia 'SAS-data-library';
proc print data=ia.passngrs;
    sum FClass BClass EClass;
run;
```

2. **Selecting Variables and Observations**

   a.
```
proc print data=ia.passngrs;
    where Dest='SEA';
run;
```

   b.
```
proc print data=ia.passngrs noobs;
    where Dest='SEA';
    var FlightID Depart FClass BClass EClass;
run;
```

   c.
```
proc print data=ia.passngrs noobs;
    where Dest='SEA' and EClass ge 120 and BClass lt 15;
    var FlightID Depart FClass BClass EClass;
run;
```

3. **Selecting Variables and Observations (Optional)**

```
proc print data=ia.employees noobs n;
    var EmpId Country Division JobCode Salary;
    sum Salary;
    where Country='CANADA';
run;
```

4. **Printing Reports with Page Breaks**

```
proc sort data=ia.passngrs out=work.passngrs;
    by Dest;
run;
proc print data=work.passngrs;
    by Dest;
    pageby Dest;
    var Depart FClass BClass EClass;
    sum FClass BClass EClass;
run;
```

5. Producing List Reports (Optional)

```
proc sort data=ia.person1 out=work.person1;
   by Gender LName;
run;
proc print data=work.person1 noobs;
   var LName FName Gender Salary;
   where State='NY' and JobCode in ('FA1' 'FA2' 'FA3');
run;
```

6. Identifying Observations and Using Page Breaks

```
proc sort data=ia.passngrs out=work.passngrs;
   by Dest;
run;
proc print data=work.passngrs;
   id Dest;
   by Dest;
   pageby Dest;
   var Depart FClass BClass EClass;
   sum FClass BClass EClass;
run;
```

7. Grouping Observations (Optional)

```
proc sort data=ia.delay out=work.delay;
   by Dest descending Mail;
run;

proc print data=work.delay;
   by Dest;
   id Dest;
   sum Mail;
   var Flight Date Mail;
   where dest ne ' ';
run;
```

8. Using Special WHERE Statement Operators

```
proc print data=ia.person1;
   where LName like 'BR%';
   var LName Fname;
run;
```

Chapter 5   Enhancing Output

5.1 Customizing Report Appearance

Objectives

- Define titles and footnotes to enhance reports.
- Define descriptive column headings.
- Use SAS system options.

3

Defining Titles and Footnotes

You use titles and footnotes to enhance reports.

General form of the TITLE statement:

TITLE*n* *'text'*;

General form of the FOOTNOTE statement:

FOOTNOTE*n* *'text'*;

Example:

```
title1 'Flight Crew Employee Listing';
footnote2 'Employee Review';
```

4

Defining Titles and Footnotes

Features of titles:

- Titles appear at the top of the page.
- The default title is **The SAS System**.
- The value of *n* can be from 1 to 10.
- An unnumbered TITLE is equivalent to TITLE1.
- Titles remain in effect until they are changed, cancelled, or you end your SAS session.
- The null TITLE statement, `title;`, cancels all titles.

5

Defining Titles and Footnotes

Features of footnotes:

- Footnotes appear at the bottom of the page.
- No footnote is printed unless one is specified.
- The value of *n* can be from 1 to 10.
- An unnumbered FOOTNOTE is equivalent to FOOTNOTE1.
- Footnotes remain in effect until they are changed or cancelled, or until you end your SAS session.
- The null FOOTNOTE statement, `footnote;`, cancels all footnotes.

6

Changing Titles and Footnotes

TITLE*n* or FOOTNOTE*n*

- replaces a previous title or footnote with the same number
- cancels all titles or footnotes with higher numbers.

7

Defining Titles and Footnotes

PROC PRINT Code	Resultant Title(s)
| ```
proc print data=work.march;
   title1 'The First Line';
   title2 'The Second Line';
run;
``` | |
| ```
proc print data=work.march;
   title2 'The Next Line';
run;
``` | |
| ```
proc print data=work.march;
   title 'The Top Line';
run;
``` | |
| ```
proc print data=work.march;
   title3 'The Third Line';
run;
``` | |
| ```
proc print data=work.march;
   title;
run;
``` | |

8

Defining Titles and Footnotes

PROC PRINT Code	Resultant Title(s)
| ```
proc print data=work.march;
   title1 'The First Line';
   title2 'The Second Line';
run;
``` | The First Line<br>The Second Line |
| ```
proc print data=work.march;
   title2 'The Next Line';
run;
``` | The First Line<br>The Next Line |
| ```
proc print data=work.march;
   title 'The Top Line';
run;
``` | The Top Line |
| ```
proc print data=work.march;
   title3 'The Third Line';
run;
``` | The Top Line<br><br>The Third Line |
| ```
proc print data=work.march;
   title;
run;
``` | |

13

Assigning Column Labels

General form of the LABEL statement:

LABEL *variable*='*label*'
        variable='*label*';

'*label*' specifies a label of up to 256 characters.

- Labels replace variable names in SAS output.
- Labels are used automatically by many procedures.
- The PRINT procedure uses labels when the LABEL or SPLIT= option is specified in the PROC PRINT statement.

14

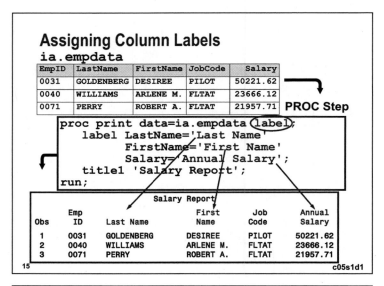

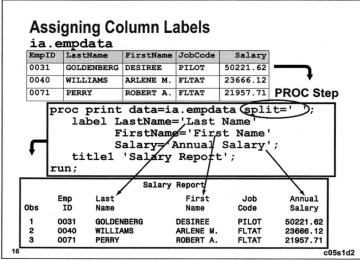

Using SAS System Options

You can use SAS system options to change the appearance of a report.

General form of the OPTIONS statement:

> **OPTIONS** *option* . . . ;

The OPTIONS statement is **not** usually included in a PROC or DATA step.

17

Using SAS System Options

Selected SAS system options:

DATE (default)	specifies to print the date and time that the SAS session began at the top of each page of the SAS output.
NODATE	specifies not to print the date and time that the SAS session began.
LINESIZE=width LS=width	specifies the line size for the SAS log and SAS output.
PAGESIZE=n PS=n	specifies the number of lines (n) that can be printed per page of SAS output.

18   *continued...*

 The DTRESET option, new in SAS®9, specifies that SAS update the date and time in the titles of the SAS log and output. The update occurs when the page is being written. This is helpful in getting a more accurate date and time stamp.

The NODTRESET option, the default, specifies that SAS not update the date and time in the titles.

Using SAS System Options

Selected SAS system options:

NUMBER (default)	specifies that page numbers be printed on the first line of each page of output.
NONUMBER	specifies that page numbers not be printed.
PAGENO=n	specifies a beginning page number (n) for the next page of SAS output.

Example:

```
options nodate nonumber ls=72;
```

19

5.2   Formatting Data Values

Objectives

- Display formatted values using SAS formats in a list report.
- Create user-defined formats using the FORMAT procedure.
- Apply user-defined formats to variables in a list report.

21

Using SAS Formats

Enhance the readability of reports by formatting the data values.

```
                        Salary Report

           Emp    Last              First      Job        Annual
    Obs    ID     Name              Name       Code        Salary

     1     0031   GOLDENBERG        DESIREE    PILOT    $50,221.62
     2     0040   WILLIAMS          ARLENE M.  FLTAT    $23,666.12
     3     0071   PERRY             ROBERT A.  FLTAT    $21,957.71
     4     0082   MCGWIER-WATTS     CHRISTINA  PILOT    $96,387.39
     5     0091   SCOTT             HARVEY F.  FLTAT    $32,278.40
     6     0106   THACKER           DAVID S.   FLTAT    $24,161.14
     7     0355   BELL              THOMAS B.  PILOT    $59,803.16
     8     0366   GLENN             MARTHA S.  PILOT   $120,202.38
```

22

Using User-defined Formats

Create custom formats to recode data values in a report.

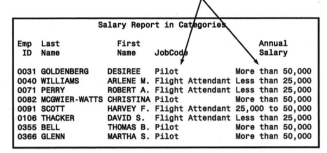

```
                    Salary Report in Categories

Emp   Last            First
ID    Name            Name       JobCode           Annual
                                                   Salary

0031  GOLDENBERG      DESIREE    Pilot             More than 50,000
0040  WILLIAMS        ARLENE M.  Flight Attendant  Less than 25,000
0071  PERRY           ROBERT A.  Flight Attendant  Less than 25,000
0082  MCGWIER-WATTS   CHRISTINA  Pilot             More than 50,000
0091  SCOTT           HARVEY F.  Flight Attendant  25,000 to 50,000
0106  THACKER         DAVID S.   Flight Attendant  Less than 25,000
0355  BELL            THOMAS B.  Pilot             More than 50,000
0366  GLENN           MARTHA S.  Pilot             More than 50,000
```

23

Formatting Data Values

You can enhance reports by using SAS formats to format data values.

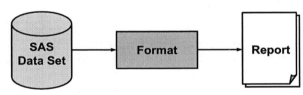

Values in the SAS data set are **not** changed.

24

Formatting Data Values

To apply a format to a specific SAS variable, use the FORMAT statement.

General form of the FORMAT statement:

> **FORMAT** *variable(s) format*;

Example:

```
proc print data=ia.empdata;
   format Salary dollar11.2;
run;
```

25

What Is a SAS Format?

A *format* is an instruction that SAS uses to write data values.

SAS formats have the following form:

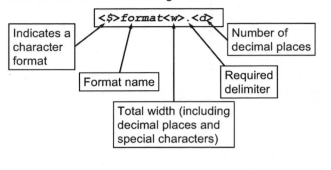

`<$>format<w>.<d>`

- Indicates a character format
- Format name
- Total width (including decimal places and special characters)
- Required delimiter
- Number of decimal places

26

SAS Formats

Selected SAS formats:

w.d 8.2	standard numeric format Width=8, 2 decimal places: 12234.21
$w. $5.	standard character format Width=5: KATHY
COMMAw.d COMMA9.2	commas in a number Width=9, 2 decimal places: 12,234.21
DOLLARw.d DOLLAR10.2	dollar signs and commas in a number Width=10, 2 decimal places: $12,234.21

27

SAS Formats

If you do not specify a format width that is large enough to accommodate a numeric value, the displayed value is automatically adjusted to fit into the width.

Stored Value	Format	Displayed Value
27134.2864	COMMA12.2	27,134.29
27134.2864	12.2	27134.29
27134.2864	DOLLAR12.2	$27,134.29
27134.2864	DOLLAR9.2	$27134.29
27134.2864	DOLLAR8.2	27134.29
27134.2864	DOLLAR5.2	27134
27134.2864	DOLLAR4.2	27E3

28

Formatting Data Values

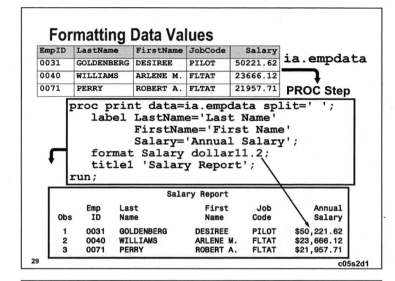

EmpID	LastName	FirstName	JobCode	Salary
0031	GOLDENBERG	DESIREE	PILOT	50221.62
0040	WILLIAMS	ARLENE M.	FLTAT	23666.12
0071	PERRY	ROBERT A.	FLTAT	21957.71

ia.empdata

PROC Step

```
proc print data=ia.empdata split=' ';
   label LastName='Last Name'
         FirstName='First Name'
         Salary='Annual Salary';
   format Salary dollar11.2;
   title1 'Salary Report';
run;
```

```
                          Salary Report

         Emp    Last             First      Job       Annual
  Obs     ID    Name             Name       Code      Salary

   1     0031   GOLDENBERG       DESIREE    PILOT   $50,221.62
   2     0040   WILLIAMS         ARLENE M.  FLTAT   $23,666.12
   3     0071   PERRY            ROBERT A.  FLTAT   $21,957.71
```

29   c05s2d1

SAS Formats

Recall that a SAS date is stored as the number of days between 01JAN1960 and the specified date.

SAS date formats display SAS date values in standard date forms.

Selected SAS date formats:

MMDDYY*w*.

Format	Displayed Value
MMDDYY6.	101601
MMDDYY8.	10/16/01
MMDDYY10.	10/16/2001

DATE*w*.

Format	Displayed Value
DATE7.	16OCT01
DATE9.	16OCT2001

30

SAS Formats

Examples:

Stored Value	Format	Displayed Value
0	MMDDYY8.	01/01/60
0	MMDDYY10.	01/01/1960
1	DATE9.	02JAN1960
-1	WORDDATE.	December 31, 1959
365	DDMMYY10.	31/12/1960
366	WEEKDATE.	Sunday, January 1, 1961

31

Exercises

For these exercises, use SAS data sets stored in a permanent SAS data library.

> Fill in the blank with the location of your SAS data library. **If you started a new SAS session since the previous lab,** submit the LIBNAME statement to assign the libref **ia** to the SAS data library.
>
> `libname ia '_____';`

1. **Enhancing List Reports**

    Create the listing described below using the **ia.passngrs** data set.

    - Do not display the date and time that the SAS session began, set the line size to 64, and start the page number at 1.
    - Sequence the report in ascending order by destination (**Dest**) and place the listing for each destination on a separate page.
    - Print only the variables **Depart**, **FClass**, **BClass**, and **EClass**.
    - Display column totals for the variables **FClass**, **BClass**, and **EClass**.
    - Place the title **San Francisco Passenger Data** on the report.
    - Display the **Depart** values with the DATE9. format and **FClass**, **BClass**, and **EClass** values with commas and zero decimal places.
    - Use the labels below to replace the variable names.

Variable	Label
Dest	Destination
Depart	Departure Date
FClass	First Class
BClass	Business Class
EClass	Economy Class

       Be sure to save your program. You use the solution to this exercise as the basis of a subsequent workshop.

SAS Output

```
                      San Francisco Passenger Data                          1

--------------------- Destination=ANC -----------------------

             Departure    First     Business    Economy
    Obs        Date       Class      Class       Class

     1       06MAY2001      13         22          150
     2       06MAY2001      14          .          133
     3       07MAY2001      16         26          143
     4       08MAY2001      14         18          137
     5       09MAY2001      14         17          144
     6       09MAY2001      13          .          142
     7       10MAY2001      15         22           99
     8       11MAY2001      15         16          137
     9       12MAY2001      15         23          105
    ----                 ------     --------     -------
    Dest                   129        144        1,190
```

```
                      San Francisco Passenger Data                          2

--------------------- Destination=HNL -----------------------

             Departure    First     Business    Economy
    Obs        Date       Class      Class       Class

    10       06MAY2001      13         24          138
    11       07MAY2001      14         25          132
    12       08MAY2001      12         21          155
    13       09MAY2001      13         22          150
    14       10MAY2001      13         14          145
    15       11MAY2001      13         24          137
    16       12MAY2001      13         19          144
    ----                 ------     --------     -------
    Dest                    91        149        1,001
```

```
                      San Francisco Passenger Data                          3

--------------------- Destination=SEA -----------------------

             Departure    First     Business    Economy
    Obs        Date       Class      Class       Class

    17       06MAY2001      10          9          132
    18       06MAY2001      11         12          111
    19       07MAY2001      12         11          126
    20       07MAY2001      12          8          119
    21       08MAY2001      12         13          115
    22       08MAY2001      12         12          136
    23       09MAY2001      10         18          128
    24       09MAY2001      11         17          105
    25       10MAY2001      11         14          131
    26       10MAY2001      11         18          104
    27       11MAY2001      12         15          106
    28       11MAY2001      10         15          111
    29       12MAY2001      12         17          131
    30       12MAY2001      10         13          113
    ----                 ------     --------     -------
    Dest                   156        192        1,668
                         ======     ========     =======
                           376        485        3,859
```

2. Enhancing List Reports (Optional)

Create the listing described below using the `ia.fltat` data set.

- Do not display the date, time, or page numbers.
- Sequence the report by `HireDate`.
- Suppress the observation column and the title (with a null TITLE statement).
- Print only the variables `EmpID`, `Location`, `JobCode`, and `Salary`.
- Run the report once, and then add the YEAR4. format to the `HireDate` variable.

Partial SAS Output

```
-------------------------- HireDate=1980 ----------------------------------

                                  Job
        EmpID       Location      Code      Salary

        E03591      LONDON        FLTAT3     47000
        E04064      FRANKFURT     FLTAT2     37000
        E01447      LONDON        FLTAT3     45000
        E00753      LONDON        FLTAT2     34000

-------------------------- HireDate=1981 ----------------------------------

                                  Job
        EmpID       Location      Code      Salary

        E02679      FRANKFURT     FLTAT1     27000
        E02606      CARY          FLTAT2     36000
        E00364      FRANKFURT     FLTAT1     25000
        E03921      CARY          FLTAT3     47000

                          .
                          .
                          .

-------------------------- HireDate=1993 ----------------------------------

                                  Job
        EmpID       Location      Code      Salary

        E02766      CARY          FLTAT2     32000
        E03631      FRANKFURT     FLTAT2     35000
        E01968      CARY          FLTAT2     33000
        E02035      FRANKFURT     FLTAT3     48000

-------------------------- HireDate=1994 ----------------------------------

                                  Job
        EmpID       Location      Code      Salary

        E03022      CARY          FLTAT1     23000
        E02397      FRANKFURT     FLTAT1     22000
```

Creating User-defined Formats

SAS also provides the FORMAT procedure, which enables you to define custom formats.

To create and use your own formats, do the following:

1. Use the FORMAT procedure to create the format.
2. Apply the format to a specific variable(s) by using a FORMAT statement.

33

Creating User-defined Formats

General form of a PROC FORMAT step:

```
PROC FORMAT;
    VALUE format-name range1='label'
                      range2='label'
                        . . . ;
RUN;
```

34

Creating User-defined Formats

A *format-name*

- names the format that you are creating
- cannot be more than 32 characters in SAS®9
- for character values, must have a dollar sign ($) as the first character, and a letter or underscore as the second character
- for numeric values, must have a letter or underscore as the first character
- cannot end in a number
- cannot be the name of a SAS format
- does not end with a period in the VALUE statement.

35

Format names in SAS 8 and earlier (that is, prior to SAS®9) are limited to 8 characters.

Creating User-defined Formats

Range(s) can be

- single values
- ranges of values
- lists of values.

Labels

- can be up to 32,767 characters in length
- are typically enclosed in quotation marks, although it is not required.

36

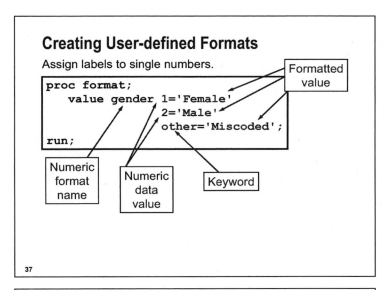

Creating User-defined Formats

Assign labels to single numbers.

```
proc format;
   value gender 1='Female'
                2='Male'
                other='Miscoded';
run;
```

Formatted value

Numeric format name

Numeric data value

Keyword

37

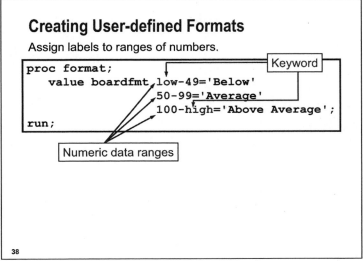

Creating User-defined Formats

Assign labels to ranges of numbers.

```
proc format;
   value boardfmt low-49='Below'
                  50-99='Average'
                  100-high='Above Average';
run;
```

Keyword

Numeric data ranges

38

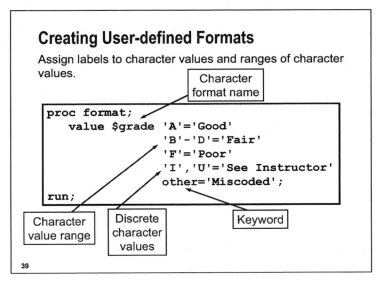

Creating User-defined Formats

Assign labels to character values and ranges of character values.

Character format name

```
proc format;
   value $grade 'A'='Good'
               'B'-'D'='Fair'
               'F'='Poor'
               'I','U'='See Instructor'
               other='Miscoded';
run;
```

Character value range

Discrete character values

Keyword

39

Creating User-defined Formats

Step 1: Create the format.

```
proc format;
   value $codefmt 'FLTAT'='Flight Attendant'
                  'PILOT'='Pilot';
run;
```

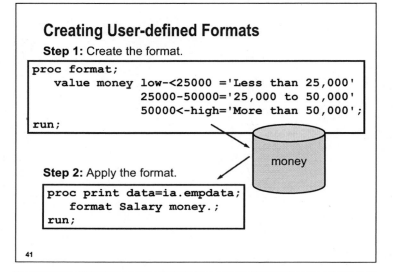

Step 2: Apply the format.

```
proc print data=ia.empdata;
   format JobCode $codefmt.;
run;
```

40

Creating User-defined Formats

Step 1: Create the format.

```
proc format;
   value money low-<25000 ='Less than 25,000'
               25000-50000='25,000 to 50,000'
               50000<-high='More than 50,000';
run;
```

money

Step 2: Apply the format.

```
proc print data=ia.empdata;
   format Salary money.;
run;
```

41

Creating User-defined Formats

You can use multiple VALUE statements in a single
PROC FORMAT step.

```
proc format;
   value $codefmt 'FLTAT'='Flight Attendant'
                  'PILOT'='Pilot';
   value money low-<25000 ='Less than 25,000'
               25000-50000='25,000 to 50,000'
               50000<-high='More than 50,000';
run;
```

c05s2d2

42

Applying User-defined Formats

```
proc print data=ia.empdata split=' ' noobs;
   label LastName='Last Name'
         FirstName='First Name'
         Salary='Annual Salary';
   format Jobcode $codefmt. Salary money.;
   title1 'Salary Report in Categories';
run;
```

```
                   Salary Report in Categories
   Emp  Last            First
   ID   Name            Name      JobCode             Annual
                                                      Salary
   0031 GOLDENBERG      DESIREE   Pilot             More than 50,000
   0040 WILLIAMS        ARLENE M. Flight Attendant  Less than 25,000
   0071 PERRY           ROBERT A. Flight Attendant  Less than 25,000
   0082 MCGWIER-WATTS    CHRISTINA Pilot             More than 50,000
   0091 SCOTT           HARVEY F. Flight Attendant  25,000 to 50,000
   0106 THACKER         DAVID S.  Flight Attendant  Less than 25,000
   0355 BELL            THOMAS B. Pilot             More than 50,000
   0366 GLENN           MARTHA S. Pilot             More than 50,000
```

43

 **Exercises**

For these exercises, use SAS data sets stored in a permanent SAS data library.

> Fill in the blank with the location of your SAS data library. **If you started a new SAS session since the previous lab**, submit the LIBNAME statement to assign the libref **ia** to the SAS data library.
>
> `libname ia'_____';`

3. **Creating User-defined Formats**

   Create a format for the variable **Dest** that assigns the following:

   • **Anchorage** to the value **ANC**

   • **Honolulu** to the value **HNL**

   • **Seattle** to the value **SEA**

4. **Applying User-defined Formats**

   Alter the program you wrote in Exercise 1 to use the format that you created in the previous exercise to display city names instead of airport codes. Reset the starting page number for the output to 1.

       Be sure to save your modified program. You use the solution to this exercise as the basis of a subsequent workshop.

   SAS Output

```
                         San Francisco Passenger Data                          1

                 ------------------ Destination=Anchorage --------------------

                   Departure    First    Business    Economy
            Obs      Date       Class      Class       Class

             1     06MAY2001      13        22          150
             2     06MAY2001      14         .          133
             3     07MAY2001      16        26          143
             4     08MAY2001      14        18          137
             5     09MAY2001      14        17          144
             6     09MAY2001      13         .          142
             7     10MAY2001      15        22           99
             8     11MAY2001      15        16          137
             9     12MAY2001      15        23          105
           ----                 ------   --------     -------
           Dest                  129       144        1,190
```

(Continued on the next page.)

```
                    San Francisco Passenger Data                          2

--------------------- Destination=Honolulu ---------------------

            Departure    First    Business    Economy
   Obs         Date      Class      Class       Class

    10      06MAY2001      13         24          138
    11      07MAY2001      14         25          132
    12      08MAY2001      12         21          155
    13      09MAY2001      13         22          150
    14      10MAY2001      13         14          145
    15      11MAY2001      13         24          137
    16      12MAY2001      13         19          144
   ----                 ------    --------    -------
   Dest                   91         149        1,001
```

```
                    San Francisco Passenger Data                          3

--------------------- Destination=Seattle ---------------------

            Departure    First    Business    Economy
   Obs         Date      Class      Class       Class

    17      06MAY2001      10          9          132
    18      06MAY2001      11         12          111
    19      07MAY2001      12         11          126
    20      07MAY2001      12          8          119
    21      08MAY2001      12         13          115
    22      08MAY2001      12         12          136
    23      09MAY2001      10         18          128
    24      09MAY2001      11         17          105
    25      10MAY2001      11         14          131
    26      10MAY2001      11         18          104
    27      11MAY2001      12         15          106
    28      11MAY2001      10         15          111
    29      12MAY2001      12         17          131
    30      12MAY2001      10         13          113
   ----                 ------    --------    -------
   Dest                  156         192        1,668
                        ======    ========    =======
                         376         485        3,859
```

5. Creating and Applying User-defined Formats (Optional)

   a. Create a user-defined format for **Model** that assigns labels as shown below.

Value(s) of Model	Label
JetCruise LF5100 JetCruise LF5200 JetCruise LF8000 JetCruise LF8100	Large Jet
JetCruise MF2100 JetCruise MF4000	Medium Jet
JetCruise SF1000	Small Jet

   b. Apply the user-defined format.

- Write a PROC PRINT step for **ia.sanfran**.
- Use the format you created for **Model**.
- Display only the variables **FlightID**, **DepartDate**, **Destination**, and **Model**.
- Suppress the title (with a null TITLE statement).

Partial SAS Output

```
            Flight      Depart
     Obs      ID         Date      Destination      Model

       1    IA11200    01DEC1999       HND        Large Jet
       2    IA01804    01DEC1999       SEA        Small Jet
       3    IA02901    02DEC1999       HNL        Large Jet
       4    IA03100    02DEC1999       ANC        Large Jet
       5    IA02901    03DEC1999       HNL        Large Jet
       6    IA03100    03DEC1999       ANC        Medium Jet
       7    IA00800    04DEC1999       RDU        Medium Jet
       8    IA01805    04DEC1999       SEA        Small Jet
       9    IA01804    06DEC1999       SEA        Large Jet
      10    IA03101    06DEC1999       ANC        Large Jet
      11    IA01802    07DEC1999       SEA        Small Jet
      12    IA11200    08DEC1999       HND        Large Jet
      13    IA03101    08DEC1999       ANC        Large Jet
      14    IA01804    08DEC1999       SEA        Small Jet
      15    IA11201    09DEC1999       HND        Large Jet
      16    IA03100    09DEC1999       ANC        Medium Jet
      17    IA01805    10DEC1999       SEA        Small Jet
       .
       .
       .
```

5.3 Creating HTML Reports

Objectives

- Create HTML reports using the Output Delivery System (ODS).

46

Business Task

Display a listing report in HTML form.

Salary Report

EmpID	LastName	FirstName	JobCode	Annual Salary
0031	GOLDENBERG	DESIREE	Pilot	More than 50,000
0040	WILLIAMS	ARLENE M.	Flight Attendant	Less than 25,000
0071	PERRY	ROBERT A.	Flight Attendant	Less than 25,000
0082	MCGWIER-WATTS	CHRISTINA	Pilot	More than 50,000
0091	SCOTT	HARVEY F.	Flight Attendant	25,000 to 50,000
0106	THACKER	DAVID S.	Flight Attendant	Less than 25,000
0355	BELL	THOMAS B.	Pilot	More than 50,000
0366	GLENN	MARTHA S.	Pilot	More than 50,000

47

The Output Delivery System

ODS statements enable you to create output in a variety
of forms.

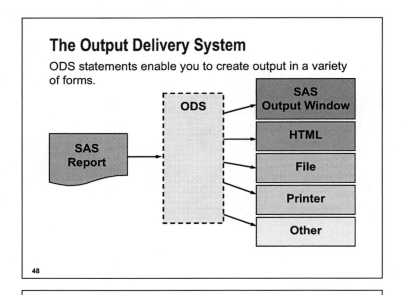

48

Generating HTML Files

The ODS HTML statement opens, closes, and manages
the HTML destination.

General form of the ODS HTML statement:

```
ODS HTML FILE='HTML-file-specification' <options>;
    SAS code that generates output
ODS HTML CLOSE;
```

49

Generating HTML Files

Output is directed to the specified HTML file until
you do one of the following:

- close the HTML destination
- specify another destination file

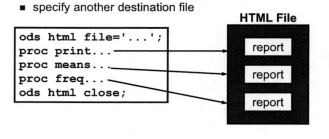

50

Creating an HTML Report

1. Open an HTML destination for the listing report.
2. Generate the report.
3. Close the HTML destination.

```
ods html file='c05s3d1.html';
proc print data=ia.empdata label noobs;
   label Salary='Annual Salary';
   format Salary money. Jobcode $codefmt.;
   title1 'Salary Report';
run;
ods html close;
```

c05s3d1

51

Creating an HTML Report

Salary Report

EmpID	LastName	FirstName	JobCode	Annual Salary
0031	GOLDENBERG	DESIREE	Pilot	More than 50,000
0040	WILLIAMS	ARLENE M.	Flight Attendant	Less than 25,000
0071	PERRY	ROBERT A.	Flight Attendant	Less than 25,000
0082	MCGWIER-WATTS	CHRISTINA	Pilot	More than 50,000
0091	SCOTT	HARVEY F.	Flight Attendant	25,000 to 50,000
0106	THACKER	DAVID S.	Flight Attendant	Less than 25,000
0355	BELL	THOMAS B.	Pilot	More than 50,000
0366	GLENN	MARTHA S.	Pilot	More than 50,000

52

 Netscape can be used to view .html files in the UNIX environment on SAS training room machines. Use the Results window to view an HTML file:

1) Locate the folder that matches the procedure output that you want to view.

2) Use the expansion icon (+) next to the folder to open its contents.

3) Select the appropriate pointer (it will have a Netscape icon), double-click the pointer or select the pointer, and then select **Open** from the menu.

The browser will start, and then the file will be displayed in a SAS Output – Netscape window.

The .pdf and .rtf files cannot be displayed on the UNIX platform because no readers have been defined for them.

Exercises

For these exercises, use SAS data sets stored in a permanent SAS data library.

> Fill in the blank with the location of your SAS data library. **If you started a new SAS session since the previous lab**, submit the LIBNAME statement to assign the libref **ia** to the SAS data library.
>
> `libname ia '_____';`

6. **Creating HTML Reports**

   Alter the program that you wrote in Exercise 4 to create an HTML report using ODS.

   ## San Francisco Passenger Data

   ### Destination=Anchorage

Obs	Departure Date	First Class	Business Class	Economy Class
1	06MAY2001	13	22	150
2	06MAY2001	14		133
3	07MAY2001	16	26	143
4	08MAY2001	14	18	137
5	09MAY2001	14	17	144
6	09MAY2001	13		142
7	10MAY2001	15	22	99
8	11MAY2001	15	16	137
9	12MAY2001	15	23	105
Dest		129	144	1,190

   (Continued on the next page.)

San Francisco Passenger Data

Destination=Honolulu

Obs	Departure Date	First Class	Business Class	Economy Class
10	06MAY2001	13	24	138
11	07MAY2001	14	25	132
12	08MAY2001	12	21	155
13	09MAY2001	13	22	150
14	10MAY2001	13	14	145
15	11MAY2001	13	24	137
16	12MAY2001	13	19	144
Dest		91	149	1,001

San Francisco Passenger Data

Destination=Seattle

Obs	Departure Date	First Class	Business Class	Economy Class
17	06MAY2001	10	9	132
18	06MAY2001	11	12	111
19	07MAY2001	12	11	126
20	07MAY2001	12	8	119
21	08MAY2001	12	13	115
22	08MAY2001	12	12	136
23	09MAY2001	10	18	128
24	09MAY2001	11	17	105
25	10MAY2001	11	14	131
26	10MAY2001	11	18	104
27	11MAY2001	12	15	106
28	11MAY2001	10	15	111
29	12MAY2001	12	17	131
30	12MAY2001	10	13	113
Dest		156	192	1,668
		376	485	3,859

7. Creating a Listing Report (Optional)

Use the **ia.newmechs** data set for this exercise.

a. Create a format for the **Gender** variable that assigns the following:
   - **Female** to the value **F**
   - **Male** to the value **M**

b. Create an HTML report of the listing described below.
   - Set the line size to 72, do not display the date and time that the SAS session began, and do not display page numbers.
   - Only print observations that have a value of **MECH01** for the variable **JobCode**.
   - Print the variables **EmpID**, **LastName**, **FirstName**, and **Gender** in the order listed here.
   - Place the title **Level I Mechanics** on the report.
   - Display the values of the variable **Gender** with the format that you created in part **a** of this exercise.

Level I Mechanics

Obs	EmpID	LastName	FirstName	Gender
1	E00007	MASSENGILL	ANNETTE M.	Female
6	E00112	WANG	ROBERT B.	Male
8	E00151	BAKER	DONALD A.	Male
16	E00308	RIPPERTON	DAVID D.	Male
19	E00417	BURT	ERICK M.	Male
34	E00449	SIU	MICHELLE	Female

5.4   Solutions to Exercises

1. **Enhancing List Reports**

```
options ls=64 nodate pageno=1;
libname ia 'SAS-data-library';
proc sort data=ia.passngrs out=work.passngrs;
   by Dest;
run;
proc print data=work.passngrs label;
   var Depart FClass BClass EClass;
   by Dest;
   pageby Dest;
   sum FClass BClass EClass;
   format Depart date9. FClass BClass EClass comma6.;
   label Dest='Destination'
         Depart='Departure Date'
         FClass='First Class'
         BClass='Business Class'
         EClass='Economy Class';
   title 'San Francisco Passenger Data';
run;
```

2. **Enhancing List Reports (Optional)**

```
options nodate nonumber;
proc sort data=ia.fltat out=work.fltat;
   by HireDate;
run;

proc print data=work.fltat noobs;
   title;
   by HireDate;
   format HireDate year.;
   var EmpID Location JobCode Salary;
run;
```

3. **Creating User-defined Formats**

```
proc format;
   value $cities  'ANC'='Anchorage'
                  'HNL'='Honolulu'
                  'SEA'='Seattle';
run;
```

4. **Applying User-defined Formats**

```
options pageno=1;
proc print data=work.passngrs label;
    var Depart FClass BClass EClass;
    by Dest;
    pageby Dest;
    sum FClass BClass EClass;
    format Depart date9. FClass BClass EClass comma6.
          Dest $cities.;
    label Dest='Destination'
          Depart='Departure Date'
          FClass='First Class'
          BClass='Business Class'
          EClass='Economy Class';
    title 'San Francisco Passenger Data';
run;
```

5. **Creating and Applying User-defined Formats (Optional)**

    a.

```
proc format;
    value $model
        'JetCruise LF5100','JetCruise LF5200',
        'JetCruise LF8000','JetCruise LF8100'
          = 'Large Jet'
        'JetCruise MF2100','JetCruise MF4000'
          = 'Medium Jet'
        'JetCruise SF1000'
          = 'Small Jet'
    ;
run;
```

    b.

```
proc print data=ia.sanfran;
    title;
    format Model $model.;
    var FlightID DepartDate Destination Model;
run;
```

6. **Creating HTML Reports**

```
options ls=64 nodate number pageno=1;
ods html file='exercise6.html';
proc print data=work.passngrs label;
   var Depart FClass BClass EClass;
   by Dest;
   pageby Dest;
   sum FClass BClass EClass;
   format Depart date9. FClass BClass EClass comma6.
          Dest $cities.;
   label Dest='Destination'
         Depart='Departure Date'
         FClass='First Class'
         BClass='Business Class'
         EClass='Economy Class';
   title 'San Francisco Passenger Data';
run;
ods html close;
```

7. **Creating a Listing Report (Optional)**

a.

```
proc format;
   value $gendfmt 'F'='Female'
                  'M'='Male';
run;
```

b.

```
options ls=72 nodate nonumber;
ods html file='exercise7.html';
proc print data=ia.newmechs;
   where JobCode='MECH01';
   var EmpID LastName FirstName Gender;
   title 'Level I Mechanics';
   format Gender $gendfmt.;
run;
ods html close;
```

Chapter 6   Creating SAS Data Sets

6.1 Reading Raw Data Files: Column Input

Objectives

- Create a temporary SAS data set from a raw data file.
- Create a permanent SAS data set from a raw data file.
- Explain how the DATA step processes data.
- Read standard data using column input.

3

Accessing Data Sources

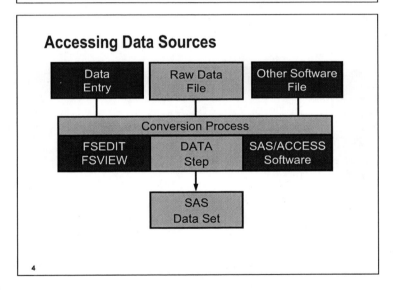

4

Reading Raw Data Files

Data for flights from New York to Dallas (DFW) and
Los Angeles (LAX) is stored in a raw data file. Create
a SAS data set from the raw data.

Description	Column
Flight Number	1- 3
Date	4-11
Destination	12-14
First Class Passengers	15-17
Economy Passengers	18-20

```
                     1       1         2
1---5----0----5----0
43912/11/00LAX 20137
92112/11/00DFW 20131
11412/12/00LAX 15170
98212/12/00dfw  5 85
43912/13/00LAX 14196
98212/13/00DFW 15116
43112/14/00LaX 17166
98212/14/00DFW  7 88
11412/15/00LAX    187
98212/15/00DFW 14 31
```

5

Creating a SAS Data Set

In order to create a SAS data set
from a raw data file, you must do
the following:

1. Start a DATA step and name
    the SAS data set being
    created (DATA statement).

2. Identify the location of
    the raw data file to read
    (INFILE statement).

3. Describe how to read
    the data fields from
    the raw data file
    (INPUT statement).

Raw Data File

```
                     1       1         2
1---5----0----5----0
43912/11/00LAX 20137
92112/11/00DFW 20131
11412/12/00LAX 15170
```

DATA Step

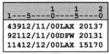
```
data SAS-data-set-name;
   infile 'raw-data-filename';
   input input-specifications;
run;
```

SAS Data Set

Flight	Date	Dest	First Class	Economy
439	12/11/00	LAX	20	137
921	12/11/00	DFW	20	131
114	12/12/00	LAX	15	170

11   ...

Creating a SAS Data Set

General form of the DATA statement:

DATA *libref.SAS-data-set(s)*;

Example: This DATA statement creates a temporary
SAS data set named **dfwlax**:

```
data work.dfwlax;
```

Example: This DATA statement creates a permanent
SAS data set named **dfwlax**:

```
libname ia 'SAS-data-library';
data ia.dfwlax;
```

12

Pointing to a Raw Data File

General form of the INFILE statement:

> **INFILE** '*filename*' *<options>*;

Examples:

```
z/OS (OS/390)
  infile 'userid.prog1.dfwlax';
UNIX
  infile '/users/userid/dfwlax.dat';
Windows
  infile 'c:\workshop\winsas\prog1\dfwlax.dat';
```

The PAD option in the INFILE statement is useful
for reading variable-length records typically found
in Windows and UNIX environments.

13

Reading Data Fields

General form of the INPUT statement:

> **INPUT** *input-specifications;*

input-specifications
- names the SAS variables
- identifies the variables as character or numeric
- specifies the locations of the fields in the raw data
- can be specified as column, formatted, list, or
  named input.

14

Reading Data Using Column Input

Column input is appropriate for reading the following:
- data in fixed columns
- standard character and numeric data

General form of a column INPUT statement:

> **INPUT** *variable <$> startcol-endcol . . . ;*

Examples of standard numeric data:

```
15   -15   15.4   +1.23   1.23E3   -1.23E-3
```

The term *standard data* refers to character and numeric
data that SAS recognizes automatically.

15

The Raw Data

Description	Column
Flight Number	1- 3
Date	4-11
Destination	12-14
First Class Passengers	15-17
Economy Passengers	18-20

```
                  1    1    2
1---5----0----5----0
43912/11/00LAX 20137
92112/11/00DFW 20131
11412/12/00LAX 15170
98212/12/00dfw  5 85
43912/13/00LAX 14196
98212/13/00DFW 15116
43112/14/00LaX 17166
98212/14/00DFW  7 88
11412/15/00LAX    187
98212/15/00DFW 14 31
```

16

Reading Data Using Column Input

Raw Data File
```
43912/11/00LAX 20137
92112/11/00DFW 20131
11412/12/00LAX 15170
```

Read the raw data file using column input.

DATA Step
```
data SAS-data-set-name;
   infile 'raw-data-filename';
   input variable <$> startcol-endcol ...;
run;
```

SAS Data Set

Flight	Date	Dest	FirstClass	Economy
439	12/11/00	LAX	20	137
921	12/11/00	DFW	20	131
114	12/12/00	LAX	15	170

17

Reading Data Using Column Input

```
                  1    1    2
1---5----0----5----0
43912/11/00LAX 20137
92112/11/00DFW 20131
11412/12/00LAX 15170
```

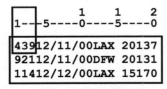

```
input Flight $ 1-3 Date $ 4-11
       Dest $ 12-14 FirstClass 15-17
       Economy 18-20;
```

18   ...

Reading Data Using Column Input

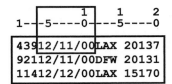

```
              1    1    2
1---5----0----5----0
43912/11/00LAX 20137
92112/11/00DFW 20131
11412/12/00LAX 15170
```

```
input Flight $ 1-3 Date $ 4-11
      Dest $ 12-14 FirstClass 15-17
      Economy 18-20;
```

19

Reading Data Using Column Input

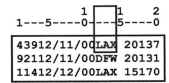

```
            1    1    2
1---5----0----5----0
43912/11/00LAX 20137
92112/11/00DFW 20131
11412/12/00LAX 15170
```

```
input Flight $ 1-3 Date $ 4-11
      Dest $ 12-14 FirstClass 15-17
      Economy 18-20;
```

20

Reading Data Using Column Input

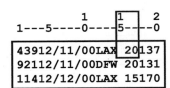

```
            1    1    2
1---5----0----5----0
43912/11/00LAX 20137
92112/11/00DFW 20131
11412/12/00LAX 15170
```

```
input Flight $ 1-3 Date $ 4-11
      Dest $ 12-14 FirstClass 15-17
      Economy 18-20;
```

21

Reading Data Using Column Input

```
          1    1        2
1---5----0----5----0
```

```
43912/11/00LAX 20137
92112/11/00DFW 20131
11412/12/00LAX 15170
```

```
input Flight $ 1-3 Date $ 4-11
      Dest $ 12-14 FirstClass 15-17
      Economy 18-20;
```

22

Creating Temporary SAS Data Sets

Store the **dfwlax** data set in the **work** library.

```
data work.dfwlax;
   infile 'raw-data-file';
   input Flight $ 1-3 Date $ 4-11
         Dest $ 12-14 FirstClass 15-17
         Economy 18-20;
run;
```

```
NOTE: The data set WORK.DFWLAX has 10 observations and
      5 variables.
```

23   c06s1d1

Examples of raw data filenames:

z/OS (OS/390)	userid.prog1.rawdata(dfwlax)
Windows	c:\workshop\winsas\prog1\dfwlax.dat
UNIX	/users/userid/dfwlax.dat

Creating Permanent SAS Data Sets

Alter the previous DATA step to permanently store the
dfwlax data set.

```
libname ia 'SAS-data-library';
data ia.dfwlax;
   infile 'raw-data-file';
   input Flight $ 1-3 Date $ 4-11
         Dest $ 12-14 FirstClass 15-17
         Economy 18-20;
run;
```

```
NOTE: The data set IA.DFWLAX has 10 observations and 5
      variables.
```

24   c06s1d2

Examples of SAS data library names:

z/OS (OS/390)	userid.prog1.sasdata
Windows	c:\workshop\winsas\prog1
UNIX	/users/userid

Looking Behind the Scenes

The DATA step is processed in two phases:
- compilation
- execution

```
data work.dfwlax;
   infile 'raw-data-file';
   input Flight $ 1-3 Date $ 4-11
         Dest $ 12-14 FirstClass 15-17
         Economy 18-20;
run;
```

25

Looking Behind the Scenes

At compile time, SAS creates the following:

- an input buffer to hold the current raw data file record that is being processed

```
                              1                   2
1 2 3 4 5 6 7 8 9 0 1 2 3 4 5 6 7 8 9 0
┌─┬─┬─┬─┬─┬─┬─┬─┬─┬─┬─┬─┬─┬─┬─┬─┬─┬─┬─┬─┐
└─┴─┴─┴─┴─┴─┴─┴─┴─┴─┴─┴─┴─┴─┴─┴─┴─┴─┴─┴─┘
```

- a program data vector (PDV) to hold the current SAS observation

Flight	Date	Dest	FirstClass	Economy
$ 3	$ 8	$ 3	N 8	N 8

- the descriptor portion of the output data set

Flight	Date	Dest	FirstClass	Economy
$ 3	$ 8	$ 3	N 8	N 8

26

Compiling the DATA Step

```
data work.dfwlax;
   infile 'raw-data-file';
   input Flight $ 1-3 Date $ 4-11
         Dest $ 12-14 FirstClass 15-17
         Economy 18-20;
run;
```

27   ...

Compiling the DATA Step

```
data work.dfwlax;
   infile 'raw-data-file';
   input Flight $ 1-3 Date $ 4-11
         Dest $ 12-14 FirstClass 15-17
         Economy 18-20;
run;
```

Input Buffer

```
                        1                   2
1 2 3 4 5 6 7 8 9 0 1 2 3 4 5 6 7 8 9 0
┌─┬─┬─┬─┬─┬─┬─┬─┬─┬─┬─┬─┬─┬─┬─┬─┬─┬─┬─┬─┐
└─┴─┴─┴─┴─┴─┴─┴─┴─┴─┴─┴─┴─┴─┴─┴─┴─┴─┴─┴─┘
```

28   ...

Compiling the DATA Step

```
data work.dfwlax;
   infile 'raw-data-file';
   input Flight $ 1-3 Date $ 4-11
         Dest $ 12-14 FirstClass 15-17
         Economy 18-20;
run;
```

Input Buffer

									1										2
1	2	3	4	5	6	7	8	9	0	1	2	3	4	5	6	7	8	9	0

PDV

Flight
$ 3

29   ...

Compiling the DATA Step

```
data work.dfwlax;
   infile 'raw-data-file';
   input Flight $ 1-3 Date $ 4-11
         Dest $ 12-14 FirstClass 15-17
         Economy 18-20;
run;
```

Input Buffer

									1										2
1	2	3	4	5	6	7	8	9	0	1	2	3	4	5	6	7	8	9	0

PDV

Flight	Date
$ 3	$ 8

30   ...

Compiling the DATA Step

```
data work.dfwlax;
   infile 'raw-data-file';
   input Flight $ 1-3 Date $ 4-11
         Dest $ 12-14 FirstClass 15-17
         Economy 18-20;
run;
```

Input Buffer

									1										2
1	2	3	4	5	6	7	8	9	0	1	2	3	4	5	6	7	8	9	0

PDV

Flight	Date	Dest
$ 3	$ 8	$ 3

31   ...

Compiling the DATA Step

```
data work.dfwlax;
   infile 'raw-data-file';
   input Flight $ 1-3 Date $ 4-11
         Dest $ 12-14 FirstClass 15-17
         Economy 18-20;
run;
```

Input Buffer

									1									2
1	2	3	4	5	6	7	8	9	0	1	2	3	4	5	6	7	8	9	0

PDV

Flight	Date	Dest	FirstClass
$ 3	$ 8	$ 3	N 8

32

Compiling the DATA Step

```
data work.dfwlax;
   infile 'raw-data-file';
   input Flight $ 1-3 Date $ 4-11
         Dest $ 12-14 FirstClass 15-17
         Economy 18-20;
run;
```

Input Buffer

									1									2
1	2	3	4	5	6	7	8	9	0	1	2	3	4	5	6	7	8	9	0

PDV

Flight	Date	Dest	FirstClass	Economy
$ 3	$ 8	$ 3	N 8	N 8

33

Compiling the DATA Step

```
data work.dfwlax;
   infile 'raw-data-file';
   input Flight $ 1-3 Date $ 4-11
         Dest $ 12-14 FirstClass 15-17
         Economy 18-20;
run;
```

Input Buffer

									1									2
1	2	3	4	5	6	7	8	9	0	1	2	3	4	5	6	7	8	9	0

PDV

Flight	Date	Dest	FirstClass	Economy

dfwlax descriptor portion

Flight	Date	Dest	FirstClass	Economy
$ 3	$ 8	$ 3	N 8	N 8

34

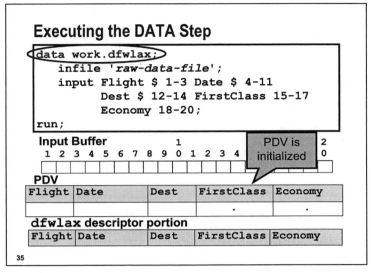

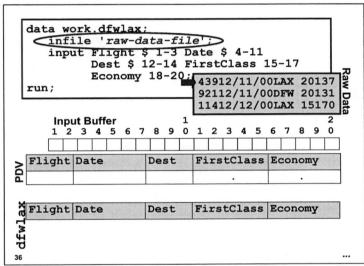

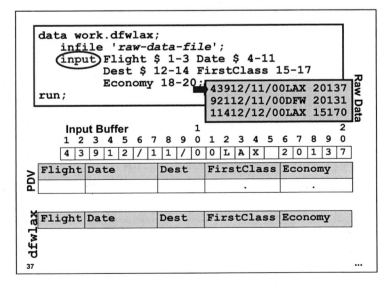

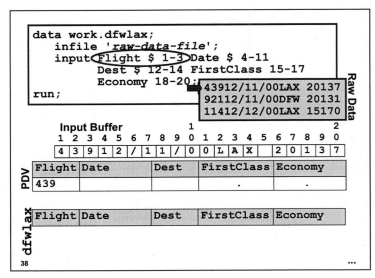

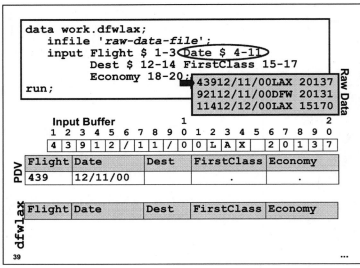

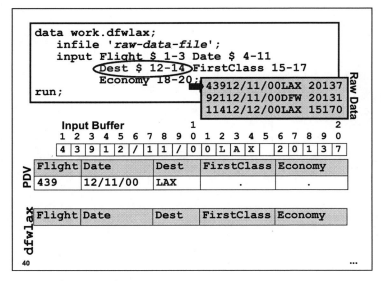

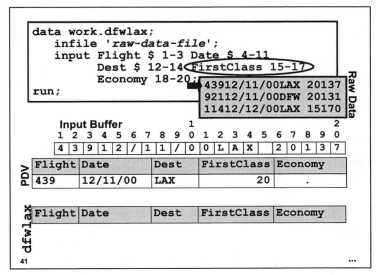

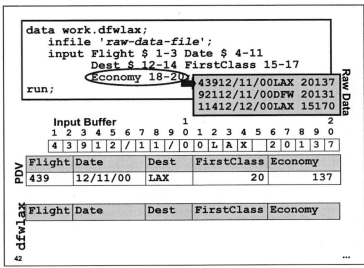

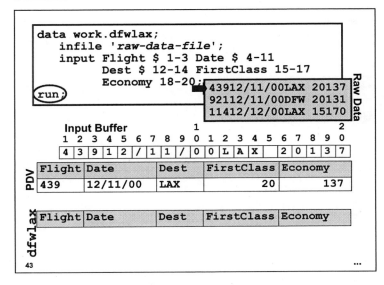

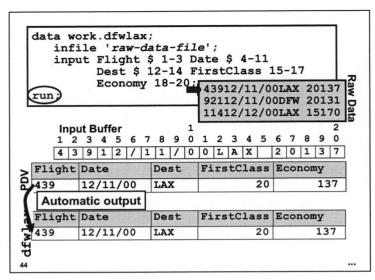

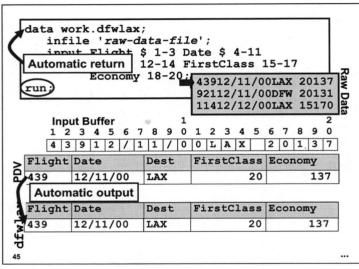

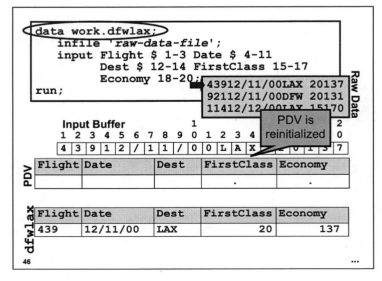

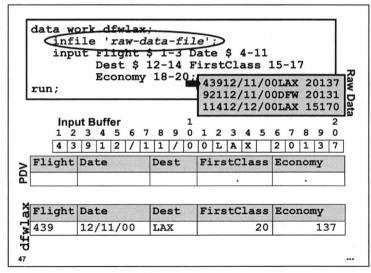

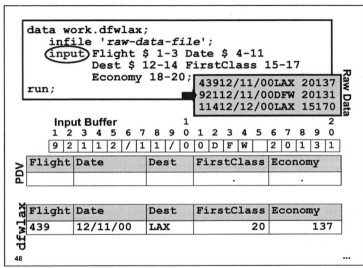

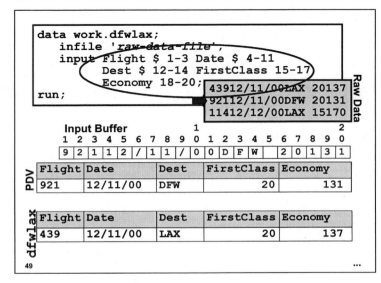

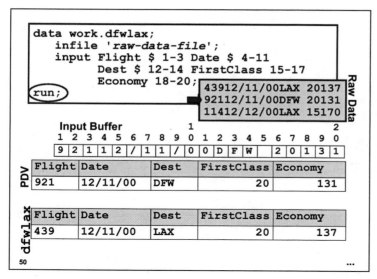

```
data work.dfwlax;
   infile 'raw-data-file';
   input Flight $ 1-3 Date $ 4-11
         Dest $ 12-14 FirstClass 15-17
         Economy 18-20;
run;
```

Raw Data

```
43912/11/00LAX 20137
92112/11/00DFW 20131
11412/12/00LAX 15170
```

Input Buffer

1	2	3	4	5	6	7	8	9	0	1	2	3	4	5	6	7	8	9	0
9	2	1	1	2	/	1	1	/	0	0	D	F	W		2	0	1	3	1

PDV

Flight	Date	Dest	FirstClass	Economy
921	12/11/00	DFW	20	131

dfwlax

Flight	Date	Dest	FirstClass	Economy
439	12/11/00	LAX	20	137

50   ...

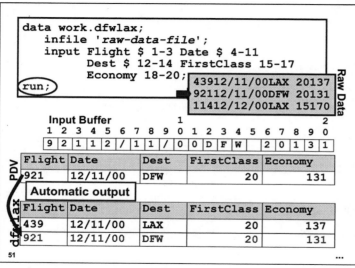

```
data work.dfwlax;
   infile 'raw-data-file';
   input Flight $ 1-3 Date $ 4-11
         Dest $ 12-14 FirstClass 15-17
         Economy 18-20;
run;
```

Raw Data

```
43912/11/00LAX 20137
92112/11/00DFW 20131
11412/12/00LAX 15170
```

Input Buffer

1	2	3	4	5	6	7	8	9	0	1	2	3	4	5	6	7	8	9	0
9	2	1	1	2	/	1	1	/	0	0	D	F	W		2	0	1	3	1

PDV

Flight	Date	Dest	FirstClass	Economy
921	12/11/00	DFW	20	131

Automatic output

dfwlax

Flight	Date	Dest	FirstClass	Economy
439	12/11/00	LAX	20	137
921	12/11/00	DFW	20	131

51   ...

```
data work.dfwlax;
   infile 'raw-data-file';
   input Flight $ 1-3 Date $ 4-11
         Dest $ 12-14 FirstClass 15-17
         Economy 18-20;
run;
```

Automatic return

Raw Data

```
43912/11/00LAX 20137
92112/11/00DFW 20131
11412/12/00LAX 15170
```

Input Buffer

1	2	3	4	5	6	7	8	9	0	1	2	3	4	5	6	7	8	9	0
9	2	1	1	2	/	1	1	/	0	0	D	F	W		2	0	1	3	1

PDV

Flight	Date	Dest	FirstClass	Economy
921	12/11/00	DFW	20	131

Automatic output

dfwlax

Flight	Date	Dest	FirstClass	Economy
439	12/11/00	LAX	20	137
921	12/11/00	DFW	20	131

52   ...

Executing the DATA Step

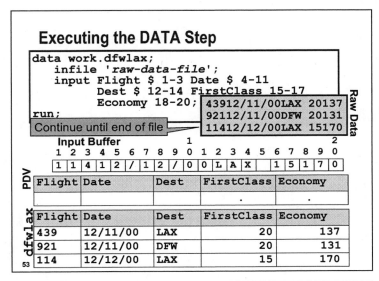

```
data work.dfwlax;
   infile 'raw-data-file';
   input Flight $ 1-3 Date $ 4-11
         Dest $ 12-14 FirstClass 15-17
         Economy 18-20;
run;
```

Continue until end of file

Raw Data

```
43912/11/00LAX 20137
92112/11/00DFW 20131
11412/12/00LAX 15170
```

Input Buffer

```
          1                   2
1 2 3 4 5 6 7 8 9 0 1 2 3 4 5 6 7 8 9 0
1 1 4 1 2 / 1 2 / 0 0 L A X   1 5 1 7 0
```

PDV

Flight	Date	Dest	FirstClass	Economy
			.	.

dfwlax

Flight	Date	Dest	FirstClass	Economy
439	12/11/00	LAX	20	137
921	12/11/00	DFW	20	131
114	12/12/00	LAX	15	170

53

DATA Step Processing: Summary

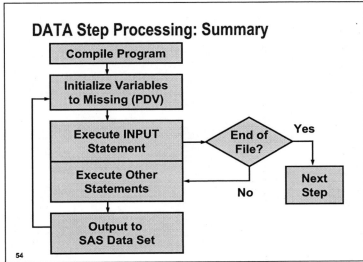

Compile Program

Initialize Variables to Missing (PDV)

Execute INPUT Statement

End of File? → Yes → Next Step

Execute Other Statements

No

Output to SAS Data Set

54

Accessing Temporary SAS Data Sets

```
proc print data=work.dfwlax;
run;
```

The SAS System

Obs	Flight	Date	Dest	First Class	Economy
1	439	12/11/00	LAX	20	137
2	921	12/11/00	DFW	20	131
3	114	12/12/00	LAX	15	170
4	982	12/12/00	dfw	5	85
5	439	12/13/00	LAX	14	196
6	982	12/13/00	DFW	15	116
7	431	12/14/00	LaX	17	166
8	982	12/14/00	DFW	7	88
9	114	12/15/00	LAX	.	187
10	982	12/15/00	DFW	14	31

c06s1d1

55

Accessing Permanent SAS Data Sets

To access a permanently stored SAS data set, perform the following tasks:

- Submit a LIBNAME statement to assign a libref to the SAS data library.
- Use the libref as the first-level name of the SAS data set.

The LIBNAME statement only needs to be submitted once per SAS session.

56

Accessing Permanent SAS Data Sets

```
libname ia 'SAS-data-library';
proc print data=ia.dfwlax;
run;
```

		The SAS System		First	
Obs	Flight	Date	Dest	Class	Economy
1	439	12/11/00	LAX	20	137
2	921	12/11/00	DFW	20	131
3	114	12/12/00	LAX	15	170
4	982	12/12/00	dfw	5	85
5	439	12/13/00	LAX	14	196
6	982	12/13/00	DFW	15	116
7	431	12/14/00	LaX	17	166
8	982	12/14/00	DFW	7	88
9	114	12/15/00	LAX	.	187
10	982	12/15/00	DFW	14	31

c06s1d2

57

 **Exercises**

For these exercises, write DATA steps that read the raw data file that contains information on flights from San Francisco to various destinations.

> Fill in the blank with the location of your raw data file. Use an INFILE statement and an INPUT statement in a DATA step to read the raw file.
>
> ```
> data ...;
>    infile '_____';
>    .
>    .
>    .
> ```

Each exercise instructs you to read **some** of the fields (identified by **bold** type in the shaded rows below) shown in the following record layout. The complete record layout for the **sfosch** raw data file is shown below.

Variable Name	Field Description	Columns	Data Type
FlightID	Flight ID Number	1–7	Character
RouteID	Route ID Number	8–14	Character
Origin	Flight Origin	15–17	Character
Destination	Flight Destination	18–20	Character
Model	Aircraft Model	21–40	Character
Date	Departure Date	41–49	Character 01JAN2000
DepartDay	Departure Day of Week	51	Numeric 1=Sunday
FClassPass	First Class Passengers	53–55	Numeric
BClassPass	Business Class Passengers	57–59	Numeric
EClassPass	Economy Class Passengers	61–63	Numeric
TotPassCap	Aircraft Capacity – Total Passengers	65–67	Numeric
CargoWt	Weight of Cargo in Pounds	69–73	Numeric
CargoRev	Revenue from Cargo in Dollars	75–79	Numeric

1. **Reading Raw Data Using Column Input**

    a. Create a SAS data set named **work.sanfran** by writing a DATA step that uses column input to create only the variables **FlightID, RouteID, Destination, Model, DepartDay,** and **TotPassCap**.

    b. Read the log to answer the following questions:

        1) How many records were read from the raw data file?

        2) How many observations does the resulting SAS data set contain?

        3) How many variables does the resulting SAS data set contain?

    c. Use PROC PRINT to display the data portion of the data set. Do not display the date and time that the SAS session started. Do not display page numbers. Set the line size to 72.

    Partial SAS Output (First 10 of 52 Observations)

    ```
                                The SAS System

                                                              Tot
           Flight                                    Depart   Pass
    Obs      ID     RouteID  Destination     Model     Day     Cap

      1    IA11200  0000112      HND     JetCruise LF8100   6     255
      2    IA01804  0000018      SEA     JetCruise SF1000   6     150
      3    IA02901  0000029      HNL     JetCruise LF5200   7     207
      4    IA03100  0000031      ANC     JetCruise LF8100   7     255
      5    IA02901  0000029      HNL     JetCruise LF5200   1     207
      6    IA03100  0000031      ANC     JetCruise MF4000   1     267
      7    IA00800  0000008      RDU     JetCruise MF4000   2     267
      8    IA01805  0000018      SEA     JetCruise SF1000   2     150
      9    IA01804  0000018      SEA     JetCruise LF5100   4     165
     10    IA03101  0000031      ANC     JetCruise LF8100   4     255
    ```

    d. Use PROC CONTENTS to display the descriptor portion of the data set.

    Partial SAS Output

    ```
                Alphabetic List of Variables and Attributes

                    #     Variable      Type     Len

                    5     DepartDay      Num       8
                    3     Destination    Char      3
                    1     FlightID       Char      7
                    4     Model          Char      20
                    2     RouteID        Char      7
                    6     TotPassCap     Num       8
    ```

    Your solution to this exercise might be useful in subsequent workshops so you should save the program for future reference.

2. Reading Raw Data Using Column Input (Optional)

Write a DATA step to read the `emplist` raw data file.

- Name the new SAS data set **work.emps**.
- Use column input.
- Write the DATA step so that the **EmpID** variable is read first and **HireDate** is not read.

The complete record layout for the **emplist** raw data file is below.

You should read all of the fields except **HireDate**.

Variable Name	Columns	Data Type
LastName	1-20	Character
FirstName	21-30	Character
EmpId	31-35	Character
JobCode	36-43	Character
HireDate	44-51	Numeric
Salary	54-59	Numeric

Write a PROC PRINT step to view the data.

- Suppress the observation column and add a suitable title.

Complete SAS Output

```
               Salary Information for Pilots and Mechanics

                             First
       EmpID    LastName     Name        JobCode     Salary

       E0029    TORRES       JAN         Pilot        50000
       E0045    LANGKAMM     SARAH       Mechanic     80000
       E0106    SMITH        MICHAEL     Mechanic     40000
       E0116    LEISTNER     COLIN       Mechanic     36000
       E0126    WADE         KIRSTEN     Pilot        85000
       E0143    TOMAS        HARALD      Pilot       105000
       E0204    WAUGH        TIM         Pilot        70000
       E0206    LEHMANN      DAGMAR      Mechanic     64000
       E0248    TRETTHAHN    MICHAEL     Pilot       100000
       E0282    TIETZ        OTTO        Pilot        45000
       E0288    O'DONOGHUE   ART         Mechanic     52000
       E0304    WALKER       THOMAS      Pilot        95000
       E0310    NOROVIITA    JOACHIM     Mechanic     78000
       E0339    OESTERBERG   ANJA        Mechanic     80000
       E0346    LAUFFER      CRAIG       Mechanic     40000
       E0428    TORR         JUGDISH     Pilot        45000
       E0449    WAGSCHAL     NADJA       Pilot        77500
       E0451    TOERMOEN     JOCHEN      Pilot        65000
```

6.2 Reading Raw Data Files: Formatted Input

Objectives
- Read standard and nonstandard character and numeric data using formatted input.
- Read date values and convert them to SAS date values.

60

Reading Data Using Formatted Input
Formatted input is appropriate for reading the following:
- data in fixed columns
- standard and nonstandard character and numeric data
- calendar values to be converted to SAS date values

61

Reading Data Using Formatted Input

General form of the INPUT statement with formatted input:

> **INPUT** *pointer-control variable informat . . . ;*

Formatted input is used to read data values by doing the following:

- moving the input pointer to the starting position of the field
- specifying a variable name
- specifying an informat

62

Reading Data Using Formatted Input

Pointer controls:

@n   moves the pointer to column *n.*

+n   moves the pointer *n* positions.

An *informat* specifies the following:

- the width of the input field
- how to read the data values that are stored in the field

63

What Is a SAS Informat?

An *informat* is an instruction that SAS uses to read data values.

SAS informats have the following form:

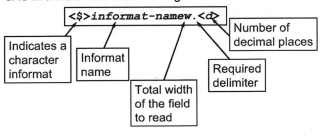

64

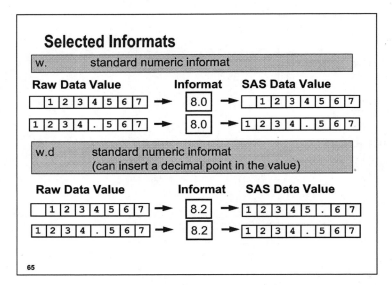

The decimal value specification in the informat is ignored if the data value being read already contains a decimal point.

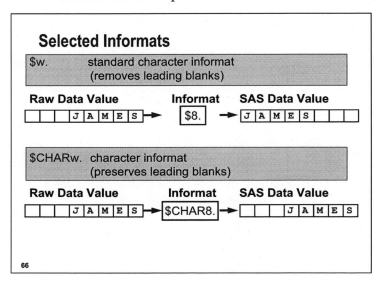

Selected Informats

COMMAw.   reads numeric data and removes selected nonnumeric characters such as dollar signs and commas.

Raw Data Value		Informat		SAS Data Value
$ 1 2 , 5 6 7	→	COMMA7.0	→	1 2 5 6 7

MMDDYYw.   reads dates of the form mm/dd/yyyy.

Raw Data Value		Informat		SAS Data Value
1 0 / 2 9 / 0 1	→	MMDDYY8.	→	1 5 2 7 7

67

Working with Date Values

Date values that are stored as SAS dates are special numeric values.

A *SAS date value* is interpreted as the number of days between January 1, 1960, and a specific date.

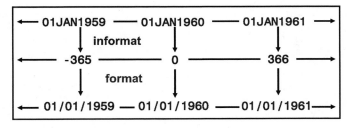

70

Converting Dates to SAS Date Values

SAS uses date **informats** to **read** and **convert** dates to SAS date values.

Examples:

Raw Data Value	Informat	Converted Value
10/29/2001	MMDDYY10.	15277
10/29/01	MMDDYY8.	15277
29OCT2001	DATE9.	15277
29/10/2001	DDMMYY10.	15277

Number of days between
01JAN1960 and 29OCT2001

71

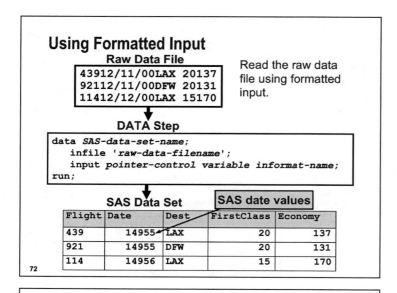

Using Formatted Input

Raw Data File

```
43912/11/00LAX 20137
92112/11/00DFW 20131
11412/12/00LAX 15170
```

Read the raw data file using formatted input.

DATA Step

```
data SAS-data-set-name;
   infile 'raw-data-filename';
   input pointer-control variable informat-name;
run;
```

SAS Data Set   SAS date values

Flight	Date	Dest	FirstClass	Economy
439	14955	LAX	20	137
921	14955	DFW	20	131
114	14956	LAX	15	170

72

Reading Data: Formatted Input

```
                    1    1    2
          1---5----0----5----0
```

Raw Data File
```
43912/11/00LAX 20137
92112/11/00DFW 20131
11412/12/00LAX 15170
```

```
data work.dfwlax;
   infile 'raw-data-file';
   input @1 Flight $3. @4 Date mmddyy8.
         @12 Dest $3. @15 FirstClass 3.
         @18 Economy 3.;
run;
```

78   c06s2d1

Examples of raw data filenames:

z/OS (OS/390)	*userid*.prog1.rawdata(dfwlax)
Windows	c:\workshop\winsas\prog1\dfwlax.dat
UNIX	/users/*userid*/dfwlax.dat

Reading Data: Formatted Input

```
proc print data=work.dfwlax;
run;
```

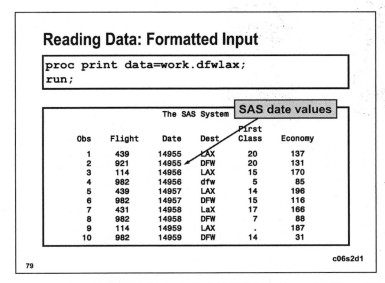

Obs	Flight	Date	Dest	First Class	Economy
1	439	14955	LAX	20	137
2	921	14955	DFW	20	131
3	114	14956	LAX	15	170
4	982	14956	dfw	5	85
5	439	14957	LAX	14	196
6	982	14957	DFW	15	116
7	431	14958	LaX	17	166
8	982	14958	DFW	7	88
9	114	14959	LAX	.	187
10	982	14959	DFW	14	31

79   c06s2d1

Reading Data: Formatted Input

```
proc print data=work.dfwlax;
   format Date date9.;
run;
```

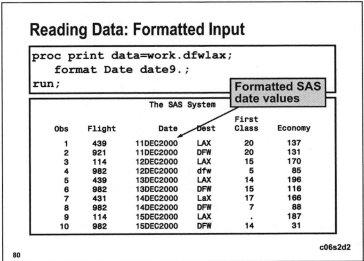

Obs	Flight	Date	Dest	First Class	Economy
1	439	11DEC2000	LAX	20	137
2	921	11DEC2000	DFW	20	131
3	114	12DEC2000	LAX	15	170
4	982	12DEC2000	dfw	5	85
5	439	13DEC2000	LAX	14	196
6	982	13DEC2000	DFW	15	116
7	431	14DEC2000	LaX	17	166
8	982	14DEC2000	DFW	7	88
9	114	15DEC2000	LAX	.	187
10	982	15DEC2000	DFW	14	31

80   c06s2d2

Exercises

For these exercises, write DATA steps that read the raw data file that contains information on flights from San Francisco to various destinations.

> Fill in the blank with the location of your raw data file. Use an INFILE statement and an INPUT statement in a DATA step to read the raw file.
>
> ```
> data ...;
>    infile '_____';
>       .
>       .
>       .
> ```

Each exercise instructs you to read **some** of the fields (identified by **bold** type in shaded rows below) shown in the following record layout. The complete record layout for the **sfosch** raw data file is shown below.

Variable Name	Field Description	Columns	Data Type
FlightID	Flight ID Number	1–7	Character
RouteID	Route ID Number	8–14	Character
Origin	Flight Origin	15–17	Character
Destination	Flight Destination	18–20	Character
Model	Aircraft Model	21–40	Character
Date	Departure Date	41–49	Numeric 01JAN2000
DepartDay	Departure Day of Week	51	Numeric 1=Sunday
FClassPass	First Class Passengers	53–55	Numeric
BClassPass	Business Class Passengers	57–59	Numeric
EClassPass	Economy Class Passengers	61–63	Numeric
TotPassCap	Aircraft Capacity – Total Passengers	65–67	Numeric
CargoWt	Weight of Cargo in Pounds	69–73	Numeric
CargoRev	Revenue from Cargo in Dollars	75–79	Numeric

3. Reading Raw Data Using Formatted Input

a. Create a SAS data set named `work.sanfran` by writing a DATA step that uses formatted input to create only the variables `FlightID`, `RouteID`, `Destination`, `Model`, `Date`, and `TotPassCap`. Store the values of `Date` as SAS date values.

   ✎   If you saved your program from Exercise 1, you can retrieve and modify the code for this workshop.

b. Use PROC PRINT to display the data portion of the data set. Display the values of `Date` in the form `12/15/2000`. Display the following labels for the column headings in place of the variable names:

Variable Name	Label
FlightID	Flight ID
RouteID	Route ID
Model	Aircraft Model
Date	Departure Date
TotPassCap	Total Passenger Capacity

Partial SAS Output (First 10 of 52 Observations)

```
                                  The SAS System

                                                               Total
              Flight  Route                          Departure Passenger
        Obs     ID     ID    Destination  Aircraft Model   Date  Capacity

          1  IA11200 0000112     HND      JetCruise LF8100 12/01/2000   255
          2  IA01804 0000018     SEA      JetCruise SF1000 12/01/2000   150
          3  IA02901 0000029     HNL      JetCruise LF5200 12/02/2000   207
          4  IA03100 0000031     ANC      JetCruise LF8100 12/02/2000   255
          5  IA02901 0000029     HNL      JetCruise LF5200 12/03/2000   207
          6  IA03100 0000031     ANC      JetCruise MF4000 12/03/2000   267
          7  IA00800 0000008     RDU      JetCruise MF4000 12/04/2000   267
          8  IA01805 0000018     SEA      JetCruise SF1000 12/04/2000   150
          9  IA01804 0000018     SEA      JetCruise LF5100 12/06/2000   165
         10  IA03101 0000031     ANC      JetCruise LF8100 12/06/2000   255
```

c. Use PROC CONTENTS to display the descriptor portion of the data set.

Partial SAS Output

```
               Alphabetic List of Variables and Attributes

                     #     Variable       Type     Len

                     5     Date           Num        8
                     3     Destination    Char       3
                     1     FlightID       Char       7
                     4     Model          Char      20
                     2     RouteID        Char       7
                     6     TotPassCap     Num        8
```

d. Save your program (DATA step, PROC PRINT step, and PROC CONTENTS step) in a file. You will use this program in a later exercise.

4. Reading Raw Data Using Formatted Input (Optional)

Write a DATA step to read the **dfwlax** raw data file.

- Name the new SAS data set **work.dfwlax**.

- Use formatted input.

The complete record layout for the **dfwlax** raw data file is below.

Variable Name	Columns	Data Type
FlightNum	1-3	Character
FlightDate	4-11	Numeric Date style: 01/01/03
Dest	12-14	Character
FirstClass	15-17	Numeric
Economy	18-20	Numeric

Write a PROC PRINT step to view the data.

- Suppress the observation column.

- Format **Economy** and **FirstClass** with commas, and add a suitable date format for **FlightDate** (for example, **date9.**, **mmddyy10.**, **ddmmyy10.**, or **worddate.**).

- Add a suitable title.

- Suppress the date, time, and page numbers.

- Add grand totals for **FirstClass** and **Economy**.

Complete SAS Output (using the DATE9. format)

```
                    Passenger Counts for Flights to LAX and DFW

            Flight      Flight                First
            Num          Date    Dest         Class      Economy

            439        11DEC2000  LAX           20          137
            921        11DEC2000  DFW           20          131
            114        12DEC2000  LAX           15          170
            982        12DEC2000  dfw            5           85
            439        13DEC2000  LAX           14          196
            982        13DEC2000  DFW           15          116
            431        14DEC2000  LaX           17          166
            982        14DEC2000  DFW            7           88
            114        15DEC2000  LAX            .          187
            982        15DEC2000  DFW           14           31
                                           =========   =========
                                              127        1,307
```

6.3   Examining Data Errors

Objectives
- Define types of data errors.
- Identify data errors.

83

What Are Data Errors?
SAS detects data errors when the following occurs:
- The INPUT statement encounters invalid data in a field.
- Illegal arguments are used in functions.
- Impossible mathematical operations are requested.

84

Examining Data Errors

When SAS encounters a data error, these events occur:

1. A note that describes the error is printed in the SAS log.

2. The input record being read is displayed in the SAS log (contents of the input buffer).

3. The values in the SAS observation being created are displayed in the SAS log (contents of the PDV).

4. A missing value is assigned to the appropriate SAS variable.

5. Execution continues.

85

Examining Data Errors

File: c06s3d1.sas
File: *userid*.prog1.sascode(c06s3d1)

- Use column input to read the raw data file.
- Examine the data error in the log.
- Use PROC PRINT to examine the data portion of the data set.

Partial Raw Data File

```
          1    1    2    2    3    3    4    4    5
1---5----0----5----0----5----0----5----0----5----0----
0031GOLDENBERG    DESIREE       PILOT1 50221.62
0040WILLIAMS      ARLENE M.     FLTAT1 23666.12
0071PERRY         ROBERT A.     FLTAT1 21957.71
0082MCGWIER-WATTSCHRISTINA      PILOT3 96387.39
0091SCOTT         HARVEY F.     FLTAT2 32278.40
0106THACKER       DAVID S.      FLTAT1 24161.14
0275GRAHAM        DEBORAH S.    FLTAT2 32024.93
0286DREWRY        SUSAN         PILOT1 55377.00
0309HORTON        THOMAS L.     FLTAT1 23705.12
0334DOWN          EDWARD        PILOT1 56%84.87
0347CHERVENY      BRENDA B.     FLTAT2 38563.45
0355BELL          THOMAS B.     PILOT1 59803.16
0366GLENN         MARTHA S.     PILOT3120202.38
0730BELL          CARLA         PILOT1 37397.93
0739SAYRE         MARCO         PILOT1 59268.61
```

1. Use a DATA step with column input to read the fields from the raw data file and create a SAS data set.

```
data work.empdata2;
    infile 'raw-data-file';
    input EmpID $ 1-4 LastName $ 5-17 FirstName $ 18-30
          JobCode $ 31-36 Salary 37-45;
run;
```

2. Examine the log.

    SAS Log

```
1      options ls=72 nodate nonumber;
2      data work.empdata2;
3         infile 'raw-data-file';
4         input EmpID $ 1-4 LastName $ 5-17 FirstName $ 18-30
5                JobCode $ 31-36 Salary 37-45;
6      run;

NOTE: The infile 'raw-data-file' is:
      File Name=raw-data-file,
      RECFM=V,LRECL=256

❶NOTE: Invalid data for Salary in line 10 37-45.
❷RULE:       ----+----1----+----2----+----3----+----4----+----5----+----6--
❸10          0334DOWN          EDWARD          PILOT1 56%84.87 45
❹EmpID=0334 LastName=DOWN FirstName=EDWARD JobCode=PILOT1 Salary=.
❺_ERROR_=1 _N_=10
 NOTE: 15 records were read from the infile 'raw-data-file'.
      The minimum record length was 45.
      The maximum record length was 45.
 NOTE: The data set WORK.EMPDATA2 has 15 observations and 5 variables.
```

❶ This note indicates that invalid data was found for the variable **Salary** in line 10 of the raw data file in columns 37-45.

❷ A ruler is drawn above the raw data record that contains the invalid data. The ruler can help you locate the invalid data in the record.

❸ SAS displays the raw data record being read (contents of the input buffer).

❹ SAS displays the observation currently being created from the raw data record (contents of the PDV). Notice that the value of **Salary** is set to missing.

❺ During the processing of every DATA step, SAS automatically creates two variables, _N_ and _ERROR_. They are **not** written to the SAS data set but are available for processing during the execution of the DATA step.

3. Use PROC PRINT to examine the data portion of the SAS data set.

```
proc print data=work.empdata2;
run;
```

SAS Output

```
                                  The SAS System

            Emp                                    Job
   Obs      ID     LastName         FirstName       Code       Salary

    1      0031    GOLDENBERG       DESIREE        PILOT1      50221.62
    2      0040    WILLIAMS         ARLENE M.      FLTAT1      23666.12
    3      0071    PERRY            ROBERT A.      FLTAT1      21957.71
    4      0082    MCGWIER-WATTS    CHRISTINA      PILOT3      96387.39
    5      0091    SCOTT            HARVEY F.      FLTAT2      32278.40
    6      0106    THACKER          DAVID S.       FLTAT1      24161.14
    7      0275    GRAHAM           DEBORAH S.     FLTAT2      32024.93
    8      0286    DREWRY           SUSAN          PILOT1      55377.00
    9      0309    HORTON           THOMAS L.      FLTAT1      23705.12
   10      0334    DOWN             EDWARD         PILOT1          .
   11      0347    CHERVENY         BRENDA B.      FLTAT2      38563.45
   12      0355    BELL             THOMAS B.      PILOT1      59803.16
   13      0366    GLENN            MARTHA S.      PILOT3     120202.38
   14      0730    BELL             CARLA          PILOT1      37397.93
   15      0739    SAYRE            MARCO          PILOT1      59268.61
```

A missing numeric value is displayed as a period, and a missing character value is displayed as a blank.

File: c06s3d2.sas
File: *userid*.prog1.sascode(c06s3d2)

- Use column input to read the raw data file again, but omit the $ after the variable **JobCode** in the INPUT statement.

- Examine the data error in the log.

1. Use a DATA step with column input to read the fields from the raw data file and create a SAS data set.

```
data work.empdata2;
    infile 'raw-data-file';
    input EmpID $ 1-4 LastName $ 5-17 FirstName $ 18-30
        JobCode 31-36 Salary 37-45;
run;
```

2. Examine the log.

SAS Log

```
1    options ls=72 nodate nonumber;
2    data work.empdata2;
3        infile 'raw-data-file';
4        input EmpID $ 1-4 LastName $ 5-17 FirstName $ 18-30
5            JobCode 31-36 Salary 37-45;
6    run;

NOTE: The infile 'raw-data-file' is:
      File Name=raw-data-file,
      RECFM=V,LRECL=256


NOTE: Invalid data for JobCode in line 1 31-36.
RULE:      ----+----1----+----2----+----3----+----4----+----5----+----6--
1          0031GOLDENBERG   DESIREE      PILOT1 50221.62 45
EmpID=0031 LastName=GOLDENBERG FirstName=DESIREE JobCode=.
Salary=50221.62 _ERROR_=1 _N_=1
NOTE: Invalid data for JobCode in line 2 31-36.
2          0040WILLIAMS     ARLENE M.    FLTAT1 23666.12 45
EmpID=0040 LastName=WILLIAMS FirstName=ARLENE M. JobCode=.
Salary=23666.12 _ERROR_=1 _N_=2
NOTE: Invalid data for JobCode in line 3 31-36.
3          0071PERRY        ROBERT A.    FLTAT1 21957.71 45
EmpID=0071 LastName=PERRY FirstName=ROBERT A. JobCode=. Salary=21957.71
_ERROR_=1 _N_=3
NOTE: Invalid data for JobCode in line 4 31-36.
4          0082MCGWIER-WATTSCHRISTINA    PILOT3 96387.39 45
EmpID=0082 LastName=MCGWIER-WATTS FirstName=CHRISTINA JobCode=.
Salary=96387.39 _ERROR_=1 _N_=4
NOTE: Invalid data for JobCode in line 5 31-36.
5          0091SCOTT        HARVEY F.    FLTAT2 32278.40 45
EmpID=0091 LastName=SCOTT FirstName=HARVEY F. JobCode=. Salary=32278.4
_ERROR_=1 _N_=5
NOTE: Invalid data for JobCode in line 6 31-36.
```

(Continued on the next page.)

```
6           0106THACKER       DAVID S.     FLTAT1 24161.14 45
EmpID=0106 LastName=THACKER FirstName=DAVID S. JobCode=. Salary=24161.14
_ERROR_=1 _N_=6
NOTE: Invalid data for JobCode in line 7 31-36.
7           0275GRAHAM        DEBORAH S.   FLTAT2 32024.93 45
EmpID=0275 LastName=GRAHAM FirstName=DEBORAH S. JobCode=.
Salary=32024.93 _ERROR_=1 _N_=7
NOTE: Invalid data for JobCode in line 8 31-36.
8           0286DREWRY        SUSAN        PILOT1 55377.00 45
EmpID=0286 LastName=DREWRY FirstName=SUSAN JobCode=. Salary=55377
_ERROR_=1 _N_=8
NOTE: Invalid data for JobCode in line 9 31-36.
9           0309HORTON        THOMAS L.    FLTAT1 23705.12 45
EmpID=0309 LastName=HORTON FirstName=THOMAS L. JobCode=. Salary=23705.12
_ERROR_=1 _N_=9
NOTE: Invalid data for JobCode in line 10 31-36.
NOTE: Invalid data for Salary in line 10 37-45.
10          0334DOWN          EDWARD       PILOT1 56%84.87 45
EmpID=0334 LastName=DOWN FirstName=EDWARD JobCode=. Salary=. _ERROR_=1
_N_=10
NOTE: Invalid data for JobCode in line 11 31-36.
11          0347CHERVENY      BRENDA B.    FLTAT2 38563.45 45
EmpID=0347 LastName=CHERVENY FirstName=BRENDA B. JobCode=.
Salary=38563.45 _ERROR_=1 _N_=11
NOTE: Invalid data for JobCode in line 12 31-36.
12          0355BELL          THOMAS B.    PILOT1 59803.16 45
EmpID=0355 LastName=BELL FirstName=THOMAS B. JobCode=. Salary=59803.16
_ERROR_=1 _N_=12
NOTE: Invalid data for JobCode in line 13 31-36.
13          0366GLENN         MARTHA S.    PILOT3120202.38 45
EmpID=0366 LastName=GLENN FirstName=MARTHA S. JobCode=. Salary=120202.38
_ERROR_=1 _N_=13
NOTE: Invalid data for JobCode in line 14 31-36.
14          0730BELL          CARLA        PILOT1 37397.93 45
EmpID=0730 LastName=BELL FirstName=CARLA JobCode=. Salary=37397.93
_ERROR_=1 _N_=14
NOTE: Invalid data for JobCode in line 15 31-36.
15          0739SAYRE         MARCO        PILOT1 59268.61 45
EmpID=0739 LastName=SAYRE FirstName=MARCO JobCode=. Salary=59268.61
_ERROR_=1 _N_=15
NOTE: 15 records were read from the infile 'raw-data-file'.
      The minimum record length was 45.
      The maximum record length was 45.
NOTE: The data set WORK.EMPDATA2 has 15 observations and 5 variables.
```

By default, the error message for invalid data for **JobCode** will be printed a maximum of 20 times.

3. Use PROC PRINT to examine the data portion of the SAS data set.

```
proc print data=work.empdata2;
run;
```

SAS Output

```
                              The SAS System

           Emp                                      Job
   Obs     ID      LastName        FirstName        Code      Salary

     1    0031     GOLDENBERG      DESIREE           .        50221.62
     2    0040     WILLIAMS        ARLENE M.         .        23666.12
     3    0071     PERRY           ROBERT A.         .        21957.71
     4    0082     MCGWIER-WATTS   CHRISTINA         .        96387.39
     5    0091     SCOTT           HARVEY F.         .        32278.40
     6    0106     THACKER         DAVID S.          .        24161.14
     7    0275     GRAHAM          DEBORAH S.        .        32024.93
     8    0286     DREWRY          SUSAN             .        55377.00
     9    0309     HORTON          THOMAS L.         .        23705.12
    10    0334     DOWN            EDWARD            .           .
    11    0347     CHERVENY        BRENDA B.         .        38563.45
    12    0355     BELL            THOMAS B.         .        59803.16
    13    0366     GLENN           MARTHA S.         .       120202.38
    14    0730     BELL            CARLA             .        37397.93
    15    0739     SAYRE           MARCO             .        59268.61
```

 **Exercises**

For these exercises, write DATA steps that read the raw data file that contains information on flights from San Francisco to various destinations.

> Fill in the blank with the location of your raw data file. Use an INFILE statement in a DATA step to read the raw file.
>
> ```
> data ...;
>    infile '_____';
>    .
>    .
>    .
> ```

Each exercise instructs you to read **some** of the fields shown (identified by **bold** type in shaded rows below) in the following record layout. The complete record layout for the **sfosch** raw data file is shown below.

Variable Name	Field Description	Columns	Data Type
FlightID	Flight ID Number	1–7	Character
RouteID	Route ID Number	8–14	Character
Origin	Flight Origin	15–17	Character
Destination	Flight Destination	18–20	Character
Model	Aircraft Model	21–40	Character
Date	Departure Date	41–49	Numeric 01JAN2000
DepartDay	Departure Day of Week	51	Numeric 1=Sunday
FClassPass	First Class Passengers	53–55	Numeric
BClassPass	Business Class Passengers	57–59	Numeric
EClassPass	Economy Class Passengers	61–63	Numeric
TotPassCap	Aircraft Capacity – Total Passengers	65–67	Numeric
CargoWt	Weight of Cargo in Pounds	69–73	Numeric
CargoRev	Revenue from Cargo in Dollars	75–79	Numeric

5. Examining Data Errors

a. Create a SAS data set named **work.passngrs** by writing a DATA step that uses formatted input to create only the variables **FlightID**, **Destination**, **Date**, **FClassPass**, **BClassPass**, and **EClassPass**. Store the values of **Date** as SAS date values.

b. Read the log and answer the following questions:

   1) How many records were read from the raw data file?

   2) How many observations are in the resulting SAS data set?

   3) How many variables are in the resulting SAS data set?

   4) What data errors are indicated in the SAS log?

c. Use PROC PRINT to display the data portion of the data set. Do not display the date and time that the SAS session started. Do not display page numbers. Set the line size to 72. Use an appropriate format to display the values of **Date**.

Partial SAS Output (First 26 of 52 Observations)

The SAS System

Obs	Flight ID	Destination	Date	FClass Pass	BClass Pass	EClass Pass
1	IA11200	HND	01DEC2000	19	31	171
2	IA01804	SEA	01DEC2000	10	.	123
3	IA02901	HNL	02DEC2000	13	24	138
4	IA03100	ANC	02DEC2000	13	22	250
5	IA02901	HNL	03DEC2000	14	25	132
6	IA03100	ANC	03DEC2000	16	.	243
7	IA00800	RDU	04DEC2000	16	.	243
8	IA01805	SEA	04DEC2000	11	.	123
9	IA01804	SEA	06DEC2000	11	12	111
10	IA03101	ANC	06DEC2000	14	26	233
11	IA01802	SEA	07DEC2000	10	.	132
12	IA11200	HND	08DEC2000	17	33	194
13	IA03101	ANC	08DEC2000	13	17	242
14	IA01804	SEA	08DEC2000	12	.	119
15	IA11201	HND	09DEC2000	15	32	175
16	IA03100	ANC	09DEC2000	14	.	237
17	IA01805	SEA	10DEC2000	12	.	126
18	IA01803	SEA	11DEC2000	12	.	136
19	IA11201	HND	12DEC2000	18	31	178
20	IA11200	HND	13DEC2000	17	29	179
21	IA03100	ANC	13DEC2000	14	.	244
22	IA01802	SEA	13DEC2000	12	.	115
23	IA01804	SEA	13DEC2000	11	.	115
24	IA01805	SEA	13DEC2000	10	.	123
25	IA11201	HND	14DEC2000	16	35	163
26	IA00801	RDU	14DEC2000	14	.	222

6.4 Assigning Variable Attributes

Objectives

- Assign permanent attributes to SAS variables.
- Override permanent variable attributes.

89

Default Variable Attributes

When a variable is created in a DATA step, the following situations exist:

- The name, type, and length of the variable are automatically assigned.
- Remaining attributes such as label and format are not automatically assigned.

When the variable is used in a later step, these events occur:

- The name is displayed for identification purposes.
- The variable's value is displayed using a system-determined format.

90

Default Variable Attributes

Create the `ia.dfwlax` data set.

```
libname ia 'SAS-data-library';
data ia.dfwlax;
   infile 'raw-data-file';
   input @1 Flight $3. @4 Date mmddyy8.
         @12 Dest $3. @15 FirstClass 3.
         @18 Economy 3.;
run;
```

c06s4d1

91

Examples of raw data filenames:

z/OS (OS/390)	userid.prog1.rawdata(dfwlax)
Windows	c:\workshop\winsas\prog1\dfwlax.dat
UNIX	/users/userid/dfwlax.dat

Examples of SAS data library names:

z/OS (OS/390)	userid.prog1.sasdata
Windows	c:\workshop\winsas\prog1
UNIX	/users/userid

Default Variable Attributes

Examine the descriptor portion of the `ia.dfwlax` data set.

```
proc contents data=ia.dfwlax;
run;
```

Partial Output

```
Alphabetic List of Variables and Attributes

   #   Variable     Type    Len

   2   Date         Num      8
   3   Dest         Char     3
   5   Economy      Num      8
   4   FirstClass   Num      8
   1   Flight       Char     3
```

c06s4d1

92

Specifying Variable Attributes

Use LABEL and FORMAT statements in the following steps:

- PROC step to temporarily assign the attributes (for the duration of the step only)
- DATA step to permanently assign the attributes (stored in the data set descriptor portion)

93

Temporary Variable Attributes

Use LABEL and FORMAT statements in a PROC step to temporarily assign attributes.

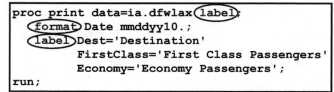

```
proc print data=ia.dfwlax label;
   format Date mmddyy10.;
   label Dest='Destination'
         FirstClass='First Class Passengers'
         Economy='Economy Passengers';
run;
```

Labels are not used automatically by PROC PRINT. You must specify the LABEL or SPLIT= option in the PROC statement.

95   c06s4d1

Temporary Variable Attributes

| | | | | First Class | Economy |
Obs	Flight	Date	Destination	Passengers	Passengers
1	439	12/11/2000	LAX	20	137
2	921	12/11/2000	DFW	20	131
3	114	12/12/2000	LAX	15	170
4	982	12/12/2000	dfw	5	85
5	439	12/13/2000	LAX	14	196
6	982	12/13/2000	DFW	15	116
7	431	12/14/2000	LaX	17	166
8	982	12/14/2000	DFW	7	88
9	114	12/15/2000	LAX	.	187
10	982	12/15/2000	DFW	14	31

The SAS System

96

Permanent Variable Attributes

Assign labels and formats in the DATA step.

```
libname ia 'SAS-data-library';
data ia.dfwlax;
   infile 'raw-data-file';
   input @1 Flight $3. @4 Date mmddyy8.
         @12 Dest $3. @15 FirstClass 3.
         @18 Economy 3.;
   format Date mmddyy10.;
   label Dest='Destination'
         FirstClass='First Class Passengers'
         Economy='Economy Passengers';
run;
```

97   c06s4d2

Examples of raw data filenames:

z/OS (OS/390)	userid.prog1.rawdata(dfwlax)
Windows	c:\workshop\winsas\prog1\dfwlax.dat
UNIX	/users/userid/dfwlax.dat

Examples of SAS data library names:

z/OS (OS/390)	userid.prog1.sasdata
Windows	c:\workshop\winsas\prog1
UNIX	/users/userid

Permanent Variable Attributes

Examine the descriptor portion of the **ia.dfwlax** data set.

```
proc contents data=ia.dfwlax;
run;
```

Partial Output

```
          Alphabetic List of Variables and Attributes

#   Variable    Type    Len    Format      Label

2   Date        Num      8     MMDDYY10.
3   Dest        Char     3                 Destination
5   Economy     Num      8                 Economy Passengers
4   FirstClass  Num      8                 First Class Passengers
1   Flight      Char     3
```

98   c06s4d2

Permanent Variable Attributes

```
proc print data=ia.dfwlax label;
run;
```

```
                           The SAS System

                                          First
                                          Class      Economy
    Obs   Flight        Date  Destination Passengers Passengers

      1    439   12/11/2000     LAX          20        137
      2    921   12/11/2000     DFW          20        131
      3    114   12/12/2000     LAX          15        170
      4    982   12/12/2000     dfw           5         85
      5    439   12/13/2000     LAX          14        196
      6    982   12/13/2000     DFW          15        116
      7    431   12/14/2000     LaX          17        166
      8    982   12/14/2000     DFW           7         88
      9    114   12/15/2000     LAX           .        187
     10    982   12/15/2000     DFW          14         31
```

99   c06s4d2

Override Permanent Attributes

Use a FORMAT statement in a PROC step to temporarily override the format stored in the data set descriptor.

```
proc print data=ia.dfwlax label;
    format Date date9.;
run;
```

100   c06s4d3

Override Permanent Attributes

```
                           The SAS System

                                          First
                                          Class      Economy
    Obs   Flight        Date  Destination Passengers Passengers

      1    439   11DEC2000      LAX          20        137
      2    921   11DEC2000      DFW          20        131
      3    114   12DEC2000      LAX          15        170
      4    982   12DEC2000      dfw           5         85
      5    439   13DEC2000      LAX          14        196
      6    982   13DEC2000      DFW          15        116
      7    431   14DEC2000      LaX          17        166
      8    982   14DEC2000      DFW           7         88
      9    114   15DEC2000      LAX           .        187
     10    982   15DEC2000      DFW          14         31
```

101

 **Exercises**

6. Assigning Variable Attributes

a. In the formatted input workshop, you wrote a program and stored it in a file. (The program creates a SAS data set named **work.sanfran**, prints the data set, and shows the contents of the descriptor portion of the data set.) Retrieve the program and submit it.

1) View the PROC PRINT output. The **Date** values are displayed in the form **12/01/2000**. Labels should be used for all column headings except for the variable **Destination**.

Partial SAS Output (First 5 of 52 Observations)

```
                              The SAS System

                                                                Total
         Flight  Route                             Departure Passenger
   Obs     ID     ID    Destination  Aircraft Model      Date  Capacity

     1  IA11200 0000112     HND      JetCruise LF8100 12/01/2000   255
     2  IA01804 0000018     SEA      JetCruise SF1000 12/01/2000   150
     3  IA02901 0000029     HNL      JetCruise LF5200 12/02/2000   207
     4  IA03100 0000031     ANC      JetCruise LF8100 12/02/2000   255
     5  IA02901 0000029     HNL      JetCruise LF5200 12/03/2000   207
```

2) View the PROC CONTENTS output. Are the labels permanently stored in the data set descriptor? Is the DATE format stored in the descriptor for the variable **Date**?

Partial SAS Log

```
         Alphabetic List of Variables and Attributes

         #    Variable       Type    Len

         5    Date           Num      8
         3    Destination    Char     3
         1    FlightID       Char     7
         4    Model          Char     20
         2    RouteID        Char     7
         6    TotPassCap     Num      8
```

b. Alter your program so that the labels and the DATE format are stored in the descriptor portion of the data set. Submit the program again.

1) View the PROC PRINT output. Are the labels still displayed? Are the values of **Date** still formatted correctly?

Partial SAS Output (First 5 of 52 Observations)

```
                                   The SAS System

                                                                 Total
              Flight   Route                            Departure Passenger
       Obs     ID       ID    Destination  Aircraft Model     Date  Capacity

         1   IA11200  0000112     HND      JetCruise LF8100 12/01/2000    255
         2   IA01804  0000018     SEA      JetCruise SF1000 12/01/2000    150
         3   IA02901  0000029     HNL      JetCruise LF5200 12/02/2000    207
         4   IA03100  0000031     ANC      JetCruise LF8100 12/02/2000    255
         5   IA02901  0000029     HNL      JetCruise LF5200 12/03/2000    207
```

2) View the PROC CONTENTS output. Are the labels permanently stored in the data set descriptor? Is the DATE format stored in the descriptor for the variable **Date**?

Partial SAS Log

```
              Alphabetic List of Variables and Attributes

       #     Variable      Type    Len    Format        Label

       5     Date          Num      8    MMDDYY10.    Departure Date
       3     Destination   Char     3
       1     FlightID      Char     7                 Flight ID
       4     Model         Char    20                 Aircraft Model
       2     RouteID       Char     7                 Route ID
       6     TotPassCap    Num      8                 Total Passenger Capacity
```

6.5   Changing Variable Attributes (Self-Study)

Objectives

- Use features in the windowing environment to change variable attributes.
- Use programming statements to change variable attributes.

104

Changing Variable Attributes under Windows

Change the name of the variable **Dest** to **Destination**.

1. If the Explorer window is not active, select **View** ➪ **Contents Only**.

2. Double-click **Libraries** to view a list of currently defined libraries.

The functionality of the SAS Explorer is similar to explorers for Windows-based systems. In addition to this view, you can view a list of folders and files, or you can specify a tree view.

3. Double-click **Ia** to show all members of that library.

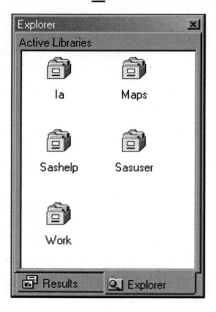

4. Right-click on the **Dfwlax** data set and select **View Columns**.

5. Right-click on the **Dest** variable and select **Modify**.

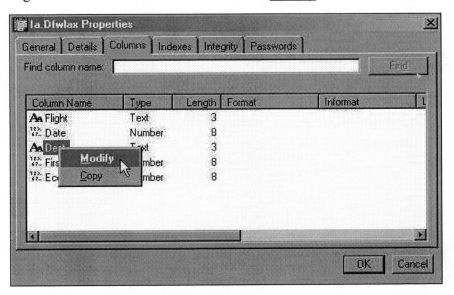

6. Type the new name, **Destination**, over the old name and select **OK**.

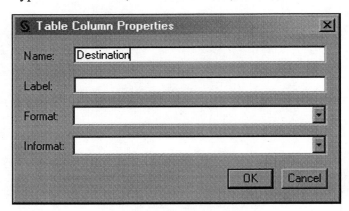

7. The new name is displayed for the variable.

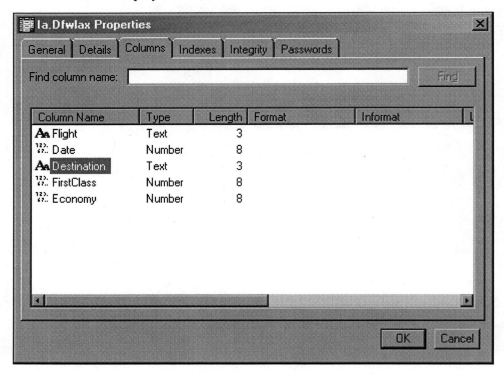

Changing Variable Attributes under UNIX

Change the name of the variable **Dest** to **Destination**.

1. If the Explorer window is not active, select **View** ⇨ **Contents Only**.

2. Double-click **Libraries** to view a list of currently defined libraries.

3. Double-click **Ia** to show all members of that library.

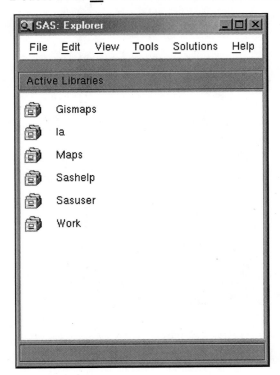

4. Right-click on the **Dfwlax** data set and select **View Columns**.

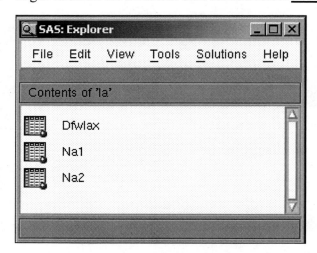

5. Right-click on the **Dest** variable and select **Modify**.

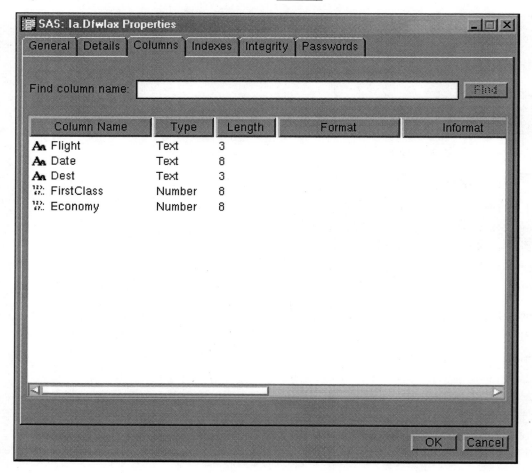

6. Type the new name, **Destination**, over the old name and select **OK**.

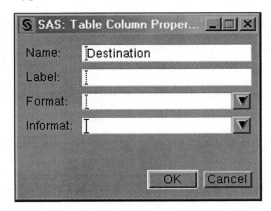

7. The new name is displayed for the variable.

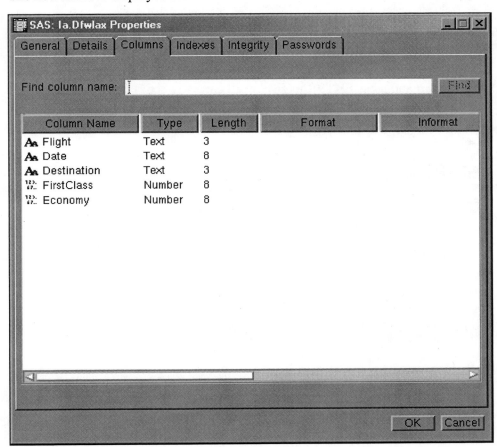

Changing Variable Attributes under z/OS (OS/390)

Change the name of the variable **Dest** to **Destination**.

1. If the Explorer window is not active, type **pmenu** on the command line and press the ENTER key.

2. Select <u>**View**</u> ⇨ <u>**Contents Only**</u>.

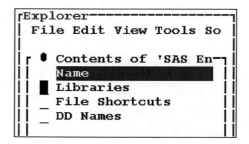

3. Type **s** beside **Libraries** and press ENTER to display all currently active SAS data libraries.

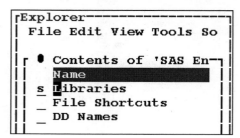

4. Type **s** beside **Ia** and press ENTER to show all members of that library.

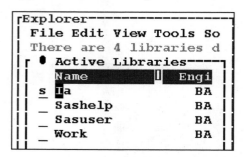

5. Type **s** beside **Dfwlax** and press ENTER to display the attributes of the variables in the **Dfwlax** data set.

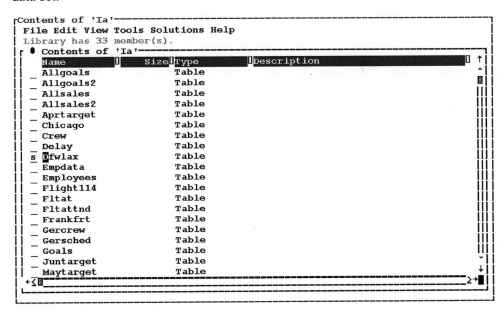

6. Type **?** beside **Dest** and press ENTER.

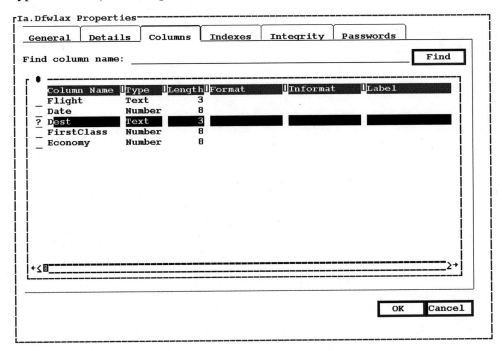

7. Select **Modify** to rename the variable.

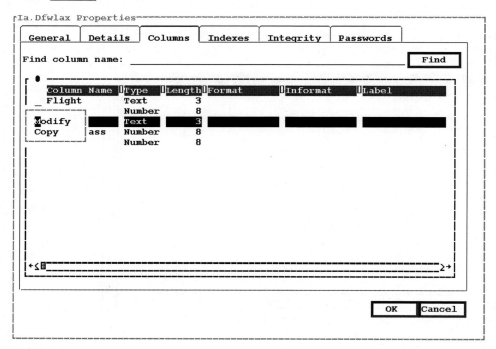

8. Type the new name, **Destination**, over the old name and select **OK**.

```
┌Table Column Properties────────────────────────────────────────────────┐
│ Name:      Destination█                                                │
│                                                                        │
│ Label:     _____        │
│                                                                        │
│ Format:    [_____[V]       │
│                                                                        │
│ Informat:  [_____[V]       │
│                                                                        │
│                                                                        │
│                                                                        │
│                                                                        │
│                                                                        │
│                                                                        │
│                                                                        │
│                                                                        │
│                                                                        │
│                                                                        │
│                                                                        │
│                                                                        │
│                                                 ┌────┐  ┌──────┐        │
│                                                 │ OK │  │Cancel│        │
│                                                 └────┘  └──────┘        │
└────────────────────────────────────────────────────────────────────────┘
```

9. The new name is displayed for the variable.

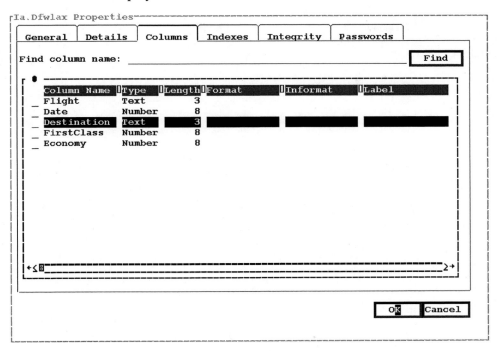

The DATASETS Procedure

You can use the DATASETS procedure to modify the following attributes of a variable:

- name
- label
- format
- informat

106

The DATASETS Procedure

General form of PROC DATASETS for changing variable attributes:

```
PROC DATASETS LIBRARY=libref ;
    MODIFY SAS-data-set ;
    RENAME old-name-1=new-name-1
            <. . . old-name-n=new-name-n>;
    LABEL variable-1='label-1'
            <. . . variable-n='label-n'>;
    FORMAT variable-list-1 format-1
            <. . . variable-list-n format-n>;
    INFORMAT variable-list-1 informat-1
            <. . . variable-list-n informat-n>;
RUN;
QUIT;
```

107

Data Set Contents

Business Task: Use the DATASETS procedure to change the name of the variable **Dest** to **Destination**.

Step 1: Look at the original attributes of the variables in the **ia.dfwlax** data set.

```
proc contents data=ia.dfwlax;
run;
```

```
      Alphabetic List of Variables and Attributes

          #    Variable     Type    Len

          2    Date         Num     8
          3    Dest         Char    3
          5    Economy      Num     8
          4    FirstClass   Num     8
          1    Flight       Char    3
```

108   c06s5d1

The DATASETS Procedure

Step 2: Use the DATASETS procedure to rename the
variable **Dest** to **Destination**.

```
proc datasets library=ia;
   modify dfwlax;
   rename Dest=Destination;
run;
quit;
```

109   c06s5d1

Data Set Contents

Step 3: Look at the attributes of the variables in
the **ia.dfwlax** data set after you run
PROC DATASETS.

```
proc contents data=ia.dfwlax;
run;
```

Alphabetic List of Variables and Attributes			
#	Variable	Type	Len
2	Date	Num	8
3	Destination	Char	3
5	Economy	Num	8
4	FirstClass	Num	8
1	Flight	Char	3

110   c06s5d1

Exercises

For these exercises, use the **passngrs** data set stored in a permanent SAS data library.

> Fill in the blank with the location of your SAS data library. **If you started a new SAS session since the previous lab**, submit the LIBNAME statement to assign the libref **ia** to the SAS data library.
>
> ```
> libname ia '_____';
> ```

7. **Changing Variable Attributes**

   a. Use the SAS windowing environment to change the following attributes of the **FClass** variable.

   1) Rename the variable to **FirstClass**.

   2) Assign the label **First Class Passengers** to the variable.

   3) Run PROC CONTENTS to verify that the changes were made.

   Partial Output

   ```
                Alphabetic List of Variables and Attributes

        #    Variable    Type    Len    Label

        5    BClass      Num      8
        3    Depart      Num      8
        2    Dest        Char     3
        6    EClass      Num      8
        4    FirstClass  Num      8     First Class Passengers
        1    FlightID    Char     7
   ```

   b. Use program statements to change the following attributes of the **Depart** variable:

   1) Assign the DATE9. format to the variable.

   2) Assign the label **Departure Date** to the variable.

   3) Run PROC CONTENTS to verify that the changes were made.

   Partial Output

   ```
                Alphabetic List of Variables and Attributes

        #    Variable    Type    Len    Format    Label

        5    BClass      Num      8
        3    Depart      Num      8     DATE9.    Departure Date
        2    Dest        Char     3
        6    EClass      Num      8
        4    FirstClass  Num      8               First Class Passengers
        1    FlightID    Char     7
   ```

6.6 Reading Microsoft Excel Spreadsheets (Self-Study)

Objectives

- Create a SAS data set from a Microsoft Excel spreadsheet using the Import Wizard.
- Create a SAS data set from an Excel spreadsheet using the IMPORT procedure.

113

✐   The IMPORT procedure and the Import Wizard are not available on z/OS.

Business Task

The flight data for Dallas and Los Angeles is in an Excel spreadsheet. Read the data into a SAS data set.

Excel Spreadsheet

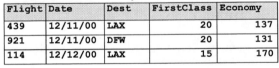

	A	B	C	D	E
1	Flight	Date	Dest	FirstClass	Economy
2	439	12/11/00	LAX	20	137
3	921	12/11/00	DFW	20	131
4	114	12/12/00	LAX	15	170

SAS Data Set

Flight	Date	Dest	FirstClass	Economy
439	12/11/00	LAX	20	137
921	12/11/00	DFW	20	131
114	12/12/00	LAX	15	170

114

The Import Wizard

The *Import Wizard* is a point-and-click graphical interface that enables you to create a SAS data set from several types of external files including the following:

- dBASE files (*.DBF)
- Excel spreadsheets (*.XLS)
- Microsoft Access tables (*.MDB)
- JMP data files (*.JMP)
- delimited files (*.*)
- comma-separated values (*.CSV)

115

The data sources available to you depend on your operating environment and the SAS/ACCESS products that you licensed. If you do not have any SAS/ACCESS products licensed, the only types of data source files available to you are as follows:

- .CSV
- .TXT
- delimited files

Excel spreadsheets and delimited files do not have column names, but they often contain column headings. For these file formats, you can specify that column headings be used to create SAS variable names. If the headings are not valid SAS names, or if the file does not contain headings, SAS uses default variable names. For example, for a delimited file, the default variable names are **VAR1**, **VAR2**, **VAR3**, and so on.

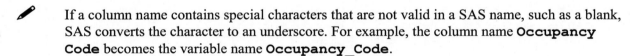

If a column name contains special characters that are not valid in a SAS name, such as a blank, SAS converts the character to an underscore. For example, the column name **Occupancy Code** becomes the variable name **Occupancy_Code**.

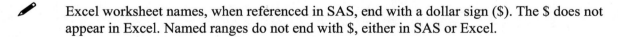

Excel worksheet names, when referenced in SAS, end with a dollar sign ($). The $ does not appear in Excel. Named ranges do not end with $, either in SAS or Excel.

Reading Excel Data with the Import Wizard

Use the Import Wizard to import the file **DallasLA.xls** into SAS. This is an Excel file that contains flight information. Name the resulting data set **work.dfwlax**.

1. Select **File** ⇨ **Import Data...**. The Import Wizard – Select import type window opens.

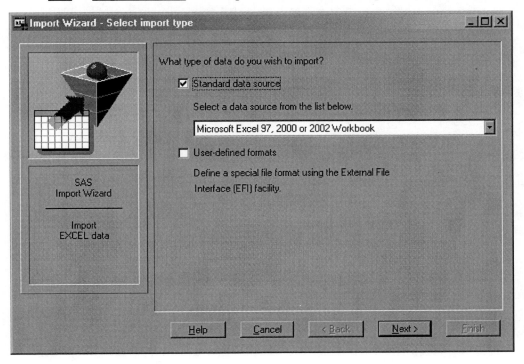

2. Select the down arrow at the end of the field.

3. From the list box, select **Microsoft Excel 97, 2000 or 2002 Workbook**.

4. Select **Next >**. The Connect to MS Excel dialog box opens.

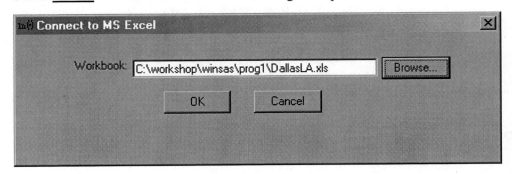

5. Type **DallasLA.xls**, which is the name of the workbook file to be imported.

   You can also select **Browse...** to specify a workbook file to import from the Open window. After you select the pathname, select **Open** to complete your selections and return to the Connect to MS Excel dialog box.

6. Select **OK**. The Import Wizard – Select Table window opens.

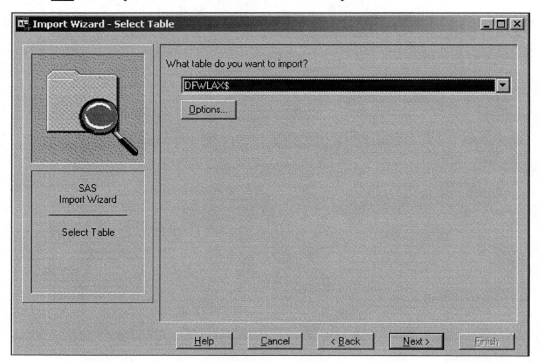

7. Select **DFWLAX$**, the name of the worksheet to be imported.

   ✎ A table name ending **with** $ represents a worksheet. A table name **without** $ represents a named range.

   ✎ Excel worksheet names, when referenced in SAS, end with a dollar sign ($). The $ does not appear in Excel. Named ranges do not end with $, either in SAS or Excel.

   ✎ You can select **Options...** to change default import settings through the SAS Import: Spreadsheet Options dialog box.

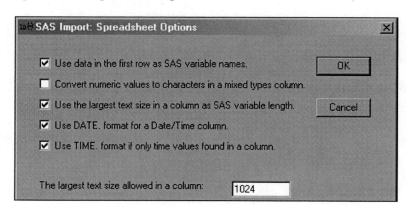

8. Select **Next >** to open the Import Wizard – Select library and member window, where you specify the storage location for the imported file.

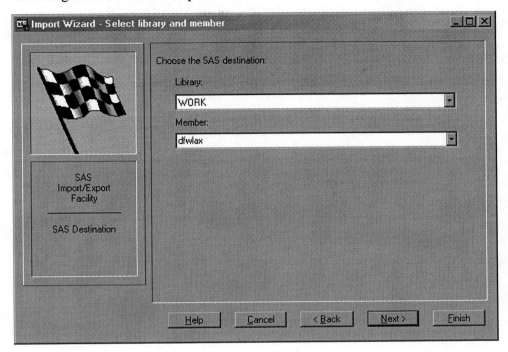

9. In the Library box, leave the library as **WORK**. In the Member box, type **dfwlax**.

    You can also select the down arrow in the Library box and select a different library. You can select the down arrow in the Member box to select an existing data set. If you select an existing data set, you will be asked later to verify that you want to replace it.

10. Select **Next >** to move to the next window or **Finish** to create the SAS data set from the Excel spreadsheet.

    If you select **Finish** and you select the name of an existing SAS data set for the name of your new SAS data set (in the Import Wizard – Select library and member window), you are prompted to determine whether or not you want to replace the existing data set. Select **OK** or **Cancel**.

If you select **Next >**, you are taken to the Import Wizard – Create SAS Statements window.

11. Type **DallasLAImport.sas**, which is the name of the location where you want to store the SAS code.

    You can also select **Browse...** to specify a location from the Save As window. After you select the pathname, select **Save** to complete your selections and return to the Import Wizard – Create SAS Statements window.

    If the file already exists, you are prompted to replace the existing file, append to the existing file, or cancel the save.

12. Select **Finish**.

13. Check the log to see that the SAS data set is successfully created.

```
NOTE: WORK.DFWLAX was successfully created.
```

14. Go to the Program Editor window and write SAS code to print the data set.

File: c06s6d1.sas

```
proc print data=work.dfwlax;
run;
```

SAS Output

```
                              The SAS System

                                            First
            Obs    Flight    Date      Dest  Class    Economy

             1      439      12/11/00   LAX    20       137
             2      921      12/11/00   DFW    20       131
             3      114      12/12/00   LAX    15       170
             4      982      12/12/00   dfw     5        85
             5      439      12/13/00   LAX    14       196
             6      982      12/13/00   DFW    15       116
             7      431      12/14/00   LaX    17       166
             8      982      12/14/00   DFW     7        88
             9      114      12/15/00   LAX     .       187
            10      982      12/15/00   DFW    14        31
```

15. Go to the Program Editor window and open the SAS code created by the Import Wizard.

File: DallasLAImport.sas

```
PROC IMPORT OUT=WORK.DFWLAX
        DATAFILE="C:\workshop\winsas\prog1\DallasLA.xls"
            DBMS=EXCEL REPLACE;
        SHEET="DFWLAX$";
        GETNAMES=YES;
        MIXED=NO;
        SCANTEXT=YES;
        USEDATE=YES;
        SCANTIME=YES;
RUN;
```

✎   For additional documentation related to statements used when reading Microsoft Excel files with the IMPORT procedure, see *Base SAS® 9.1 Procedures Guide, Volumes 1, 2*, and *3* and *SAS/ACCESS® 9.1 Interface to PC Files: Reference*.

The IMPORT Procedure

General form of the IMPORT procedure:

```
PROC IMPORT OUT=SAS-data-set
            DATAFILE='external-file-name'
            < DBMS=file-type > <REPLACE>;
RUN;
```

REPLACE   overwrites an existing SAS data set.

117

Available DBMS Specifications

Identifier	Input Data Source	Extension
ACCESS	Microsoft Access table	.MDB
CSV	delimited file (comma-separated values)	.CSV
DBF	dBASE 5.0, IV, III+, and II files	.DBF
DLM	delimited file (default delimiter is a blank)	.*
EXCEL	Microsoft Excel spreadsheet	.XLS
JMP	JMP table	.JMP
TAB	delimited file (tab-delimited values)	.TXT
WK1	Lotus 1-2-3 Release 2 spreadsheet	.WK1
WK3	Lotus 1-2-3 Release 3 spreadsheet	.WK3
WK4	Lotus 1-2-3 Release 4 or 5 spreadsheet	.WK4

If *external-file-name* contains a valid extension so that PROC IMPORT can recognize the type of data, you can omit the DBMS= option.

If you specify DBMS=ACCESS to import a Microsoft Access table, PROC IMPORT can distinguish whether the table is in Access 97, 2000, or 2002 format.

If you specify DBMS=EXCEL to import a Microsoft Excel spreadsheet, PROC IMPORT can distinguish between Excel 2002, 2000, 97, 5.0, and 4.0 spreadsheets.

Reading Excel Data with PROC IMPORT

This PROC IMPORT code reads the same Excel file
previously processed through the Import Wizard:

```
proc import out=work.dfwlax
            datafile="DallasLA.xls"
            dbms=excel2000 replace;
   mixed=yes;
run;
```

MIXED=YES; converts numeric data values into
               character data values for a column
               that contains mixed data types.

c06s6d2

118

The default is MIXED=NO, which means that numeric data will be imported as missing values
in a character column. The MIXED= option is available only for reading Excel data.

When you use the Import Wizard, you can set the MIXED=YES option by selecting **Convert numeric
values to characters in a mixed types column** in the SAS Import: Spreadsheet Options dialog box.

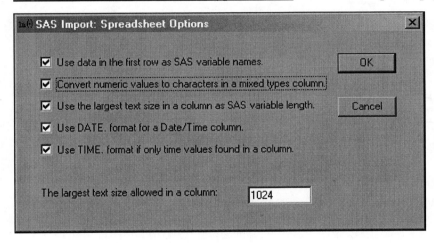

Other commonly used PROC IMPORT data source statements include the following:

GETNAMES=NO;

> Do not attempt to generate SAS variable names from the column names in the input file's first
> row of data.

SHEET="*spreadsheet-name*";

> Read a particular spreadsheet from a file that contains multiple spreadsheets.

Reading Tab-delimited Data

What if the data in the previous example were stored in a tab-delimited file?

Change the PROC IMPORT code to read the tab-delimited file.

```
proc import out=work.dfwlax
            datafile="DallasLA.txt"
            dbms=tab replace;
run;
```

119   c06s6d3

Excel SAS/ACCESS LIBNAME Engine

If you want to access Excel data without making a copy as a SAS data set, use the LIBNAME statement.

General form of a LIBNAME statement to access an Excel workbook:

LIBNAME *libref 'location-of-Excel-workbook' <options>*;

Example:

```
libname myxls 'c:\temp\sales.xls';
```

120

The Excel SAS/ACCESS LIBNAME engine is available in SAS 9.1.

    Due to the .xls extension, SAS recognizes the library path as an Excel workbook. Unlike other SAS/ACCESS interfaces, the Excel engine need not be specified in the LIBNAME statement.

Excel SAS/ACCESS LIBNAME Engine

The entire Excel workbook is treated in the same way as a SAS library.

Individual worksheets and named ranges are considered equivalent to SAS data sets.

Use PROC PRINT to display data from the DFWLAX$ worksheet in the Excel workbook named DallasLA.xls:

```
libname xlsdata 'DallasLA.xls';

proc print data=xlsdata."dfwlax$"n;
run;
```

c06s6d4

121

The MIXED=YES and GETNAMES=NO options are supported by the LIBNAME statement when you use the Excel SAS/ACCESS LIBNAME engine.

   SAS name literal syntax is required for the following:

- all Excel worksheet names because they end with $
- named ranges that do not satisfy SAS naming conventions

 **Exercises**

(Applicable Only for Microsoft Windows Users)

8. **Reading a Microsoft Excel Spreadsheet**

    a. The Excel spreadsheet **sfosch.xls** contains information about International Airlines flights originating in San Francisco.

        Use the Import Wizard to create a SAS data set named **work.sfoexcel** from the Excel spreadsheet.

        Save the PROC IMPORT code that is generated to a file named **ImportSFO.sas**.

        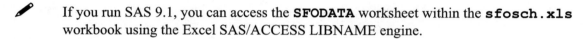 If you run SAS 9.1, you can access the **SFODATA** worksheet within the **sfosch.xls** workbook using the Excel SAS/ACCESS LIBNAME engine.

    b. Use PROC PRINT to display the data portion of the SAS data set **work.sfoexcel**. Do not display the date and time that the SAS session started. Do not display page numbers. Set the line size to 72.

        Partial output is shown on the next page.

Partial SAS Output (First 15 of 52 Observations)

```
                                 The SAS System

       Flight
 Obs   ID        RouteID  Origin   Destination  Model              Date

   1   IA11200   0000112  0000112  HND          JetCruise LF8100   01DEC2000
   2   IA01804   0000018  0000018  SEA          JetCruise SF1000   01DEC2000
   3   IA02901   0000029  0000029  HNL          JetCruise LF5200   02DEC2000
   4   IA03100   0000031  0000031  ANC          JetCruise LF8100   02DEC2000
   5   IA02901   0000029  0000029  HNL          JetCruise LF5200   03DEC2000
   6   IA03100   0000031  0000031  ANC          JetCruise MF4000   03DEC2000
   7   IA00800   0000008  0000008  RDU          JetCruise MF4000   04DEC2000
   8   IA01805   0000018  0000018  SEA          JetCruise SF1000   04DEC2000
   9   IA01804   0000018  0000018  SEA          JetCruise LF5100   06DEC2000
  10   IA03101   0000031  0000031  ANC          JetCruise LF8100   06DEC2000
  11   IA01802   0000018  0000018  SEA          JetCruise SF1000   07DEC2000
  12   IA11200   0000112  0000112  HND          JetCruise LF8100   08DEC2000
  13   IA03101   0000031  0000031  ANC          JetCruise LF8100   08DEC2000
  14   IA01804   0000018  0000018  SEA          JetCruise SF1000   08DEC2000
  15   IA11201   0000112  0000112  HND          JetCruise LF8100   09DEC2000


                                                Tot
       Depart    FClass   BClass   EClass       Pass   Cargo    Cargo
 Obs   Day       Pass     Pass     Pass         Cap    Wt       Rev

   1    6         19       31       171         255    61300    79077
   2    6         10        .       123         150    10300    13287
   3    7         13       24       138         207    47400    61146
   4    7         13       22       250         255    24800    31992
   5    1         14       25       132         207    48200    62178
   6    1         16        .       243         267    25600    33024
   7    2         16        .       243         267    25600    33024
   8    2         11        .       123         150    10100    13029
   9    4         11       12       111         165    12500    16125
  10    4         14       26       233         255    28000    36120
  11    5         10        .       132         150     8500    10965
  12    6         17       33       194         255    56700    73143
  13    6         13       17       242         255    26400    34056
  14    6         12        .       119         150    10700    13803
  15    7         15       32       175         255    61100    78819
```

c. Use PROC CONTENTS to display the descriptor portion of the **work.sfoexcel** data set.

Partial SAS Output

```
              -----Alphabetic List of Variables and Attributes-----

   #   Variable      Type   Len   Pos   Format   Informat   Label
   -----------------------------------------------------------------------
   9   BClassPass    Num     8    16                         BClassPass
  13   CargoRev      Num     8    48                         CargoRev
  12   CargoWt       Num     8    40                         CargoWt
   6   Date          Char    9    96    $9.      $9.         Date
   7   DepartDay     Num     8     0                         DepartDay
   4   Destination   Char    3    77    $3.      $3.         Destination
  10   EClassPass    Num     8    24                         EClassPass
   8   FClassPass    Num     8     8                         FClassPass
   1   FlightID      Char    7    56    $7.      $7.         FlightID
   5   Model         Char   16    80    $16.     $16.        Model
   3   Origin        Char    7    70    $7.      $7.         Origin
   2   RouteID       Char    7    63    $7.      $7.         RouteID
  11   TotPassCap    Num     8    32                         TotPassCap
```

9. Reading a Comma-delimited File

a. The file named **sfosch.csv** (delimited file with comma-separated values) contains the same information about International Airlines flights as the Excel spreadsheet named **sfosch.xls**.

Open the file named **ImportSFO.sas** that you saved in the previous exercise. Alter the PROC IMPORT statement so that it creates a SAS data set named **work.sfocsv** from the comma-delimited file.

b. Use PROC PRINT to display the data portion of the **work.sfocsv** data set. Do not display the date and time that the SAS session started. Do not display page numbers. Set the line size to 72. Partial output is shown on the next page.

Partial SAS Output (First 9 of 52 Observations)

```
                                 The SAS System

        Flight
Obs     ID              RouteID         Origin   Destination   Model

  1     IA11200           112             112        HND        JetCruise LF8100
  2     IA01804            18              18        SEA        JetCruise SF1000
  3     IA02901            29              29        HNL        JetCruise LF5200
  4     IA03100            31              31        ANC        JetCruise LF8100
  5     IA02901            29              29        HNL        JetCruise LF5200
  6     IA03100            31              31        ANC        JetCruise MF4000
  7     IA00800             8               8        RDU        JetCruise MF4000
  8     IA01805            18              18        SEA        JetCruise SF1000
  9     IA01804            18              18        SEA        JetCruise LF5100


Obs     Date            DepartDay      FClassPass      BClassPass      EClassPass

  1     01DEC2000           6              19              31              171
  2     01DEC2000           6              10               .              123
  3     02DEC2000           7              13              24              138
  4     02DEC2000           7              13              22              250
  5     03DEC2000           1              14              25              132
  6     03DEC2000           1              16               .              243
  7     04DEC2000           2              16               .              243
  8     04DEC2000           2              11               .              123
  9     06DEC2000           4              11              12              111


Obs        TotPassCap          CargoWt          CargoRev

  1            255              61300             79077
  2            150              10300             13287
  3            207              47400             61146
  4            255              24800             31992
  5            207              48200             62178
  6            267              25600             33024
  7            267              25600             33024
  8            150              10100             13029
  9            165              12500             16125
```

6.7 Solutions to Exercises

1. **Reading Raw Data Using Column Input**

    a.

```
data work.sanfran;
   infile 'raw-data-file';
   input FlightID $ 1-7 RouteID $ 8-14
         Destination $ 18-20 Model $ 21-40
         DepartDay 51 TotPassCap 65-67;
run;
```

    b.

    1) Fifty-two records were read.

    2) Fifty-two observations were stored in the SAS data set.

    3) Six variables were stored in the SAS data set.

    c.

```
options nodate nonumber ls=72;
proc print data=work.sanfran;
run;
```

    d.

```
proc contents data=work.sanfran;
run;
```

2. **Reading Raw Data Using Column Input (Optional)**

```
data work.emps;
   infile 'raw-data-filename';
   input EmpID      $ 31-35
         LastName   $  1-20
         FirstName  $ 21-30
         JobCode    $ 36-43
         Salary       54-59;
run;

proc print data=work.emps noobs;
   title 'Salary Information for Pilots and Mechanics';
run;
```

3. Reading Raw Data Using Formatted Input

a.

```
data work.sanfran;
   infile 'raw-data-file';
   input @1 FlightID $7. @8 RouteID $7.
         @18 Destination $3. @21 Model $20.
         @41 Date date9. @65 TotPassCap 3.;
run;
```

b.

```
proc print data=work.sanfran label;
   format Date mmddyy10.;
   label FlightID='Flight ID'
         RouteID='Route ID'
         Model='Aircraft Model'
         Date='Departure Date'
         TotPassCap='Total Passenger Capacity';
run;
```

c.

```
proc contents data=work.sanfran;
run;
```

d. Use the FILE command or select **Save As** from the File menu.

4. Reading Raw Data Using Formatted Input (Optional)

```
data work.dfwlax;
   infile 'raw-data-filename';
   input @1  FlightNum  $3.
         @4  FlightDate  mmddyy8.
         @12 Dest       $3.
         @18 Economy     3.
         @15 FirstClass  3.;
run;

options nodate nonumber;
proc print data=work.dfwlax noobs;
   title 'Passenger Counts for Flights to LAX and DFW';
   sum Economy FirstClass;
   format Economy FirstClass comma9. FlightDate date9.;
run;
```

5. Examining Data Errors

a.

```
data work.passngrs;
   infile 'raw-data-file';
   input @1 FlightID $7.    @18 Destination $3.
         @41 Date date9.    @53 FClassPass 3.
         @57 BClassPass 3.  @61 EClassPass 3.;
run;
```

b.

1) Fifty-two records were read.

2) Fifty-two observations are in the resulting data set.

3) Six variables are in the resulting data set.

4) There is invalid data for **BClassPass** in record numbers 11 and 26.

c.

```
options ls=72 nodate nonumber;
proc print data=work.passngrs;
   format Date date9.;
run;
```

6. Assigning Variable Attributes

a.

```
data work.sanfran;
   infile 'raw-data-file';
   input @1 FlightID $7.     @8 RouteID $7.
         @18 Destination $3. @21 Model $20.
         @41 Date date9.     @65 TotPassCap 3.;
run;

proc print data=work.sanfran label;
   format Date mmddyy10.;
   label FlightID='Flight ID'
         RouteID='Route ID'
         Model='Aircraft Model'
         Date='Departure Date'
         TotPassCap='Total Passenger Capacity';
run;

proc contents data=work.sanfran;
run;
```

1) **Date** values are formatted properly. Labels are displayed.

2) Labels are not in the descriptor. The DATE format is not in the descriptor.

b.

```
data work.sanfran;
   infile 'raw-data-file';
   input @1 FlightID $7.     @8 RouteID $7.
         @18 Destination $3. @21 Model $20.
         @41 Date date9.     @65 TotPassCap 3.;
   format Date mmddyy10.;
   label FlightID='Flight ID'
         RouteID='Route ID'
         Model='Aircraft Model'
         Date='Departure Date'
         TotPassCap='Total Passenger Capacity';
run;
proc print data=work.sanfran label;
run;
proc contents data=work.sanfran;
run;
```

1) Yes, the labels are displayed. Yes, the **Date** values are formatted correctly.

2) Yes, the labels are in the descriptor. Yes, the DATE format is in the descriptor.

7. **Changing Variable Attributes**

   a.

   1) Use the demonstration for your operating system shown in the lecture portion of this section for changing the name of a variable.

   2) You can type the variable label in the same window where you rename the variable.

   3)
   ```
   libname ia 'SAS-data-library';
   proc contents data=ia.passngrs;
   run;
   ```

   b.

   ```
   proc datasets library=ia;
      modify passngrs;
      format Depart date9.;
      label Depart='Departure Date';
   run;
   quit;
   proc contents data=ia.passngrs;
   run;
   ```

8. Reading an Excel Spreadsheet

a.

1) Select **Import Data** from the File menu.

2) Select **Excel 97, 2000 or 2002 Workbook** as the data source and select **Next >**.

3) Select **Browse** to locate the spreadsheet **sfosch.xls** and select **OK**.

4) Select the worksheet named **SFODATA$** and select **Next >**.

5) Leave **Work** as the library. Type **sfoexcel** in the Member field and select **Next >**.

6) Select **Browse** to locate the directory where you want to store the program and name the program **ImportSFO.sas**.

7) Select **Save** ⇨ **Finish**.

b.

```
options ls=72 nodate nonumber;
proc print data=work.sfoexcel;
run;
```

c.

```
proc contents data=work.sfoexcel;
run;
```

 An alternate solution using the Excel LIBNAME engine is shown below:

```
libname sfoxls 'sfosch.xls';
options ls=72 nodate nonumber;
proc print data=sfoxls."sfodata$"n;
run;
proc contents data=sfoxls."sfodata$"n;
run;
```

9. Reading a Comma-delimited File

a.

```
PROC IMPORT OUT= WORK.sfocsv
           DATAFILE= "sfosch.csv"
           DBMS=csv REPLACE;
RUN;
```

b.

```
options ls=72 nodate nonumber;
proc print data=work.sfocsv;
run;
```

Chapter 7 DATA Step Programming

7.1   Reading SAS Data Sets and Creating Variables

Objectives

- Create a SAS data set using another SAS data set as input.
- Create SAS variables.
- Use operators and SAS functions to manipulate data values.
- Control which variables are included in a SAS data set.

3

Reading a SAS Data Set

Create a temporary SAS data set named **onboard** from the permanent SAS data named **ia.dfwlax** and create a variable that represents the total passengers on board.
Sum **FirstClass** and **Economy** values to compute **Total**.

SAS date values

New Variable

ia.dfwlax

Flight	Date	Dest	FirstClass	Economy	Total
439	14955	LAX	20	137	157
921	14955	DFW	20	131	151
114	14956	LAX	15	170	185

4

Reading a SAS Data Set

To create a SAS data set using a SAS data set as input, you must use the following:

- DATA statement to start a DATA step and name the SAS data set being created (output data set: **onboard**)
- SET statement to identify the SAS data set being read (input data set: **ia.dfwlax**)

To create a variable, you must use an assignment statement to add the values of the variables **FirstClass** and **Economy** and assign the sum to the variable **Total**.

5

You **cannot** use INFILE and INPUT statements to read SAS data sets. They can only read raw data files.

You **cannot** use a SET statement to read raw data files. A SET statement can only read SAS data sets.

Reading a SAS Data Set

General form of a DATA step:

```
DATA output-SAS-data-set;
    SET input-SAS-data-set;
    <additional SAS statements>
RUN;
```

By default, the SET statement reads all of the following:

- observations from the input SAS data set
- variables from the input SAS data set

6

Assignment Statements

An assignment statement does the following:

- evaluates an expression
- assigns the resulting value to a variable

General form of an assignment statement:

> *variable=expression;*

7

SAS Expressions

An *expression* contains operands and operators
that form a set of instructions that produce a value.

Operands are	Operators are
▪ variable names ▪ constants.	▪ symbols that request arithmetic calculations ▪ SAS functions.

8

Using Operators

Selected operators for basic arithmetic calculations in an assignment statement:

Operator	Action	Example	Priority
**	Exponentiation	Raise=x**y;	I
–	Negative prefix	Negative=-x;	I
*	Multiplication	Mult=x*y;	II
/	Division	Divide=x/y;	II
+	Addition	Sum=x+y;	III
–	Subtraction	Diff=x-y;	III

9

Rules for Operators

- Operations of priority I are performed before operations of priority II, and so on.
- Consecutive operations with the same priority are performed in this sequence:
  - from right to left within priority I
  - from left to right within priority II and III
- Parentheses can be used to control the order of operations.

Compiling the DATA Step

```
libname ia 'SAS-data-library';
data onboard;
   set ia.dfwlax;
   Total=FirstClass+Economy;
run;
```

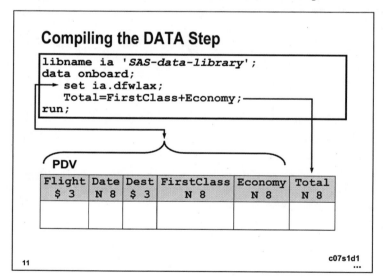

PDV

Flight	Date	Dest	FirstClass	Economy	Total
$ 3	N 8	$ 3	N 8	N 8	N 8

11   c07s1d1
                                                        ...

Executing the DATA Step

`ia.dfwlax`

Flight	Date	Dest	FirstClass	Economy
439	14955	LAX	20	137
921	14955	DFW	20	131
114	14956	LAX	15	170

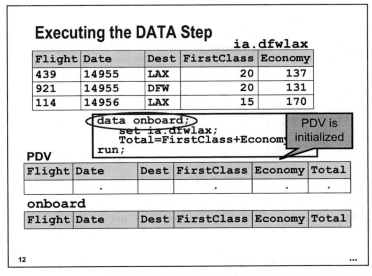

```
data onboard;
   set ia.dfwlax;
   Total=FirstClass+Economy
run;
```

PDV is initialized

PDV

Flight	Date	Dest	FirstClass	Economy	Total
	.		.	.	.

onboard

Flight	Date	Dest	FirstClass	Economy	Total

12 ...

Executing the DATA Step

`ia.dfwlax`

Flight	Date	Dest	FirstClass	Economy
➡ 439	14955	LAX	20	137
921	14955	DFW	20	131
114	14956	LAX	15	170

```
data onboard;
   set ia.dfwlax;
   Total=FirstClass+Economy;
run;
```

PDV

Flight	Date	Dest	FirstClass	Economy	Total
439	14955	LAX	20	137	.

onboard

Flight	Date	Dest	FirstClass	Economy	Total

13 ...

Executing the DATA Step

`ia.dfwlax`

Flight	Date	Dest	FirstClass	Economy
➡ 439	14955	LAX	20	137
921	14955	DFW	20	131
114	14956	LAX	15	170

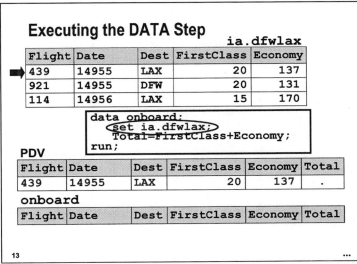

```
data onboard;
   set ia.dfwlax;
   Total=FirstClass+Economy;
run;
```

PDV

Flight	Date	Dest	FirstClass	Economy	Total
439	14955	LAX	20	137	157

onboard

Flight	Date	Dest	FirstClass	Economy	Total

14 ...

Executing the DATA Step

ia.dfwlax

Flight	Date	Dest	FirstClass	Economy
439	14955	LAX	20	137
921	14955	DFW	20	131
Automatic Return		LAX	15	170

```
data onboard;
   set ia.dfwlax;
   Total=FirstClass+Economy;
run;
```

PDV

Flight	Date	Dest	FirstClass	Economy	Total
439	14955	LAX	20	137	157

onboard   Automatic output

Flight	Date	Dest	FirstClass	Economy	Total
439	14955	LAX	20	137	157

17

Executing the DATA Step

ia.dfwlax

Flight	Date	Dest	FirstClass	Economy
439	14955	LAX	20	137
921	14955	DFW		
114	14956	LAX		

Reinitialize Total to missing

```
data onboard;
   set ia.dfwlax;
   Total=FirstClass+Economy;
run;
```

PDV

Flight	Date	Dest	FirstClass	Economy	Total
439	14955	LAX	20	137	.

onboard

Flight	Date	Dest	FirstClass	Economy	Total
439	14955	LAX	20	137	157

18

Executing the DATA Step

ia.dfwlax

Flight	Date	Dest	FirstClass	Economy
439	14955	LAX	20	137
921	14955	DFW	20	131
114	14956	LAX	15	170

```
data onboard;
   set ia.dfwlax;
   Total=FirstClass+Economy;
run;
```

PDV

Flight	Date	Dest	FirstClass	Economy	Total
921	14955	DFW	20	131	.

onboard

Flight	Date	Dest	FirstClass	Economy	Total
439	14955	LAX	20	137	157

19

Executing the DATA Step

`ia.dfwlax`

Flight	Date	Dest	FirstClass	Economy
439	14955	LAX	20	137
➡ 921	14955	DFW	20	131
114	14956	LAX	15	170

```
data onboard;
   set ia.dfwlax;
      Total=FirstClass+Economy;
   run;
```

PDV

Flight	Date	Dest	FirstClass	Economy	Total
921	14955	DFW	20	131	151

onboard

Flight	Date	Dest	FirstClass	Economy	Total
439	14955	LAX	20	137	157

20   ...

Executing the DATA Step

`ia.dfwlax`

Flight	Date	Dest	FirstClass	Economy
439	14955	LAX	20	137
➡ 921	14955	DFW	20	131
Automatic return		LAX	15	170

```
data onboard;
   set ia.dfwlax;
      Total=FirstClass+Economy;
   run;
```

PDV

Flight	Date	Dest	FirstClass	Economy	Total
921	14955	DFW	20	131	151

onboard Automatic output

Flight	Date	Dest	FirstClass	Economy	Total
439	14955	LAX	20	137	157
921	14955	DFW	20	131	151

23   ...

Executing the DATA Step

`ia.dfwlax`

Flight	Date	Dest	FirstClass	Economy
439	14955	LAX	20	137
921	14955	DFW	20	131
114	14956	LAX	15	170

Continue until end of file

```
data onboard;
   set ia.dfwlax;
      Total=FirstClass+Economy;
   run;
```

PDV

Flight	Date	Dest	FirstClass	Economy	Total
114	14956	LAX	15	170	185

onboard

Flight	Date	Dest	FirstClass	Economy	Total
439	14955	LAX	20	137	157
921	14955	DFW	20	131	151
114	14956	LAX	15	170	185

24

Assignment Statements

```
proc print data=onboard;
    format Date date9.;
run;
```

```
                        The SAS System
                                    First
Obs    Flight      Date      Dest   Class   Economy   Total

  1     439    11DEC2000    LAX      20       137      157
  2     921    11DEC2000    DFW      20       131      151
  3     114    12DEC2000    LAX      15       170      185
  4     982    12DEC2000    dfw       5        85       90
  5     439    13DEC2000    LAX      14       196      210
  6     982    13DEC2000    DFW      15       116      131
  7     431    14DEC2000    LaX      17       166      183
  8     982    14DEC2000    DFW       7        88       95
  9     114    15DEC2000    LAX       .       187        .
 10     982    15DEC2000    DFW      14        31       45
```

Why is **Total** missing in observation 9?   c07s1d1

25

Using SAS Functions

A *SAS function* is a routine that returns a value that is determined from specified arguments.

General form of a SAS function:

function-name(argument1,argument2, . . .)

Example:

```
Total=sum(FirstClass,Economy);
```

26

Using SAS Functions

SAS functions can do the following:
- perform arithmetic operations
- compute sample statistics (for example: sum, mean, and standard deviation)
- manipulate SAS dates and process character values
- perform many other tasks

Sample statistics functions ignore missing values.

27

Using the SUM Function

```
data onboard;
   set ia.dfwlax;
   Total=sum(FirstClass,Economy);
run;
```

c07s1d2

28

Using the SUM Function

```
proc print data=onboard;
   format Date date9.;
run;
```

```
                          The SAS System
                                      First
Obs     Flight        Date     Dest   Class    Economy    Total

 1       439       11DEC2000    LAX     20        137       157
 2       921       11DEC2000    DFW     20        131       151
 3       114       12DEC2000    LAX     15        170       185
 4       982       12DEC2000    dfw      5         85        90
 5       439       13DEC2000    LAX     14        196       210
 6       982       13DEC2000    DFW     15        116       131
 7       431       14DEC2000    LaX     17        166       183
 8       982       14DEC2000    DFW      7         88        95
 9       114       15DEC2000    LAX      .        187       187
10       982       15DEC2000    DFW     14         31        45
```

c07s1d2

29

Using Date Functions

You can use SAS date functions to do the following:

- create SAS date values
- extract information from SAS date values

30

Date Functions: Create SAS Dates

TODAY()	obtains the date value from the system clock.
MDY(*month,day,year*)	uses numeric *month*, *day*, and *year* values to return the corresponding SAS date value.

31

Date Functions: Extracting Information

YEAR(*SAS-date*)	extracts the year from a SAS date and returns a four-digit value for year.
QTR(*SAS-date*)	extracts the quarter from a SAS date and returns a number from 1 to 4.
MONTH(*SAS-date*)	extracts the month from a SAS date and returns a number from 1 to 12.
WEEKDAY(*SAS-date*)	extracts the day of the week from a SAS date and returns a number from 1 to 7, where 1 represents Sunday, and so on.

32

Using the WEEKDAY Function

Add an assignment statement to the DATA step to create a variable that shows the day of the week that the flight occurred.

```
data onboard;
   set ia.dfwlax;
   Total=sum(FirstClass,Economy);
   DayOfWeek=weekday(Date);
run;
```

Print the data set, but do not display the variables **FirstClass** and **Economy**.

c07s1d3

33

Using the WEEKDAY Function

```
proc print data=onboard;
    var Flight Dest Total DayOfWeek Date;
    format Date weekdate.;
run;
```

```
                              The SAS System
                              Day
                              Of
   Obs   Flight   Dest   Total   Week            Date
    1     439      LAX     157     2      Monday, December 11, 2000
    2     921      DFW     151     2      Monday, December 11, 2000
    3     114      LAX     185     3      Tuesday, December 12, 2000
    4     982      dfw      90     3      Tuesday, December 12, 2000
    5     439      LAX     210     4      Wednesday, December 13, 2000
    6     982      DFW     131     4      Wednesday, December 13, 2000
    7     431      LaX     183     5      Thursday, December 14, 2000
    8     982      DFW      95     5      Thursday, December 14, 2000
    9     114      LAX     187     6      Friday, December 15, 2000
   10     982      DFW      45     6      Friday, December 15, 2000
```

What if you do not want the variables **FirstClass**
and **Economy** in the data set?

c07s1d3

34

Selecting Variables

You can use a DROP or KEEP statement
in a DATA step to control which variables
are **written to** the new SAS data set.

General form of DROP and KEEP statements:

> **DROP** *variables;*
>
> **KEEP** *variables;*

35

Selecting Variables

Do **not** store the variables **FirstClass** and
Economy in the **onboard** data set.

```
data onboard;
    set ia.dfwlax;
    drop FirstClass Economy;
    Total=sum(FirstClass,Economy);
run;
```

```
    keep Flight Date Dest Total;
```

Equivalent

PDV

Flight	Date	Dest	FirstClass	Economy	Total
	.		.	.	.

c07s1d4

36

Selecting Variables

```
proc print data=onboard;
   format Date date9.;
run;
```

```
                        The SAS System

          Obs    Flight        Date    Dest    Total

           1      439      11DEC2000   LAX      157
           2      921      11DEC2000   DFW      151
           3      114      12DEC2000   LAX      185
           4      982      12DEC2000   dfw       90
           5      439      13DEC2000   LAX      210
           6      982      13DEC2000   DFW      131
           7      431      14DEC2000   LaX      183
           8      982      14DEC2000   DFW       95
           9      114      15DEC2000   LAX      187
          10      982      15DEC2000   DFW       45
```

c07s1d4

37

Selecting Variables

```
proc contents data=onboard;
run;
```

Partial Output

```
        Alphabetic List of Variables and Attributes

           #    Variable    Type    Len

           2    Date        Num      8
           3    Dest        Char     3
           1    Flight      Char     3
           4    Total       Num      8
```

38

 **Exercises**

For these exercises, use SAS data sets stored in a permanent SAS data library.

> Fill in the blank with the location of your SAS data library. **If you started a new SAS session since the previous lab**, submit the LIBNAME statement to assign the libref **ia** to the SAS data library.
>
> `libname ia '_____';`

1. **Reading SAS Data Sets and Creating Variables**

    a. Use the **ia.fltattnd** data set to create a temporary SAS data set named **bonus**.

        • Create a variable named **BonusAmt** that contains an annual bonus amount for each employee. Calculate the bonus amount as 8% of **Salary**.

        • Create a variable named **AnnivMo** that contains the employment month for each employee. Hint: Determine the month portion of the employee's date of hire (**HireDate**).

        • The **bonus** data set should contain only the variables **EmpID**, **Salary**, **BonusAmt**, **HireDate**, and **AnnivMo**.

    b. Use the PRINT procedure to display the data portion of the **bonus** data set. Display the values of **Salary** and **BonusAmt** with dollar signs, commas, and no decimal places.

    SAS Output

Obs	HireDate	EmpID	Salary	BonusAmt	Anniv Mo
1	23MAY1982	E01483	$30,000	$2,400	5
2	19MAY1986	E01384	$38,000	$3,040	5
3	02JUN1983	E00223	$18,000	$1,440	6
4	09OCT1981	E00632	$40,000	$3,200	10
5	22NOV1991	E03884	$38,000	$3,040	11
6	02AUG1984	E00034	$28,000	$2,240	8
7	14JAN1980	E03591	$43,000	$3,440	1
8	18FEB1980	E04064	$37,000	$2,960	2
9	06DEC1984	E01996	$20,000	$1,600	12
10	12MAY1992	E04356	$34,000	$2,720	5
11	25SEP1980	E01447	$35,000	$2,800	9
12	02JAN1981	E02679	$31,000	$2,480	1
13	09JAN1981	E02606	$26,000	$2,080	1
14	10DEC1987	E03323	$22,000	$1,760	12

2. Reading SAS Data Sets and Creating Variables (Optional)

a. Write a DATA step to read a SAS data set and create a new variable.

- Use the **ia.weekrev** SAS data set to create a temporary SAS data set named **temprev**.
- Create a variable named **TotalRev** by adding **CargoRev** and **PasRev**.
- Add a statement that drops **CargoRev** and **PasRev** from the **temprev** data set.

b. Write a PROC PRINT step to view the **temprev** data set.

- Suppress the observation column.
- Display an appropriate report title.
- Display the values of **TotalRev** with dollar signs, commas, and no decimal places.
- Add a grand total for **TotalRev**.
- Display only the variables **FlightID**, **Origin**, **Date**, and **TotalRev**.

Partial SAS Output

```
                           Revenue Data for
                        Flights to San Francisco

          Flight
           ID        Origin      Date        TotalRev

          IA02402     DFW      01DEC2000      $13,552
          IA02403     DFW      01DEC2000      $13,647
          IA02400     JFK      01DEC2000      $13,710
          IA02401     JFK      01DEC2000      $13,632
          IA02406     JFK      01DEC2000      $12,941
          IA02402     DFW      02DEC2000      $13,715
          IA02403     DFW      02DEC2000      $13,359
          IA02400     JFK      02DEC2000      $13,607
                        .
                        .
                        .
          IA02405     YYZ      05DEC2000      $13,389
          IA02402     DFW      06DEC2000      $13,547
          IA02403     DFW      06DEC2000      $13,439
          IA02400     JFK      06DEC2000      $13,429
          IA02401     JFK      06DEC2000      $13,625
          IA02400     JFK      07DEC2000      $13,710
          IA02401     JFK      07DEC2000      $13,394
          IA02404     YYZ      07DEC2000      $13,364
          IA02405     YYZ      07DEC2000      $13,509
                                             ============
                                              $462,544
```

7.2   Conditional Processing

Objectives

- Execute statements conditionally using IF-THEN logic.
- Control the length of character variables explicitly with the LENGTH statement.
- Select rows to include in a SAS data set.
- Use SAS date constants.

41

Conditional Execution

International Airlines wants to compute revenue for Los Angeles and Dallas flights based on the prices in the table below.

DESTINATION	CLASS	AIRFARE
LAX	First	2000
	Economy	1200
DFW	First	1500
	Economy	900

42

Conditional Execution

General form of IF-THEN and ELSE statements:

```
IF expression THEN statement;
ELSE statement;
```

An *expression* contains operands and operators that form a set of instructions that produce a value.

Operands are	Operators are

• variable names
• constants.
	• symbols that request
	  – a comparison
	  – a logical operation
	  – an arithmetic calculation
	• SAS functions.

Only one executable statement is allowed in an IF-THEN or ELSE statement.

43

Conditional Execution

Compute revenue figures based on flight destination.

DESTINATION	CLASS	AIRFARE
LAX	First	2000
	Economy	1200
DFW	First	1500
	Economy	900

```
data flightrev;
   set ia.dfwlax;
   Total=sum(FirstClass,Economy);
   if Dest='LAX' then
      Revenue=sum(2000*FirstClass,1200*Economy);
   else if Dest='DFW' then
      Revenue=sum(1500*FirstClass,900*Economy);
run;
```

44   c07s2d1

Conditional Execution

```
data flightrev;   TRUE
   set ia.dfwlax;
   Total=sum(FirstClass,Economy);
   if Dest='LAX' then
      Revenue=sum(2000*FirstClass,1200*Economy);
   else if Dest='DFW' then
      Revenue=sum(1500*FirstClass,900*Economy);
run;
```

PDV (First Observation)

Flight	Date	Dest	First Class	Economy	Total	Revenue
439	14955	LAX	20	137	157	204400

47   ...

Conditional Execution

```
data flightrev;
   set ia.dfwlax;
   Total=sum(FirstClass,Economy);
   if Dest='LAX' then
      Revenue=sum(2000*FirstClass,1200*Economy);
   else if Dest='DFW' then
      Revenue=sum(1500*FirstClass,900*Economy);
run;
```

PDV (Fourth Observation)

Flight	Date	Dest	First Class	Economy	Total	Revenue
982	14956	dfw	5	85	90	.

49

Conditional Execution

```
data flightrev;      FALSE
   set ia.dfwlax;
   Total=sum(FirstClass,Economy);
   if Dest='LAX' then
      Revenue=sum(2000*FirstClass,1200*Economy);
   else if Dest='DFW' then
      Revenue=sum(1500*FirstClass,900*Economy);
run;
```

PDV (Fourth Observation)

Flight	Date	Dest	First Class	Economy	Total	Revenue
982	14956	dfw	5	85	90	.

50

Conditional Execution

```
data flightrev;   FALSE
   set ia.dfwlax;
   Total=sum(FirstClass,Economy);
   if Dest='LAX' then
      Revenue=sum(2000*FirstClass,1200*Economy);
   else if Dest='DFW' then
      Revenue=sum(1500*FirstClass,900*Economy);
run;
```

PDV (Fourth Observation)

Flight	Date	Dest	First Class	Economy	Total	Revenue
982	14956	dfw	5	85	90	.

52

Conditional Execution

```
proc print data=flightrev;
   format Date date9.;
run;
```

```
                    The SAS System
                           First
 Obs  Flight      Date  Dest Class  Economy  Total  Revenue

   1    439   11DEC2000  LAX    20     137     157   204400
   2    921   11DEC2000  DFW    20     131     151   147900
   3    114   12DEC2000  LAX    15     170     185   234000
   4    982   12DEC2000  dfw     5      85      90       .
   5    439   13DEC2000  LAX    14     196     210   263200
   6    982   13DEC2000  DFW    15     116     131   126900
   7    431   14DEC2000  LaX    17     166     183       .
   8    982   14DEC2000  DFW     7      88      95    89700
   9    114   15DEC2000  LAX     .     187     187   224400
  10    982   15DEC2000  DFW    14      31      45    48900
```

Why are two **Revenue** values missing?

c07s2d1

54

The UPCASE Function

You can use the UPCASE function to convert letters from lowercase to uppercase.

General form of the UPCASE function:

UPCASE *(argument)*

55

Conditional Execution

Use the UPCASE function to convert the **Dest** values to uppercase for the comparison.

```
data flightrev;
   set ia.dfwlax;
   Total=sum(FirstClass,Economy);
   if upcase(Dest)='LAX' then
      Revenue=sum(2000*FirstClass,1200*Economy);
   else if upcase(Dest)='DFW' then
      Revenue=sum(1500*FirstClass,900*Economy);
run;
```

c07s2d2

56

Conditional Execution

```
data flightrev;
   set ia.dfwlax;
   Total=sum(FirstClass,Economy);
   if upcase(Dest)='LAX' then
      Revenue=sum(2000*FirstClass,1200*Economy);
   else if upcase(Dest)='DFW' then
      Revenue=sum(1500*FirstClass,900*Economy);
run;
```

PDV (Fourth Observation)   upcase('dfw')='DFW'

Flight	Date	Dest	First Class	Economy	Total	Revenue
982	14956	dfw	5	85	90	.

58

Conditional Execution

FALSE

```
data flightrev;
   set ia.dfwlax;
   Total=sum(FirstClass,Economy);
   if upcase(Dest)='LAX' then
      Revenue=sum(2000*FirstClass,1200*Economy);
   else if upcase(Dest)='DFW' then
      Revenue=sum(1500*FirstClass,900*Economy);
run;
```

PDV (Fourth Observation)   upcase('dfw')='DFW'

Flight	Date	Dest	First Class	Economy	Total	Revenue
982	14956	dfw	5	85	90	.

59

Conditional Execution

TRUE

```
data flightrev;
   set ia.dfwlax;
   Total=sum(FirstClass,Economy);
   if upcase(Dest)='LAX' then
      Revenue=sum(2000*FirstClass,1200*Economy);
   else if upcase(Dest)='DFW' then
      Revenue=sum(1500*FirstClass,900*Economy);
run;
```

PDV (Fourth Observation)   upcase('dfw')='DFW'

Flight	Date	Dest	First Class	Economy	Total	Revenue
982	14956	dfw	5	85	90	84000

61

Conditional Execution

```
proc print data=flightrev;
   format Date date9.;
run;
```

```
                    The SAS System
                          First
 Obs  Flight      Date  Dest  Class  Economy  Total  Revenue

  1    439    11DEC2000  LAX    20     137     157    204400
  2    921    11DEC2000  DFW    20     131     151    147900
  3    114    12DEC2000  LAX    15     170     185    234000
  4    982    12DEC2000  dfw     5      85      90     84000
  5    439    13DEC2000  LAX    14     196     210    263200
  6    982    13DEC2000  DFW    15     116     131    126900
  7    431    14DEC2000  LaX    17     166     183    233200
  8    982    14DEC2000  DFW     7      88      95     89700
  9    114    15DEC2000  LAX     .     187     187    224400
 10    982    15DEC2000  DFW    14      31      45     48900
```

62   c07s2d2

Conditional Execution

You can use the DO and END statements to
execute a group of statements based on a condition.

General form of the DO and END statements:

```
IF expression THEN DO;
   executable statements
END;
ELSE DO;
   executable statements
END;
```

63

Conditional logic can include one or more ELSE IF statements:

```
IF condition THEN statement;
<ELSE IF condition THEN statement;>
...
<ELSE statement;>
```

For greater efficiency, construct your IF-THEN/ELSE statement with conditions of decreasing
probability.

Conditional Execution

Use DO and END statements to execute a group
of statements based on a condition.

```
data flightrev;
   set ia.dfwlax;
   Total=sum(FirstClass,Economy);
   if upcase(Dest)='DFW' then do;
      Revenue=sum(1500*FirstClass,900*Economy);
      City='Dallas';
   end;
   else if upcase(Dest)='LAX' then do;
      Revenue=sum(2000*FirstClass,1200*Economy);
      City='Los Angeles';
   end;
run;
```

64   c07s2d3

Conditional Execution

```
proc print data=flightrev;
   var Dest City Flight Date Revenue;
   format Date date9.;
run;
```

			The SAS System		
Obs	Dest	City	Flight	Date	Revenue
1	LAX	Los An	439	11DEC2000	204400
2	DFW	Dallas	921	11DEC2000	147900
3	LAX	Los An	114	12DEC2000	234000
4	dfw	Dallas	982	12DEC2000	84000
5	LAX	Los An	439	13DEC2000	263200
6	DFW	Dallas	982	13DEC2000	126900
7	LaX	Los An	431	14DEC2000	233200
8	DFW	Dallas	982	14DEC2000	89700
9	LAX	Los An	114	15DEC2000	224400
10	DFW	Dallas	982	15DEC2000	48900

Why are `City` values truncated?

65   c07s2d3

Variable Lengths

At compile time, the length of a variable is determined
the first time that the variable is encountered.

```
data flightrev;
   set ia.dfwlax;
   Total=sum(FirstClass,Economy);
   if upcase(Dest)='DFW' then do;
      Revenue=sum(1500*FirstClass,900*Economy);
      City='Dallas';
   end;
   else if upcase(Dest)='LAX' then do;
      Revenue=sum(2000*First...
      City='Los Angeles';
   end;
run;
```

Six characters between the quotation marks: Length=6

67

The LENGTH Statement

You can use the LENGTH statement to define
the length of a variable explicitly.

General form of the LENGTH statement:

```
LENGTH variable(s) $ length;
```

Example:

```
length City $ 11;
```

68

The LENGTH Statement

```
data flightrev;
   set ia.dfwlax;
   length City $ 11;
   Total=sum(FirstClass,Economy);
   if upcase(Dest)='DFW' then do;
      Revenue=sum(1500*FirstClass,900*Economy);
      City='Dallas';
   end;
   else if upcase(Dest)='LAX' then do;
      Revenue=sum(2000*FirstClass,1200*Economy);
      City='Los Angeles';
   end;
run;
```

69   c07s2d4

The LENGTH Statement

```
proc print data=flightrev;
   var Dest City Flight Date Revenue;
   format Date date9.;
run;
```

```
                      The SAS System
   Obs   Dest    City          Flight      Date      Revenue
    1    LAX     Los Angeles    439     11DEC2000    204400
    2    DFW     Dallas         921     11DEC2000    147900
    3    LAX     Los Angeles    114     12DEC2000    234000
    4    dfw     Dallas         982     12DEC2000     84000
    5    LAX     Los Angeles    439     13DEC2000    263200
    6    DFW     Dallas         982     13DEC2000    126900
    7    LaX     Los Angeles    431     14DEC2000    233200
    8    DFW     Dallas         982     14DEC2000     89700
    9    LAX     Los Angeles    114     15DEC2000    224400
   10    DFW     Dallas         982     15DEC2000     48900
```

70   c07s2d4

Subsetting Rows

In a DATA step, you can subset the rows (observations) in a SAS data set with the following statements:

- WHERE statement
- DELETE statement
- subsetting IF statement

The WHERE statement in a DATA step is the same as the WHERE statement you saw in a PROC step.

71

Deleting Rows

You can use a DELETE statement to control which rows are not written to the SAS data set.

General form of the DELETE statement:

IF *expression* **THEN DELETE**;

The *expression* can be any SAS expression.
The DELETE statement is valid only in a DATA step.

72

Deleting Rows

Delete rows that have a **Total** value that is less than or equal to 175.

```
data over175;
   set ia.dfwlax;
   length City $ 11;
   Total=sum(FirstClass,Economy);
   if Total le 175 then delete;
   if upcase(Dest)='DFW' then do;
      Revenue=sum(1500*FirstClass,900*Economy);
      City='Dallas';
   end;
   else if upcase(Dest)='LAX' then do;
      Revenue=sum(2000*FirstClass,1200*Economy);
      City='Los Angeles';
   end;
run;
```

73   c07s2d5

Deleting Rows

```
proc print data=over175;
   var Dest City Flight Date Total Revenue;
   format Date date9.;
run;
```

```
                        The SAS System

Obs    Dest      City       Flight      Date     Total    Revenue

 1     LAX    Los Angeles     114     12DEC2000    185     234000
 2     LAX    Los Angeles     439     13DEC2000    210     263200
 3     LaX    Los Angeles     431     14DEC2000    183     233200
 4     LAX    Los Angeles     114     15DEC2000    187     224400
```

c07s2d5

74

Selecting Rows

You can use a subsetting IF statement to control
which rows are written to the SAS data set.

General form of the subsetting IF statement:

> **IF** *expression*;

The *expression* can be any SAS expression.

The subsetting IF statement is valid only
in a DATA step.

75

Process Flow of a Subsetting IF

Subsetting IF:

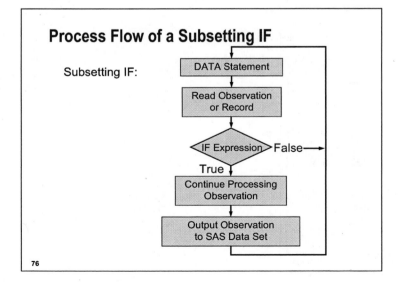

76

Selecting Rows

Select rows that have a **Total** value that is greater than 175.

```
data over175;
   set ia.dfwlax;
   length City $ 11;
   Total=sum(FirstClass,Economy);
   if Total gt 175;
   if upcase(Dest)='DFW' then do;
      Revenue=sum(1500*FirstClass,900*Economy);
      City='Dallas';
   end;
   else if upcase(Dest)='LAX' then do;
      Revenue=sum(2000*FirstClass,1200*Economy);
      City='Los Angeles';
   end;
run;
```

c07s2d6

77

Selecting Rows

```
proc print data=over175;
   var Dest City Flight Date Total Revenue;
   format Date date9.;
run;
```

```
                      The SAS System

Obs   Dest    City        Flight      Date    Total   Revenue

 1    LAX     Los Angeles   114    12DEC2000    185    234000
 2    LAX     Los Angeles   439    13DEC2000    210    263200
 3    LaX     Los Angeles   431    14DEC2000    183    233200
 4    LAX     Los Angeles   114    15DEC2000    187    224400
```

c07s2d6

78

Selecting Rows

The variable **Date** in the **ia.dfwlax** data set contains SAS date values (numeric values).

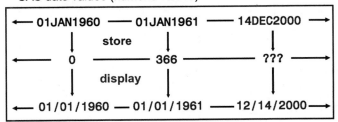

What if you only want flights that were before a specific date, such as **14DEC2000**?

79

Using SAS Date Constants

The constant **'ddMMMyyyy'd** (example: '14dec2000'd) creates a SAS date value from the date enclosed in quotation marks.

dd	is a one- or two-digit value for the day.
MMM	is a three-letter abbreviation for the month (JAN, FEB, MAR, and so on).
yyyy	is a four-digit value for the year.
d	is required to convert the quoted string to a SAS date.

80

Using SAS Date Constants

```
data over175;
   set ia.dfwlax;
   length City $ 11;
   Total=sum(FirstClass,Economy);
   if Total gt 175 and Date lt '14dec2000'd;
   if upcase(Dest)='DFW' then do;
      Revenue=sum(1500*FirstClass,900*Economy);
      City='Dallas';
   end;
   else if upcase(Dest)='LAX' then do;
      Revenue=sum(2000*FirstClass,1200*Economy);
      City='Los Angeles';
   end;
run;
```

81   c07s2d7

Using SAS Date Constants

```
proc print data=over175;
   var Dest City Flight Date Total Revenue;
   format Date date9.;
run;
```

		The SAS System				
Obs	Dest	City	Flight	Date	Total	Revenue
1	LAX	Los Angeles	114	12DEC2000	185	234000
2	LAX	Los Angeles	439	13DEC2000	210	263200

82   c07s2d7

Subsetting Data

What if the data were in a raw data file instead
of a SAS data set?

```
data over175;
   infile 'raw-data-file';
   input @1 Flight $3. @4 Date mmddyy8.
         @12 Dest $3. @15 FirstClass 3.
         @18 Economy 3.;
   length City $ 11;
   Total=sum(FirstClass,Economy);
   if Total gt 175 and Date lt '14dec2000'd;
   if upcase(Dest)='DFW' then do;
      Revenue=sum(1500*FirstClass,900*Economy);
      City='Dallas';
   end;
   else if upcase(Dest)='LAX' then do;
      Revenue=sum(2000*FirstClass,1200*Economy);
      City='Los Angeles';
   end;
run;
```
c07s2d8

You can use the $UPCASE informat in the INPUT statement to translate the **Dest** values
to uppercase as they are read from the raw data file.

Subsetting Data

```
proc print data=over175;
   var Dest City Flight Date Total Revenue;
   format Date date9.;
run;
```

```
                       The SAS System

Obs   Dest      City      Flight       Date   Total   Revenue

 1    LAX    Los Angeles    114    12DEC2000    185    234000
 2    LAX    Los Angeles    439    13DEC2000    210    263200
```

c07s2d8

84

WHERE or Subsetting IF?

Step and Usage	WHERE	IF
PROC step	Yes	No
DATA step (source of variable)		
INPUT statement	No	Yes
Assignment statement	No	Yes
SET statement (single data set)	Yes	Yes
SET/MERGE (multiple data sets)		
Variable in ALL data sets	Yes	Yes
Variable not in ALL data sets	No	Yes

85

WHERE or Subsetting IF?

Use a WHERE statement and a subsetting IF statement
in the same step.

```
data over175;
   set ia.dfwlax;
   where Date lt '14dec2000'd;
   length City $ 11;
   Total=sum(FirstClass,Economy);
   if Total gt 175;
   if upcase(Dest)='DFW' then do;
      Revenue=sum(1500*FirstClass,900*Economy);
      City='Dallas';
   end;
   else if upcase(Dest)='LAX' then do;
      Revenue=sum(2000*FirstClass,1200*Economy);
      City='Los Angeles';
   end;
run;
```

86   c07s2d9

WHERE or Subsetting IF?

```
proc print data=over175;
   var Dest City Flight Date Total Revenue;
   format Date date9.;
run;
```

```
                      The SAS System

Obs   Dest      City      Flight      Date    Total   Revenue

 1    LAX    Los Angeles   114    12DEC2000    185    234000
 2    LAX    Los Angeles   439    13DEC2000    210    263200
```

c07s2d9

87

 **Exercises**

For these exercises, use SAS data sets stored in a permanent SAS data library.

> Fill in the blank with the location of your SAS data library. **If you started a new SAS session since the previous lab**, submit the LIBNAME statement to assign the libref **ia** to the SAS data library.
>
> ```
> libname ia '_____';
> ```

3. **Creating Variables Using Conditional Execution**

   a. Use the **ia.fltattnd** data set to create a temporary SAS data set named **raises**.

      - Create a variable named **Increase** that contains an annual salary increase amount for each employee. Calculate the **Increase** values as shown below:
        - 10% of **Salary** when **JobCode='FLTAT1'**
        - 8% of **Salary** when **JobCode='FLTAT2'**
        - 6% of **Salary** when **JobCode='FLTAT3'**

      - Create a variable named **NewSal** that contains the new annual salary for each employee by adding the raise to the original salary.

      - The **raises** data set should contain only the variables **EmpID**, **Salary**, **Increase**, and **NewSal**.

   b. Use the PRINT procedure to display the data portion of the **raises** data set. Display the values of **Salary**, **Increase**, and **NewSal** with dollar signs, commas, and no decimal places.

      SAS Output

Obs	EmpID	Salary	Increase	NewSal
		The SAS System		
1	E01483	$30,000	$2,400	$32,400
2	E01384	$38,000	$2,280	$40,280
3	E00223	$18,000	$1,080	$19,080
4	E00632	$40,000	$2,400	$42,400
5	E03884	$38,000	$3,040	$41,040
6	E00034	$28,000	$1,680	$29,680
7	E03591	$43,000	$4,300	$47,300
8	E04064	$37,000	$2,220	$39,220
9	E01996	$20,000	$1,200	$21,200
10	E04356	$34,000	$2,720	$36,720
11	E01447	$35,000	$3,500	$38,500
12	E02679	$31,000	$3,100	$34,100
13	E02606	$26,000	$2,600	$28,600
14	E03323	$22,000	$1,760	$23,760

4. Selecting Rows

a. Alter the DATA step that you wrote in Exercise 3 by creating another variable named **BonusAmt** that contains an annual bonus for each employee based on the employee's current salary (before the increase). Calculate the **BonusAmt** as shown below:

- 15% of **Salary** when **JobCode='FLTAT1'**
- 12% of **Salary** when **JobCode='FLTAT2'**
- 10% of **Salary** when **JobCode='FLTAT3'**

Hint: Remember that there is a way to execute more than one statement based on the result of an IF expression.

Include only observations (rows) that have a **BonusAmt** value that exceeds 2000 dollars. The **raises** data set should contain only the variables **EmpID**, **Salary**, **Increase**, **NewSal**, and **BonusAmt**.

b. Use the PRINT procedure to display the data portion of the **raises** data set. Display the values of **Salary**, **Increase**, **NewSal**, and **BonusAmt** with dollar signs, commas, and no decimal places.

SAS Output

```
                                 The SAS System

         Obs    EmpID      Salary     Increase     BonusAmt      NewSal

          1     E01483    $30,000     $2,400       $3,600       $32,400
          2     E01384    $38,000     $2,280       $3,800       $40,280
          3     E00632    $40,000     $2,400       $4,000       $42,400
          4     E03884    $38,000     $3,040       $4,560       $41,040
          5     E00034    $28,000     $1,680       $2,800       $29,680
          6     E03591    $43,000     $4,300       $6,450       $47,300
          7     E04064    $37,000     $2,220       $3,700       $39,220
          8     E04356    $34,000     $2,720       $4,080       $36,720
          9     E01447    $35,000     $3,500       $5,250       $38,500
         10     E02679    $31,000     $3,100       $4,650       $34,100
         11     E02606    $26,000     $2,600       $3,900       $28,600
         12     E03323    $22,000     $1,760       $2,640       $23,760
```

5. Creating Variables Using Conditional Execution

a. Alter the DATA step that you wrote in exercise **4.a** by creating a character variable named **JobTitle** that contains the following values:

- **Flight Attendant I**, when **JobCode='FLTAT1'**
- **Flight Attendant II**, when **JobCode='FLTAT2'**
- **Senior Flight Attendant** when **JobCode='FLTAT3'**

Remember to include the new variable **JobTitle** in your data set.

b. Use the PRINT procedure to display the data portion of the **raises** data set. Display the values of **Salary**, **Increase**, **NewSal**, and **BonusAmt** with dollar signs, commas, and no decimal places. Verify that the values of the variable **JobTitle** are not truncated.

SAS Output

```
                              The SAS System

        Obs EmpID   Salary       JobTitle           Increase BonusAmt  NewSal

          1 E01483  $30,000 Flight Attendant II      $2,400   $3,600  $32,400
          2 E01384  $38,000 Senior Flight Attendant  $2,280   $3,800  $40,280
          3 E00632  $40,000 Senior Flight Attendant  $2,400   $4,000  $42,400
          4 E03884  $38,000 Flight Attendant II      $3,040   $4,560  $41,040
          5 E00034  $28,000 Senior Flight Attendant  $1,680   $2,800  $29,680
          6 E03591  $43,000 Flight Attendant I       $4,300   $6,450  $47,300
          7 E04064  $37,000 Senior Flight Attendant  $2,220   $3,700  $39,220
          8 E04356  $34,000 Flight Attendant II      $2,720   $4,080  $36,720
          9 E01447  $35,000 Flight Attendant I       $3,500   $5,250  $38,500
         10 E02679  $31,000 Flight Attendant I       $3,100   $4,650  $34,100
         11 E02606  $26,000 Flight Attendant I       $2,600   $3,900  $28,600
         12 E03323  $22,000 Flight Attendant II      $1,760   $2,640  $23,760
```

7.3   Dropping and Keeping Variables (Self-Study)

Objectives

- Compare DROP and KEEP statements to DROP= and KEEP= data set options.

90

Selecting Variables

You can use a DROP= or KEEP= data set option in a DATA statement to control which variables are **written to** the new SAS data set.

General form of the DROP= and KEEP= data set options:

> *SAS-data-set*(**DROP=***variables*)
> or
> *SAS-data-set*(**KEEP=***variables*)

91

Selecting Variables

Do not store the variables **FirstClass** and **Economy** in the **onboard** data set.

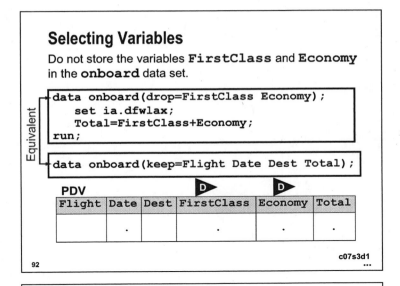

```
data onboard(drop=FirstClass Economy);
   set ia.dfwlax;
   Total=FirstClass+Economy;
run;
```

```
data onboard(keep=Flight Date Dest Total);
```

PDV

Flight	Date	Dest	FirstClass	Economy	Total
	.		.	.	.

c07s3d1

92

Selecting Variables

```
proc print data=onboard;
   format Date date9.;
run;
```

```
                    The SAS System

    Obs    Flight        Date    Dest    Total

      1     439      11DEC2000    LAX      157
      2     921      11DEC2000    DFW      151
      3     114      12DEC2000    LAX      185
      4     982      12DEC2000    dfw       90
      5     439      13DEC2000    LAX      210
      6     982      13DEC2000    DFW      131
      7     431      14DEC2000    LaX      183
      8     982      14DEC2000    DFW       95
      9     114      15DEC2000    LAX        .
     10     982      15DEC2000    DFW       45
```

c07s3d1

93

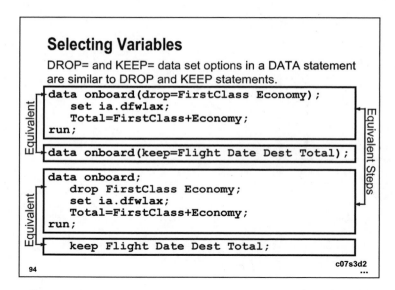

Selecting Variables

DROP= and KEEP= data set options in a DATA statement
are similar to DROP and KEEP statements.

```
data onboard(drop=FirstClass Economy);
   set ia.dfwlax;
   Total=FirstClass+Economy;
run;
```

```
data onboard(keep=Flight Date Dest Total);
```

```
data onboard;
   drop FirstClass Economy;
   set ia.dfwlax;
   Total=FirstClass+Economy;
run;
```

```
   keep Flight Date Dest Total;
```

94   c07s3d2

When specified for a data set named in the DATA statement, the DROP= and KEEP= data set
options are similar to DROP and KEEP statements. However, the DROP= and KEEP= data set
options can be used in situations where the DROP and KEEP statements cannot. For example,
DROP= and KEEP= data set options can be specified on a data set named in a SET statement
to control which variables are loaded into the program data vector. They can also be used in a
PROC step to control which variables are available for processing by the procedure.

 **Exercises**

For these exercises, use SAS data sets stored in a permanent SAS data library.

> Fill in the blank with the location of your SAS data library. **If you started a new SAS session since the previous lab**, submit the LIBNAME statement to assign the libref **ia** to the SAS data library.
>
> ```
> libname ia '_____';
> ```

6. **Reading SAS Data Sets and Creating Variables**

    a. Use the **ia.fltattnd** data set to create a data set named **bonus**.

       - Create a variable named **BonusAmt** that contains an annual bonus amount for each employee. Calculate the bonus amount as 8% of **Salary**.

       - Create a variable named **AnnivMo** that contains the employment month for each employee. Hint: Determine the month portion of the employee's date of hire (**HireDate**).

       - The **bonus** data set should contain only the variables **EmpID**, **Salary**, **BonusAmt**, **HireDate**, and **AnnivMo**. Use a DROP= or KEEP= data set option instead of a DROP or KEEP statement.

    b. Use the PRINT procedure to display the data portion of the **bonus** data set. Display the values of **Salary** and **BonusAmt** with dollar signs, commas, and no decimal places.

    SAS Output

					Anniv
Obs	HireDate	EmpID	Salary	BonusAmt	Mo
1	23MAY1982	E01483	$30,000	$2,400	5
2	19MAY1986	E01384	$38,000	$3,040	5
3	02JUN1983	E00223	$18,000	$1,440	6
4	09OCT1981	E00632	$40,000	$3,200	10
5	22NOV1991	E03884	$38,000	$3,040	11
6	02AUG1984	E00034	$28,000	$2,240	8
7	14JAN1980	E03591	$43,000	$3,440	1
8	18FEB1980	E04064	$37,000	$2,960	2
9	06DEC1984	E01996	$20,000	$1,600	12
10	12MAY1992	E04356	$34,000	$2,720	5
11	25SEP1980	E01447	$35,000	$2,800	9
12	02JAN1981	E02679	$31,000	$2,480	1
13	09JAN1981	E02606	$26,000	$2,080	1
14	10DEC1987	E03323	$22,000	$1,760	12

The SAS System

7.4 Reading Excel Spreadsheets Containing Date Fields (Self-Study)

Objectives

- Create a SAS data set from an Excel spreadsheet that contains date fields.
- Create a SAS data set from an Excel spreadsheet that contains datetime fields.

97

Business Task

The flight data for Dallas and Los Angeles are in an Excel spreadsheet. The departure date is stored as a date field in the spreadsheet.

Excel Spreadsheet

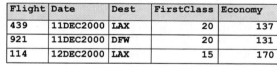

SAS Data Set

Flight	Date	Dest	FirstClass	Economy
439	11DEC2000	LAX	20	137
921	11DEC2000	DFW	20	131
114	12DEC2000	LAX	15	170

98

Importing Date Fields

Use the IMPORT procedure to create a SAS data set from the spreadsheet containing date fields.

```
proc import out=work.dfwlaxdates
            datafile='datefields.xls'
            dbms=excel2000 replace;
run;

proc print data=work.dfwlaxdates;
run;
```

c07s4d1

99

Importing Date Fields

PROC IMPORT automatically converts the spreadsheet date fields to SAS date values and assigns the DATE9. format.

```
                        The SAS System

                                           First
   Obs    Flight       Date     Dest       Class     Economy

    1      439      11DEC2000    LAX         20         137
    2      921      11DEC2000    DFW         20         131
    3      114      12DEC2000    LAX         15         170
    4      982      12DEC2000    dfw          5          85
    5      439      13DEC2000    LAX         14         196
    6      982      13DEC2000    DFW         15         116
    7      431      14DEC2000    LAX         17         166
    8      982      14DEC2000    DFW          7          88
    9      114      15DEC2000    LAX          .         187
   10      982      15DEC2000    DFW         14          31
```

100

The Import Wizard and the Excel LIBNAME engine also convert spreadsheet dates to SAS date values and assign the DATE9. format.

Importing Date-Time Fields

PROC IMPORT also converts spreadsheet fields that
contain datetime information into SAS date values
and assigns the DATE9. format.

Excel Spreadsheet

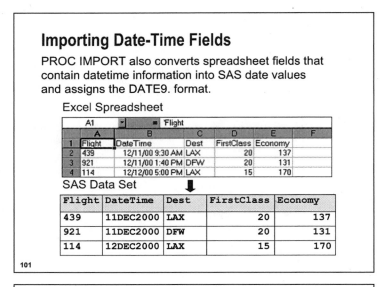

SAS Data Set

Flight	DateTime	Dest	FirstClass	Economy
439	11DEC2000	LAX	20	137
921	11DEC2000	DFW	20	131
114	12DEC2000	LAX	15	170

101

Importing Date-Time Fields

To import datetime fields as SAS datetime values, add
the USEDATE=NO statement to the PROC IMPORT step.

```
proc import out=work.dfwlaxdatetimes
            datafile='datetimefields.xls'
            dbms=excel2000 replace;
   usedate=no;
run;

proc print data=work.dfwlaxdatetimes;
run;
```

102   c07s4d2

The LIBNAME statement supports the USEDATE=NO option with the Excel SAS/ACCESS engine.

To read datetime fields as SAS datetime values using the Import Wizard, deselect
Use DATE. format for a Date/Time column in the SAS Import: Spreadsheet Options
dialog box.

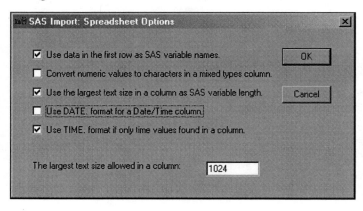

SAS Datetime Values

A *SAS datetime value* is interpreted as the number of seconds between midnight, January 1, 1960, and a specific date and time.

01JAN1960:00:00:00

31DEC1959:23:59:00   01JAN1960:00:01:00

informat

◄— -3600 —— -60 — 0 – 60 —— 3600 —►

format

31DEC1959:23:00:00   01JAN1960:01:00:00

103

Importing Date-Time Fields

The DATETIME19. format is assigned to the SAS datetime values.

```
                    The SAS System

                                        First
Obs    Flight         DateTime    Dest  Class   Economy

 1      439    11DEC2000:09:30:00  LAX    20      137
 2      921    11DEC2000:13:40:00  DFW    20      131
 3      114    12DEC2000:17:00:00  LAX    15      170
 4      982    12DEC2000:18:10:00  dfw     5       85
 5      439    13DEC2000:09:30:00  LAX    14      196
 6      982    13DEC2000:18:10:00  DFW    15      116
 7      431    14DEC2000:13:00:00  LAX    17      166
 8      982    14DEC2000:18:10:00  DFW     7       88
 9      114    15DEC2000:17:00:00  LAX     .      187
10      982    15DEC2000:18:10:00  DFW    14       31
```

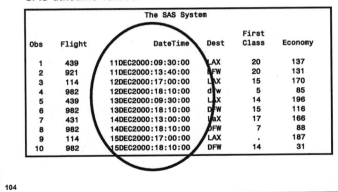

104

The DATEPART Function

You can use the DATEPART function to extract the date portion of a SAS datetime value.

DATEPART(*SASdatetime*)   returns the SAS date value from a SAS datetime value.

```
data convert;
   Time='01DEC00:09:15'dt;
   Date=datepart(Time);
run;
```

PDV

Time	Date
1291281300	14945

105

 **Exercises**

(Applicable Only to Windows Users)

7. Reading an Excel Spreadsheet Containing Date Fields

The Excel spreadsheet **sfoschdates.xls** contains information about International Airlines flights originating in San Francisco.

a. Use the Import Wizard or PROC IMPORT to create a SAS data set named **work.sfodatetime** from the Excel spreadsheet.

b. Use PROC PRINT to display the data portion of the SAS data set **work.sfodatetime**. Do not display the date and time that the SAS session started. Do not display page numbers. Set the line size to 72.

> If you use the Excel LIBNAME engine, you can display the data directly from the Excel worksheet named **SFODATA** found in **sfoschdates.xls**.

Partial SAS Output (First 8 of 52 Observations)

```
                               The SAS System

         Flight
Obs ID          RouteID  Origin   Destination  Model              Date

  1 IA11200     0000112  0000112      HND       JetCruise LF8100  01DEC2000
  2 IA01804     0000018  0000018      SEA       JetCruise SF1000  01DEC2000
  3 IA02901     0000029  0000029      HNL       JetCruise LF5200  02DEC2000
  4 IA03100     0000031  0000031      ANC       JetCruise LF8100  02DEC2000
  5 IA02901     0000029  0000029      HNL       JetCruise LF5200  03DEC2000
  6 IA03100     0000031  0000031      ANC       JetCruise MF4000  03DEC2000
  7 IA00800     0000008  0000008      RDU       JetCruise MF4000  04DEC2000
  8 IA01805     0000018  0000018      SEA       JetCruise SF1000  04DEC2000


                                                 Tot
         Depart   FClass    BClass    EClass    Pass   Cargo   Cargo
Obs      Day      Pass      Pass      Pass      Cap    Wt      Rev

  1       6        19        31        171      255   61300   79077
  2       6        10         .        123      150   10300   13287
  3       7        13        24        138      207   47400   61146
  4       7        13        22        250      255   24800   31992
  5       1        14        25        132      207   48200   62178
  6       1        16         .        243      267   25600   33024
  7       2        16         .        243      267   25600   33024
  8       2        11         .        123      150   10100   13029
```

7.5 Solutions to Exercises

1. Reading SAS Data Sets and Creating Variables

a.

```
data bonus;
   set ia.fltattnd;
   keep EmpID Salary BonusAmt HireDate AnnivMo;
   BonusAmt=.08*Salary;
   AnnivMo=month(HireDate);
run;
```

b.

```
proc print data=bonus;
   format Salary BonusAmt dollar8.0;
run;
```

2. Reading SAS Data Sets and Creating Variables (Optional)

a.

```
data work.temprev;
   set ia.weekrev;
   TotalRev=sum(CargoRev,PasRev);
   drop CargoRev PasRev;
run;
```

b.

```
proc print data=work.temprev noobs;
   title1 'Revenue Data for';
   title2 'Flights to San Francisco';
   var FlightID Origin Date TotalRev;
   sum TotalRev;
   format TotalRev dollar12.;
run;
```

3. Creating Variables Using Conditional Execution

a.

```
data raises;
   set ia.fltattnd;
   keep EmpID Salary Increase NewSal;
   if JobCode='FLTAT1' then Increase=.10*Salary;
   else if JobCode='FLTAT2' then Increase=.08*Salary;
   else if JobCode='FLTAT3' then Increase=.06*Salary;
   NewSal=sum(Salary,Increase);
run;
```

b.

```
proc print data=raises;
   format Salary Increase NewSal dollar8.0;
run;
```

4. **Selecting Rows**

    a.

```
data raises;
   set ia.fltattnd;
   keep EmpID Salary Increase NewSal BonusAmt;
   if JobCode='FLTAT1' then do;
      Increase=.10*Salary;
      BonusAmt=.15*Salary;
   end;
   else if JobCode='FLTAT2' then do;
      Increase=.08*Salary;
      BonusAmt=.12*Salary;
   end;
   else if JobCode='FLTAT3' then do;
      Increase=.06*Salary;
      BonusAmt=.10*Salary;
   end;
   if BonusAmt gt 2000;
   NewSal=sum(Salary,Increase);
run;
```

    b.

```
proc print data=raises;
   format Salary Increase NewSal BonusAmt dollar8.0;
run;
```

5. **Creating Variables Using Conditional Execution**

    a.

```
data raises;
   set ia.fltattnd;
   keep EmpID Salary Increase NewSal BonusAmt JobTitle;
   length JobTitle $ 23;
   if JobCode='FLTAT1' then do;
      Increase=.10*Salary;
      BonusAmt=.15*Salary;
      Jobtitle='Flight Attendant I';
   end;
   else if JobCode='FLTAT2' then do;
      Increase=.08*Salary;
      BonusAmt=.12*Salary;
      Jobtitle='Flight Attendant II';
   end;
   else if JobCode='FLTAT3' then do;
      Increase=.06*Salary;
      BonusAmt=.10*Salary;
      Jobtitle='Senior Flight Attendant';
   end;
   if BonusAmt gt 2000;
   NewSal=sum(Salary,Increase);
run;
```

b.

```
proc print data=raises;
    format Salary Increase NewSal BonusAmt dollar8.0;
run;
```

6. **Reading SAS Data Sets and Creating Variables**

   a.

```
data bonus(keep=EmpID Salary BonusAmt HireDate AnnivMo);
    set ia.fltattnd;
    BonusAmt=.08*Salary;
    AnnivMo=month(HireDate);
run;
```

   b.

```
proc print data=bonus;
    format Salary BonusAmt dollar8.0;
run;
```

7. **Reading an Excel Spreadsheet Containing Date Fields**

   a.

```
proc import out=work.sfodatetime
            datafile='sfoschdates.xls'
            dbms=excel2000;
run;
```

   b.

```
options ls=72 nodate nonumber;
proc print data=work.sfodatetime;
run;
```

   ✎   Using the Excel LIBNAME engine:

```
libname sfoxls 'sfoschdates.xls';
options ls=72 nodate nonumber;
proc print data=sfoxls."sfodata$"n;
run;
```

Chapter 8   Combining SAS Data Sets

8.1 Concatenating SAS Data Sets

Objectives
- Use the SET statement in a DATA step to concatenate two or more SAS data sets.
- Use the RENAME= data set option to change the names of variables.
- Use the SET and BY statements in a DATA step to interleave two or more SAS data sets.

3

Concatenating SAS Data Sets
Use the SET statement in a DATA step to concatenate SAS data sets.

General form of a DATA step concatenation:

```
DATA SAS-data-set ;
    SET SAS-data-set1 SAS-data-set2 . . . ;
    <additional SAS statements>
RUN;
```

4

Concatenating SAS Data Sets

You can read any number of SAS data sets with a single
SET statement.

**SAS
Data Sets**

```
data work.qtr1;
    set work.jan work.feb
        work.mar;
run;
```

jan

feb

mar

work.qtr1

jan

feb

mar

6

Business Task

Two SAS data sets, **na1** and **na2**, contain data for newly
hired navigators. Concatenate the data sets into a new
data set named **newhires**.

na1

Name	Gender	JobCode
TORRES	M	NA1
LANG	F	NA1
SMITH	F	NA1

na2

Name	Gender	JobCode
LISTER	M	NA2
TORRES	F	NA2

The data sets contain the same variables.

7

Concatenating SAS Data Sets: Compilation

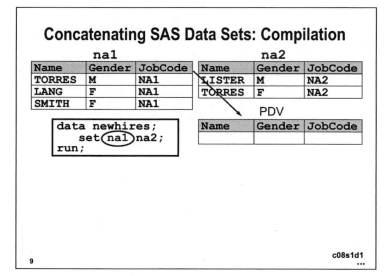

na1

Name	Gender	JobCode
TORRES	M	NA1
LANG	F	NA1
SMITH	F	NA1

na2

Name	Gender	JobCode
LISTER	M	NA2
TORRES	F	NA2

```
data newhires;
    set na1 na2;
run;
```

PDV

Name	Gender	JobCode

9

c08s1d1

...

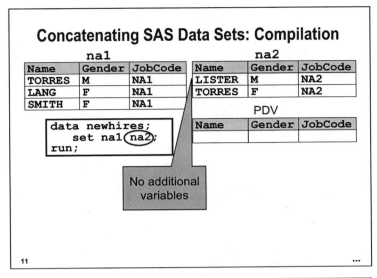

Concatenating SAS Data Sets: Compilation

na1		
Name	Gender	JobCode
TORRES	M	NA1
LANG	F	NA1
SMITH	F	NA1

na2		
Name	Gender	JobCode
LISTER	M	NA2
TORRES	F	NA2

```
data newhires;
   set na1 na2;
run;
```

PDV

Name	Gender	JobCode

No additional variables

11

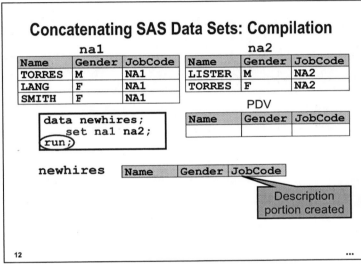

Concatenating SAS Data Sets: Compilation

na1		
Name	Gender	JobCode
TORRES	M	NA1
LANG	F	NA1
SMITH	F	NA1

na2		
Name	Gender	JobCode
LISTER	M	NA2
TORRES	F	NA2

```
data newhires;
   set na1 na2;
run;
```

PDV

Name	Gender	JobCode

newhires

Name	Gender	JobCode

Description portion created

12

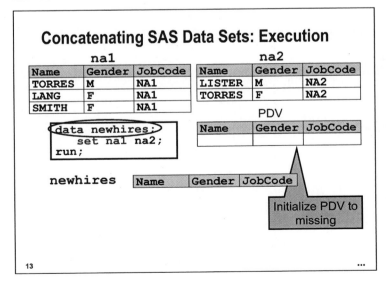

Concatenating SAS Data Sets: Execution

na1		
Name	Gender	JobCode
TORRES	M	NA1
LANG	F	NA1
SMITH	F	NA1

na2		
Name	Gender	JobCode
LISTER	M	NA2
TORRES	F	NA2

```
data newhires;
   set na1 na2;
run;
```

PDV

Name	Gender	JobCode

newhires

Name	Gender	JobCode

Initialize PDV to missing

13

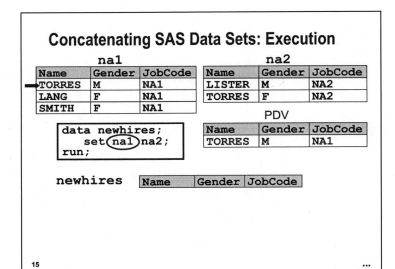

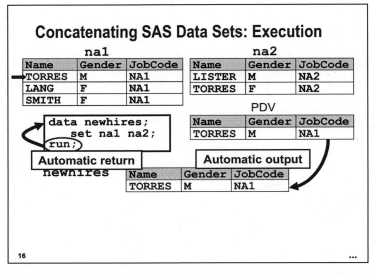

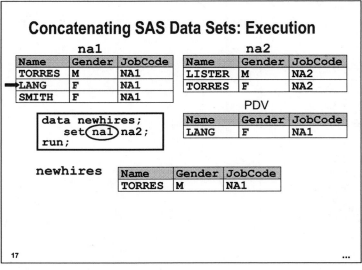

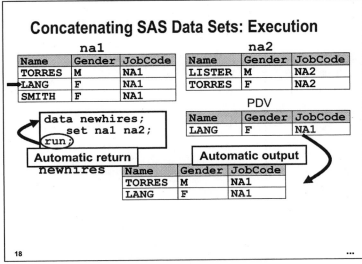

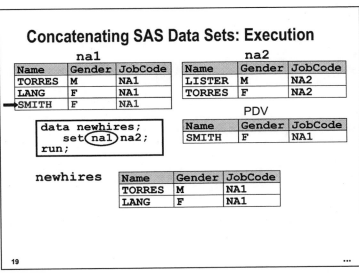

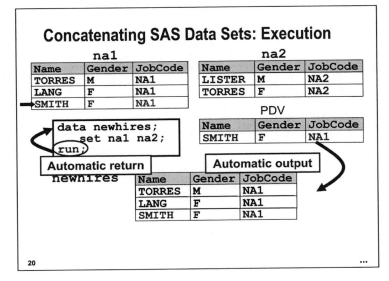

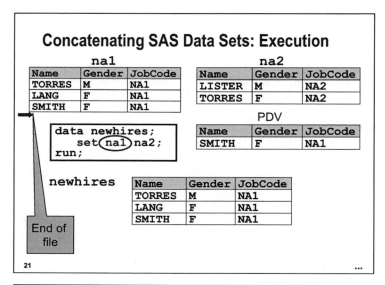

Concatenating SAS Data Sets: Execution

na1

Name	Gender	JobCode
TORRES	M	NA1
LANG	F	NA1
SMITH	F	NA1

na2

Name	Gender	JobCode
LISTER	M	NA2
TORRES	F	NA2

PDV

Name	Gender	JobCode
SMITH	F	NA1

```
data newhires;
   set na1 na2;
run;
```

newhires

Name	Gender	JobCode
TORRES	M	NA1
LANG	F	NA1
SMITH	F	NA1

End of file

21

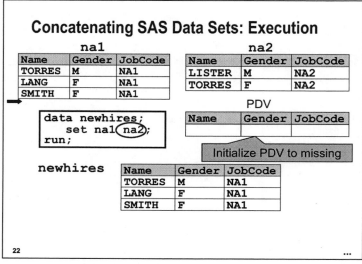

Concatenating SAS Data Sets: Execution

na1

Name	Gender	JobCode
TORRES	M	NA1
LANG	F	NA1
SMITH	F	NA1

na2

Name	Gender	JobCode
LISTER	M	NA2
TORRES	F	NA2

PDV

Name	Gender	JobCode

```
data newhires;
   set na1 na2;
run;
```

Initialize PDV to missing

newhires

Name	Gender	JobCode
TORRES	M	NA1
LANG	F	NA1
SMITH	F	NA1

22

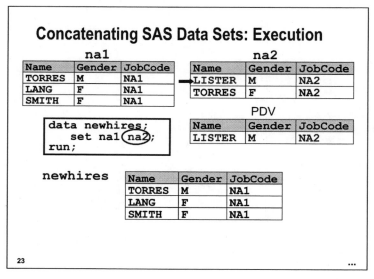

Concatenating SAS Data Sets: Execution

na1

Name	Gender	JobCode
TORRES	M	NA1
LANG	F	NA1
SMITH	F	NA1

na2

Name	Gender	JobCode
LISTER	M	NA2
TORRES	F	NA2

PDV

Name	Gender	JobCode
LISTER	M	NA2

```
data newhires;
   set na1 na2;
run;
```

newhires

Name	Gender	JobCode
TORRES	M	NA1
LANG	F	NA1
SMITH	F	NA1

23

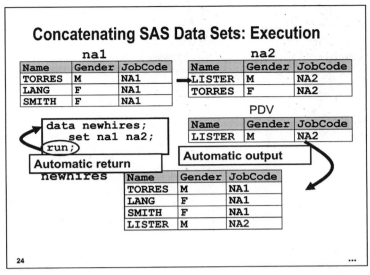

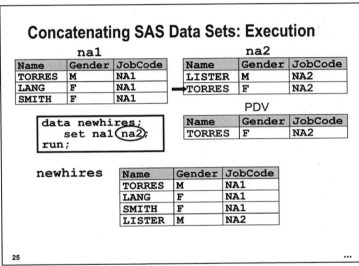

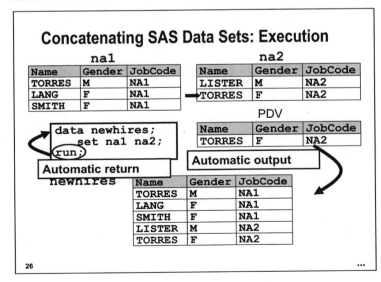

Concatenating SAS Data Sets: Execution

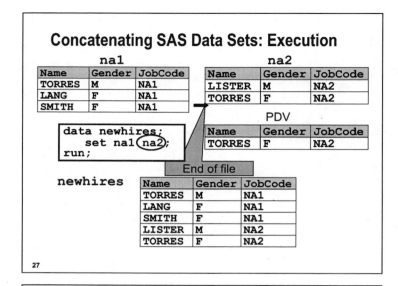

na1		
Name	Gender	JobCode
TORRES	M	NA1
LANG	F	NA1
SMITH	F	NA1

na2		
Name	Gender	JobCode
LISTER	M	NA2
TORRES	F	NA2

```
data newhires;
    set na1 na2;
run;
```

PDV

Name	Gender	JobCode
TORRES	F	NA2

End of file

newhires

Name	Gender	JobCode
TORRES	M	NA1
LANG	F	NA1
SMITH	F	NA1
LISTER	M	NA2
TORRES	F	NA2

27

Concatenating SAS Data Sets: Execution

When SAS reaches end of file on the last data set, DATA step execution ends.

newhires

Name	Gender	JobCode
TORRES	M	NA1
LANG	F	NA1
SMITH	F	NA1
LISTER	M	NA2
TORRES	F	NA2

28

Business Task

Two SAS data sets, **fa1** and **fa2**, contain data for newly hired flight attendants. Concatenate the data sets into a new data set named **newfa**.

fa1		
Name	Gender	JobCode
KENT	F	FA1
PATEL	M	FA1
JONES	F	FA1

fa2		
Name	JCode	Gender
LOPEZ	FA2	F
GRANT	FA2	F

The data sets contain similar data, but the variable names are different (**JobCode** versus **JCode**).

29

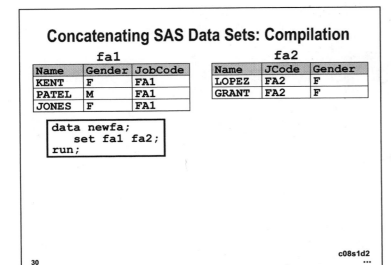

Concatenating SAS Data Sets: Compilation

fa1

Name	Gender	JobCode
KENT	F	FA1
PATEL	M	FA1
JONES	F	FA1

fa2

Name	JCode	Gender
LOPEZ	FA2	F
GRANT	FA2	F

```
data newfa;
   set fa1 fa2;
run;
```

c08s1d2

30

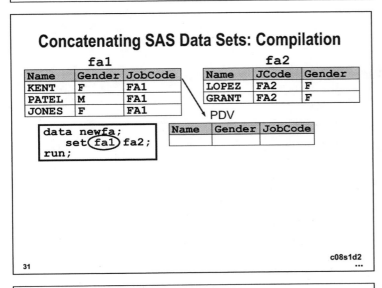

Concatenating SAS Data Sets: Compilation

fa1

Name	Gender	JobCode
KENT	F	FA1
PATEL	M	FA1
JONES	F	FA1

fa2

Name	JCode	Gender
LOPEZ	FA2	F
GRANT	FA2	F

PDV

Name	Gender	JobCode

```
data newfa;
   set fa1 fa2;
run;
```

c08s1d2

31

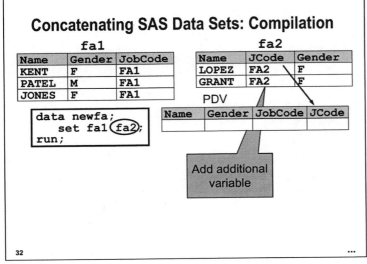

Concatenating SAS Data Sets: Compilation

fa1

Name	Gender	JobCode
KENT	F	FA1
PATEL	M	FA1
JONES	F	FA1

fa2

Name	JCode	Gender
LOPEZ	FA2	F
GRANT	FA2	F

PDV

Name	Gender	JobCode	JCode

```
data newfa;
   set fa1 fa2;
run;
```

Add additional variable

32

Concatenating SAS Data Sets: Compilation

fa1

Name	Gender	JobCode
KENT	F	FA1
PATEL	M	FA1
JONES	F	FA1

fa2

Name	JCode	Gender
LOPEZ	FA2	F
GRANT	FA2	F

PDV

Name	Gender	JobCode	JCode

```
data newfa;
    set fa1 fa2;
run;
```

newfa

Name	Gender	JobCode	JCode

33   c08s1d2
                                                                ...

Concatenating SAS Data Sets: Execution

fa1

Name	Gender	JobCode
KENT	F	FA1
PATEL	M	FA1
JONES	F	FA1

fa2

Name	JCode	Gender
LOPEZ	FA2	F
GRANT	FA2	F

PDV

Name	Gender	JobCode	JCode

```
data newfa;
    set fa1 fa2;
run;
```

newfa

Name	Gender	JobCode	JCode
KENT	F	FA1	
PATEL	M	FA1	
JONES	F	FA1	
LOPEZ	F		FA2
GRANT	F		FA2

34

The RENAME= Data Set Option

You can use the RENAME= data set option to change the name of a variable.

General form of the RENAME= data set option:

SAS-data-set(**RENAME=**(*old-name-1=new-name-1*
                        old-name-2=new-name-2
                        .
                        .
                        .
                        old-name-n=new-name-n))

35

The RENAME= Data Set Option

fa1

Name	Gender	JobCode
KENT	F	FA1
PATEL	M	FA1
JONES	F	FA1

fa2

Name	JCode	Gender
LOPEZ	FA2	F
GRANT	FA2	F

```
data newfa;
    set fa1 fa2(rename=(JCode=JobCode));
run;
```

c08s1d3

36

...

The RENAME= Data Set Option

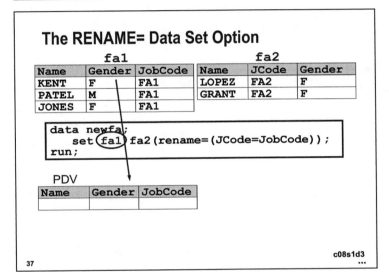

fa1

Name	Gender	JobCode
KENT	F	FA1
PATEL	M	FA1
JONES	F	FA1

fa2

Name	JCode	Gender
LOPEZ	FA2	F
GRANT	FA2	F

```
data newfa;
    set fa1 fa2(rename=(JCode=JobCode));
run;
```

PDV

Name	Gender	JobCode

c08s1d3

37

...

The RENAME= Data Set Option

fa1

Name	Gender	JobCode
KENT	F	FA1
PATEL	M	FA1
JONES	F	FA1

fa2

Name	JCode	Gender
LOPEZ	FA2	F
GRANT	FA2	F

```
data newfa;
    set fa1 fa2(rename=(JCode=JobCode));
run;
```

PDV

Name	Gender	JobCode

38

...

The RENAME= Data Set Option

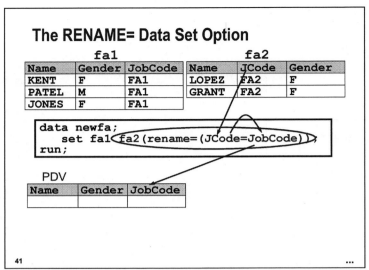

```
data newfa;
    set fa1 fa2(rename=(JCode=JobCode));
run;
```

41   ...

The RENAME= Data Set Option

fa1			fa2		
Name	Gender	JobCode	Name	JCode	Gender
KENT	F	FA1	LOPEZ	FA2	F
PATEL	M	FA1	GRANT	FA2	F
JONES	F	FA1			

```
data newfa;
    set fa1 fa2(rename=(JCode=JobCode));
run;
```

PDV

Name	Gender	JobCode

newfa

Name	Gender	JobCode

42   ...

The RENAME= Data Set Option

fa1			fa2		
Name	Gender	JobCode	Name	JCode	Gender
KENT	F	FA1	LOPEZ	FA2	F
PATEL	M	FA1	GRANT	FA2	F
JONES	F	FA1			

```
data newfa;
    set fa1 fa2(rename=(JCode=JobCode));
run;
```

PDV

Name	Gender	JobCode

newfa

Name	Gender	JobCode
KENT	F	FA1
PATEL	M	FA1
JONES	F	FA1
LOPEZ	F	FA2
GRANT	F	FA2

43

Interleaving SAS Data Sets

Use the SET statement with a BY statement
in a DATA step to interleave SAS data sets.

General form of a DATA step interleave:

DATA *SAS-data-set*;
    SET *SAS-data-set1 SAS-data-set2 . . .* ;
    BY *BY-variable*;
    <other SAS statements>
RUN;

44

Interleaving SAS Data Sets

Interleaving SAS data sets simply concatenates SAS data
sets so that the observations in the resulting data set are
in order.

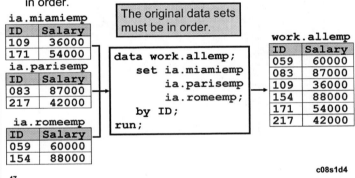

The original data sets
must be in order.

```
data work.allemp;
   set ia.miamiemp
        ia.parisemp
        ia.romeemp;
   by ID;
run;
```

ia.miamiemp

ID	Salary
109	36000
171	54000

ia.parisemp

ID	Salary
083	87000
217	42000

ia.romeemp

ID	Salary
059	60000
154	88000

work.allemp

ID	Salary
059	60000
083	87000
109	36000
154	88000
171	54000
217	42000

c08s1d4

47

Interleaving SAS Data Sets

Interleave the **fa1** and **fa2** data sets by **Name**.

fa1

Name	Gender	JobCode
KENT	F	FA1
PATEL	M	FA1
JONES	F	FA1

fa2

Name	JCode	Gender
LOPEZ	FA2	F
GRANT	FA2	F

c08s1d5

48

Interleaving SAS Data Sets

Interleave the **fa1** and **fa2** data sets by **Name**.

fa1

Name	Gender	JobCode
KENT	F	FA1
PATEL	M	FA1
JONES	F	FA1

fa2

Name	JCode	Gender
LOPEZ	FA2	F
GRANT	FA2	F

The data sets must be sorted first.

```
proc sort data=fa1;
   by name;
run;
```
```
proc sort data=fa2;
   by name;
run;
```

Name	Gender	JobCode
JONES	F	FA1
KENT	F	FA1
PATEL	M	FA1

Name	JCode	Gender
GRANT	FA2	F
LOPEZ	FA2	F

50

c08s1d5

...

Interleaving SAS Data Sets

fa1

Name	Gender	JobCode
JONES	F	FA1
KENT	F	FA1
PATEL	M	FA1

fa2

Name	JCode	Gender
GRANT	FA2	F
LOPEZ	FA2	F

```
data newfa;
   set fa1 fa2(rename=(JCode=JobCode));
   by Name;
run;
```

51

...

Interleaving SAS Data Sets

fa1

Name	Gender	JobCode
JONES	F	FA1
KENT	F	FA1
PATEL	M	FA1

fa2

Name	JCode	Gender
GRANT	FA2	F
LOPEZ	FA2	F

```
data newfa;
   set fa1 fa2(rename=(JCode=JobCode));
   by Name;
run;
```

PDV

Name	Gender	JobCode

newfa

Name	Gender	JobCode

52

...

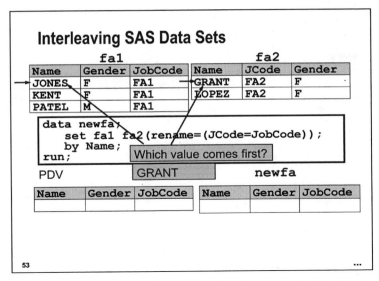

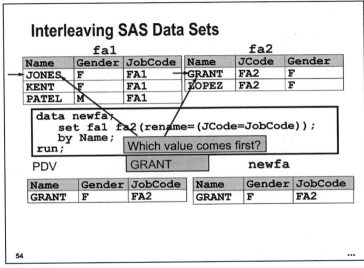

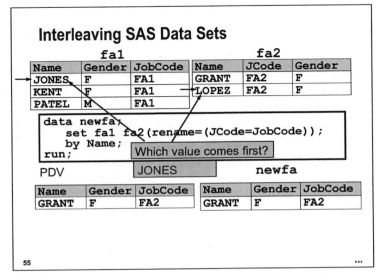

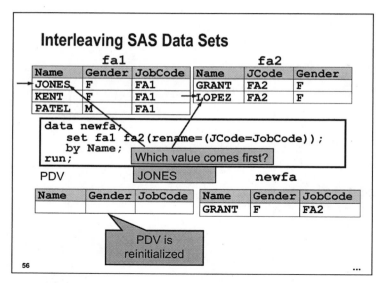

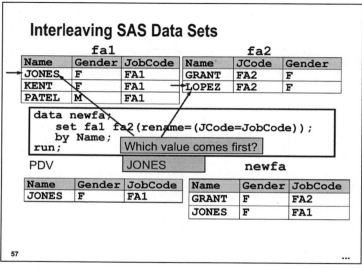

Interleaving SAS Data Sets

fa1

Name	Gender	JobCode
JONES	F	FA1
KENT	F	FA1
PATEL	M	FA1

fa2

Name	JCode	Gender
GRANT	FA2	F
LOPEZ	FA2	F

```
data newfa;
   set fa1 fa2(rename=(JCode=JobCode));
   by Name;
run;
```

PDV

Name	Gender	JobCode

newfa

Name	Gender	JobCode
GRANT	F	FA2
JONES	F	FA1
KENT	F	FA1
LOPEZ	F	FA2
PATEL	M	FA1

58

In the case where the data values are equal, the observation is always read from the first data set listed in the SET statement. For example:

fa1

Name	Gender	JobCode
JONES	F	FA1
LOPEZ	F	FA1
PATEL	M	FA1

fa2

Name	Gender	JobCode
GRANT	F	FA2
LOPEZ	M	FA2

The program below:

```
data newfa;
   set fa1 fa2;
   by Name;
run;
```

results in the following:

newfa

Name	Gender	JobCode
GRANT	F	FA2
JONES	F	FA1
LOPEZ	F	FA1
LOPEZ	M	FA2
PATEL	M	FA1

 **Exercises**

1. **Concatenating SAS Data Sets**

   The goal is to create a second-quarter data set for International Airlines' Vienna hub.

   Combine target information for April, May, and June into one data set. This data is currently stored in separate data sets by month as follows:

   - `ia.aprtarget`
   - `ia.maytarget`
   - `ia.juntarget`

   a. Browse the descriptor portion of each data set to determine the number of observations, as well as the number of variables and their attributes.

      How many observations does each data set contain?

      `ia.aprtarget` _____

      `ia.maytarget` _____

      `ia.juntarget` _____

      What are the names of the variables in each data set?

      `ia.aprtarget` _____

      _____

      `ia.maytarget` _____

      _____

      `ia.juntarget` _____

      _____

   b. Concatenate the three data sets and create a new data set named **work.q2vienna**. Rename any variables as necessary.

   c. Browse the SAS log. There should be no warning or error messages.
      - How many observations are written to the new data set?
      - How many variables does the new data set contain?

d. Submit a PROC PRINT step to verify the data.

Partial Output (First 9 of 307 Observations)

```
                                    The SAS System

                      D
                      e
                      s
              F       t
              l       i              F    E
              i       n              T    T
              g       a              a    a
              h       t      D       r    r           F                E
         O    t       i      a       g    g           R                R
         b    I       o      t       e    e           e                e
         s    D       n      e       t    t           v                v

         1   IA06100  CDG  01APR2000   8   85      $3,328.00       $11,730.00
         2   IA05900  CDG  01APR2000   8   85      $2,392.00        $8,415.00
         3   IA07200  FRA  01APR2000  10   97      $1,720.00        $5,432.00
         4   IA04700  LHR  01APR2000  14  120      $2,576.00        $7,320.00
         5   IA06100  CDG  02APR2000   8   85      $3,328.00       $11,730.00
         6   IA05900  CDG  02APR2000   8   85      $2,392.00        $8,415.00
         7   IA07200  FRA  02APR2000  10   97      $1,720.00        $5,432.00
         8   IA04700  LHR  02APR2000  14  120      $2,576.00        $7,320.00
         9   IA06100  CDG  03APR2000   8   85      $3,328.00       $11,730.00
```

e. Recall the DATA step and modify it to create two new variables: **TotTar** and **TotRev**.

- **TotTar** is the total targeted number of economy and first-class passengers.
- **TotRev** is the total revenue expected from economy and first-class passengers.

Keep only the variables **FlightID**, **Destination**, **Date**, **TotTar**, and **TotRev**.

f. Submit a PROC PRINT step to verify the data.

Partial Output (First 9 of 307 Observations)

```
                              The SAS System

              Flight                              Tot    Tot
        Obs     ID     Destination      Date      Tar    Rev

         1   IA06100       CDG       01APR2000     93    15058
         2   IA05900       CDG       01APR2000     93    10807
         3   IA07200       FRA       01APR2000    107     7152
         4   IA04700       LHR       01APR2000    134     9896
         5   IA06100       CDG       02APR2000     93    15058
         6   IA05900       CDG       02APR2000     93    10807
         7   IA07200       FRA       02APR2000    107     7152
         8   IA04700       LHR       02APR2000    134     9896
         9   IA06100       CDG       03APR2000     93    15058
```

8.2 Merging SAS Data Sets

Objectives

- Prepare data for merging using the SORT procedure.
- Merge SAS data sets on a single common variable.

61

Merging SAS Data Sets

Use the MERGE statement in a DATA step to join corresponding observations from two or more SAS data sets.

General form of a DATA step match-merge:

```
DATA SAS-data-set;
   MERGE SAS-data-sets;
   BY BY-variable(s);
   <additional SAS statements>
RUN;
```

62

Merging SAS Data Sets

You can read any number of SAS data sets with a single
MERGE statement.

SAS Data Sets

| costs | sales | | goals | taxes |

```
data compare;
   merge costs sales goals taxes;
   by Month;
run;
```

compare

| costs | sales | goals | taxes |

63

Merging combines data sets horizontally by a common variable.

Business Task

International Airlines is
comparing monthly sales
performance to monthly
sales goals.

The sales and goals data
are stored in separate
SAS data sets.

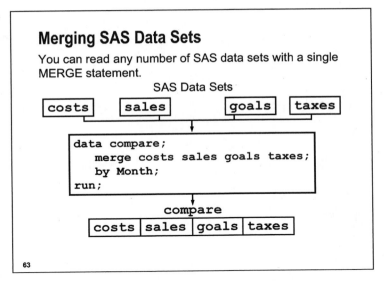

64

Business Task

To calculate the difference between revenues and goals, the **performance** and **goals** data sets must be merged.

ia.performance

Month	Sales
1	2118223
2	1960034

ia.goals

Month	Goal
1	2130000
2	1920000

Match-merge the data sets by **Month** and compute the difference between the variable values for **Sales** and **Goal**.

ia.compare

Month	Sales	Goal	Difference
1	2118223	2130000	-11777
2	1960034	1920000	40034

65

Merging SAS Data: Compilation

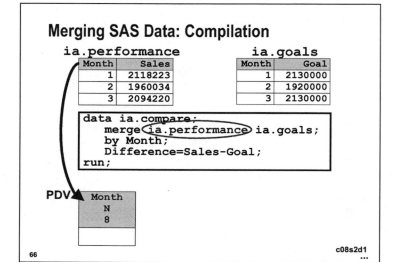

ia.performance

Month	Sales
1	2118223
2	1960034
3	2094220

ia.goals

Month	Goal
1	2130000
2	1920000
3	2130000

```
data ia.compare;
   merge ia.performance ia.goals;
   by Month;
   Difference=Sales-Goal;
run;
```

PDV

Month
N
8

66   c08s2d1
...

Merging SAS Data: Compilation

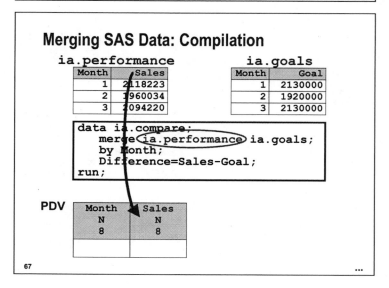

ia.performance

Month	Sales
1	2118223
2	1960034
3	2094220

ia.goals

Month	Goal
1	2130000
2	1920000
3	2130000

```
data ia.compare;
   merge ia.performance ia.goals;
   by Month;
   Difference=Sales-Goal;
run;
```

PDV

Month	Sales
N	N
8	8

67   ...

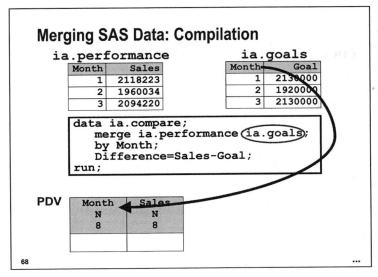

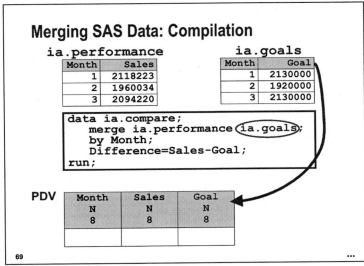

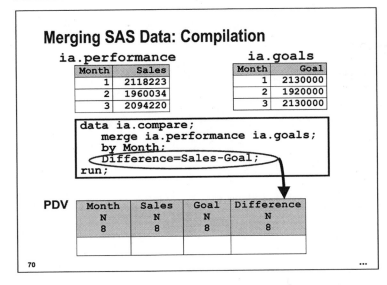

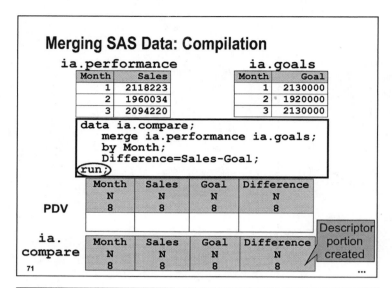

Merging SAS Data: Compilation

`ia.performance`

Month	Sales
1	2118223
2	1960034
3	2094220

`ia.goals`

Month	Goal
1	2130000
2	1920000
3	2130000

```
data ia.compare;
   merge ia.performance ia.goals;
   by Month;
   Difference=Sales-Goal;
run;
```

PDV

Month N 8	Sales N 8	Goal N 8	Difference N 8

ia. compare

Month N 8	Sales N 8	Goal N 8	Difference N 8

Descriptor portion created

71

...

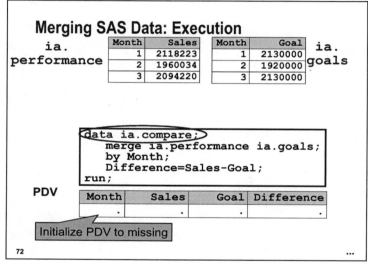

Merging SAS Data: Execution

ia. performance

Month	Sales
1	2118223
2	1960034
3	2094220

Month	Goal
1	2130000
2	1920000
3	2130000

ia. goals

```
data ia.compare;
   merge ia.performance ia.goals;
   by Month;
   Difference=Sales-Goal;
run;
```

PDV

Month	Sales	Goal	Difference
.	.	.	.

Initialize PDV to missing

72   ...

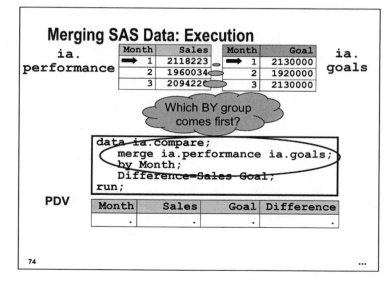

Merging SAS Data: Execution

ia. performance

Month	Sales
➡ 1	2118223
2	1960034
3	2094220

Month	Goal
➡ 1	2130000
2	1920000
3	2130000

ia. goals

Which BY group comes first?

```
data ia.compare;
   merge ia.performance ia.goals;
   by Month;
   Difference=Sales-Goal;
run;
```

PDV

Month	Sales	Goal	Difference
.	.	.	.

74   ...

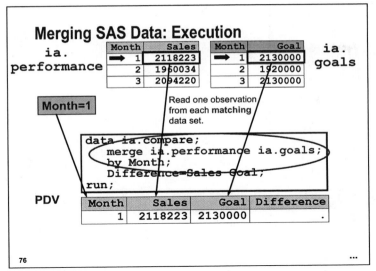

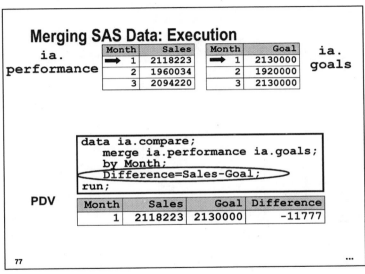

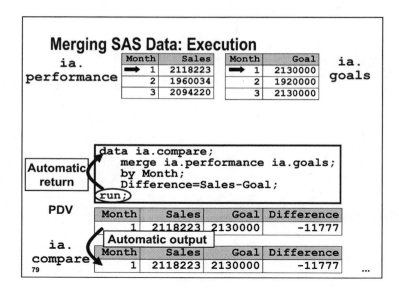

✏ By default, SAS outputs all variables from the PDV to the SAS data set.

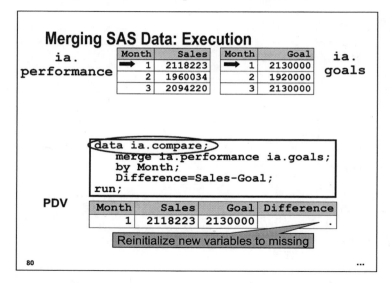

SAS reinitializes variables created in the DATA step to missing at the start of every DATA step iteration.

Before reading additional observations during a match-merge, SAS first determines if there are observations remaining for the current BY group.

• If there are observations remaining for the current BY group, they are read into the PDV, processed, and written to the output data set.

• If there are no more observations for the current BY group, SAS reinitializes the remainder of the PDV, identifies the next BY group, and reads the corresponding observations.

This process is repeated until SAS reads all of the observations in both data sets.

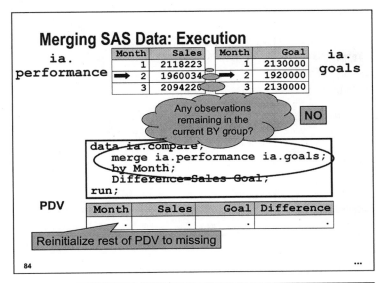

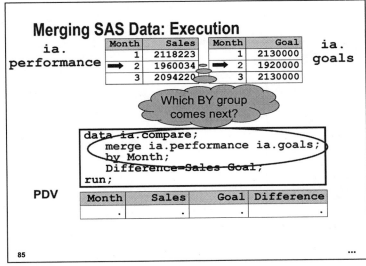

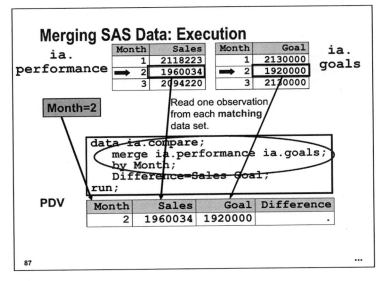

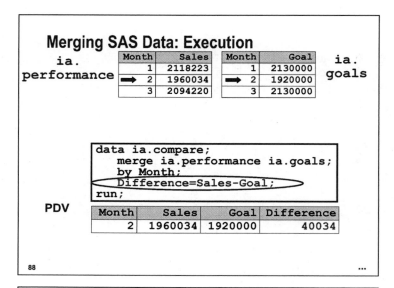

Merging SAS Data: Execution

88

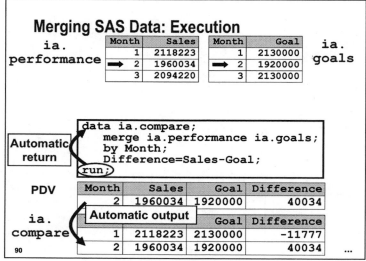

Merging SAS Data: Execution

90

The same process is repeated until SAS reaches the end of both data sets.

Merging SAS Data: Execution

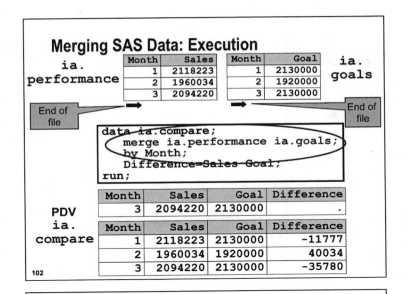

```
data ia.compare;
  merge ia.performance ia.goals;
  by Month;
  Difference=Sales-Goal;
run;
```

PDV

Month	Sales	Goal	Difference
3	2094220	2130000	.

ia. compare

Month	Sales	Goal	Difference
1	2118223	2130000	-11777
2	1960034	1920000	40034
3	2094220	2130000	-35780

102

Business Task

Merge two data sets to acquire the names of the German crew who are scheduled to fly next week.

ia.gercrew

EmpID	LastName
E00632	STRAUSS
E01483	SCHELL-HAUNGS
E01996	WELLHAEUSSER
E04064	WASCHK

ia.gersched

EmpID	FlightNum
E04064	5105
E00632	5250
E01996	5501

To match-merge the data sets by **EmpID**, the data sets must be ordered by **EmpID**.

```
proc sort data=ia.gersched
             out=work.gersched;
  by EmpID;
run;
```

103   c08s2d2

Merging SAS Data: Execution

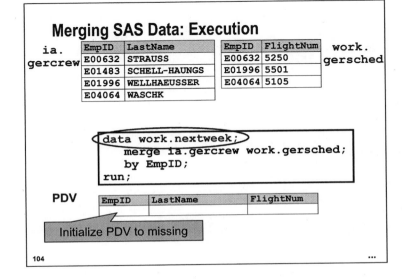

```
data work.nextweek;
  merge ia.gercrew work.gersched;
  by EmpID;
run;
```

PDV

EmpID	LastName	FlightNum

Initialize PDV to missing

104   ...

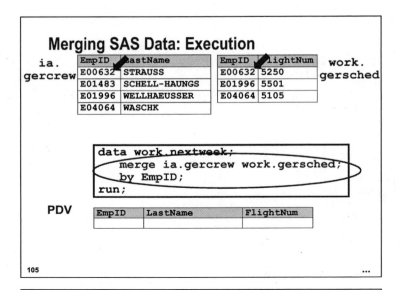

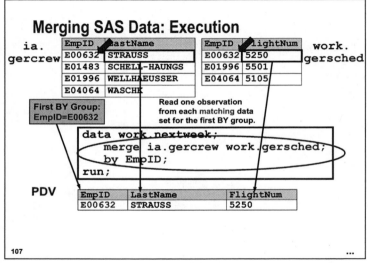

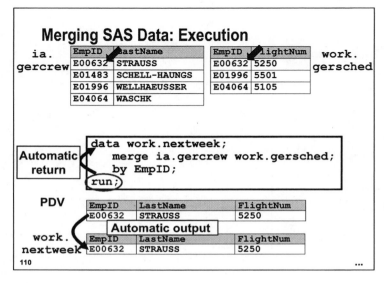

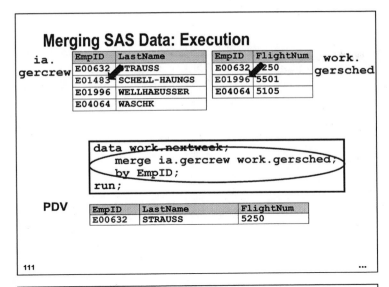

Merging SAS Data: Execution

ia.
gercrew

EmpID	LastName
E00632	TRAUSS
E01483	SCHELL-HAUNGS
E01996	WELLHAEUSSER
E04064	WASCHK

EmpID	FlightNum
E00632	250
E01996	5501
E04064	5105

work.
gersched

```
data work.nextweek;
    merge ia.gercrew work.gersched;
    by EmpID;
run;
```

PDV

EmpID	LastName	FlightNum
E00632	STRAUSS	5250

111   ...

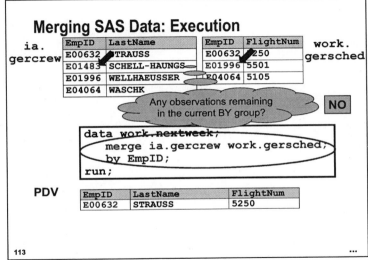

Merging SAS Data: Execution

ia.
gercrew

EmpID	LastName
E00632	TRAUSS
E01483	SCHELL-HAUNGS
E01996	WELLHAEUSSER
E04064	WASCHK

EmpID	FlightNum
E00632	250
E01996	5501
E04064	5105

work.
gersched

Any observations remaining
in the current BY group?   NO

```
data work.nextweek;
    merge ia.gercrew work.gersched;
    by EmpID;
run;
```

PDV

EmpID	LastName	FlightNum
E00632	STRAUSS	5250

113   ...

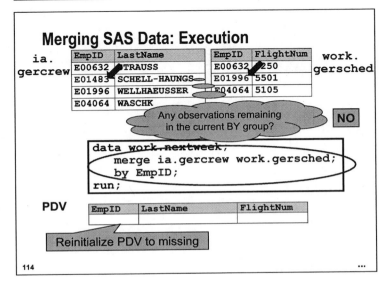

Merging SAS Data: Execution

ia.
gercrew

EmpID	LastName
E00632	TRAUSS
E01483	SCHELL-HAUNGS
E01996	WELLHAEUSSER
E04064	WASCHK

EmpID	FlightNum
E00632	250
E01996	5501
E04064	5105

work.
gersched

Any observations remaining
in the current BY group?   NO

```
data work.nextweek;
    merge ia.gercrew work.gersched;
    by EmpID;
run;
```

PDV

EmpID	LastName	FlightNum

Reinitialize PDV to missing

114   ...

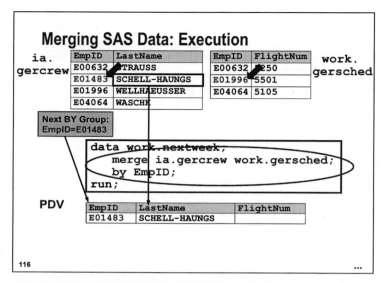

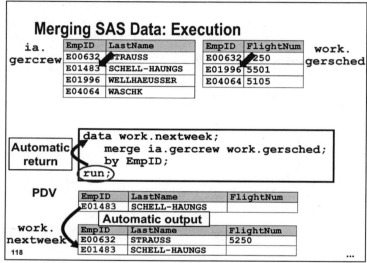

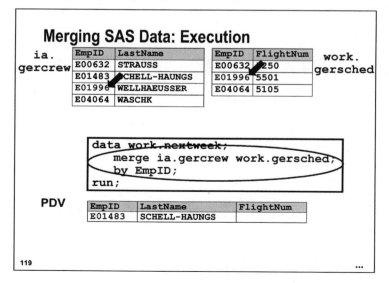

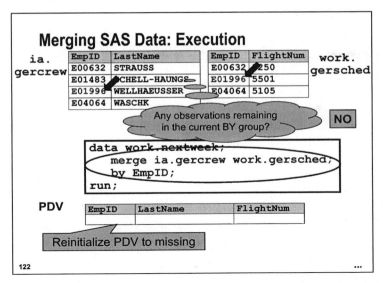

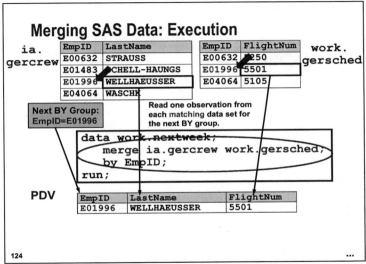

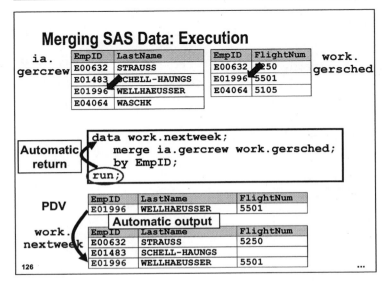

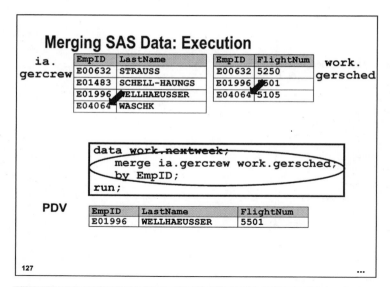

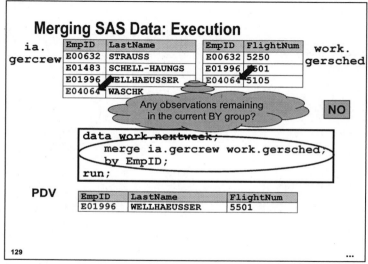

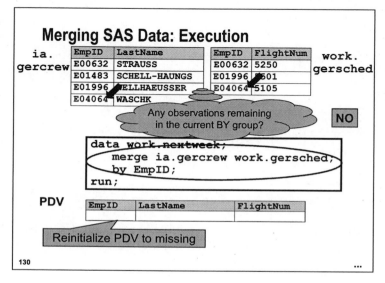

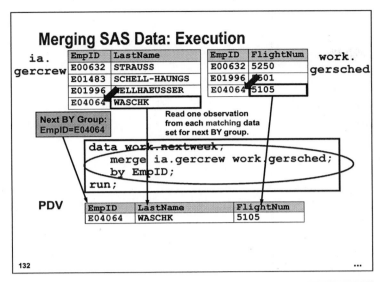

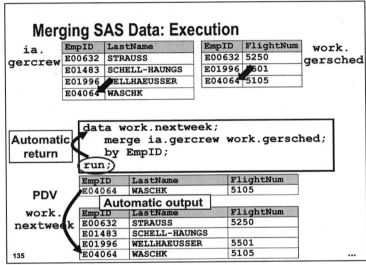

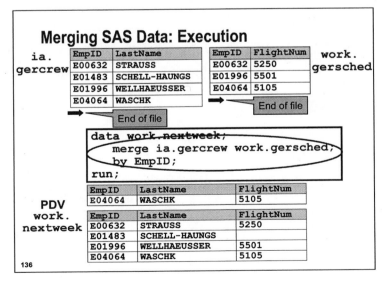

Eliminating Nonmatches

Exclude from the data set crew members who are
not scheduled to fly next week.

ia.gercrew

EmpID	LastName
E00632	STRAUSS
E01483	SCHELL-HAUNGS
E01996	WELLHAEUSSER
E04064	WASCHK

work.gersched

EmpID	FlightNum
E00632	5250
E01996	5501
E04064	5105

137

The data set **work.gersched** contains only employees who are scheduled to fly next week.

The IN= Data Set Option

Use the IN= data set option to determine which
data set(s) contributed to the current observation.

General form of the IN= data set option:

> *SAS-data-set*(**IN=***variable*)

variable is a temporary numeric variable that has
two possible values:

0 indicates that the data set did not contribute
to the current observation.

1 indicates that the data set did contribute to
the current observation.

138

The variable created with the IN= data set option is only available during execution and is not
written to the SAS data set.

The IN= Data Set Option

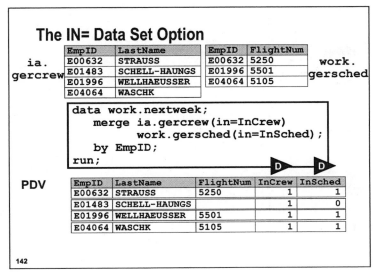

142

Eliminating Nonmatches

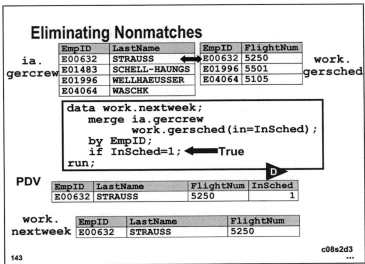

143

c08s2d3
...

The subsetting IF controls which observations are written to the SAS data set. If the condition evaluates to **true**, the observation is written to the SAS data set. If the condition is evaluated to **false**, the observation is not written to the SAS data set.

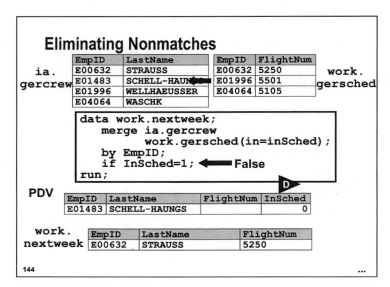

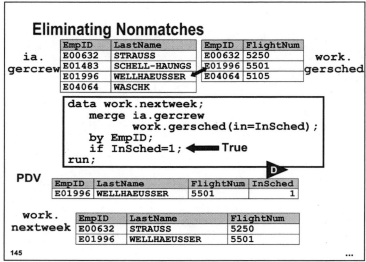

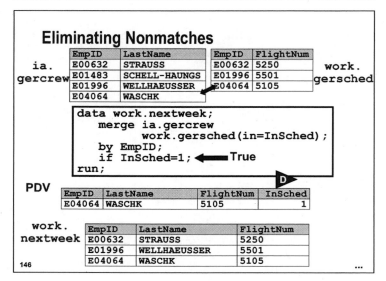

 **Exercises**

2. Merging SAS Data Sets

The weather in Birmingham, Alabama, on December 15, 1999, might have caused some customers to alter their shipping plans. Investigate how much cargo revenue was lost on all flights out of Birmingham by comparing the targeted revenue with the actual revenue.

a. Sort the data set **ia.target121999** into a temporary data set named **sortb**. Sort by the variable **FlightID**. Use the WHERE statement to create a subset for Birmingham on December 15, 1999.

```
where Date='15dec1999'd and Origin='BHM';
```

b. Sort the data set **ia.sales121999** into a temporary data set named **sorts**. Sort by the variable **FlightID**. Use the WHERE statement to create a subset for Birmingham on December 15, 1999.

```
where Date='15dec1999'd and Origin='BHM';
```

c. Create a new temporary data set named **compare** by merging the **sortb** and **sorts** data sets by the variable **FlightID**. Subtract **CargoRev** from **CargoTarRev** to create a new variable named **LostCargoRev**.

d. Print the data set **compare**. (Print only the variables **CargoTarRev**, **CargoRev**, and **LostCargoRev**.) Label the **LostCargoRev** variable. Format the **LostCargoRev** variable with a dollar sign and two decimal digits.

SAS Output

	The SAS System		
Obs	Target Revenue from Cargo	Revenue from Cargo	Lost Cargo Revenue
1	$3,441.00	$3,751.00	$-310.00
2	$3,441.00	$3,441.00	$0.00
3	$3,441.00	$2,821.00	$620.00
4	$3,441.00	$3,751.00	$-310.00
5	$3,441.00	$2,883.00	$558.00
6	$3,441.00	$2,945.00	$496.00

3. Identifying Data Set Contributors (Optional)

The **ia.frankfrt** data set contains information about flights to Frankfurt. The data set contains the variables **Flight** (the flight number), **Date** (the date of the flight), and **IDNo** (the ID number of the pilot who is assigned to the flight).

The **ia.pilots** data set contains pilot information and includes the variable **IDNum** (the ID number of each pilot).

a. Merge the **ia.pilots** and **ia.frankfrt** data sets by ID number to create a temporary data set named **schedule** that contains a work schedule for the pilots. The ID number of each pilot does not have the same variable name in each data set. The **schedule** data set should contain only the variables **IDNum**, **LName**, **FName**, **Date**, and **Flight**.

- Check the log to ensure that no errors occurred.
- Use PROC PRINT to verify that the data sets were merged properly. Notice that some pilots did not fly to Frankfurt.

SAS Output

```
                              The SAS System

          Obs    IDNum    LName         FName         Date      Flight

            1     1076    VENTER        RANDALL      04MAR00      821
            2     1076    VENTER        RANDALL      05MAR00      821
            3     1106    MARSHBURN     JASPER          .
            4     1107    THOMPSON      WAYNE           .
            5     1118    DENNIS        ROGER        06MAR00      821
            6     1333    BLAIR         JUSTIN       02MAR00      821
            7     1404    CARTER        DONALD       01MAR00      219
            8     1404    CARTER        DONALD       02MAR00      219
            9     1407    GRANT         DANIEL       01MAR00      821
           10     1410    HARRIS        CHARLES      06MAR00      219
           11     1428    BRADY         CHRISTINE       .
           12     1439    HARRISON      FELICIA      03MAR00      821
           13     1442    NEWKIRK       SANDRA          .
           14     1478    NEWTON        JAMES        03MAR00      219
           15     1545    HUNTER        CLYDE           .
           16     1556    PENNINGTON    MICHAEL         .
           17     1739    BOYCE         JONATHAN     05MAR00      219
           18     1777    LUFKIN        ROY             .
           19     1830    TRIPP         KATHY        04MAR00      219
           20     1830    TRIPP         KATHY        07MAR00      219
           21     1890    STEPHENSON    ROBERT          .
           22     1905    GRAHAM        ALVIN           .
           23     1928    UPCHURCH      LARRY           .
```

b. Alter the DATA step to create a temporary data set named **schedule** that contains only pilots who had Frankfurt assignments.

- Use PROC PRINT to verify that the data sets were merged properly.

SAS Output

```
                              The SAS System

           Obs    IDNum    LName      FName       Date     Flight

            1     1076     VENTER     RANDALL     04MAR00    821
            2     1076     VENTER     RANDALL     05MAR00    821
            3     1118     DENNIS     ROGER       06MAR00    821
            4     1333     BLAIR      JUSTIN      02MAR00    821
            5     1404     CARTER     DONALD      01MAR00    219
            6     1404     CARTER     DONALD      02MAR00    219
            7     1407     GRANT      DANIEL      01MAR00    821
            8     1410     HARRIS     CHARLES     06MAR00    219
            9     1439     HARRISON   FELICIA     03MAR00    821
           10     1478     NEWTON     JAMES       03MAR00    219
           11     1739     BOYCE      JONATHAN    05MAR00    219
           12     1830     TRIPP      KATHY       04MAR00    219
           13     1830     TRIPP      KATHY       07MAR00    219
```

c. Alter the DATA step to create a temporary data set named **nofrank** that contains only pilots who did **not** have Frankfurt assignments.

- Use a KEEP statement to restrict the **nofrank** data set to contain only the variables **IDNum**, **LName**, and **FName**.

- Use PROC PRINT to verify that the data sets were merged properly.

SAS Output

```
                          The SAS System

           Obs    IDNum    LName         FName

            1     1106     MARSHBURN     JASPER
            2     1107     THOMPSON      WAYNE
            3     1428     BRADY         CHRISTINE
            4     1442     NEWKIRK       SANDRA
            5     1545     HUNTER        CLYDE
            6     1556     PENNINGTON    MICHAEL
            7     1777     LUFKIN        ROY
            8     1890     STEPHENSON    ROBERT
            9     1905     GRAHAM        ALVIN
           10     1928     UPCHURCH      LARRY
```

8.3 Combining SAS Data Sets: Additional Features (Self-Study)

Objectives

- Define types of DATA step merges.
- Illustrate how the DATA step handles different types of merges.

149

Other Merges

In addition to one-to-one merges, the DATA step merge works with many other kinds of data combinations:

one-to-many   Unique BY values are in one data set and duplicate matching BY values are in the other data set.

many-to-many   Duplicate matching BY values are in both data sets.

150

One-to-Many Merging

`work.one`

X	Y
1	A
2	B
3	C

`work.two`

X	Z
1	A1
1	A2
2	B1
3	C1
3	C2

```
data work.three;
   merge work.one work.two;
   by X;
run;
```

151   ...

One-to-Many Merging

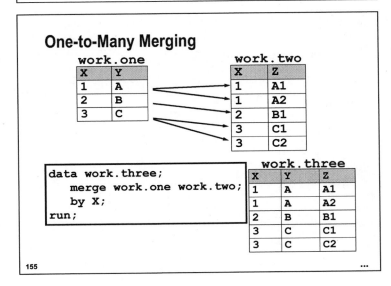

`work.one`

X	Y
1	A
2	B
3	C

`work.two`

X	Z
1	A1
1	A2
2	B1
3	C1
3	C2

```
data work.three;
   merge work.one work.two;
   by X;
run;
```

`work.three`

X	Y	Z
1	A	A1
1	A	A2
2	B	B1
3	C	C1
3	C	C2

155   ...

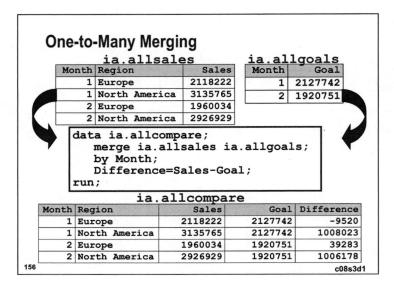

In a one-to-many merge, when SAS reads the last observation from a BY-group in one data set, SAS retains its values in the program data vector for all variables that are unique to that data set until all observations for that BY-group have been read from all data sets.

The total number of observations in the final data set is the sum of the maximum number of observations in a BY-group from either data set.

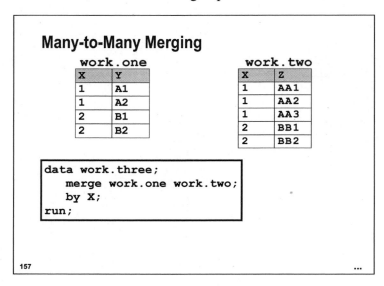

Many-to-Many Merging

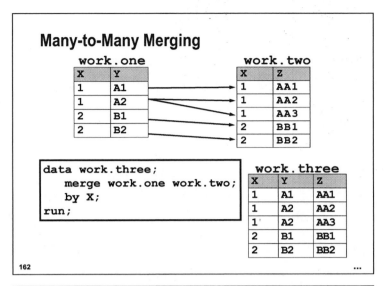

```
data work.three;
    merge work.one work.two;
    by X;
run;
```

162

Many-to-Many Merging

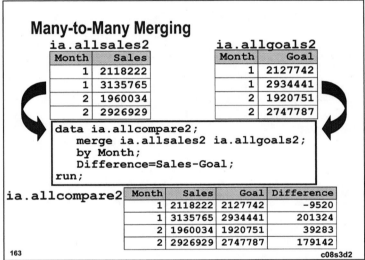

```
data ia.allcompare2;
    merge ia.allsales2 ia.allgoals2;
    by Month;
    Difference=Sales-Goal;
run;
```

ia.allcompare2

Month	Sales	Goal	Difference
1	2118222	2127742	-9520
1	3135765	2934441	201324
2	1960034	1920751	39283
2	2926929	2747787	179142

163   c08s3d2

In a many-to-many merge, a note is issued to the log that states, "NOTE: MERGE statement has more than one data set with repeats of BY values." This message is meant to be informational.

A DATA step that performs a many-to-many merge does not produce a Cartesian product.

PROC SQL creates all possible combinations when joining tables. This can be controlled by specifying a WHERE clause.

Understanding the nature of a many-to-many merge will ensure that you chose the correct method to combine your data to obtain the desired results.

8.4 Solutions to Exercises

1. **Concatenating SAS Data Sets**

   a.

   Each data set contains observations in the amounts shown below:
   - `ia.aprtarget` __120__
   - `ia.maytarget` __67__
   - `ia.juntarget` __120__

   The variable names in each data set are as follows:

   `ia.aprtarget`   Flight, Destination, Date, FClassTar, EClassTar, FRev, ERev

   `ia.maytarget`   FlightID, Destination, Date, FTarget, ETarget, FRev, ERev

   `ia.juntarget`   FlightID, Destination, Date, FTarget, ETarget, FRev, ERev

   b.
   ```
   data work.q2vienna;
     set ia.aprtarget(rename=(Flight=FlightID
                              FClassTar=FTarget
                              EClassTar=ETarget))
         ia.maytarget ia.juntarget;
   run;
   ```

   c.
   - There are __307__ observations written to the new data set.
   - There are __7__ variables in the new data set.

   d.
   ```
   proc print data=work.q2vienna;
   run;
   ```

   e.
   ```
   data work.q2vienna;
      keep FlightID Destination Date TotTar TotRev;
      set ia.aprtarget(rename=(Flight=FlightID
                               FClassTar=FTarget
                               EClassTar=ETarget))
          ia.maytarget ia.juntarget;
      TotTar=sum(FTarget,ETarget);
      TotRev=sum(FRev,ERev);
   run;
   ```

   f.
   ```
   proc print data=work.q2vienna;
   run;
   ```

2. **Merging SAS Data Sets**

You must sort both SAS data sets prior to merging. Within PROC SORT, you can add a WHERE statement to subset the observations written to the new SAS data sets created with the OUT= option.

✐   When you use a WHERE statement in PROC SORT, be sure to specify an OUT= option. Otherwise, you permanently subset the data.

```
proc sort data=ia.target121999 out=sortb;
   by FlightID;
   where Date='15dec1999'd and Origin='BHM';
run;
proc sort data=ia.sales121999 out=sorts;
   by FlightID;
   where Date='15dec1999'd and Origin='BHM';
run;
data compare;
   merge sortb sorts;
   by FlightID;
   LostCargoRev=CargoTarRev-CargoRev;
run;
proc print data=compare label;
   format LostCargoRev dollar12.2;
   var CargoTarRev CargoRev LostCargoRev;
   label LostCargoRev='Lost Cargo Revenue';
run;
```

3. **Identifying Data Set Contributors (Optional)**

a.

```
proc sort data=ia.pilots out=pilots;
   by IDNum;
run;
proc sort data=ia.frankfrt out=frankfrt;
   by IDNo;
run;
data schedule;
   keep IDNum LName FName Date Flight;
   merge pilots frankfrt(rename=(IDNo=IDNum));
   by IDNum;
run;
proc print data=schedule;
run;
```

b.

```
data schedule;
   keep IDNum LName FName Date Flight;
   merge pilots frankfrt(in=inFrank rename=(IDNo=IDNum));
   by IDNum;
   if inFrank=1;
run;
proc print data=schedule;
run;
```

c.

```
data nofrank;
   keep IDNum LName FName;
   merge pilots frankfrt(in=inFrank rename=(IDNo=IDNum));
   by IDNum;
   if inFrank=0;
run;
proc print data=nofrank;
run;
```

Chapter 9 Producing Summary Reports

9.1   Introduction to Summary Reports

Objectives

- Identify the different report writing procedures.

3

Summary Reports

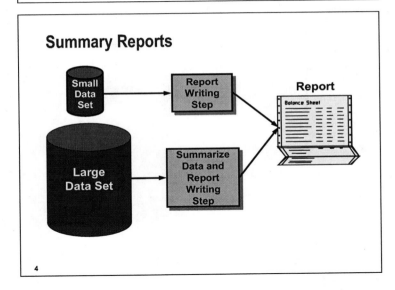

4

Summary Report Procedures

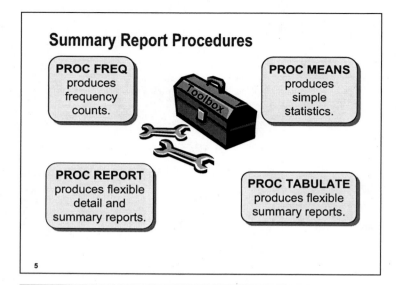

PROC FREQ
produces
frequency
counts.

PROC MEANS
produces
simple
statistics.

PROC REPORT
produces flexible
detail and
summary reports.

PROC TABULATE
produces flexible
summary reports.

5

PROC FREQ Output

```
              Distribution of Job Code Values

                    The FREQ Procedure

Job                                 Cumulative    Cumulative
Code       Frequency    Percent     Frequency      Percent

FLTAT1        14         20.29          14          20.29
FLTAT2        18         26.09          32          46.38
FLTAT3        12         17.39          44          63.77
PILOT1         8         11.59          52          75.36
PILOT2         9         13.04          61          88.41
PILOT3         8         11.59          69         100.00
```

6

PROC MEANS Output

```
                    Salary by Job Code

                   The MEANS Procedure

                 Analysis Variable : Salary

Job      N
Code    Obs   N       Mean      Std Dev     Minimum      Maximum

FLTAT1   14  14    25642.86     2951.07    21000.00     30000.00

FLTAT2   18  18    35111.11     1906.30    32000.00     38000.00

FLTAT3   12  12    44250.00     2301.19    41000.00     48000.00

PILOT1    8   8    69500.00     2976.10    65000.00     73000.00

PILOT2    9   9    80111.11     3756.48    75000.00     86000.00

PILOT3    8   8    99875.00     7623.98    92000.00    112000.00
```

7

PROC REPORT Output

```
                    Salary Analysis
        Job Code  Home Base           Salary

        FLTAT1    CARY              $131,000
                  FRANKFURT         $100,000
                  LONDON            $128,000
        FLTAT2    CARY              $245,000
                  FRANKFURT         $181,000
                  LONDON            $206,000
        FLTAT3    CARY              $217,000
                  FRANKFURT         $134,000
                  LONDON            $180,000
        PILOT1    CARY              $211,000
                  FRANKFURT         $135,000
                  LONDON            $210,000
        PILOT2    CARY              $323,000
                  FRANKFURT         $240,000
                  LONDON            $158,000
        PILOT3    CARY              $300,000
                  FRANKFURT         $205,000
                  LONDON            $294,000
                                  ==========
                                  $3,598,000
```

8

PROC TABULATE Output

Average Salary for Cary and Frankfurt

	Location		All
	CARY	FRANKFURT	
	Salary	Salary	Salary
	Mean	Mean	Mean
JobCode			
FLTAT1	$26,200	$25,000	$25,667
FLTAT2	$35,000	$36,200	$35,500
FLTAT3	$43,400	$44,667	$43,875
All	$34,882	$34,583	$34,759

9

9.2 Basic Summary Reports

Objectives

- Create one-way and two-way frequency tables using the FREQ procedure.
- Specify the variables to be processed by the FREQ procedure.
- Generate simple descriptive statistics using the MEANS procedure.
- Group observations of a SAS data set for analysis using the CLASS statement in the MEANS procedure.

11

Goal Report 1

International Airlines wants to know how many employees are in each job code.

```
              Distribution of Job Code Values

                  The FREQ Procedure

Job                              Cumulative   Cumulative
Code     Frequency    Percent    Frequency     Percent

FLTAT1      14         20.29         14         20.29
FLTAT2      18         26.09         32         46.38
FLTAT3      12         17.39         44         63.77
PILOT1       8         11.59         52         75.36
PILOT2       9         13.04         61         88.41
PILOT3       8         11.59         69        100.00
```

12

Goal Report 2

Categorize job code and salary values to determine
how many employees are in each group.

```
                Salary Distribution by Job Codes
                       The FREQ Procedure
                     Table of JobCode by Salary

JobCode             Salary

Frequency
Percent
Row Pct
Col Pct          Less tha 25,000 t More tha   Total
                 n 25,000 o 50,000 n 50,000

Flight Attendant       5       39        0        44
                    7.25    56.52     0.00     63.77
                   11.36    88.64     0.00
                  100.00   100.00     0.00

Pilot                  0        0       25        25
                    0.00     0.00    36.23     36.23
                    0.00     0.00   100.00
                    0.00     0.00   100.00

Total                  5       39       25        69
                    7.25    56.52    36.23    100.00
```

13

Creating a Frequency Report

PROC FREQ displays frequency counts of the
data values in a SAS data set.

General form of a simple PROC FREQ step:

```
PROC FREQ DATA=SAS-data-set;
RUN;
```

Example:

```
proc freq data=ia.crew;
run;
```

14

Creating a Frequency Report

By default, PROC FREQ does the following:

- analyzes every variable in the SAS data set
- displays each distinct data value
- calculates the number of observations in which
  each data value appears (and the corresponding
  percentage)
- indicates for each variable how many observations
  have missing values

15

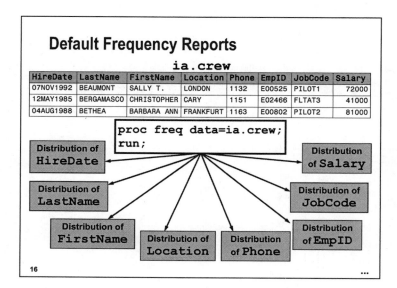

By default, PROC FREQ creates a report on every variable in the data set. For example, the **EmpID** report displays every unique value of **EmpID**, counts how many observations have each value, and provides percentages and cumulative statistics. This is not a useful report because each employee has his or her own unique employee ID.

You do not typically create frequency reports for variables with a large number of distinct values, such as **EmpID**, or for analysis variables, such as **Salary**. You usually create frequency reports for categorical variables, such as **JobCode**. You can group variables into categories by creating and applying formats.

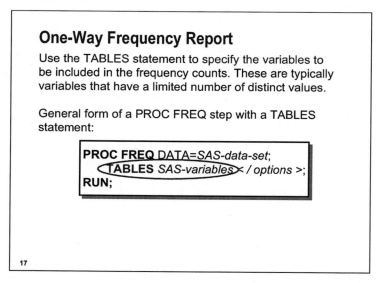

If you specify more than one variable in the TABLES statement, separate the variable names by a space. This creates one table for each variable. For example:

```
tables JobCode Location;
```

Creating a Frequency Report

```
proc freq data=ia.crew;
   tables JobCode;
   title 'Distribution of Job Code Values';
run;
```

Distribution of Job Code Values				
The FREQ Procedure				
Job Code	Frequency	Percent	Cumulative Frequency	Cumulative Percent
FLTAT1	14	20.29	14	20.29
FLTAT2	18	26.09	32	46.38
FLTAT3	12	17.39	44	63.77
PILOT1	8	11.59	52	75.36
PILOT2	9	13.04	61	88.41
PILOT3	8	11.59	69	100.00

c09s2d1

18

Displaying the Number of Levels

Use the NLEVELS option in the PROC FREQ statement
to display the number of levels for the variables included
in the frequency counts.

```
proc freq data=ia.crew nlevels;
   tables Location;
   title 'Distribution of Location Values';
run;
```

c09s2d1a

19

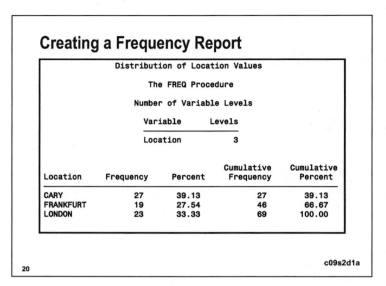

Creating a Frequency Report

```
               Distribution of Location Values

                   The FREQ Procedure

                Number of Variable Levels

                 Variable        Levels

                 Location          3


                                   Cumulative    Cumulative
Location      Frequency   Percent   Frequency      Percent

CARY             27        39.13        27          39.13
FRANKFURT        19        27.54        46          66.67
LONDON           23        33.33        69         100.00
```

c09s2d1a

20

To display the number of levels without displaying the frequency counts, add the NOPRINT option to the TABLES statement.

```
proc freq data=ia.crew nlevels;
   tables JobCode Location / noprint;
   title 'Number of Levels for Job Code and Location';
run;
```

To display the number of levels for all variables without displaying any frequency counts, use the _ALL_ keyword and the NOPRINT option in the TABLES statement.

```
proc freq data=ia.crew nlevels;
   tables _all_ / noprint;
   title 'Number of Levels for All Variables';
run;
```

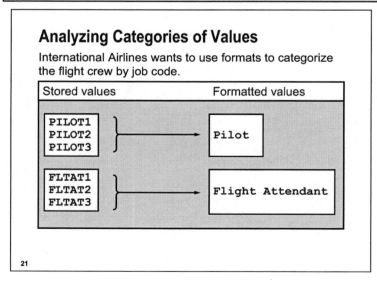

Analyzing Categories of Values

International Airlines wants to use formats to categorize the flight crew by job code.

Stored values	Formatted values
PILOT1 PILOT2 PILOT3	Pilot
FLTAT1 FLTAT2 FLTAT3	Flight Attendant

21

Analyzing Categories of Values

```
proc format;
   value $codefmt
           'FLTAT1'-'FLTAT3'='Flight Attendant'
           'PILOT1'-'PILOT3'='Pilot';
run;
proc freq data = ia.crew;
   format JobCode $codefmt.;
   tables JobCode;
run;
```

c09s2d2

22

Analyzing Categories of Values

Distribution of Job Code Values

The FREQ Procedure

JobCode	Frequency	Percent	Cumulative Frequency	Cumulative Percent
Flight Attendant	44	63.77	44	63.77
Pilot	25	36.23	69	100.00

23

PROC FREQ automatically groups the data by a variable's formatted value if a format is associated with that variable.

Crosstabular Frequency Reports

A two-way, or *crosstabular*, frequency report analyzes all possible combinations of the distinct values of two variables.

The asterisk (*) operator in the TABLES statement is used to cross variables.

General form of the FREQ procedure to create a crosstabular report:

```
PROC FREQ DATA=SAS-data-set;
    TABLES variable1*variable2;
RUN;
```

24

Crosstabular Frequency Reports

```
proc format;
   value $codefmt
         'FLTAT1'-'FLTAT3'='Flight Attendant'
         'PILOT1'-'PILOT3'='Pilot';
   value money
         low-<25000 ='Less than 25,000'
         25000-50000='25,000 to 50,000'
         50000<-high='More than 50,000';
run;
proc freq data=ia.crew;
   tables JobCode*Salary;
   format JobCode $codefmt. Salary money.;
   title 'Salary Distribution by Job Codes';
run;
```

25   c09s2d3

In a crosstabular report, the values of the first variable in the TABLES statement form the rows of the frequency table and the values of the second variable form the columns.

Crosstabular Frequency Reports

```
                Salary Distribution by Job Codes

                     The FREQ Procedure

                  Table of JobCode by Salary

     JobCode          Salary

     Frequency
     Percent
     Row Pct
     Col Pct       Less tha 25,000 t More tha   Total
                   n 25,000 o 50,000 n 50,000

     Flight Attendant      5       39        0      44
                        7.25    56.52     0.00   63.77
                       11.36    88.64     0.00
                      100.00   100.00     0.00

     Pilot                 0        0       25      25
                        0.00     0.00    36.23   36.23
                        0.00     0.00   100.00
                        0.00     0.00   100.00

     Total                 5       39       25      69
                        7.25    56.52    36.23  100.00
```

26

Crosstabular Frequency Reports

To display the crosstabulation results in a listing form,
add the CROSSLIST option to the TABLES statement.

```
proc freq data=ia.crew;
   tables JobCode*Location / crosslist;
   title 'Location Distribution for Job Codes';
run;
```

c09s2d3a

27

Crosstabular Frequency Reports

Partial Output

```
                Location Distribution for Job Codes

                       The FREQ Procedure

                  Table of JobCode by Location

     Job                                 Row      Column
     Code   Location  Frequency  Percent  Percent   Percent

     FLTAT1 CARY           5       7.25    35.71    18.52
            FRANKFURT      4       5.80    28.57    21.05
            LONDON         5       7.25    35.71    21.74

            Total         14      20.29   100.00
     -------------------------------------------------------
     FLTAT2 CARY           7      10.14    38.89    25.93
            FRANKFURT      5       7.25    27.78    26.32
            LONDON         6       8.70    33.33    26.09

            Total         18      26.09   100.00
     -------------------------------------------------------
```

28

Business Task

International Airlines wants to determine the minimum, maximum, and average salaries for each job code.

29

Calculating Summary Statistics

The MEANS procedure displays simple descriptive statistics for the numeric variables in a SAS data set.

General form of a simple PROC MEANS step:

> **PROC MEANS** DATA=*SAS-data-set*;
> **RUN**;

Example:

```
proc means data=ia.crew;
   title 'Salary Analysis';
run;
```

30   c09s2d4

Calculating Summary Statistics

Salary Analysis					
The MEANS Procedure					
Variable	N	Mean	Std Dev	Minimum	Maximum
HireDate	69	9812.78	1615.44	7318.00	12690.00
Salary	69	52144.93	25521.78	21000.00	112000.00

31

Calculating Summary Statistics

By default, PROC MEANS does the following:

- analyzes every numeric variable in the SAS data set
- prints the statistics N, MEAN, STD, MIN, and MAX
- excludes missing values before calculating statistics

32

Default statistics are shown below:

N	number of rows with nonmissing values
MEAN	arithmetic mean (or average)
STD	standard deviation
MIN	minimum value
MAX	maximum value

Other statistics include the following:

RANGE	difference between lowest and highest values
MEDIAN	50th percentile value
SUM	total
NMISS	number of rows with missing values

Selecting Variables

The VAR statement identifies the analysis variables
and their order in the PROC MEANS output.

General form of the VAR statement:

> **VAR** *SAS-variable(s)*;

33

Selecting Variables

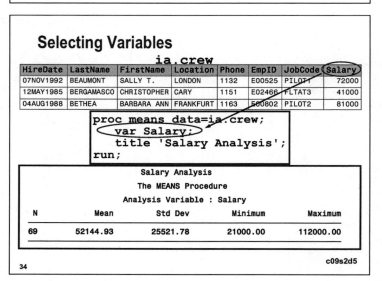

ia.crew

HireDate	LastName	FirstName	Location	Phone	EmpID	JobCode	Salary
07NOV1992	BEAUMONT	SALLY T.	LONDON	1132	E00525	PILOT1	72000
12MAY1985	BERGAMASCO	CHRISTOPHER	CARY	1151	E02466	FLTAT3	41000
04AUG1988	BETHEA	BARBARA ANN	FRANKFURT	1163	E00802	PILOT2	81000

```
proc means data=ia.crew;
   var Salary;
   title 'Salary Analysis';
run;
```

```
                 Salary Analysis
              The MEANS Procedure
           Analysis Variable : Salary

  N        Mean       Std Dev      Minimum      Maximum

  69      52144.93    25521.78     21000.00    112000.00
```

34   c09s2d5

Grouping Observations

The CLASS statement in the MEANS procedure
groups the observations of the SAS data set for analysis.

General form of the CLASS statement:

> **CLASS** *SAS-variable(s)*;

35

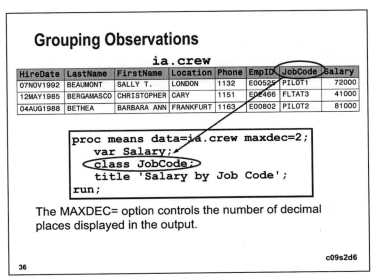

Grouping Observations

ia.crew

HireDate	LastName	FirstName	Location	Phone	EmpID	JobCode	Salary
07NOV1992	BEAUMONT	SALLY T.	LONDON	1132	E00525	PILOT1	72000
12MAY1985	BERGAMASCO	CHRISTOPHER	CARY	1151	E02466	FLTAT3	41000
04AUG1988	BETHEA	BARBARA ANN	FRANKFURT	1163	E00802	PILOT2	81000

```
proc means data=ia.crew maxdec=2;
   var Salary;
   class JobCode;
   title 'Salary by Job Code';
run;
```

The MAXDEC= option controls the number of decimal
places displayed in the output.

c09s2d6

36

Grouping Observations

```
                  Salary by Job Code

                  The MEANS Procedure

               Analysis Variable : Salary

Job      N
Code    Obs   N      Mean      Std Dev     Minimum      Maximum

FLTAT1  14   14   25642.86    2951.07    21000.00     30000.00

FLTAT2  18   18   35111.11    1906.30    32000.00     38000.00

FLTAT3  12   12   44250.00    2301.19    41000.00     48000.00

PILOT1   8    8   69500.00    2976.10    65000.00     73000.00

PILOT2   9    9   80111.11    3756.48    75000.00     86000.00

PILOT3   8    8   99875.00    7623.98    92000.00    112000.00
```

37

PROC MEANS might not always print two digits to the right of the decimal point. To control
the maximum number of decimal places for PROC MEANS to use in printing results, use the
MAXDEC= option in the PROC MEANS statement.

General form of the PROC MEANS statement with the MAXDEC= option:

> **PROC MEANS** DATA=*SAS-data-set* MAXDEC=*number*;
> **RUN;**

 **Exercises**

1. Creating Frequency Reports

a. Use PROC FREQ to create a report using the **ia.sanfran** data set that displays the frequency count for each **DepartDay**. Add an appropriate title.

SAS Output

```
                      Flights from San Francisco by Day of Week

                               The FREQ Procedure

                                              Cumulative      Cumulative
         DepartDay    Frequency     Percent    Frequency        Percent
         ─────────────────────────────────────────────────────────────
             1            6         11.54          6            11.54
             2           13         25.00         19            36.54
             3            5          9.62         24            46.15
             4            7         13.46         31            59.62
             5            7         13.46         38            73.08
             6            8         15.38         46            88.46
             7            6         11.54         52           100.00
```

b. Use PROC FREQ to create a report using the **ia.sanfran** data set that displays the frequency count for each **Destination**. Add an appropriate title.

SAS Output

```
                          Flights from San Francisco

                               The FREQ Procedure

                                              Cumulative      Cumulative
         Destination   Frequency    Percent    Frequency        Percent
         ─────────────────────────────────────────────────────────────
         ANC              10        19.23         10            19.23
         HND               8        15.38         18            34.62
         HNL               3         5.77         21            40.38
         RDU               6        11.54         27            51.92
         SEA              25        48.08         52           100.00
```

c. **(Optional)** You can specify many options in the TABLES statement to control the calculations and appearance of a frequency table. The NOCUM option suppresses the printing of the cumulative frequencies and cumulative percentages. You can specify options in a TABLES statement in the following way:

```
tables variable / options;
```

Recall your program from Exercise **1.b** and add the NOCUM option to the TABLES statement.

SAS Output

```
                         Flights from San Francisco

                            The FREQ Procedure

            Destination     Frequency      Percent

               ANC             10          19.23
               HND              8          15.38
               HNL              3           5.77
               RDU              6          11.54
               SEA             25          48.08
```

d. Use PROC FREQ to create a report using the **ia.sanfran** data set, which displays the frequency count for each **Destination** by **DepartDay**.

Partial SAS Output

```
                        Flights from San Francisco

                           The FREQ Procedure

                    Table of Destination by DepartDay

       Destination
                DepartDay

       Frequency
       Percent
       Row Pct
       Col Pct          1|       2|       3|       4|  Total

       ANC              0|       3|       1|       1|     10
                     0.00|    5.77|    1.92|    1.92|  19.23
                     0.00|   30.00|   10.00|   10.00|
                     0.00|   23.08|   20.00|   14.29|

       HND              1|       2|       1|       3|      8
                     1.92|    3.85|    1.92|    5.77|  15.38
                    12.50|   25.00|   12.50|   37.50|
                    16.67|   15.38|   20.00|   42.86|

       HNL              0|       0|       0|       0|      3
                     0.00|    0.00|    0.00|    0.00|   5.77
                     0.00|    0.00|    0.00|    0.00|
                     0.00|    0.00|    0.00|    0.00|

       RDU              2|       1|       1|       0|      6
                     3.85|    1.92|    1.92|    0.00|  11.54
                    33.33|   16.67|   16.67|    0.00|
                    33.33|    7.69|   20.00|    0.00|
```

The presentation of the output might vary depending on the line size of the page. This is only partial output.

2. Validating Data with PROC FREQ (Optional)

a. PROC FREQ is useful in checking the validity and completeness of data. Use PROC FREQ to check the validity of the variables **Gender** and **JobCode** in the **ia.mechanics** data set.

1) What do you notice about the values of the variable **Gender**?

2) What do you notice about the values of the variable **JobCode**?

SAS Output

```
                              The FREQ Procedure

                                       Cumulative    Cumulative
     Gender    Frequency    Percent    Frequency      Percent

       B            1         2.94          1           2.94
       F           17        50.00         18          52.94
       G            1         2.94         19          55.88
       M           15        44.12         34         100.00


     Job                                Cumulative    Cumulative
     Code      Frequency    Percent     Frequency      Percent

     MECHO1         6        18.18          6          18.18
     MECHO2        12        36.36         18          54.55
     MECHO3        15        45.45         33         100.00

                          Frequency Missing = 1
```

b. Modify the previous report to display the frequency count for each **Gender** by **JobCode**. What are the **JobCode** values for the invalid values of **Gender**? (The output is not shown because it provides the answer.)

3. Creating Basic Summary Reports

a. Generate a PROC MEANS report using the **ia.sanfran** data set as input to display statistics for the variables **CargoRev** and **TotPassCap** only. Remove any titles currently in effect.

SAS Output

```
                              The MEANS Procedure

   Variable     N        Mean        Std Dev       Minimum        Maximum

   CargoRev    52     33433.50      23731.72       9417.00       84495.00
   TotPassCap  52   203.8076923   52.4494298    150.0000000    267.0000000
```

b. Modify the previous report to display the data for each **Destination**. Limit the number of decimal places in the output to two. The output shown below is only partial output; all statistics should appear in your report.

Partial SAS Output

```
                           The MEANS Procedure

                  N
Destination      Obs    Variable       N        Mean       Std Dev
─────────────────────────────────────────────────────────────────
ANC              10     CargoRev      10     35811.30      4458.74
                        TotPassCap    10       257.60        11.69

HND               8     CargoRev       8     78625.50      3251.06
                        TotPassCap     8       250.50         8.33

HNL               3     CargoRev       3     59684.00      3464.64
                        TotPassCap     3       207.00         0.00

RDU               6     CargoRev       6     37840.00      4787.04
                        TotPassCap     6       267.00         0.00

SEA              25     CargoRev      25     13813.32      2316.59
                        TotPassCap    25       151.80         4.97
```

4. Requesting Specific Statistics through PROC MEANS (Optional)

You can request specific statistics by listing the names in a PROC MEANS statement. For example, to request N (the frequency of non-missing values), and only N, use the following PROC MEANS step:

```
proc means data=SAS-data-set-name n;
run;
```

Modify the report from Exercise 3, and alter the PROC MEANS statement to request only the minimum (MIN), maximum (MAX), and mean (MEAN) statistics.

SAS Output

```
                           The MEANS Procedure

                N
Destination    Obs  Variable     Minimum      Maximum        Mean
─────────────────────────────────────────────────────────────────
ANC            10   CargoRev     31992.00     44643.00     35811.30
                    TotPassCap     238.00       267.00       257.60

HND             8   CargoRev     73143.00     84495.00     78625.50
                    TotPassCap     237.00       255.00       250.50

HNL             3   CargoRev     55728.00     62178.00     59684.00
                    TotPassCap     207.00       207.00       207.00

RDU             6   CargoRev     31734.00     43344.00     37840.00
                    TotPassCap     267.00       267.00       267.00

SEA            25   CargoRev      9417.00     17931.00     13813.32
                    TotPassCap     150.00       165.00       151.80
```

5. Creating HTML Output (Optional)

Modify the previous report by adding an ODS statement to create the output as HTML.

The MEANS Procedure

Destination	N Obs	Variable	Minimum	Maximum	Mean
ANC	10	CargoRev	31992.00	44643.00	35811.30
		TotPassCap	238.00	267.00	257.60
HND	8	CargoRev	73143.00	84495.00	78625.50
		TotPassCap	237.00	255.00	250.50
HNL	3	CargoRev	55728.00	62178.00	59684.00
		TotPassCap	207.00	207.00	207.00
RDU	6	CargoRev	31734.00	43344.00	37840.00
		TotPassCap	267.00	267.00	267.00
SEA	25	CargoRev	9417.00	17931.00	13813.32
		TotPassCap	150.00	165.00	151.80

9.3 The REPORT Procedure

Objectives

- Use the REPORT procedure to create a listing report.
- Apply the ORDER usage type to sort the data on a listing report.
- Apply the GROUP usage type to create a summary report.
- Use the RBREAK statement to produce a grand total.

40

REPORT Procedure Features

PROC REPORT enables you to do the following:

- create listing reports
- create summary reports
- enhance reports
- request separate subtotals and grand totals
- generate reports in an interactive point-and-click or programming environment

41

PROC REPORT versus PROC PRINT

FEATURE	REPORT	PRINT
Detail Report	Yes	Yes
Summary Report	Yes	No
Crosstabular Report	Yes	No
Grand Totals	Yes	Yes
Subtotals	Yes	Yes, but not without Grand Total
Labels used automatically	Yes	No
Sort data for report	Yes	No

42

Creating a List Report

General form of a simple PROC REPORT step:

PROC REPORT DATA=*SAS-data-set <options>*;
RUN;

Selected options:

WINDOWS | WD   invokes the procedure in an interactive REPORT window (default).

NOWINDOWS | NOWD   displays the report in the OUTPUT window.

```
proc report data=ia.crew nowd;
run;
```

43

The REPORT Procedure

The default listing has a detail row for each observation in the data set. In addition, the listing is displayed with

- each data value as it is stored in the data set, or a formatted value if a format is stored with the data
- variable names or labels as report column headings
- a default width for the report columns
- character values left-justified
- numeric values right-justified
- observations in the order in which they are stored in the data set.

44

Printing Selected Variables

You can use a COLUMN statement to do the following:

- select the variables to appear in the report
- order the variables in the report

General form of the COLUMN statement:

> **COLUMN** *SAS-variables*;

45

The COLUMN statement lists the report items to include in the columns of the report and describes the arrangement of the columns. A report item can be

- a data set variable
- a statistic calculated by the procedure
- a variable that you compute from other items in the report.

Omit the COLUMN statement if you want to include all the variables in the input data set in the same order as they occur in the data set.

Sample Listing Report

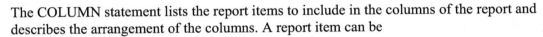

```
title 'Salary Analysis';
proc report data=ia.crew nowd;
   column JobCode Location Salary;
run;
```

Partial
SAS
Output

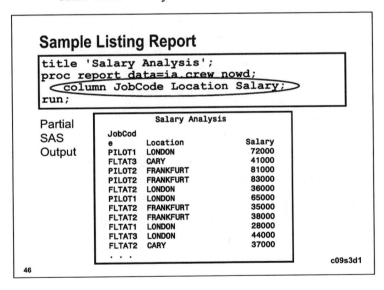

```
              Salary Analysis
JobCod
e       Location        Salary
PILOT1  LONDON           72000
FLTAT3  CARY             41000
PILOT2  FRANKFURT        81000
PILOT2  FRANKFURT        83000
FLTAT2  LONDON           36000
PILOT1  LONDON           65000
FLTAT2  FRANKFURT        35000
FLTAT2  FRANKFURT        38000
FLTAT1  LONDON           28000
FLTAT3  LONDON           44000
FLTAT2  CARY             37000
 . . .
```

c09s3d1

46

The DEFINE Statement

You can enhance the report by using DEFINE statements to accomplish the following:

- define how each variable is used in the report
- assign formats to variables
- specify report column headers and column widths
- change the order of the rows in the report

47

The DEFINE Statement

General form of the DEFINE statement:

> **DEFINE** *variable / <usage> <attribute-list>*;

You can define options (usage and attributes) in the DEFINE statement in any order.

48

The DEFINE Statement

Variable Type	Default Usage	Report Produced
Character	Display	Listing
Numeric	Analysis	Summary

The ANALYSIS usage for numeric variables

- uses a default statistic of SUM
- has no effect when producing a listing report that contains character variables, so the original data value is displayed.

49

Character and Numeric Variables

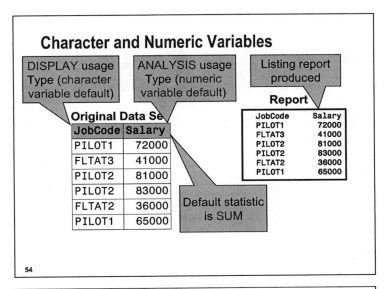

Numeric Variables Only

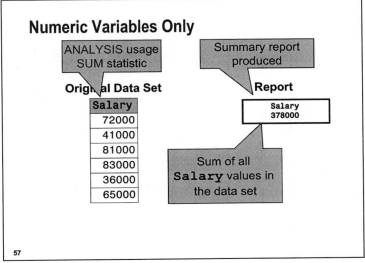

The DEFINE Statement

Selected attributes:

' *report-column-header* '   defines the report column header.

If there is a label stored for the variable in the descriptor portion of the data set, it is the default header.

The DEFINE Statement

Selected attributes:

FORMAT=   assigns a format to a variable.

If there is a format stored for the variable in the descriptor portion of the data set, it is used as the default format.

WIDTH=   controls the width of a report column.

The default width is
- the variable length for character variables
- 9 for numeric variables
- the format width if there is a format stored for the variable in the descriptor portion of the data set.

59

Enhancing the Listing Report

- Change column headings.
- Increase the column widths.
- Add a format to display **Salary** with dollar signs and commas.

```
proc report data=ia.crew nowd;
   column JobCode Location Salary;
   define JobCode / width=8 'Job Code';
   define Location / 'Home Base';
   define Salary / format=dollar10.;
run;
```

60   c09s3d2

Enhancing the Listing Report

Partial SAS Output

Job Code	Home Base	Salary
PILOT1	LONDON	$72,000
FLTAT3	CARY	$41,000
PILOT2	FRANKFURT	$81,000
PILOT2	FRANKFURT	$83,000
FLTAT2	LONDON	$36,000
PILOT1	LONDON	$65,000
FLTAT2	FRANKFURT	$35,000
FLTAT2	FRANKFURT	$38,000
FLTAT1	LONDON	$28,000

. . .

61

ORDER Usage Type

Selected attributes:

ORDER	orders the rows in the report.

- Orders the report in ascending order. Include the DESCENDING option in the DEFINE statement to force the order to be descending.
- Suppresses repetitive printing of values.
- Does **not** need data to be previously sorted.

62

ORDER Usage Type

Display the data in ascending order by **JobCode**.

```
proc report data=ia.crew nowd;
   column JobCode Location Salary;
   define JobCode / order width=8 'Job Code';
   define Location / 'Home Base';
   define Salary / format=dollar10.;
run;
```

63   c09s3d3

ORDER Usage Type

Partial SAS Output

```
                    Salary Analysis

   Job Code  Home Base          Salary
   FLTAT1    LONDON            $28,000
             FRANKFURT         $25,000
             CARY              $23,000
                . . .
             FRANKFURT         $27,000
             LONDON            $22,000
   FLTAT2    LONDON            $36,000
             FRANKFURT         $35,000
                . . .
             FRANKFURT         $33,000
             CARY              $38,000
```

64

Business Task

International Airlines wants to summarize **Salary** by **JobCode** for each **Location**.

65

Desired Report

```
                    Salary Analysis

          Job Code  Home Base         Salary
          FLTAT1    CARY            $131,000
                    FRANKFURT       $100,000
                    LONDON          $128,000
          FLTAT2    CARY            $245,000
                    FRANKFURT       $181,000
                    LONDON          $206,000
          FLTAT3    CARY            $217,000
                    FRANKFURT       $134,000
                    LONDON          $180,000
          PILOT1    CARY            $211,000
                    FRANKFURT       $135,000
                    LONDON          $210,000
          PILOT2    CARY            $323,000
                    FRANKFURT       $240,000
                    LONDON          $158,000
          PILOT3    CARY            $300,000
                    FRANKFURT       $205,000
                    LONDON          $294,000
                                   ==========
                                 $3,598,000
```

66

Defining Group Variables

Use the REPORT procedure to create a summary report by defining variables as **group** variables.

All observations whose group variables have the same values are collapsed into a single row in the report.

67

Defining Group Variables

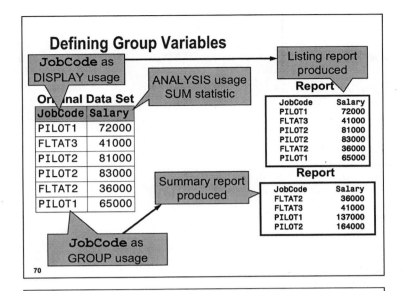

70

Defining Group Variables

You can define more than one variable as a group variable.

Nesting of group variables is determined by the order of the variables in the COLUMN statement.

```
column JobCode Location Salary;
```

71

Defining Group Variables

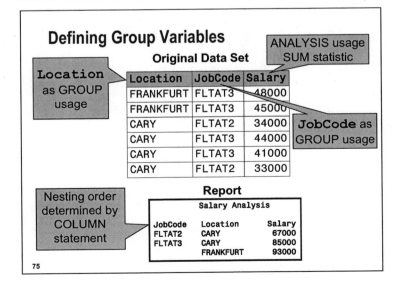

75

Defining Group Variables

If you want a summary report, there must be no display or order variables in the report definition.

- Display and order variables produce listing reports (one row for each observation).
- Group variables produce summary reports (observations collapsed into groups).
- One or more display or order variables (without associated statistics) in a report definition will result in a listing report, even if group variables are also present.

76

Defining Analysis Variables

Default usage for numeric variables is ANALYSIS with a default statistic of SUM.

- If the report contains group variables, the report displays the sum of the numeric variables' values for each group.
- If the report contains at least one display or order variable and no group variables, the report lists all of the values of the numeric variable.
- If the report contains only numeric variables with a usage of ANALYSIS, the report displays grand totals for the numeric variables.

77

Defining Analysis Variables

Selected statistics include the following:

SUM	sum (default)
N	number of nonmissing values
MEAN	average
MAX	maximum value
MIN	minimum value

To specify a statistic other than SUM, type the name of the statistic after the slash in the DEFINE statement.

Example:

```
define Salary / mean format=dollar10.;
```

78

Summarizing the Data

Use the GROUP usage in the DEFINE statement
to specify the variables that define groups.

```
proc report data=ia.crew nowd;
   column JobCode Location Salary;
   define JobCode / group width=8 'Job Code';
   define Location / group 'Home Base';
   define Salary / format=dollar10.;
run;
```

c09s3d4

79

Summarizing the Data

Partial SAS Output

```
                   Salary Analysis
         Job Code  Home Base          Salary
         FLTAT1    CARY             $131,000
                   FRANKFURT        $100,000
                   LONDON           $128,000
         FLTAT2    CARY             $245,000
                   FRANKFURT        $181,000
                   LONDON           $206,000
         FLTAT3    CARY             $217,000
                   FRANKFURT        $134,000
                   LONDON           $180,000
         PILOT1    CARY             $211,000
                   FRANKFURT        $135,000
                   LONDON           $210,000
         PILOT2    CARY             $323,000
                   FRANKFURT        $240,000
                   LONDON           $158,000
         PILOT3    CARY             $300,000
                   FRANKFURT        $205,000
                   LONDON           $294,000
```

80

Printing Grand Totals

You can use an RBREAK statement to add the following:

- the grand total to the top or bottom of the report
- a line before the grand total
- a line after the grand total

General form of the RBREAK statement:

RBREAK BEFORE | AFTER </options>;

81

Printing Grand Totals

Selected options:

SUMMARIZE	prints the total.
OL	prints a single line above the total.
DOL	prints a double line above the total.
UL	prints a single line below the total.
DUL	prints a double line below the total.

82

The RBREAK Statement

Use the RBREAK statement to display the grand total at the bottom of the report.

```
proc report data=ia.crew nowd;
   column JobCode Location Salary;
   define JobCode / group width=8 'Job Code';
   define Location / group 'Home Base';
   define Salary / format=dollar10.;
   rbreak after / summarize dol;
run;
```

83   c09s3d5

The RBREAK Statement

```
                    Salary Analysis

         Job Code  Home Base         Salary
         FLTAT1    CARY            $131,000
                   FRANKFURT       $100,000
                   LONDON          $128,000
         FLTAT2    CARY            $245,000
                   FRANKFURT       $181,000
                   LONDON          $206,000
         FLTAT3    CARY            $217,000
                   FRANKFURT       $134,000
                   LONDON          $180,000
         PILOT1    CARY            $211,000
                   FRANKFURT       $135,000
                   LONDON          $210,000
         PILOT2    CARY            $323,000
                   FRANKFURT       $240,000
                   LONDON          $158,000
         PILOT3    CARY            $300,000
                   FRANKFURT       $205,000
                   LONDON          $294,000
                                 ==========
                                 $3,598,000
```

84

Enhancing the Report

You can use the HEADLINE and HEADSKIP options in the PROC REPORT statement to make the report more readable.

```
proc report data=ia.crew nowd headline headskip;
   column JobCode Location Salary;
   define JobCode / group width=8 'Job Code';
   define Location / group 'Home Base';
   define Salary / format=dollar10.;
   rbreak after / summarize dol;
run;
```

c09s3d6

85

Enhancing the Report

```
                    Salary Analysis
        Job Code  Home Base          Salary

        FLTAT1    CARY             $131,000
                  FRANKFURT        $100,000
                  LONDON           $128,000
        FLTAT2    CARY             $245,000
                  FRANKFURT        $181,000
                  LONDON           $206,000
        FLTAT3    CARY             $217,000
                  FRANKFURT        $134,000
                  LONDON           $180,000
        PILOT1    CARY             $211,000
                  FRANKFURT        $135,000
                  LONDON           $210,000
        PILOT2    CARY             $323,000
                  FRANKFURT        $240,000
                  LONDON           $158,000
        PILOT3    CARY             $300,000
                  FRANKFURT        $205,000
                  LONDON           $294,000
                                 ==========
                                 $3,598,000
```

86

 **Exercises**

6. **Creating a List Report**

    Use PROC REPORT and the **ia.employees** data set to produce a list report with the following characteristics:

    *   Output should be sent to the Output window.
    *   The report should display only the variables **Division**, **City**, and **Salary**.
    *   Each variable displayed should have a descriptive report column heading.
    *   Salary should be displayed with dollar signs, commas, and no decimals.
    *   The columns of the report should be wide enough so that individual data values are not truncated.
    *   The observations on the report should be ordered by the values of **Division**.
    *   The report should be titled **Employee Salary Data**.

    Partial PROC REPORT Output

    ```
                            Employee Salary Data

          Division Name        City Based          Salary
          AIRPORT OPERATIONS   CARY               $29,000
                               CARY               $41,000
                               CARY               $23,000
                               CARY               $17,000
                               CARY               $32,000
                               CARY               $39,000
                               TORONTO            $29,000
                               CARY               $33,000
    ```

7. **Creating a Sorted List Report (Optional)**

    Modify the previous report so that both **Division** and **City** appear in sorted order.

    Partial PROC REPORT Output

    ```
                            Employee Salary Data

          Division Name        City Based          Salary
          AIRPORT OPERATIONS   AUSTIN             $22,000
                                                  $37,000
                                                  $35,000
                               BRUSSELS           $16,000
                                                  $38,000
                               CARY               $29,000
                                                  $41,000
    ```

8. Creating a Summary Report

Use PROC REPORT and the `ia.employees` data set to produce a summary report with the following characteristics:

- The report should display only the variables **Division**, **City**, and **Salary**.
- Each variable displayed should have a descriptive report column heading.
- Salary should be displayed with dollar signs, commas, and no decimals.
- The columns of the report should be wide enough so that individual data values are not truncated.
- The observations on the report should be summarized by the values of **City** for each **Division**.
- The report should be titled **Employee Salary Data by Division / City**.

Partial PROC REPORT Output

```
              Employee Salary Data by Division / City

    Division Name        City Based          Salary
    AIRPORT OPERATIONS    AUSTIN             $94,000
                          BRUSSELS           $54,000
                          CARY            $2,510,000
                          COPENHAGEN        $254,000
                          FRANKFURT         $285,000
                          GENEVA             $72,000
                          LONDON            $122,000
                          PARIS             $147,000
                          ROCKVILLE          $79,000
                          ROME              $112,000
                          SYDNEY            $108,000
                          TOKYO              $73,000
                          TORONTO           $137,000
    CORPORATE OPERATIONS  ATLANTA           $105,000
                          CARY              $210,000
```

9. Adding a Grand Total to the Report

Modify the previous report so that a grand total appears with a single line above the total and a double line below the total.

Partial PROC REPORT Output (Bottom of Report)

```
                          PITTSBURGH         $52,000
                          ROCKVILLE          $81,000
                          SAN FRANCISCO      $41,000
                          SAN JOSE           $21,000
                          SINGAPORE          $63,000
                          TOKYO             $101,000
                          TORONTO            $83,000
                                          -----------
                                          $16,290,000
                                          ===========
```

9.4 The TABULATE Procedure (Self-Study)

Objectives

- Create one- and two-dimensional tabular reports using the TABULATE procedure.
- Produce totals for one dimension.
- Produce totals for both dimensions.

89

Introduction

The report-writing features of PROC TABULATE include the following:

- control of table construction
- differentiating between classification variables and analysis variables
- specifying statistics
- formatting of values
- labeling variables and statistics

90

PROC TABULATE versus PROC REPORT

FEATURE	REPORT	TABULATE
Detail Report	Yes	No
Summary Report	Yes	Yes
Crosstabular Report	Yes	Yes
Grand Totals	Yes	Yes
Dividing Lines	Yes	Yes
Labels used automatically	Yes	Yes
Ability to create computed columns	Yes	No

91

PROC TABULATE Syntax

General form of a PROC TABULATE step:

```
PROC TABULATE DATA=SAS-data-set <options>;
     CLASS class-variables;
     VAR analysis-variables;
     TABLE page-expression,
           row-expression,
           column-expression </ option(s)>;
RUN;
```

92

A CLASS statement or a VAR statement must be specified, but both statements together are not required.

Specifying Classification Variables

A CLASS statement identifies variables to be used as classification, or grouping, variables.

```
PROC TABULATE DATA=SAS-data-set <options>;
    CLASS class-variables;
    VAR analysis-variables;
    TABLE page-expression,
          row-expression,
          column-expression </ option(s)>;
RUN;
```

Examples of class variables are **Location**, **Gender**, and **JobCode**.

93

Class variables

- can be numeric or character
- identify classes or categories on which calculations are done
- represent discrete categories if they are numeric (for example, **Year**).

Specifying Analysis Variables

A VAR statement identifies variables to be used as analysis variables.

```
PROC TABULATE DATA=SAS-data-set <options>;
    CLASS class-variables;
    VAR analysis-variables;
    TABLE page-expression,
          row-expression,
          column-expression </ option(s)>;
RUN;
```

Examples of analysis variables are **Salary**, **CargoWt**, and **Revenue**.

94

Analysis variables

- are always numeric
- tend to be continuous
- are appropriate for calculating averages, sums, or other statistics.

Specifying Table Structure

A TABLE statement identifies table structure and format.

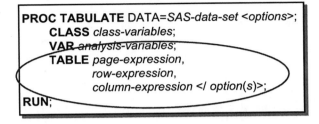

PROC TABULATE DATA=*SAS-data-set <options>*;
    CLASS *class-variables*;
    VAR *analysis-variables*;
    TABLE *page-expression*,
            row-expression,
            column-expression </ option(s)>;
RUN;

95

The TABLE Statement

You specify the table format and the desired statistics
with expressions in the TABLE statement.

A simple expression consists of elements and operators.

Elements include these items:

- variables
- statistics

96

TABLE statement operators control the format of the table. These operators include the following:

Operator	Action
Comma ,	Go to new table dimension.
Blank	Concatenate table information.
Asterisk *	Cross, nest, or subgroup information.

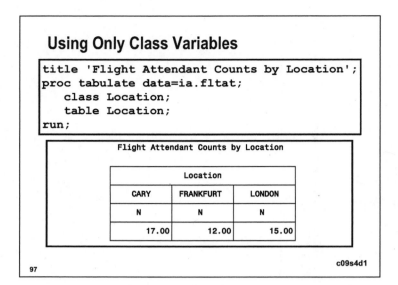

If there are only class variables in the TABLE statement, the default statistic is N, or the number of non-missing values.

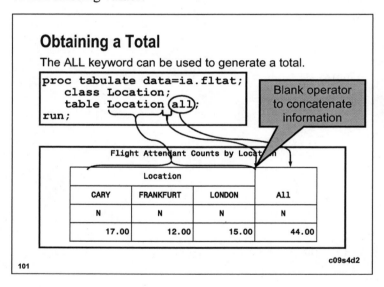

Two-Dimensional Tables

The comma in the TABLE statement directs the table
to move to a different dimension.

```
title2 'by JobCode';
proc tabulate data=ia.fltat;
   class Location JobCode;
   table JobCode, Location;
run;
```

Variables in the
dimension closest to
the column dimension
are in the row
dimension.

The comma
operator
moves to a
new dimension.

The variable closest
to the semicolon is
always in the column
dimension.

c09s4d3

104

Two-Dimensional Tables

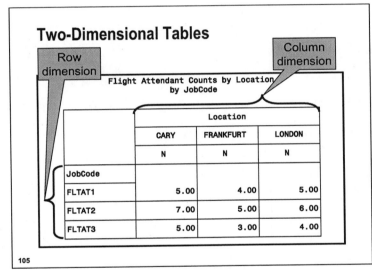

Row dimension

Column dimension

Flight Attendant Counts by Location
by JobCode

	Location		
	CARY	FRANKFURT	LONDON
	N	N	N
JobCode			
FLTAT1	5.00	4.00	5.00
FLTAT2	7.00	5.00	6.00
FLTAT3	5.00	3.00	4.00

105

Subsetting the Data

The WHERE statement can be used in PROC TABULATE
to subset the data.

```
title 'Counts for Cary and Frankfurt';
proc tabulate data=ia.fltat;
   where Location in ('CARY', 'FRANKFURT');
   class Location JobCode;
   table JobCode, Location;
run;
```

c09s4d4

106

Subsetting the Data

Counts for Cary and Frankfurt		
	Location	
	CARY	**FRANKFURT**
	N	N
JobCode		
FLTAT1	5.00	4.00
FLTAT2	7.00	5.00
FLTAT3	5.00	3.00

107

Two-Dimensional Tables

The ALL keyword generates a total for the dimension in which it is specified.

```
proc tabulate data=ia.fltat;
   where Location in ('CARY', 'FRANKFURT');
   class Location JobCode;
   table JobCode all, Location all;
run;
```

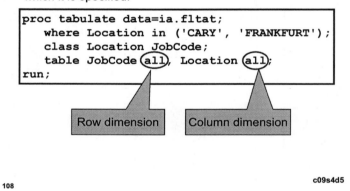

Row dimension   Column dimension

108   c09s4d5

Two-Dimensional Tables

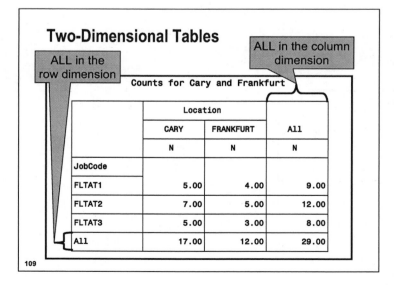

ALL in the row dimension

ALL in the column dimension

Counts for Cary and Frankfurt			
	Location		
	CARY	**FRANKFURT**	**All**
	N	N	N
JobCode			
FLTAT1	5.00	4.00	9.00
FLTAT2	7.00	5.00	12.00
FLTAT3	5.00	3.00	8.00
All	17.00	12.00	29.00

109

Using Analysis Variables

The asterisk (*) operator in the TABLE statement is used to nest information.

If there are analysis variables in the TABLE statement, the default statistic is SUM.

```
title 'Total Salary for Cary and Frankfurt';
proc tabulate data=ia.fltat;
   where Location in ('CARY', 'FRANKFURT');
   class Location JobCode;
   var Salary;
   table JobCode, Location*Salary;
run;
```

c09s4d6

110

Using Analysis Variables

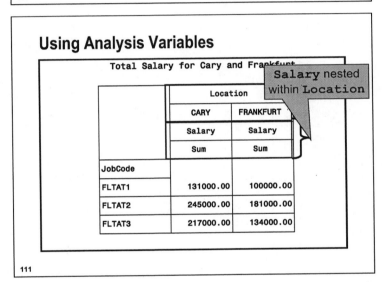

		Location	
		CARY	FRANKFURT
		Salary	Salary
		Sum	Sum
JobCode			
FLTAT1		131000.00	100000.00
FLTAT2		245000.00	181000.00
FLTAT3		217000.00	134000.00

Total Salary for Cary and Frankfurt

Salary nested within Location

111

Formatting the Statistic Data

To format the statistics in the cells, use the FORMAT= option in the PROC TABULATE statement.

```
proc tabulate data=ia.fltat format=dollar12;
   where Location in ('CARY', 'FRANKFURT');
   class Location JobCode;
   var Salary;
   table JobCode, Location*Salary;
run;
```

112   c09s4d7

🖋 The FORMAT **statement** can be used to control data values in the exterior of the report (values of the class variables).

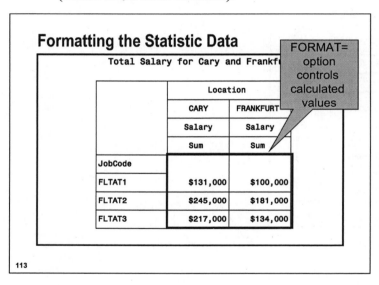

Formatting the Statistic Data

Total Salary for Cary and Frankf...

FORMAT=
option
controls
calculated
values

JobCode	Location	
	CARY	FRANKFURT
	Salary	Salary
	Sum	Sum
FLTAT1	$131,000	$100,000
FLTAT2	$245,000	$181,000
FLTAT3	$217,000	$134,000

113

Specifying a Statistic

To specify a different statistic in the cells, follow the analysis variable with the asterisk operator and the desired statistic.

```
title 'Average Salary for Cary and Frankfurt';
proc tabulate data=ia.fltat format=dollar12.;
   where Location in ('CARY', 'FRANKFURT');
   class Location JobCode;
   var Salary;
   table JobCode, Location*Salary*mean;
run;
```

c09s4d8

114

Selected statistics in PROC TABULATE include the following:

NMISS   number of missing observations

STD   standard deviation

MIN   minimum value

MAX   maximum value

RANGE   range of values

MEDIAN   middle value

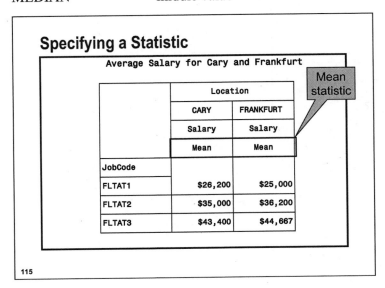

115

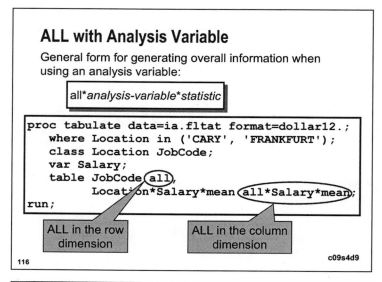

ALL with Analysis Variable

General form for generating overall information when using an analysis variable:

all*analysis-variable*statistic

```
proc tabulate data=ia.fltat format=dollar12.;
   where Location in ('CARY', 'FRANKFURT');
   class Location JobCode;
   var Salary;
   table JobCode all,
         Location*Salary*mean all*Salary*mean;
run;
```

ALL in the row dimension

ALL in the column dimension

116   c09s4d9

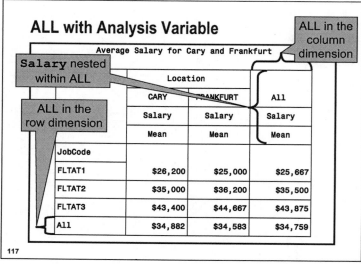

ALL with Analysis Variable

ALL in the column dimension

Average Salary for Cary and Frankfurt

Salary nested within ALL

ALL in the row dimension

	Location		All
	CARY	FRANKFURT	
	Salary	Salary	Salary
	Mean	Mean	Mean
JobCode			
FLTAT1	$26,200	$25,000	$25,667
FLTAT2	$35,000	$36,200	$35,500
FLTAT3	$43,400	$44,667	$43,875
All	$34,882	$34,583	$34,759

117

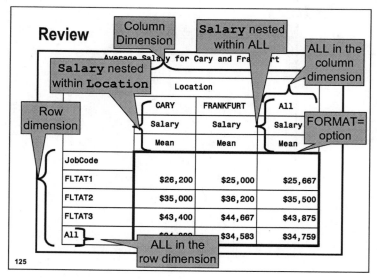

Review

Column Dimension

Salary nested within ALL

ALL in the column dimension

Average Salary for Cary and Frankfurt

Salary nested within Location

Row dimension

FORMAT= option

	Location		All
	CARY	FRANKFURT	
	Salary	Salary	Salary
	Mean	Mean	Mean
JobCode			
FLTAT1	$26,200	$25,000	$25,667
FLTAT2	$35,000	$36,200	$35,500
FLTAT3	$43,400	$44,667	$43,875
All		$34,583	$34,759

ALL in the row dimension

125

 **Exercises**

10. **Creating a One-Dimensional Frequency Report**

    Use PROC TABULATE and the `ia.employees` data set to produce a summary report that displays a frequency count for the variable **Division** with an appropriate title.

    PROC TABULATE Output

Counts by Division				
Division				
AIRPORT OPERATIONS	CORPORATE OPERATIONS	CORPORATE PLANNING	FINANCE & IT	FLIGHT OPERATIONS
N	N	N	N	N
131.00	6.00	1.00	65.00	143.00

(Continued)

Counts by Division	
Division	
HUMAN RESOURCES	SALES & MARKETING
N	N
101.00	53.00

✏ Depending on the width of your page, the report might span two separate pages, as shown in the output above.

11. Creating a Two-Dimensional Frequency Report

Modify the previous report to do the following:

- subset the data to only display divisions that have the word OPERATIONS in the name
- display the variable `City` in the row dimension
- add row and column totals
- add an appropriate title

PROC TABULATE Output

	Division			
	AIRPORT OPERATIONS	CORPORATE OPERATIONS	FLIGHT OPERATIONS	All
	N	N	N	N
City				
ATLANTA	.	1.00	.	1.00
AUSTIN	3.00	.	1.00	4.00
BRUSSELS	2.00	.	.	2.00
CARY	81.00	2.00	116.00	199.00
COPENHAGEN	8.00	.	.	8.00
FRANKFURT	10.00	.	13.00	23.00
GENEVA	2.00	.	.	2.00
LONDON	4.00	1.00	7.00	12.00
PARIS	5.00	.	.	5.00
PHOENIX	.	1.00	.	1.00
ROCKVILLE	3.00	.	.	3.00
ROME	3.00	.	.	3.00
SYDNEY	3.00	.	2.00	5.00
TOKYO	3.00	.	2.00	5.00
TORONTO	4.00	1.00	2.00	7.00
All	131.00	6.00	143.00	280.00

Counts for Operations Divisions

12. Creating a Report on an Analysis Variable

Modify the previous report to do the following:

- display the mean of the variable **Salary** in the column dimension
- display the overall mean of the variable **Salary** in the column dimension
- display the data with dollar signs, commas, and no digits after the decimal point
- add an appropriate title

PROC TABULATE Output

Average Salaries for Operations Divisions

City	| Division			| All
	AIRPORT OPERATIONS	CORPORATE OPERATIONS	FLIGHT OPERATIONS	All
	Salary	Salary	Salary	Salary
	Mean	Mean	Mean	Mean
ATLANTA	.	$105,000	.	$105,000
AUSTIN	$31,333	.	$22,000	$29,000
BRUSSELS	$27,000	.	.	$27,000
CARY	$30,988	$105,000	$32,224	$32,452
COPENHAGEN	$31,750	.	.	$31,750
FRANKFURT	$28,500	.	$34,000	$31,609
GENEVA	$36,000	.	.	$36,000
LONDON	$30,500	$125,000	$45,000	$46,833
PARIS	$29,400	.	.	$29,400
PHOENIX	.	$95,000	.	$95,000
ROCKVILLE	$26,333	.	.	$26,333
ROME	$37,333	.	.	$37,333
SYDNEY	$36,000	.	$28,500	$33,000
TOKYO	$24,333	.	$37,500	$29,600
TORONTO	$34,250	$85,000	$18,000	$36,857
All	$30,893	$103,333	$32,762	$33,400

13. Creating a Report Using HTML (Optional)

Modify the previous report to output the report to an HTML file.

PROC TABULATE Output

The SAS System				
	Division			**All**
	AIRPORT OPERATIONS	**CORPORATE OPERATIONS**	**FLIGHT OPERATIONS**	
	Salary	**Salary**	**Salary**	**Salary**
	Mean	**Mean**	**Mean**	**Mean**
City				
ATLANTA	.	$105,000	.	$105,000
AUSTIN	$31,333	.	$22,000	$29,000
BRUSSELS	$27,000	.	.	$27,000
CARY	$30,988	$105,000	$32,224	$32,452
COPENHAGEN	$31,750	.	.	$31,750
FRANKFURT	$28,500	.	$34,000	$31,609
GENEVA	$36,000	.	.	$36,000
LONDON	$30,500	$125,000	$45,000	$46,833
PARIS	$29,400	.	.	$29,400
PHOENIX	.	$95,000	.	$95,000
ROCKVILLE	$26,333	.	.	$26,333
ROME	$37,333	.	.	$37,333
SYDNEY	$36,000	.	$28,500	$33,000
TOKYO	$24,333	.	$37,500	$29,600
TORONTO	$34,250	$85,000	$18,000	$36,857
All	$30,893	$103,333	$32,762	$33,400

9.5 Solutions to Exercises

1. **Creating Frequency Reports**

   a.
   ```
   proc freq data=ia.sanfran;
      tables DepartDay;
      title 'Flights from San Francisco by Day of Week';
   run;
   ```

   b.
   ```
   proc freq data=ia.sanfran;
      tables Destination;
      title 'Flights from San Francisco';
   run;
   ```

   c. (Optional)
   ```
   proc freq data=ia.sanfran;
      tables Destination / nocum;
   run;
   ```

   d.
   ```
   proc freq data=ia.sanfran;
      tables Destination*DepartDay;
   run;
   ```

2. **Validating Data with PROC FREQ (Optional)**

   a.
   ```
   proc freq data=ia.mechanics;
      tables Gender JobCode;
   run;
   ```

   1) What do you notice about the values of the variable **Gender**? There is a **B** and a **G**.

   2) What do you notice about the values of the variable **JobCode**? There is a missing value.

   b.
   ```
   proc freq data=ia.mechanics;
      tables Gender*JobCode;
   run;
   ```

   What are the **JobCode** values for the invalid values of **Gender**? The **B** is a MECH02; the **G** is a MECH03.

3. **Creating Basic Summary Reports**

    a.

    ```
    title;
    proc means data=ia.sanfran;
       var CargoRev TotPassCap;
    run;
    ```

    b.

    ```
    proc means data=ia.sanfran maxdec=2;
       var CargoRev TotPassCap;
       class Destination;
    run;
    ```

4. **Requesting Specific Statistics through PROC MEANS (Optional)**

    ```
    proc means data=ia.sanfran min max mean maxdec=2;
       var CargoRev TotPassCap;
       class Destination;
    run;
    ```

5. **Creating HTML Output (Optional)**

    ```
    ods html file='means.html';
    proc means data=ia.sanfran min max mean maxdec=2;
       var CargoRev TotPassCap;
       class Destination;
    run;
    ods html close;
    ```

6. **Creating a List Report**

    ```
    title 'Employee Salary Data';
    proc report data=ia.employees nowd;
       column Division City Salary;
       define Division / order width=20 'Division Name';
       define City /  width=13 'City Based';
       define Salary / format=dollar14.;
    run;
    ```

7. **Creating a Sorted List Report (Optional)**

    ```
    proc report data=ia.employees nowd;
       column Division City Salary;
       define Division / order width=20 'Division Name';
       define City / order width=13 'City Based';
       define Salary / format=dollar14.;
    run;
    ```

8. **Creating a Summary Report**

```
title 'Employee Salary Data by Division / City';
proc report data=ia.employees nowd;
   column Division City Salary;
   define Division / group width=20 'Division Name';
   define City / group width=13 'City Based';
   define Salary / format=dollar14.;
run;
```

9. **Adding a Grand Total to the Report**

```
title 'Employee Salary Data by Division / City';
proc report data=ia.employees nowd;
   column Division City Salary;
   define Division / group width=20 'Division Name';
   define City / group width=13 'City Based';
   define Salary / format=dollar14.;
   rbreak after / summarize ol dul;
run;
```

10. **Creating a One-Dimensional Frequency Report**

```
title 'Counts by Division';
proc tabulate data=ia.employees;
   class Division;
   table Division;
run;
```

11. **Creating a Two-Dimensional Frequency Report**

```
title 'Counts for Operations Divisions';
proc tabulate data=ia.employees;
   where Division contains 'OPERATIONS';
   class Division City;
   table City all, Division all;
run;
```

12. **Creating a Report on an Analysis Variable**

```
title 'Average Salaries for Operations Divisions';
proc tabulate data=ia.employees format=dollar10.;
   where Division contains 'OPERATIONS';
   class Division City;
   var Salary;
   table City all, Division*Salary*mean all*Salary*mean;
run;
```

13. **Creating a Report Using HTML (Optional)**

```
ods html file='tabulate.html';
proc tabulate data=ia.employees format=dollar10.;
   where Division contains 'OPERATIONS';
   class Division City;
   var Salary;
   table City all, Division*Salary*mean all*Salary*mean;
run;
ods html close;
```

Chapter 10 Introduction to Graphics Using SAS/GRAPH (Self-Study)

10.1 Producing Bar and Pie Charts

Objectives
- Produce high-resolution bar and pie charts.
- Control the device driver used by SAS/GRAPH to create output.
- Control the statistics displayed in the chart.

3

SAS/GRAPH software is required to produce the high-resolution charts and graphs created in this chapter.

Graphically Summarizing Data

You can use bar or pie charts to graphically display the following:
- distribution of a variable's values
- average value of a variable for different categories
- total value of a variable for different categories

4

Vertical Bar Chart

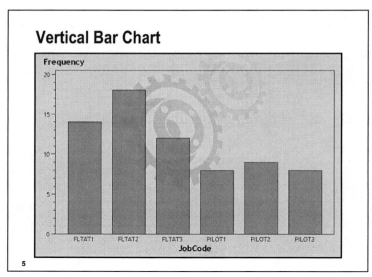

5

Horizontal Bar Chart

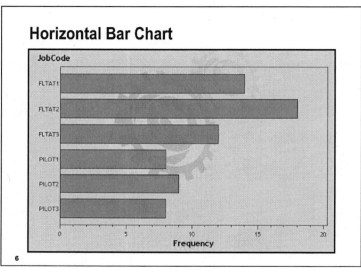

6

Pie Chart

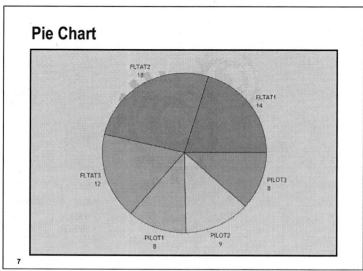

7

Specifying a Chart

When using the GCHART procedure, do the following:

- Specify the physical form of the chart.
- Identify a chart variable that determines the number of bars or pie slices to create.
- Optionally identify an analysis variable to use for calculating statistics that determine the height (or length) of the bar or the size of the slice.

By default, the height, length, or size represents a frequency count (N).

8

The GCHART Procedure

General form of the PROC GCHART statement:

PROC GCHART DATA=*SAS-data-set*;

Use one of these statements to specify the desired type of chart:

HBAR *chart-variable . . . </ options>*;
VBAR *chart-variable . . . </ options>*;
PIE *chart-variable . . . </ options>*;

9

Chart Variable

The chart variable

- determines the number of bars or slices produced within a graph
- can be character or numeric.

10

Vertical Bar Chart

Produce a vertical bar chart that displays the number of employees in each job code.

```
proc gchart data=ia.crew;
   vbar JobCode;
run;
```

JobCode is the chart variable.

11   c10s1d1

Vertical Bar Chart

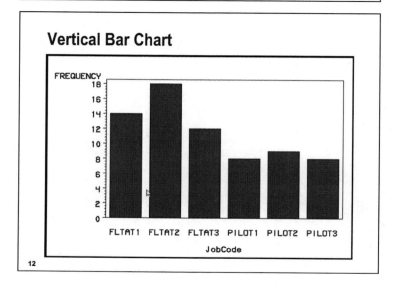

12

Specifying a Graphics Device Driver

You can route SAS/GRAPH output to a particular type of
graphics file or hardware device. To do so, specify
a graphics device driver in the GOPTIONS statement.

General form of the GOPTIONS statement:

> **GOPTIONS** *graphics-options*;

13

The GOPTIONS statement is a global statement that can be placed outside of DATA and PROC steps.
Initially, the GOPTIONS statement must be submitted prior to the GCHART procedure for the options
to be in effect for that graph. After the statement is submitted, it is in effect for the entire SAS session.

DEVICE= Option

The DEVICE= (or DEV=) graphics option in the
GOPTIONS statement specifies the device driver.

Examples:

Graphics Destination	GOPTIONS Statement
Windows display (default)	goptions dev=win;
UNIX display (default)	goptions dev=xcolor;
Windows color printer	goptions dev=winprtc;
UNIX gray scale printer	goptions dev=sasprtg;
GIF file	goptions dev=gif;
Windows Metafile	goptions dev=wmf;
JPEG file	goptions dev=jpg;

14

 There are many device drivers available. A list of device drivers can be found in the
sashelp.devices catalog.

DEVICE= Option

Some device drivers create graphics that use ODS styles
and provide Web-enabled data visualization capabilities.

Examples:

Type of Output	GOPTIONS Statement
ActiveX Control	`goptions dev=activex;`
ActiveX Image	`goptions dev=actximg;`
Java Applet	`goptions dev=java;`
Java Image	`goptions dev=javaimg;`

These drivers must be used with ODS and with a
compatible ODS destination.

15

  The ACTIVEX device driver generates interactive images for Microsoft Windows environments. Images created with this driver use the SAS/GRAPH Control for ActiveX to display interactive graphs in Web pages and OLE documents (in Microsoft Office products). The SAS/GRAPH Control for ActiveX is installed with SAS/GRAPH software on Windows systems. The control must be installed on each computer that needs to view it. If you want to publish SAS/GRAPH output for ActiveX on a Web server, you might need to install the control on your Web server.

You can generate similar images as static pictures using DEVICE= ACTXIMG. This approach does not require that the SAS/GRAPH Control for ActiveX be installed in order to view the graph.

The JAVA device driver generates interactive presentations that run in the Graph, Map, and Contour applets. The SAS/GRAPH Applets for Java are rendered by JavaScript code in an HTML file. The class files required for the applets are installed with SAS/GRAPH software. To view the graph, you open the HTML file in a Web browser that supports Java 1.1.4 or higher. If you plan to distribute your output HTML files to others, your SAS/GRAPH program might have to specify archive information that any viewing browser can use to find the class files needed to render the client graphs.

You can generate similar images as static pictures using DEVICE=JAVAIMG. This approach does not require that your program specify archive information in order for the viewing browser to display the graph.

Vertical Bar Chart

Modify the vertical bar chart to create a static image using the default ODS style within an HTML document.

```
ods html file='vbar.html';
goptions dev=javaimg;

proc gchart data=ia.crew;
    vbar JobCode;
run;

ods html close;
```

c10s1d2

16

Vertical Bar Chart

17

Horizontal Bar Chart

Produce a horizontal bar chart that displays the number of employees in each job code.

```
goptions reset=all;

proc gchart data=ia.crew;
   hbar JobCode;
run;
```

JobCode is the chart variable.

18   c10s1d3

GOPTIONS RESET=ALL resets all graphic options to their default settings, including the device driver.

Horizontal Bar Chart

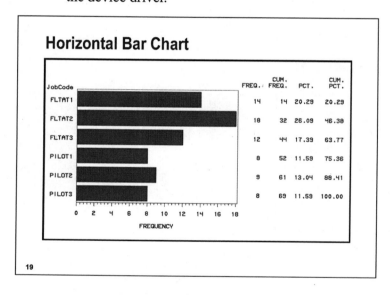

19

Horizontal Bar Chart

Modify the horizontal bar chart code to create the graph
as an ActiveX control in an HTML document.

```
ods html file='hbar.html';
goptions dev=activex;

proc gchart data=ia.crew;
   hbar JobCode;
run;

ods html close;
```

c10s1d4

20

Horizontal Bar Chart

21

For horizontal bar charts generated with the Java and ActiveX device drivers, default statistics
are not generated.

Pie Chart

Produce a pie chart that displays the number of employees in each job code. Create the graph as a static image using the default ODS style within an HTML document.

```
ods html file='piechart.html';
goptions dev=actximg;

proc gchart data=ia.crew;
   pie JobCode;
run;

ods html close;
```

JobCode is the chart variable.

22   c10s1d5

Pie Chart

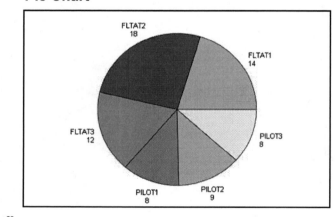

23

Character Chart Variable

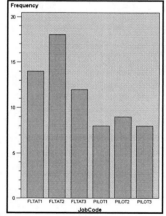

If the chart variable is character, a bar or slice is created for each unique variable value.

The chart variable is **JobCode**.

24

Numeric Chart Variable

For numeric chart variables, the variables are assumed to be continuous unless otherwise specified.

Intervals are automatically calculated and identified by midpoints.

One bar or slice is constructed for each midpoint.

25

Numeric Chart Variable

Produce a vertical bar chart on the numeric variable `Salary`.

```
ods html file='salary1.html';
goptions dev=actximg;

proc gchart data=ia.crew;
    vbar Salary;
run;

ods html close;
```

`Salary` is the chart variable.

c10s1d6

26

Numeric Chart Variable

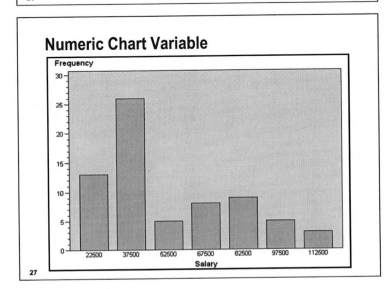

27

The DISCRETE Option

To override the default behavior for numeric chart variables, use the DISCRETE option in the HBAR, VBAR, or PIE statement.

The DISCRETE option produces a bar or slice for each unique numeric variable value; the values are no longer treated as intervals.

28

Numeric Chart Variable

Produce a vertical bar chart that displays a separate bar for each distinct value of the numeric variable **Salary**.

```
ods html file='Salary2.html';
goptions dev=actximg;

proc gchart data=ia.crew;
   vbar Salary / discrete;
run;

ods html close;
```

Salary is the chart variable, but the DISCRETE option modifies how SAS displays the values.

29   c10s1d7

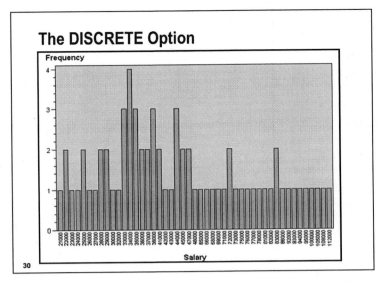

The DISCRETE Option

In this example, using intervals instead of discrete values produces a more meaningful chart.

The DISCRETE option is typically used for numeric chart variables that have only a small number of distinct values.

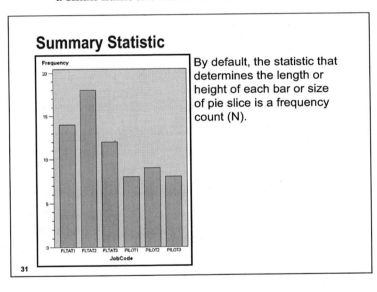

Summary Statistic

By default, the statistic that determines the length or height of each bar or size of pie slice is a frequency count (N).

Analysis Variable

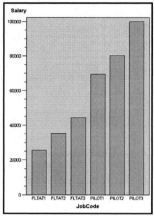

To override the default frequency count, you can use the following HBAR, VBAR, or PIE statement options:

> SUMVAR=*analysis-variable*
> TYPE=MEAN | SUM

32

SUMVAR= and TYPE= Options

SUMVAR=	identifies the analysis variable to use for the sum or mean calculation.
TYPE=	specifies that the height or length of the bar or size of the slice represents a mean or sum of the *analysis-variable* values.

If an analysis variable is
- specified, the default value of TYPE is SUM
- not specified, the default value of TYPE is FREQ.

33

Using an Analysis Variable

Produce a vertical bar chart that displays the average salary of employees in each job code.

```
ods html file='vbar2.html';
goptions dev=actximg;

proc gchart data=ia.crew;
   vbar JobCode / sumvar=Salary
                  type=mean;
run;

ods html close;
```

34   c10s1d8

PROC GCHART Output

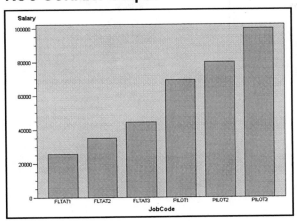

35

RUN-Group Processing

PROC GCHART supports RUN-group processing, which means that the following are true:

- The procedure executes the group of statements following the PROC statement when a RUN statement is encountered.
- Additional statements followed by another RUN statement can be submitted without resubmitting the PROC statement.
- The procedure stays active until a PROC, DATA, or QUIT statement is encountered.

36

Pie Chart

Produce a pie chart that displays the total salary of all employees in each job code.

```
ods html file='piechart.html';
goptions dev=actximg;

proc gchart data=ia.crew;
   pie JobCode / sumvar=Salary type=sum;
   format Salary dollar8.;
run;
```

c10s1d9

37

Pie Chart

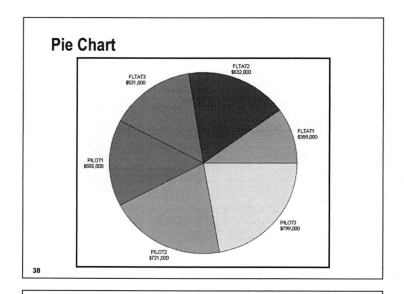

38

Pie Chart

You can use the FILL= option to specify whether to
fill the pie slices in a solid (FILL=S) or crosshatched
(FILL=X) pattern.

```
goptions dev=gif;
   pie JobCode / sumvar=Salary type=sum
                 fill=x;
   format Salary dollar8.;
run;
```

39   c10s1d9

🖉   PROC GCHART supports RUN-group processing, so it is unnecessary to resubmit
      the PROC GCHART statement.

🖉   The FILL= option is not supported by ACTIVEX and JAVA device drivers.

Pie Chart

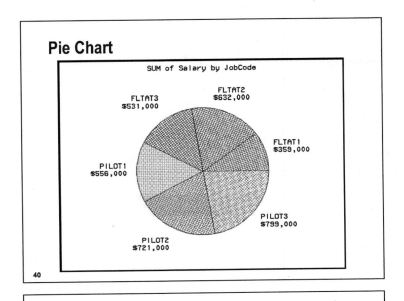

40

Exploding a Pie Slice

You can highlight individual slices of a pie chart by moving them away from the rest of the pie with the EXPLODE= option.

```
goptions dev=javaimg;
   pie JobCode / sumvar=Salary type=sum
                 explode='PILOT3';
   format Salary dollar8.;
run;
quit;
ods html close;
```

c10s1d9

41

A QUIT statement was added to the PROC GCHART code to enable SAS to stop processing the procedure.

Exploding a Pie Slice

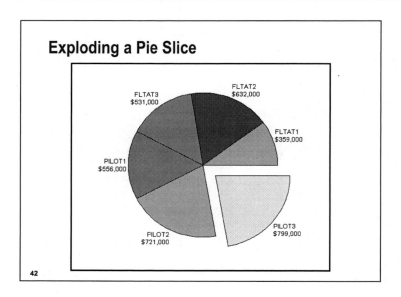

42

10.2 Enhancing Output

Objectives

- Apply an ODS style to enhance graph appearance.
- Incorporate titles and footnotes with graphs.
- Enhance graphs using color, fonts, and titles and footnotes of different sizes.

44

Apply an ODS Style

You can use ODS styles to enhance the appearance of your graphical output. The styles provide a consistent look and visual theme.

To use a style, specify the STYLE= option in an ODS statement that generates HTML output and specify an ActiveX or Java driver.

```
ods html file='piechart2.html'
         style=gears;
goptions dev=actximg;
```

c10s2d1

45

To view the list of available styles, submit the following code:

```
proc template;
   list styles;
run;
```

Apply an ODS Style

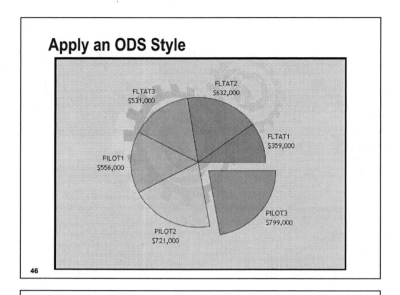

46

Adding Titles and Footnotes

You can use TITLE and FOOTNOTE statement options to modify the characteristics of text strings.

Selected options:

COLOR=color | C=color
FONT=type-font | F=type-font
HEIGHT=n | H=n

47

COLOR=   names the color to use for the text that follows the option. The default depends on the device.

FONT=   identifies the font to use for the text that follows the option. Valid fonts depend on the device driver specified. The default font also depends on the device, and possibly on ODS options. For devices other than ActiveX and Java, the default is SWISS for TITLE1 and the hardware character set for all other titles and all footnotes.

HEIGHT=   specifies the height of the characters in text that follows the option. Units of H=n can be in CELLS (default), inches (IN), centimeters (CM), or percent (PCT) of the display.

All title and footnote options must precede the quoted text string.

For ActiveX and Java drivers, TITLE and FOOTNOTE statements are produced by ODS, not the driver itself. Defaults are therefore dependent on ODS settings.

Title and Footnote Options

Examples:

```
title color=green 'Number of Pilots by Job Level';
title font=brush color=red  'March Flights';
title height=3 in  font=duplex 'Flights to RDU';
footnote height=3 "IA's Gross Revenue by Region";
footnote height=3 cm 'Average Salary by Job Level';
footnote height=3 pct 'Total Flights by Model';
```

48

Adding Titles and Footnotes

Add a title and footnote to the pie chart.

```
title1 h=.25 in c=green
        'Total Salary by Job Code';
footnote1 h=.2 in c=orange f=arial
         'Confidential';
   pie JobCode / sumvar=Salary type=sum
                 explode='PILOT3';
   format salary dollar8.;
run;
```

c10s2d1

49

Adding Titles and Footnotes

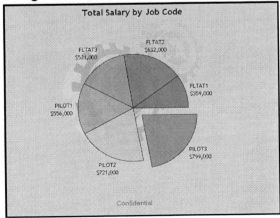

50

 **Exercises**

1. **Producing Vertical Bar Charts and Pie Charts**

    Use the **ia.personl** data set and a WHERE statement to produce the charts requested below for the ticket agents. (Note that the last character in the data set name is the lowercase letter l not the numeral 1.) The **JobCode** values are TA1, TA2, and TA3.

    ```
    where JobCode in ('TA1', 'TA2', 'TA3');
    ```

    a. Produce a vertical bar chart that displays the number of male and female ticket agents. (**Gender** values are M and F.)

    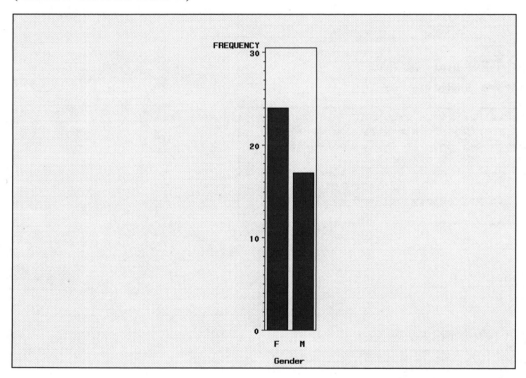

b. Modify the code to route the result to an ActiveX image within an HTML document. Add an appropriate title.

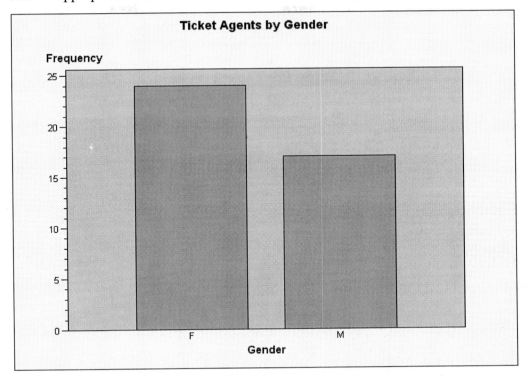

c. Create a pie chart to compare salaries of each ticket agent job level. Each pie slice should represent the average salary for one of the three **JobCode** values. Send the output to an HTML document containing the pie chart as a static JAVA image. Use the banker ODS style, and add an appropriate title. Explore the interactivity of the graph in the completed HTML document.

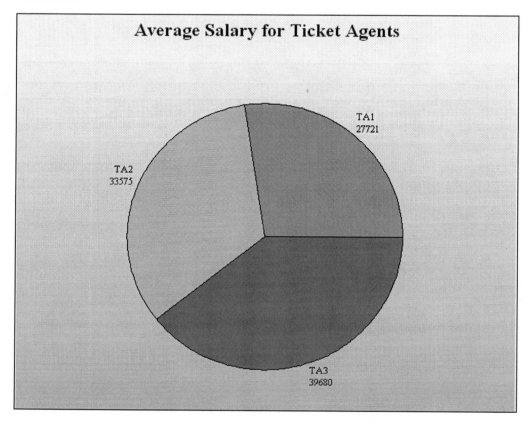

d. Enhance the pie chart by exploding the slice that represents the TA3 value of **JobCode**.
Change the font color for the title to red.

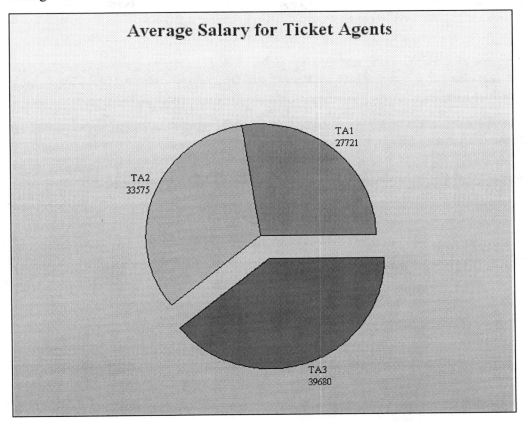

2. Producing a Horizontal Bar Chart (Optional)

Use the **ia.chicago** data set to produce a horizontal bar chart that displays the total number of passengers boarded (**Boarded**) each day of the week. Create a new variable, **Day**, which contains the day of the week, where 1 represents Sunday, 2 represents Monday, and so on.

- Place an appropriate title on the chart.
- Use the label **Day of the Week** for the variable **Day** and the label **Passengers** for the variable **Boarded**.

If the chart did not generate seven bars, add the DISCRETE option to the HBAR statement and generate the chart again.

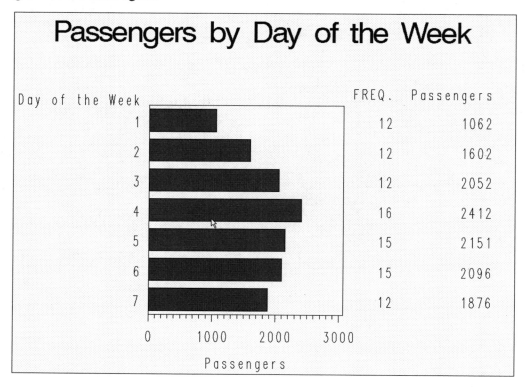

10.3 Producing Plots

Objectives

- Produce plots.
- Define plotting symbols.
- Control the appearance of the axes.

53

The GPLOT Procedure

You can use the GPLOT procedure to plot one variable against another within a set of coordinate axes.

General form of a PROC GPLOT step:

```
PROC GPLOT DATA=SAS-data-set;
    PLOT vertical-variable*horizontal-variable </ options>;
RUN;
QUIT;
```

54

The *vertical-variable* specifies the vertical axis variable. The *horizontal-variable* specifies the horizontal axis variable.

You can do the following:

- specify the symbols to represent data
- use different methods of interpolation
- specify line styles, colors, and thickness
- draw reference lines within the axes
- place one or more plot lines within the axes

    PROC GPLOT supports RUN-group processing. Use a QUIT statement to terminate the procedure.

PROC GPLOT Output

Produce a plot of the number of passengers by date for flight number 114 over a one-week period.

```
ods html file='plot.html' style=gears;
goptions dev=actximg;

proc gplot data=ia.flight114;
   where date between '02mar2001'd and
         '08mar2001'd;
   plot Boarded*Date;
   title 'Total Passengers for Flight 114';
   title2 'between 02Mar2001 and 08Mar2001';
run;
```

55   c10s3d1

PROC GPLOT Output

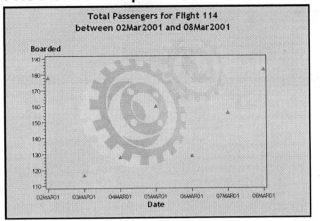

56

SYMBOL Statement

You can use the SYMBOL statement to do the following:

- define plotting symbols
- draw lines through the data points
- specify the color of the plotting symbols and lines

57

SYMBOL Statement

General form of the SYMBOL statement:

> **SYMBOL***n* options;

The value of *n* can range from 1 to 255.

If *n* is omitted, the default is 1.

58

SYMBOL Statement

SYMBOL statements have the following characteristics:

global	After they are defined, they remain in effect until changed or until the end of the SAS session.
additive	Specifying the value of one option does not affect the values of other options.

59

SYMBOL Statement Options

You can specify the plotting symbol that you want with the VALUE= option in the SYMBOL statement:

VALUE=_symbol_ | **V=**_symbol_

Selected _symbol_ values include the following:

PLUS	DIAMOND
STAR	TRIANGLE
SQUARE	NONE (no plotting symbol)

60

SYMBOL Statement Options

You can use the I= option in the SYMBOL statement to draw lines between the data points.

I=_interpolation_

Selected _interpolation_ values:

JOIN	joins the points with straight lines.
SPLINE	joins the points with a smooth line.
NEEDLE	draws vertical lines from the points to the zero point on horizontal axis.

61

SYMBOL Statement Options

Use a square as the plotting symbol and join the points
with straight lines.

```
   plot Boarded*Date;
   symbol value=square i=join;
run;
```

c10s3d1

62

PROC GPLOT supports RUN-group processing and is still running, so it is unnecessary
to resubmit the PROC GPLOT statement when you submit other PLOT statements.

The subsetting WHERE statement submitted earlier also remains in effect due to RUN-group
processing.

SYMBOL Statement Options

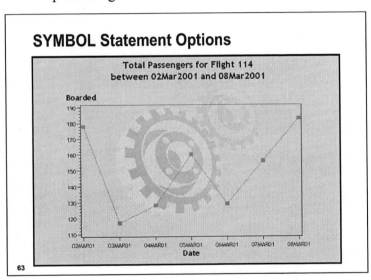

63

Additional SYMBOL Statement Options

You can enhance the appearance of the plots with the following selected options:

WIDTH=width **W=**width	specifies the thickness of the line.
COLOR=color **C=**color	specifies the symbol and line color.

64

Color and Width Options

Show the line in red with double thickness.

```
   plot Boarded*Date;
   symbol c=red w=2;
run;
```

65   c10s3d1

Previous options (**value=square** and **i=join**) are still in effect due to the additive characteristic of the SYMBOL statement.

Color and Width Options

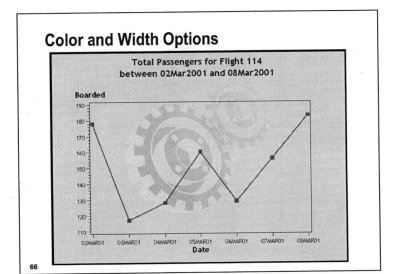

66

✎   The line appears in red with a width of 2.

Modifying the SYMBOL Statement

Set the attributes for SYMBOL1.

```
symbol1 c=blue v=diamond;
```

Modify only the color of SYMBOL1, not the V= option setting.

```
symbol1 c=green;
```

67

Canceling SYMBOL Statements

You can cancel a SYMBOL statement by submitting
a null SYMBOL statement.

```
symbol1;
```

To cancel all SYMBOL statements, submit the following
statement:

```
goptions reset=symbol;
```

68

Controlling the Axis Appearance

You can modify the appearance of the axes that
PROC GPLOT produces with the following:
- PLOT statement options
- the LABEL statement
- the FORMAT statement

69

PLOT Statement Options

You can use PLOT statement options to control the
scaling and color of the axes, and the color of the
axis text.

Selected PLOT statement options for axis control:

HAXIS=*values*	scales the horizontal axis.
VAXIS=*values*	scales the vertical axis.
CAXIS=*color*	specifies the color of both axes.
CTEXT=*color*	specifies the color of the text on both axes.

70

PLOT Statement Options

Define the scale on the vertical axis and display the
axis text in blue.

```
    plot Boarded*Date / vaxis=100 to 200 by 25
                        ctext=blue;
run;
```

c10s3d1

71

PLOT Statement Options

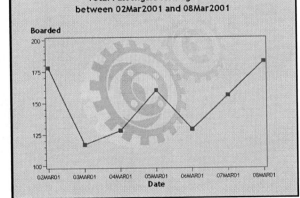

72

The line appears in red with a width of 2, and the axis text is blue.

Adding Labels

Place labels on the axes.

```
   plot Boarded*Date / vaxis=100 to 200 by 25
                       ctext=blue;
   label Boarded='Passengers Boarded'
         Date='Departure Date';
run;
quit;

ods html close;
```

73   c10s3d1

Adding Labels

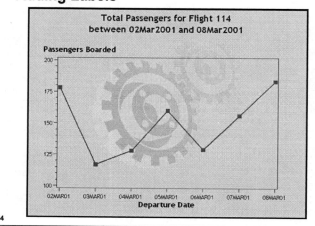

The axis text color is blue.

Exercises

3. Producing a Two-Dimensional Plot

The data set **ia.delay** contains dates and delays in minutes for International Airlines flights. Use the data set and an appropriate WHERE statement to select flights to Copenhagen (**Dest='CPH'**) and produce the plot described below:

- Create the plot as an ActiveX control within an HTML document.
- Use the ODS style named Normal.
- Plot the variable **Delay** on the vertical axis and the variable **Date** along the horizontal axis.
- Adjust the scale on the vertical axis to start at **-15** and end at **30** with a tick mark every **15** minutes.
- Display the title **Flights to Copenhagen** in red.
- Display the points as red squares.
- Use the NEEDLE interpolation technique to connect the points to the zero point on the horizontal axis.

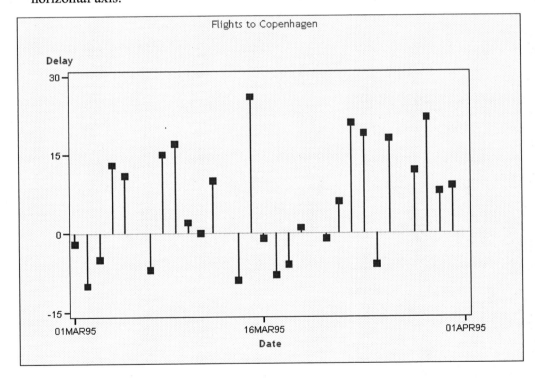

10.4 Solutions to Exercises

1. **Producing Vertical Bar Charts and Pie Charts**

   a.

   ```
   proc gchart data=ia.personl;
      where JobCode in ('TA1', 'TA2', 'TA3');
      vbar Gender;
   run;
   ```

   b.

   ```
   ods html file='MyBarChart.html';
   goptions dev=actximg;
   title 'Ticket Agents by Gender';
   proc gchart data=ia.personl;
      vbar gender;
      where jobcode in('TA1','TA2','TA3');
   run;

   quit;
   ods html close;
   ```

   c.

   ```
   ods html file='MyPieChart.html' style=banker;
   goptions dev=javaimg;
   title 'Average Salary for Ticket Agents';

   proc gchart data=ia.personl;
      pie JobCode/type=mean sumvar=salary;
      where jobcode in('TA1','TA2','TA3');
   run;
   quit;
   ods html close;
   ```

   d.

   ```
   ods html file='MyPieChart.html' style=banker;
   goptions dev=javaimg;
   title c=red 'Average Salary for Ticket Agents';

   proc gchart data=ia.personl;
      pie JobCode/type=mean sumvar=salary explode='TA3';
      where jobcode in('TA1','TA2','TA3');
   run;
   quit;
   ods html close;
   ```

2. **Producing a Horizontal Bar Chart (Optional)**

```
data chicago;
    set ia.chicago;
    Day=weekday(Date);
run;
proc gchart data=chicago;
    hbar Day / sumvar=Boarded type=sum discrete;
    label Boarded='Passengers';
    title c=blue 'Passengers by Day of the Week';
run;
```

3. **Producing a Two-Dimensional Plot**

```
goptions dev=activex;
ods html file='myplot.html' style=normal;
proc gplot data=ia.delay;
    where Dest='CPH';
    plot Delay*Date / vaxis = -15 to 30 by 15;
    title c=red 'Flights to Copenhagen';
    symbol i=needle c=red v=square;
run;
quit;
ods html close;
```

Chapter 11   Additional Resources

11.1 Where Do I Go from Here?

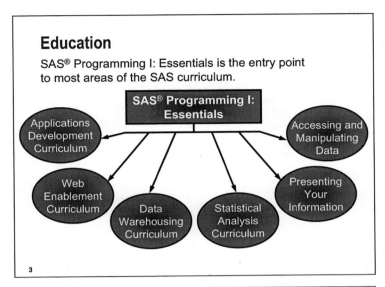

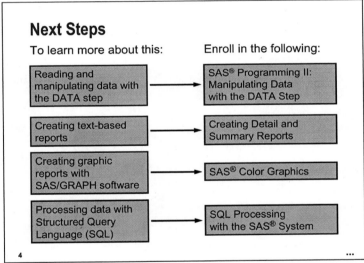

SAS Certified Professional Program

Consider taking a certification exam to assess your knowledge of SAS software. For a current listing of certification exams and registration information, visit support.sas.com/certify.

5

11.2 SAS Resources

Services

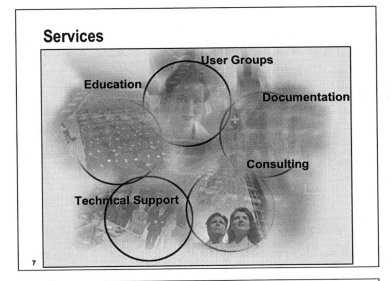

Education

Computer-based:
- e-Learning

Conferences:
- Data Mining Technology Conference

Education

Refer to the SAS Training Web site for more information on these classes and the broad curriculum of courses available.

support.sas.com/training

9

SAS Training Home Page

support.sas.com/training/us

10

100% Customer Satisfaction Guarantee

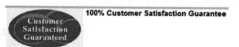

At SAS Education, satisfaction is 100% guaranteed.

"At SAS Education we take great pride in the fact that our customers consistently rank our training as excellent. That's no accident. From the moment you register, during your training, and even after you're back at work, we strive to provide you with the highest level of customer care possible. Our goal is to help you learn how to use SAS more effectively. So, if you're not satisfied with your training experience, let us know and we will make things right. I promise."

Dr. Herbert J. Kirk, SAS Education Vice President

11

Value Beyond the Classroom

More than 2,100 SAS students who took training in the
first three months of 2006 were surveyed to determine
the impact of SAS training on their job performance. The
survey was given between 60 and 120 days on the job
after training to allow a fair judgment on how SAS training
might have helped them. Here are some results:

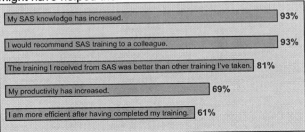

My SAS knowledge has increased.	93%
I would recommend SAS training to a colleague.	93%
The training I received from SAS was better than other training I've taken.	81%
My productivity has increased.	69%
I am more efficient after having completed my training.	61%

12

Consulting Services

Services provided include the following:
- knowledge transfer
- application development
- analytical consulting
- implement business solutions

13

Technical Support

Goals:
- Provide support to SAS users to solve any problems
  that they encounter when using SAS software.
- Free unlimited support.
- Local support at each site with a designated
  SAS consultant.

World Wide Web Services:
- Report/resolve problems
- Frequently asked questions
- SASware Ballot suggestions/results
- Download zaps/fixes/patches
- Upload code/data
- Search SAS notes
- Alert notes

14

Technical Support (North America)

Problem Tracking System

Telephone: 9:00 a.m. until 8:00 p.m. Eastern Time
Monday–Friday
(919) 677-8008

E-mail: support@sas.com – report problems
suggest@sas.com – software suggestions

Web: **support.sas.com/techsup/**

15

Documentation

Documenting SAS:
- Reference Guides
- Getting Started Guides
- User's Guides
- Companions
- Changes and Enhancements

Current products and services:
- Publications Catalog
- SAS Press
- Online Documentation

16

Documentation

Reference guides:
- SAS online documentation
- Delivered on a CD-ROM
- Shipped free with software
- Single copies available
- Hard-copy books to purchase

support.sas.com/documentation

17

SAS Publishing

support.sas.com > SAS Publishing

SAS Publishing

Home

Browse Bookstore

SAS Press Titles

SAS Documentation

Shrink-Wrap Software

New Books

Complete Catalog

Detailed Search

Browse SAS Publishing

New to SAS?

For Instructors

SAS Press Home

Available Soon!

Welcome to SAS Publishing

SAS Publishing is a global enterprise committed to providing SAS customers and prospects with the highest-quality resources for learning SAS. Here you'll find information about books, e-learning, online documentation and e-books that support SAS, the world's leader in business intelligence.

We look forward to assisting you in your pursuit of learning SAS. If you have questions or comments, please contact SAS Publishing at sasbook@sas.com

sas publishing

STARTING POINTS

New to SAS | For Instructors | SAS Press Home | e-Books | Resources | Contact Us

support.sas.com/publishing

18

User Groups

Benefits:

- Enhance your understanding of SAS software and services.
- Exchange ideas about using your software and hardware most productively.
- Learn of new SAS products and services as soon as they become available.
- Have more influence over the direction of SAS software and services.

19

International Users Groups

SAS Global Forum (formerly SUGI)
>   Annual conference held March or April in
>   North America

SAS Forum International (formerly SEUGI)
>   Annual conference held May or June in
>   Europe

SUGA (SAS Users Group of Australia)
>   Annual conference held August or September
>   in Australia

20

Regional User Groups

SESUG   Southeastern United States
NESUG   Northeastern United States
MWSUG   Midwestern United States
SCSUG   South-Central United States
WUSS   Western United States

All regional conferences are usually held in September or October.

21

Other Users Groups

Local   City or area user group. Often
                              hold multiple meetings per year.

Special Interest Industry-specific user groups.

In-house   Single organization or company
                              user group.

Worldwide   Most countries have their own
                              users groups.

support.sas.com/usergroups

22

Newsgroups

There is a newsgroup named **comp.soft-sys.sas**. This is a bulletin board for users to post questions, answers, and discuss SAS software.

To view this newsgroup, use any newsgroup viewer, such as **groups.google.com**.

23

Newsgroups

This newsgroup is also gated to a listserv. To subscribe
to the listserv, send e-mail to any of the mail servers:

- listserv@listserv.uga.edu   University of Georgia
- listserv@vm.marist.edu   Marist University
- listserv@listserv.vt.edu   Virginia Polytechnic
                                 University

- listserv@AKH-WIEN.AC.AT   University of Vienna

The subject line is ignored and the body should contain
the command: `subscribe sas-l your name`.
For example, `subscribe sas-l Tom Smith` is
how Tom Smith would subscribe.

24

Additional Information

Access the SAS Web site at **www.sas.com** to learn
more about available software, support, and services
and to take advantage of these offerings.

25

Appendix A Using SAS Enterprise Guide to Complete Exercises

A.1 Introduction

SAS Enterprise Guide is a software package that is designed to create reports and analyses using SAS via a point-and-click, drag-and-drop Windows interface. In many processing situations, knowledge of code and syntax is not required. However, SAS programmers can still include and develop their own code within the SAS Enterprise Guide interface. This appendix is intended for SAS programmers who will use SAS Enterprise Guide rather than the SAS Windowing Environment to develop SAS code.

This appendix documents the steps that are necessary to perform SAS Programming I course exercises within the SAS Enterprise Guide interface. In many instances, the same results that are achieved by the programs developed could be created without writing code using the interactive point-and-click menus in SAS Enterprise Guide. Because the goal of the Programming I course is to provide an introduction to SAS programming, this appendix will focus on the methods to achieve the results programmatically rather than interactively. However, Appendix B illustrates the point-and-click approach to creating the graphical results in Chapter 10 of the course.

This appendix was prepared using SAS Enterprise Guide 4.1. Menus and screens for other versions of SAS Enterprise Guide will differ somewhat.

A.2 Creating the Files Needed for the Course

1. If the SAS programming course that you are taking is being taught in a SAS public training center, then minimize all the applications that are open on your Windows desktop. If you are taking the course elsewhere, your instructor will provide instructions for accessing the course files.

2. Double-click on the Courseware icon. The Training System Application opens.

3. Within the list box of Available Courses, scroll down and select **SAS Programming I**. Select **OK**. This will launch the SAS®9 windowing environment, as well as load a series of data sets, programs, and raw data files to be used during the course. The default location for these files is c:\workshop\winsas\prog1.

4. From the menu in the upper-left corner of SAS®9, select **File** ⇨ **Exit**. You will use SAS Enterprise Guide and not the windowing environment for the course.

5. Return to the Training System for Windows Application and scroll to the course description **Querying and Reporting Using SAS Enterprise Guide.** Click on this entry and select **OK**. The Welcome to SAS Enterprise Guide window opens.

6. Select **New Project**.

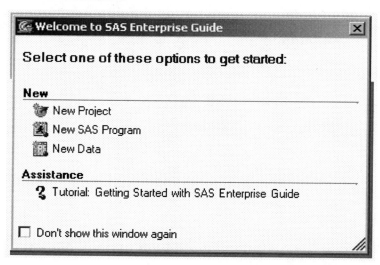

A.3 Understanding Functional Areas in SAS Enterprise Guide

When you select **New Project**, a display similar to the one shown below appears. By default, four major areas appear in the interface:

- Project Explorer
- Workspace
- Task List window
- Task Status window

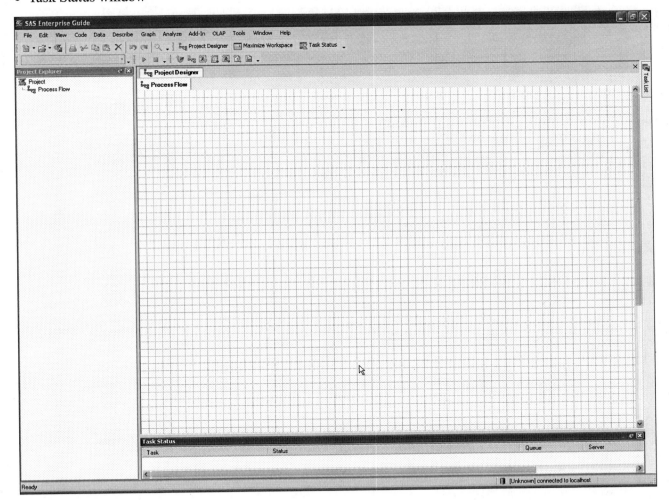

The Project Explorer keeps track of all the data sources, output, tasks, and programs that were created or used in the SAS Enterprise Guide project.

When SAS Enterprise Guide is opened, the Project Designer appears in the workspace by default. The Process Flow window in the Project Designer displays your data sources, tasks, programs, and output in a flow diagram format. When you execute a program, the results are automatically opened in the workspace as well, typically as HTML output. The code and log from different programs can also be displayed in this same area. Tabs at the top of the Workspace window correspond to each of the items that are open in the workspace and enable you to select the item that you want to view.

The Task List window at the right side of the display enables you to select and open one of the point-and-click task dialog boxes that are available in SAS Enterprise Guide. By default, this window is hidden or *pinned*. You can access it by moving your cursor over the Task List tab at the upper-right of the display.

🖋   This appendix does not address or explore the Task List window. All results created in this course are generated by typing and submitting SAS code, or by bringing existing SAS code into SAS Enterprise Guide.

The Task Status window is shown at the bottom of the interface. This window displays the status of any tasks that are currently running.

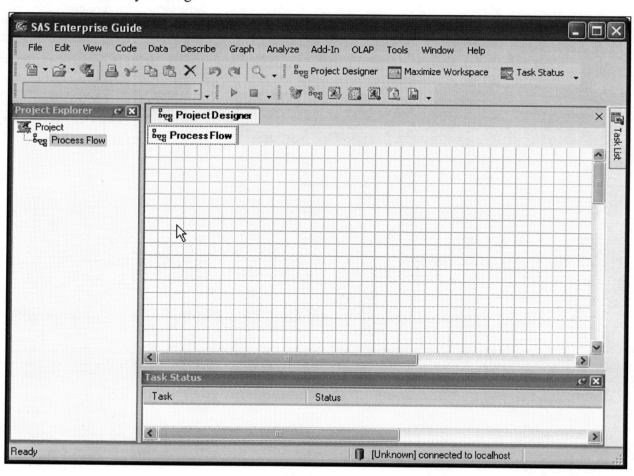

A.4 Naming the Project

1. From the menu bar, select **File** ⇨ **Save Project As...**.

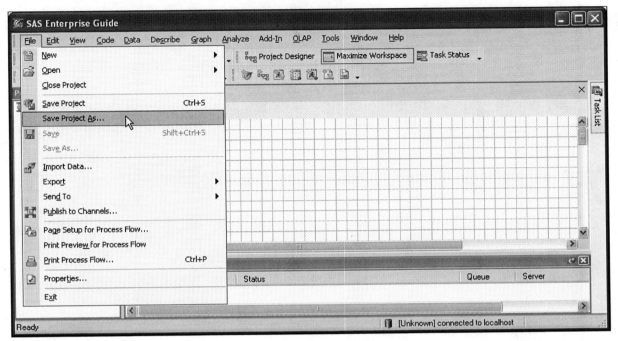

2. Save the project to your local computer by selecting **Local Computer** in the Save Project To dialog box.

3. In the Save As window, navigate to the default directory location for Programming I, (c:\workshop\winsas\prog1), or to the location specified by your instructor.

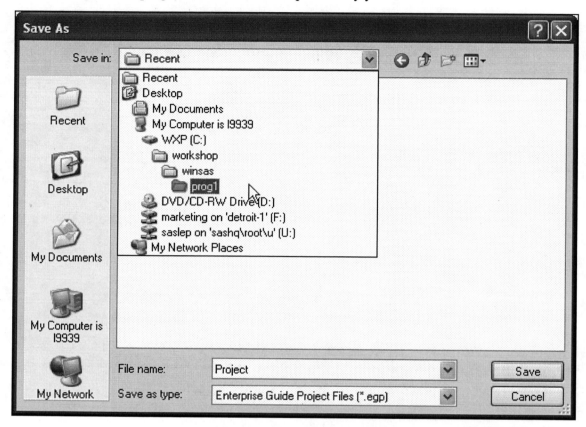

4. Type **Programming1** in the `File name` field as the name of the project, with **Enterprise Guide Project Files (*.egp)** selected as the type.

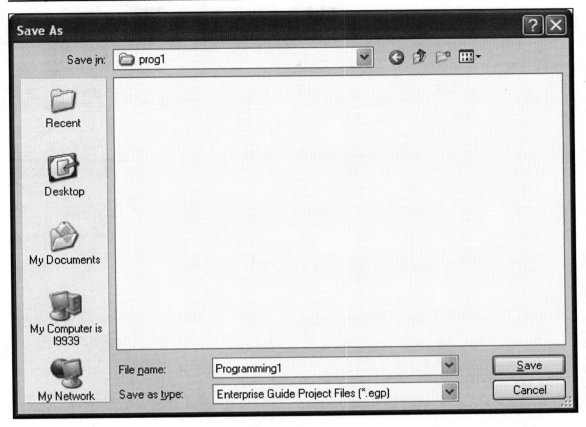

5. Select **Save**.

A.5 Working with Existing Code

Bring a SAS Programming I demonstration into SAS Enterprise Guide, execute the code, and look at the log and the results.

1. From the menu bar, select **File** ⇨ **Open** ⇨ **Code...**.

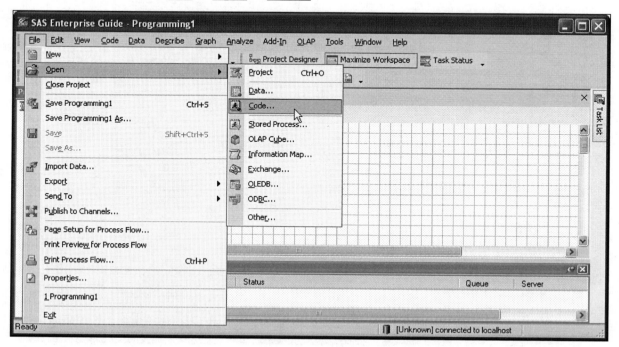

2. In the Open Code From dialog box, select **Local Computer**.

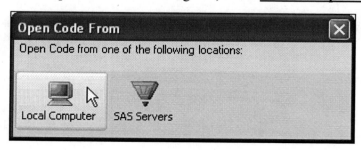

3. In the Open From My Computer window, navigate in the drop-down list box to the location where the Programming I programs are stored. The default directory location for the course is c:\workshop\winsas\prog1.

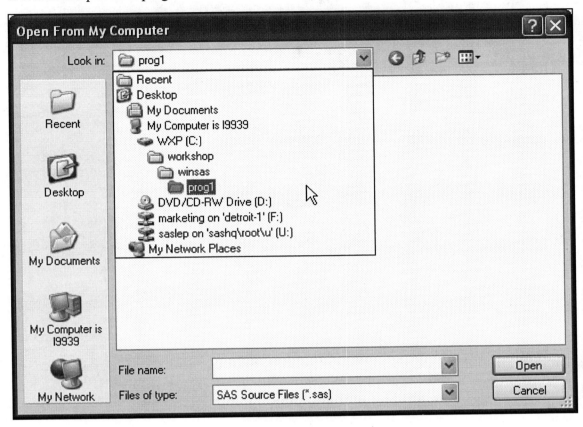

4.   Double-click on the program entry **c02s2d1.sas**. This is one of the demonstration programs used in Chapter 2 of the course. The name **c02s2d1** indicates Chapter 2, Section 2, Demonstration 1.

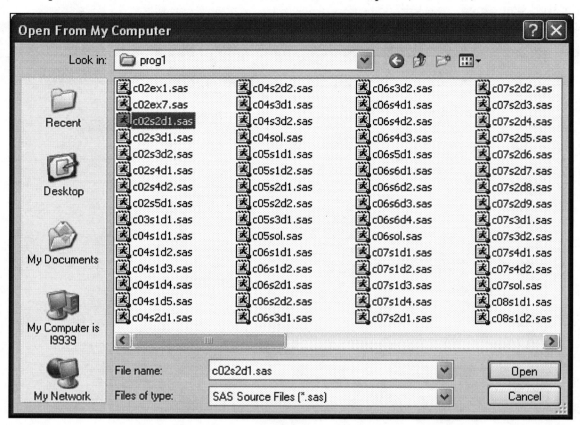

5.   Select **Open**.

After you select the program, an icon representing the program is added to the Project Explorer
and the code automatically appears in the workspace.

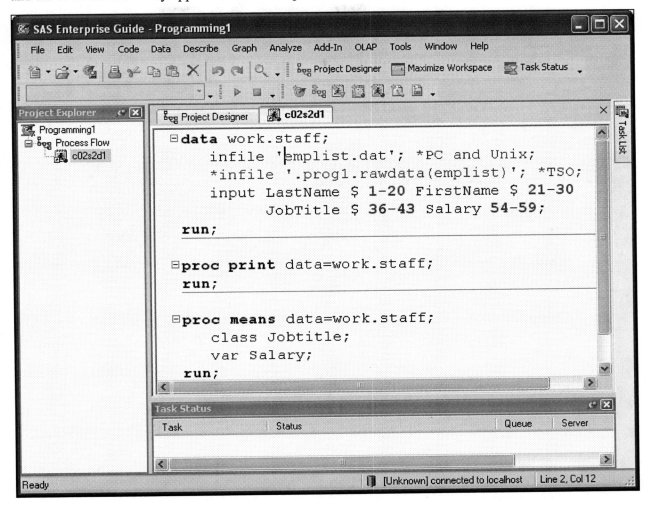

A.6 Resizing Windows in SAS Enterprise Guide

The size of the various windows can be increased or decreased in an SAS Enterprise Guide session. You might want to maximize the size of the workspace when you develop code or view results. To do so, click Maximize Workspace on the toolbar, or select **View** ⇨ **Maximize Workspace**.

When you maximize the workspace, windows other than the workspace will be *pinned* or hidden. Tabs corresponding to each of the pinned windows appear at the edge of the display. You can access a pinned window by moving your mouse over the tab for the window. The window remains accessible until you move your mouse beyond it.

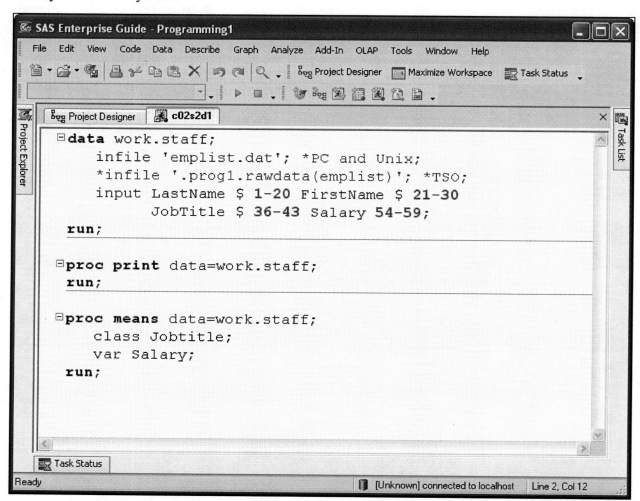

To restore the hidden windows, click again on the Maximize Workspace icon or select **View** ⇨ **Maximize Workspace**.

You can also manually resize individual windows using the resize handles that appear when the mouse is slowly moved over the border between two windows.

A.7 Modifying Demonstration Code

Before this program is executed, a change to the syntax is necessary. The SAS Programming I demonstrations are written to take advantage of a default directory location used by the traditional SAS windowing environment. In some situations, that default directory path is assumed and does not need to be specified in a program. However, SAS Enterprise Guide has a different default location than the windowing environment, which means that you must specify a full path in this code. Specifically, the filename specified in the INFILE statement of the program must be modified.

Add the appropriate path specification to the INFILE statement. This path should point to the location of your Programming I data files, and be entered within the quotation marks prior to the filename **emplist.dat**. The default path is c:\workshop\winsas\PROG1. Your instructor will indicate if you should use a different path.

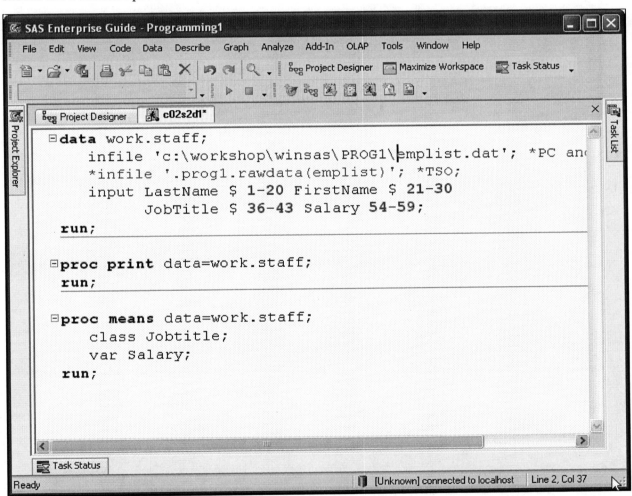

A.8 Executing SAS Code

1. To execute the modified code, right-click anywhere inside the code window displayed in the workspace.

2. A menu appears with a choice to **Run On** *your active server*. The default server is **SASMain**. The instructor will indicate if your server name is different.

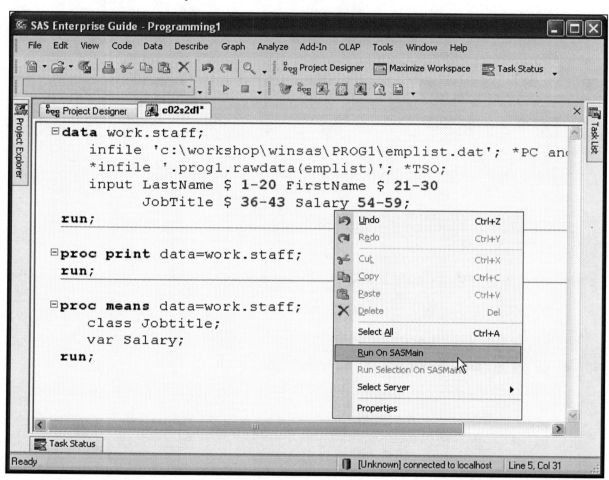

A.9 Viewing SAS Enterprise Guide Output

If the modified code executed correctly, the following HTML report appears in the workspace.

The first part of the report is the output of the PRINT procedure included in the program.

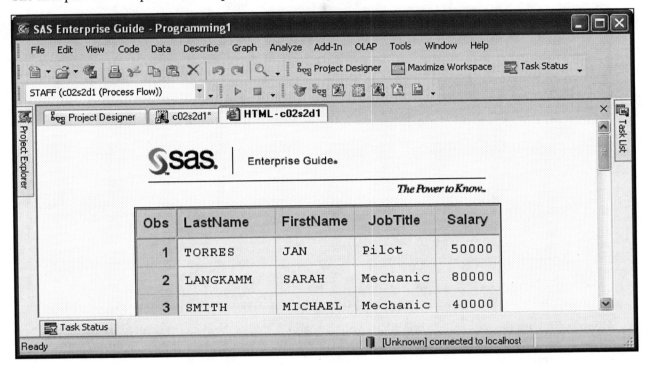

1. Scroll down in the HTML report displayed in the workspace to view the output created by the MEANS procedure in this SAS program.

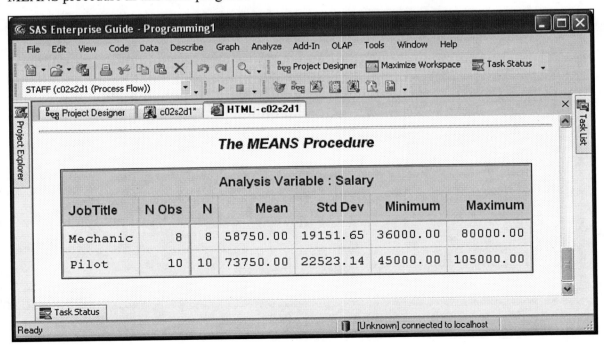

2. Click on the **Project Designer** tab at the top of the workspace to view the Process Flow window. The process flow for your project has two new entries in it. One represents the HTML report created by the program and the other represents a data set. The entry associated with the HTML report was viewed in the last slide.

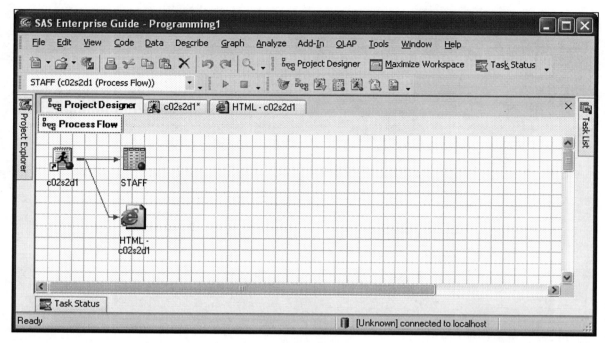

3. Double-click on the icon labeled **STAFF**. The data grid displays the data set created by the program c02s2d1.sas. The fields with red pyramids to the left of the column name are character variables. Blue circles, currency symbols, and calendar icons indicate numeric variables.

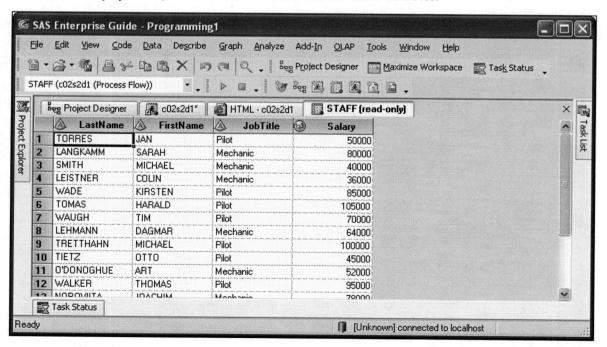

A.10 Diagnosing and Correcting Syntax Errors

A red X appears on the code icon in the Process Flow or Project Explorer windows when a syntax error occurs. When this happens, the error must be investigated and the code corrected.

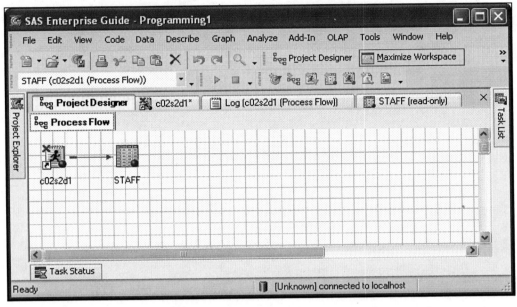

1. By default, SAS Enterprise Guide automatically displays the SAS log in the workspace when errors occur. View the log by selecting the tab labeled **Log** with the name of the program. You can scroll through the log to find errors. The log below indicates a single syntax error in the code. The default directory location for the Programming I course was typed incorrectly. It should be as follows:

```
infile 'c:\workshop\winsas\prog1\emplist.dat'
```

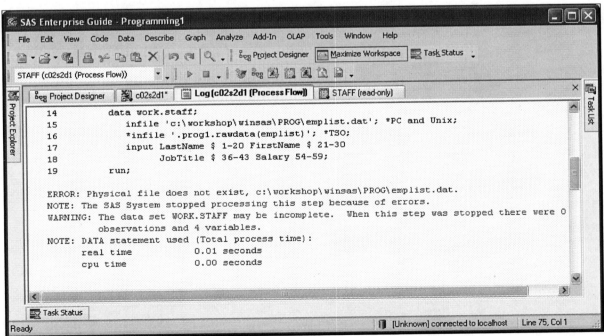

2. To correct the code, select the tab with the program name (**c02s2d1***) in the Project Designer window.
    If the code was closed in the Project Designer window, you can reopen it by double-clicking on the
    code icon in the Process Flow window or by right-clicking and selecting **Open**.

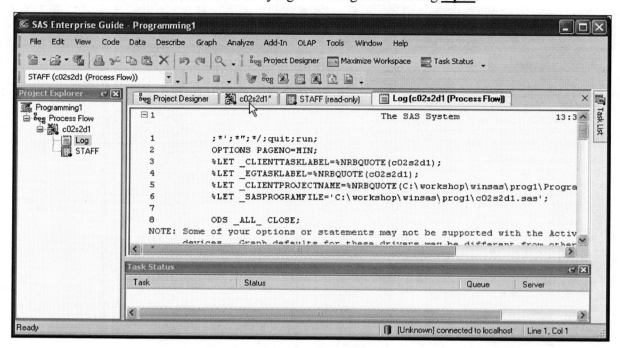

✎   Do not select **Open Last Submitted Code** instead of **Open** from the menu. This selection
      opens a read-only copy of the code as it was last submitted in SAS Enterprise Guide. If you
      try to edit the program, you will be asked if you want to create a modifiable version of the
      code. If you say yes, you will have two copies of the code in your project. Select **Open Last
      Submitted Code** only if you want to create a copy (for example, as the starting point for a
      new program) or if you want to view a read-only version of the code. Always select **Open**
      from the menu when you want to modify the existing code.

3. Make the required corrections to the code. Right-click on the code icon in the Process Flow window, or right-click anywhere inside the open code item in the workspace, as shown below, to execute the revised program.

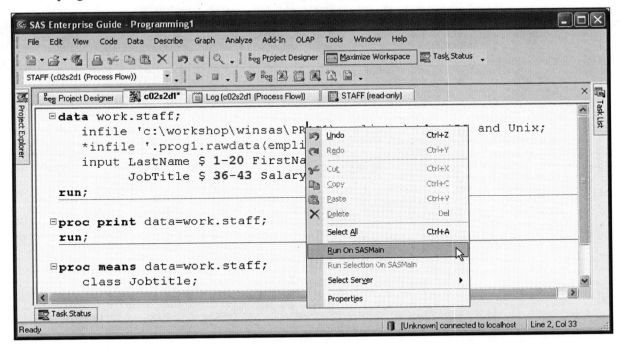

If the code is successfully changed and executed, then two new icons appear in the Process Flow window and an HTML report opens in the Work Area.

✎   If the program still did not execute correctly, get help from the instructor.

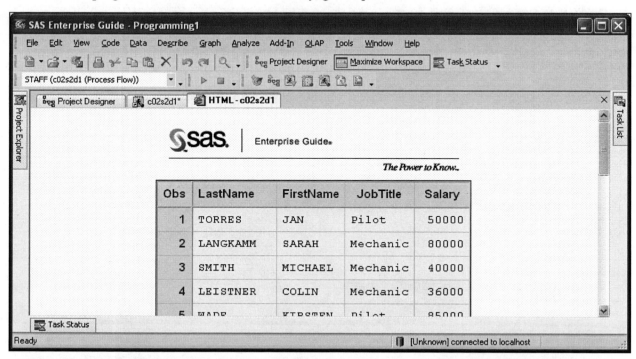

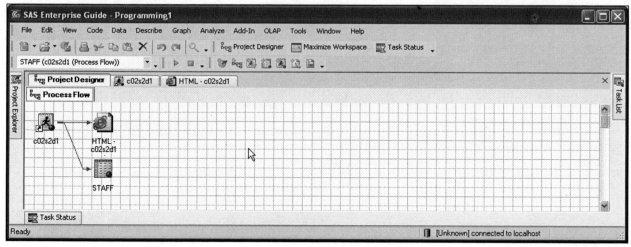

A.11 Creating SAS Programs to Complete Exercises

To complete exercises from various courses, students might be required to either modify existing sections of SAS code using methods presented earlier, or create a solution entirely by typing a SAS program.

1.   From the menu bar of SAS Enterprise Guide, select **File** ⇨ **New** ⇨ **Code**.

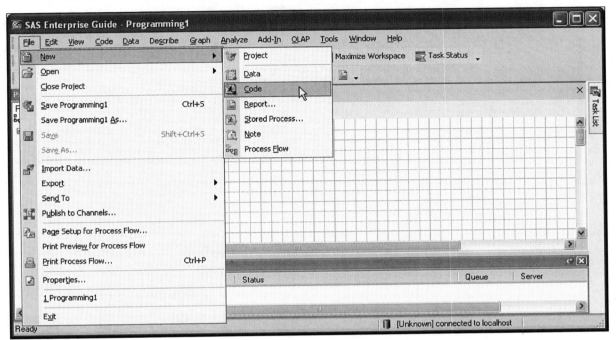

A new code window opens in the workspace.

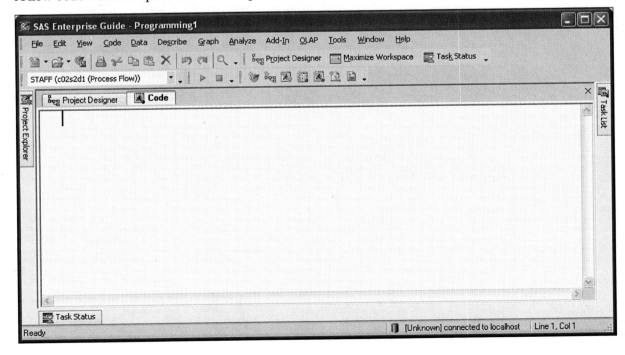

2. As in the Program Editor window of a SAS session, the programming statements for the new program can be typed into the code window. In this case, the code being entered is from Exercise 4 in Section 4.2 of the SAS Programming I course.

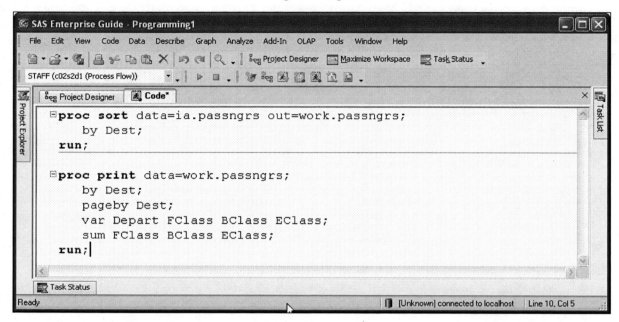

A.12 Accessing Data Sources with the LIBNAME Statement

The code for the program is almost complete, but one addition is required. The PROC SORT step is pointing to a data set stored in a SAS data library named IA. However, this library was not defined in the SAS Enterprise Guide session. A LIBNAME statement must be added to define this library. The LIBNAME statement for the SAS Programming 1 course is as follows:

```
libname ia 'c:\workshop\winsas\prog1';
```

Go back to the code that was created for Exercise 4 in Chapter 4 and add the appropriate LIBNAME statement.

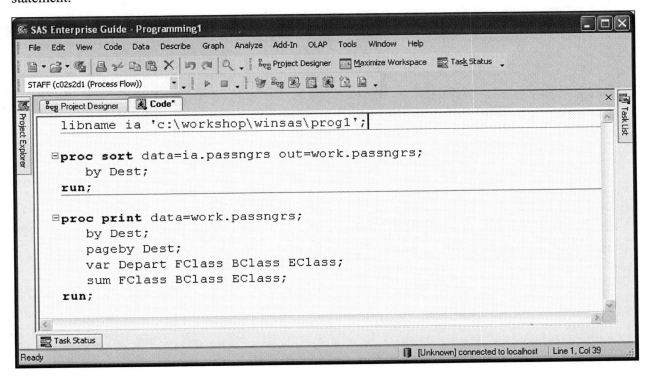

A.13 Renaming a Code Node in the Process Flow Window

Give the created SAS program a formal name.

1. View the process flow by clicking on the **Process Designer** tab at the top of the workspace. New code entries will be named Code, Code2, Code3, and so on, by default. Highlight the newly created code item, right-click, and select **Rename**.

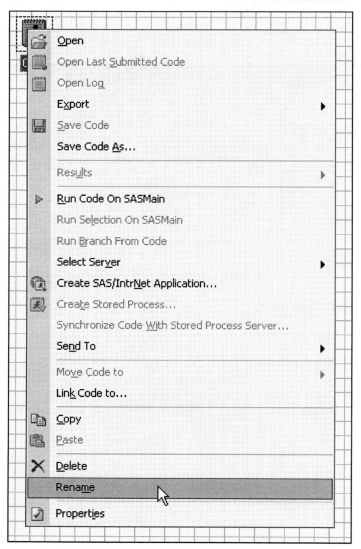

2. Change the name of this code node from **Code1** to **ch4ex4**.

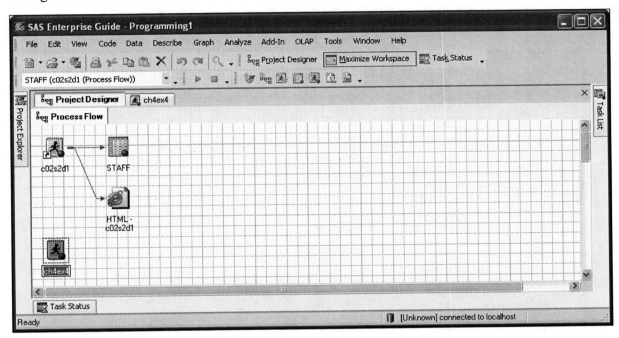

A.14 Submitting Exercise Programs

1. Execute this program (or others like it) by right-clicking on this entry and selecting **Run ch4ex4 On SASMain** from the menu.

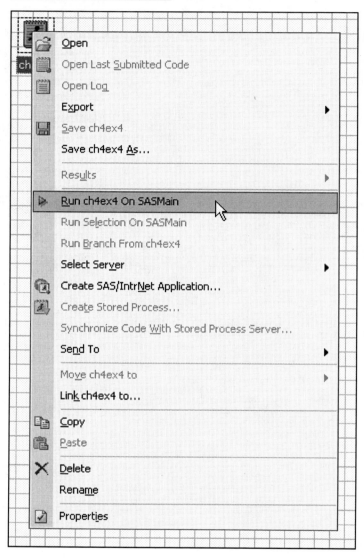

✐   You can also right-click anywhere inside the code window displayed in the workspace and select **Run On SASMain** to submit the code.

2. If the program successfully executes, then the following report appears in the workspace and two new icons associated with Ch4ex4 appear in the Process Flow window. If a red X appears on the code icon for Ch4ex4, then an error occurred and the program must be corrected.

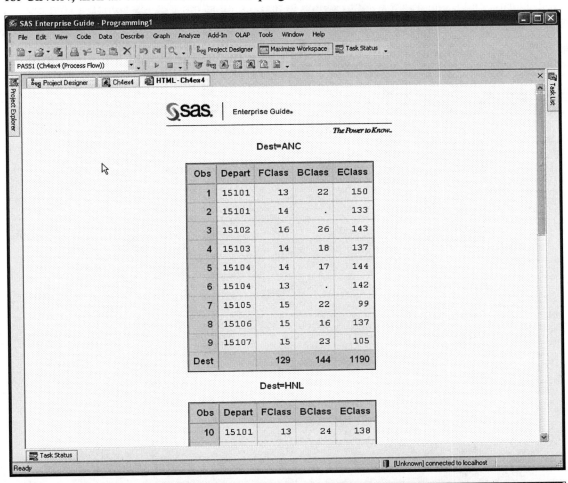

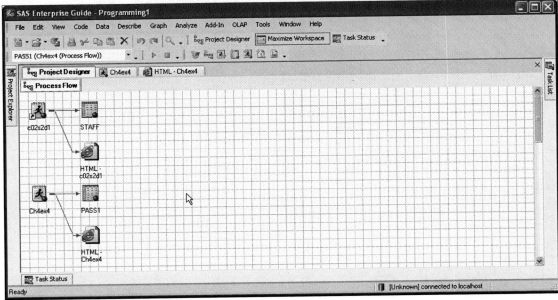

3. The default results produced by SAS Enterprise Guide do not look the same as those produced by default in the SAS windowing environment. By default, SAS Enterprise Guide creates results in HTML format with an ODS style applied. The traditional SAS interface creates text output by default. During class, you might want to switch to text output to more easily compare your exercise results to those displayed in this book.

> The classical listing output can be generated by selecting **Tools** ⇨ **Options** ⇨ **Results Tab**, deselecting **HTML**, and then selecting the **Text output** check box.

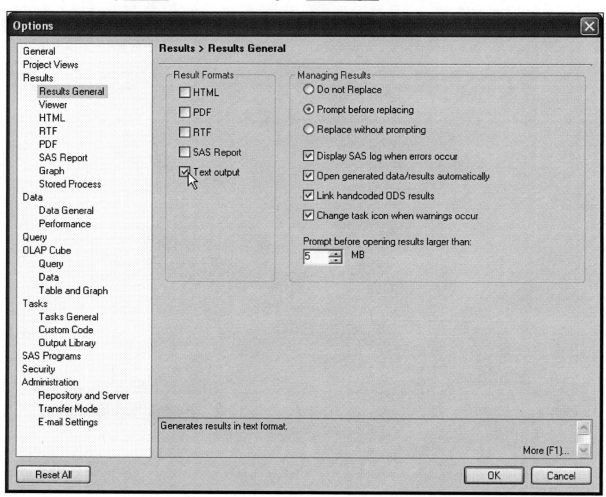

A.15 Saving Projects

Whenever a significant change is made to a project in SAS Enterprise Guide, it is a good idea to save the current contents.

From the SAS Enterprise Guide menu bar, select **File** ⇨ **Save Programming1**.

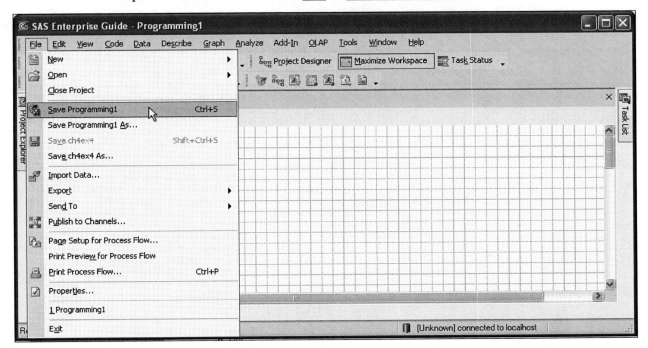

A.16 The Output Delivery System and SAS Enterprise Guide

At several points in the course exercises, you are asked to create results in HTML format using the Output Delivery System (ODS). In the traditional SAS windowing environment, this is achieved using programming statements. By default, SAS Enterprise Guide uses ODS to create HTML output with no coding required. Therefore, you can decide to skip the exercises pertaining to this topic.

A.17 Copying SAS Programs within a Project

1. Some of the exercises created during one part of the course are used as the starting point for the next. To create a new code node, right-click on an existing node. A menu appears. Scroll down in the menu and select **Copy**.

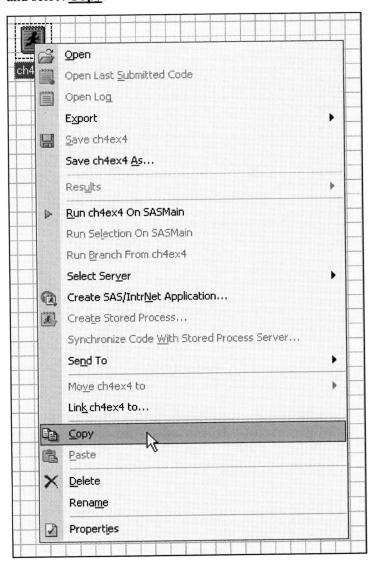

2. Move the mouse to any location on the process flow, right-click, and select **Paste** from the menu. This creates a new code item with the same name as the original.

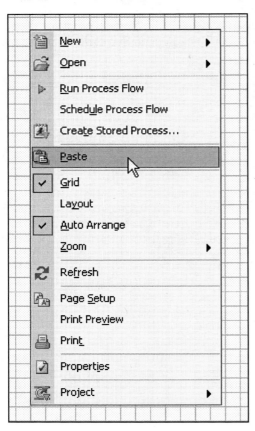

3. To rename the copy of the code used for the next exercise, right-click on the code in the Process Flow window. Select **<u>Rename</u>** from the menu. Backspace over the copy of the program and type the name **Ch5ex1**. The first exercise in Chapter 5 can use the code from Chapter 4 as a starting point.

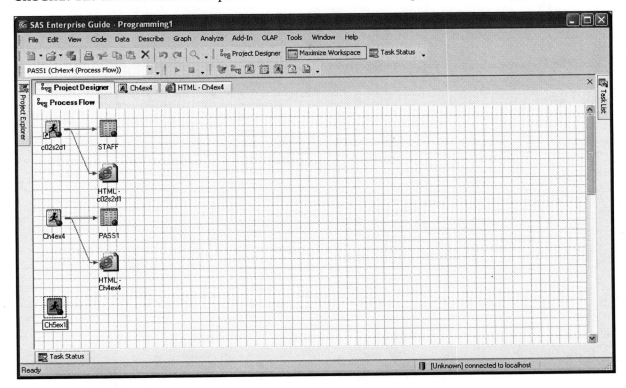

4. Save the current contents of your project.

Appendix B Introduction to Graphics Using SAS Enterprise Guide

B.1 Introduction to Graphics Using SAS Enterprise Guide

Appendix A documented the steps to complete the SAS Programming I course exercises using the SAS Enterprise Guide interface by developing and submitting code. However, in many instances the same results can be achieved using the interactive menus in SAS Enterprise Guide. This section documents the steps necessary to create the graphical exercises from Chapter 10 of the course using a point-and-click rather than a programmatic approach.

This appendix was prepared using SAS Enterprise Guide 4.1. Menus and screens for other versions of SAS Enterprise Guide will differ somewhat.

Before beginning these exercises, be certain that your IA library is defined in your current SAS Enterprise Guide project. Launch SAS Enterprise Guide, and create and name a new project. Create a new code item containing the appropriate LIBNAME statement to define the IA library. Submit the code.

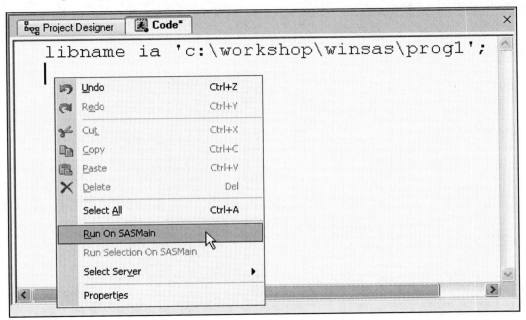

See Appendix A for information on creating projects and code items and submitting code.

This LIBNAME statement points to the default data path for the Programming I course. If your instructor has specified a different path, use that instead.

B.2 Exercise 1a: Producing a Vertical Bar Chart

Before beginning this exercise, verify that your IA library is defined as documented in Section B.1.

Use the **ia.person1** data set and a WHERE statement to produce the charts requested below for the ticket agents (**JobCode** values of TA1, TA2, and TA3).

```
where JobCode in ('TA1', 'TA2', 'TA3');
```

Produce a vertical bar chart that displays the number of male and female ticket agents. (**Gender** values are M and F.)

1. In order to use the interactive SAS Enterprise Guide task dialog boxes and wizards, bring the data of interest into the project. From the menu, select **File** ⇨ **Open** ⇨ **Data**.

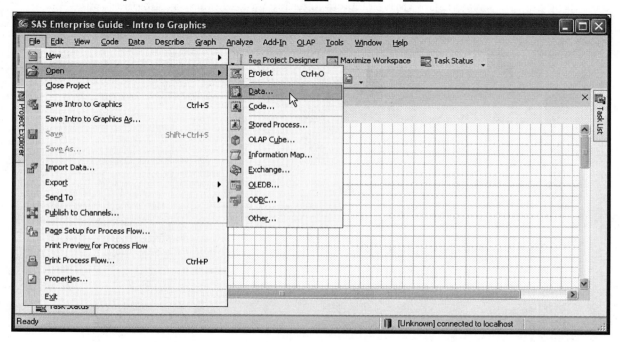

2. The Open Data From dialog box appears. Select **SAS Servers** to select a data source in the IA library.

✎   The default location for the IA library is on the local network. In such a case, you could also select **Local Computer** and navigate to the directory (for example, c:\workshop\winsas\prog1) to select a data source.

3. Your server list contains a single server named SASMain by default. Highlight the displayed server name and select **Open**.

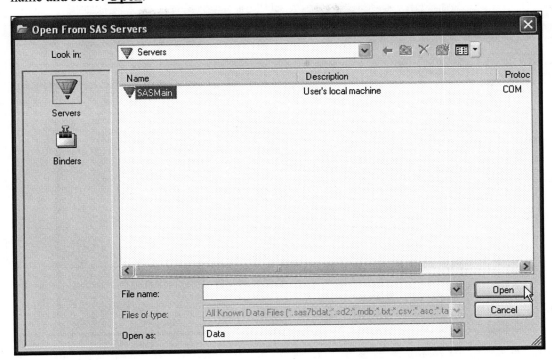

4. Highlight the **Libraries** icon and select **Open** to see a list of SAS data libraries defined on the server.

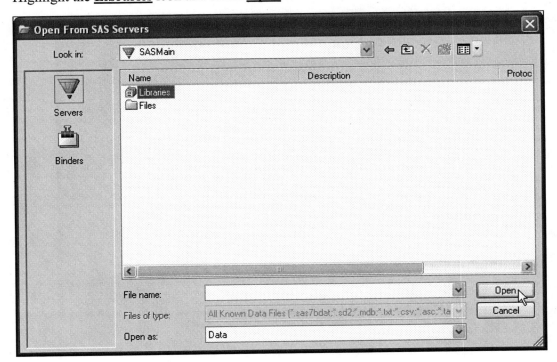

5. A list of libraries defined on the server is displayed. Highlight the **IA** library and select **Open**.

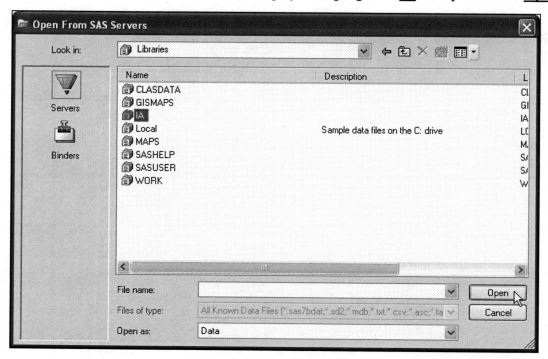

6. A list of data sets in the IA library is displayed. Scroll down to find the **PERSONL** data set, highlight the data set, and select **Open**.

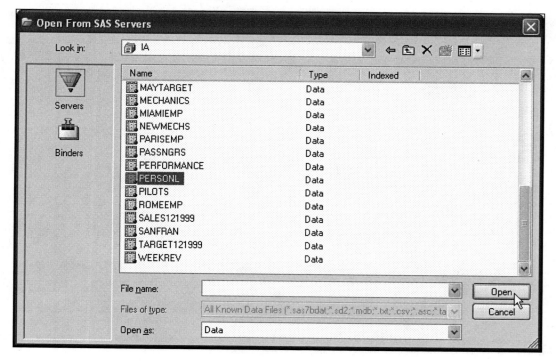

7. An icon representing the **PERSONL** data set now appears in the Project Explorer window, and a snapshot of the data is displayed in the workspace.

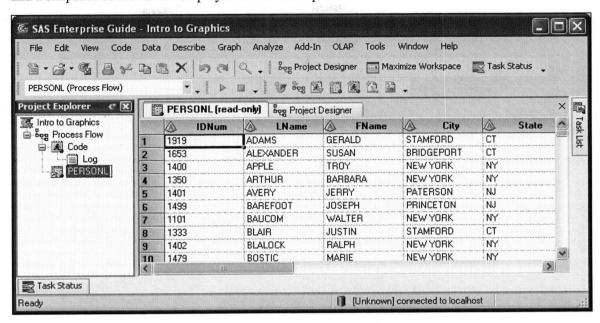

✏ If you maximized the Workspace window, you need to hold your cursor over the Project Explorer tab in order to view the contents of the window.

8. Filter the **IA.PERSONL** data set to include ticket agents only. Highlight the **PERSONL** icon in the Project Explorer window, right-click, and select **Filter and Query...**.

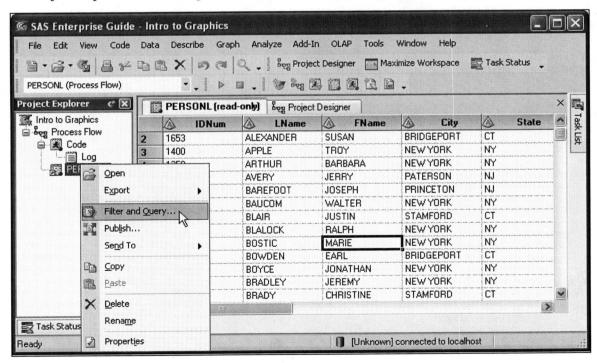

9. The Query Builder opens. The Query Builder enables you to extract data from one or more data sets according to criteria that you specify.

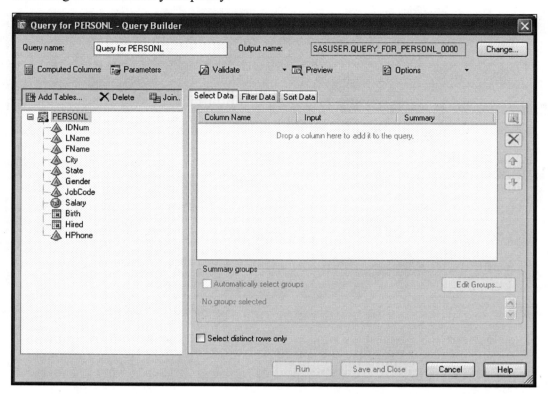

10. The default names for the Query Task to be displayed in the SAS Enterprise Guide interface and for the output data set to be created appear at the top of the window. To give the query a more meaningful name, type **Ticket Agent Query** in the `Query name` field.

11. Specify the library and name for the output table by selecting [Change...] next to Output Name.

12. To change the library in which to save the data set, select the down arrow next to Save in and select **Libraries**.

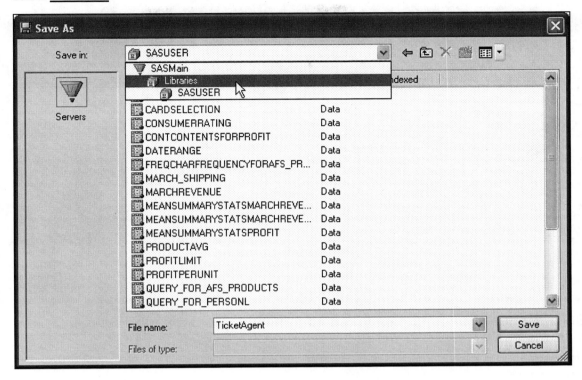

13. Double-click to select **IA**.

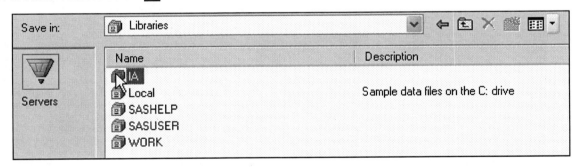

14. Type **TicketAgent** in the `File name` field and select **<u>Save</u>**.

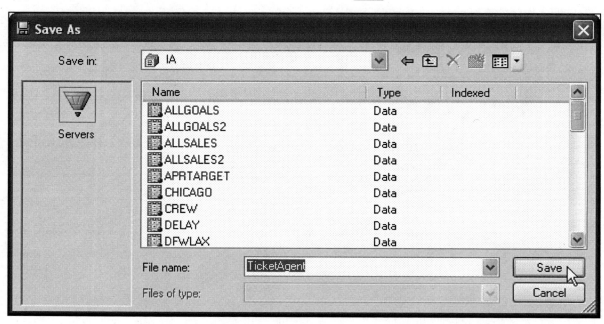

15. The Save As window is closed, and the new data set name appears at the top of the Query Builder window.

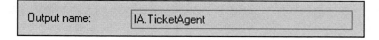

16. The Select Data tab enables you to specify the variables to be included in the query result. To include all of the variables from **IA.PERSONL**, highlight the data set name, right-click, and select **Add All Columns to Selection**. The list of columns appears in the Select Data tab.

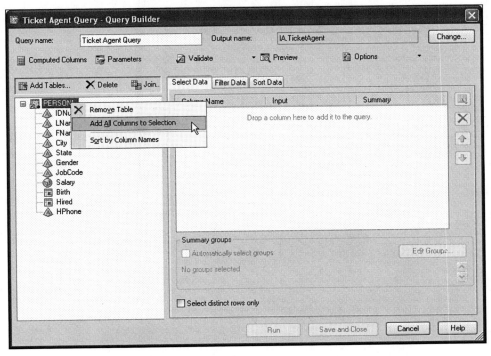

🖉   You can also drag and drop individual variables into the Select Data window.

17. To specify a filter for ticket agents only, select the **Filter Data** tab. Highlight the variable **JobCode** in the list of available variables on the left, and drag it into the box labeled Filter the raw data.

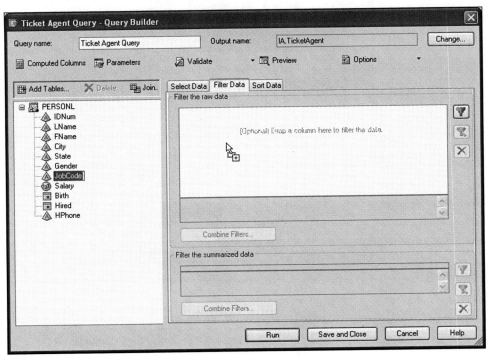

18. The Edit Filter window opens. Click the down arrow next to **<u>Operator</u>** and select **<u>In a list of values</u>**.

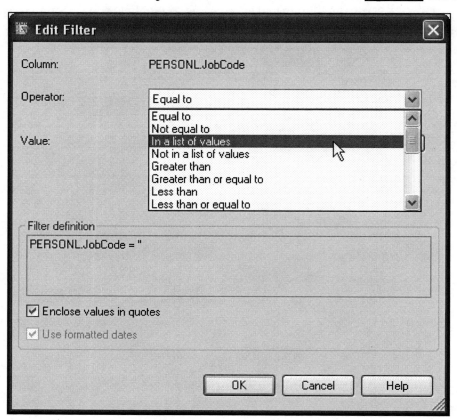

19. To specify the list of values, select **<u>Add</u>** ⇨ **<u>Get Values</u>**.

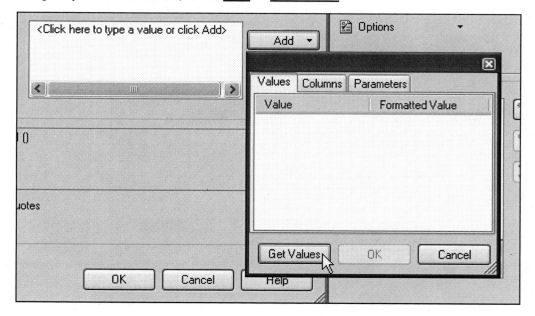

20. The window is populated with a list of the values of the **JobCode** variable. Scroll down and select the ticket agent codes of interest, **TA1**, **TA2**, and **TA3**. Select **OK** ⇨ **OK** to complete the filter definition.

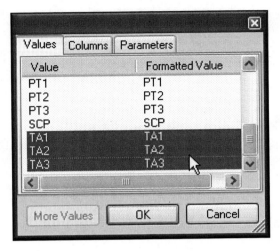

🖉   Hold down the Shift or CTRL key to make multiple selections in the Values window.

21. The query definition is complete. Select **Run**.

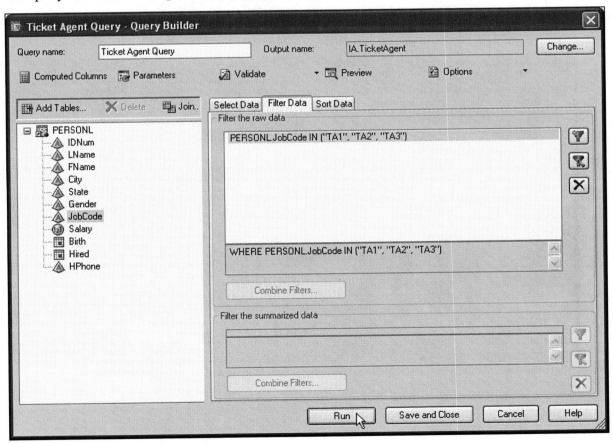

Icons representing the query task and the associated code, log, and output data set appear in the Project Explorer window. A snapshot of data from the **IA.TicketAgent** data set is opened in the workspace.

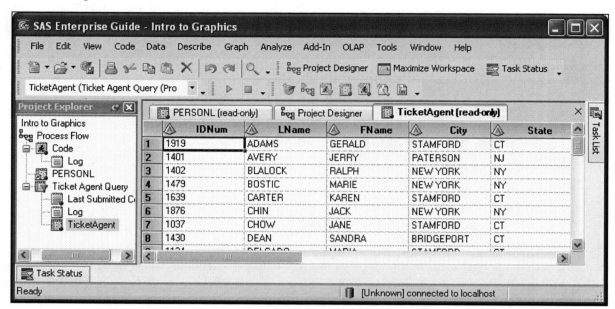

22. To create a bar chart based on the **TicketAgent** data set, highlight the data set icon in the Project Explorer window and select **Graph** ⇨ **Bar Chart…**.

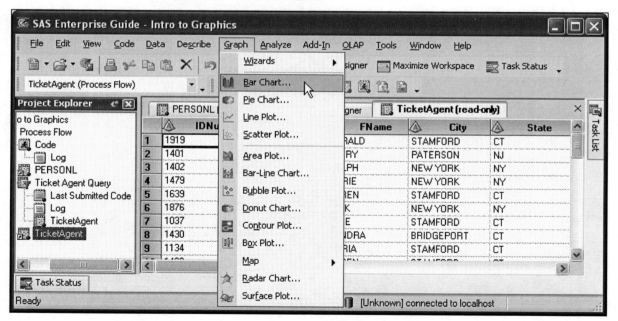

23. The Bar Chart task dialog box opens. Options for creating the bar chart are grouped into sections or *panes* along the left of the dialog box. The Bar Chart pane, which enables you to select the general form of the chart, is presented first. Select **Simple Vertical Bar**.

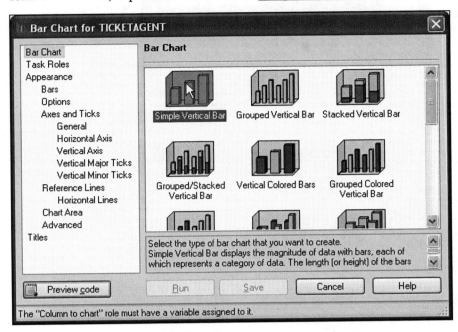

24. Select the **Task Roles** pane at the left of the window to specify how variables from the **TicketAgent** data set will be used in creating the chart. The Task Roles pane shows a list of available variables from the selected data set on the left, and a list of available roles for the Bar Chart task on the right. To assign a variable to a role, highlight it in the list and then drag and drop it onto the desired role.

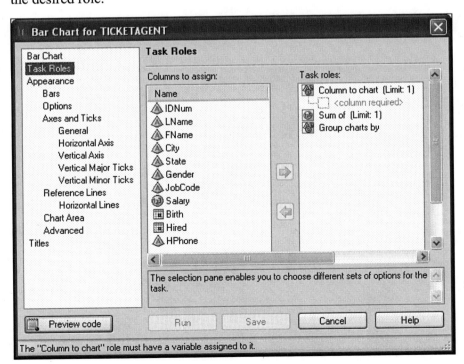

25. The chart that you will create has a bar for each gender value. Therefore, **Gender** is the column to chart. Highlight **Gender** and drag it onto the Column to chart role.

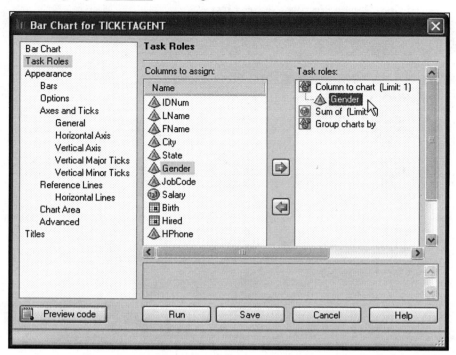

26. You specified all of the information necessary to create a bar chart. The settings in the other panes can remain at their default values. Select **Run**.

27. When the task runs successfully, icons representing the task, code, log, and results for the bar chart are added to the Project Explorer window under the node for the **TicketAgent** data set, and a report showing the results is opened in the workspace.

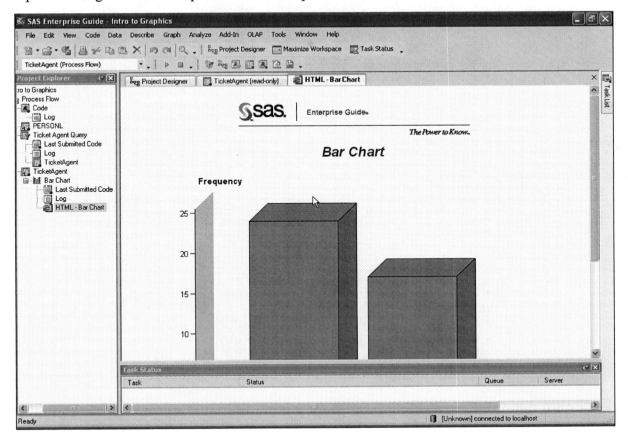

B.3 Exercise 1b: Modifying the Bar Chart

Modify the bar chart task created in Exercise 1a to save the result as an ActiveX image within an HTML document. Add an appropriate title.

1. By default, SAS Enterprise Guide creates results in HTML format using a default ODS style, and the default graphic format is an interactive ActiveX graphic. You can generate similar images as static pictures using the ActiveX image format. As presented in Chapter 10, you can control the type of image created in the SAS windowing environment using programming statements. In SAS Enterprise Guide, you can also control the output and graphic formats using the interactive menus. To modify the graphic format for this bar chart (leaving the default settings as is), highlight the **Bar Chart** task icon in the Project Explorer, right-click, and select **Properties**.

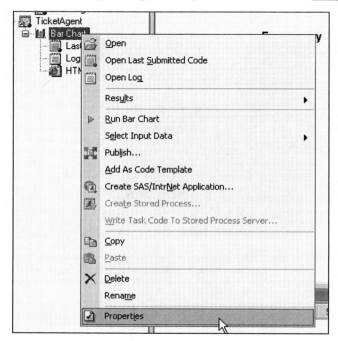

✎   See Chapter 10 for more information on the differences between the interactive and static ActiveX and Java graphics, and for details on the steps necessary to distribute the interactive graphics.

2. Select the **Results** pane, and then check the box next to **Override the preferences set in Tools →
    Options**. Click on the down arrow next to Graphic Format, and select **ActiveX image (SAS V9)**.
    Select **OK**.

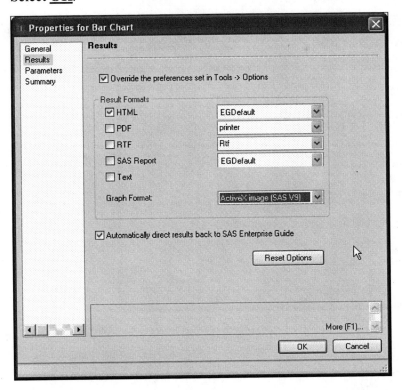

3. To modify the title for the chart, right-click on the **Bar Chart** task in the Project Explorer window
    and select **Open**.

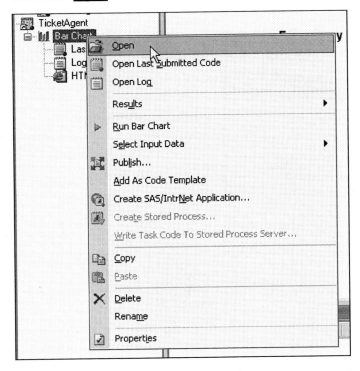

4. The bar chart task reopens, with the previous settings retained. Select the **Titles** pane.

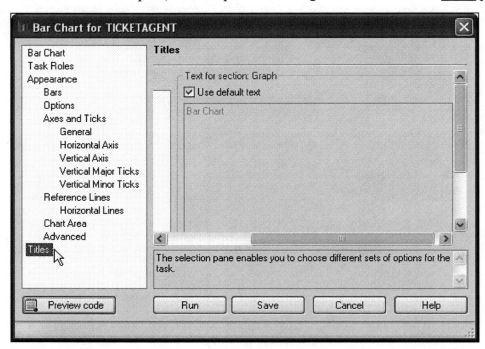

5. Select **Graph** in the Section window. Uncheck **Use default text**, and enter an appropriate title.

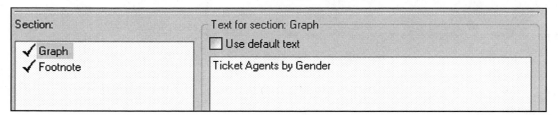

6. Select **Run**, and then select **Yes** to replace the results from the previous run.

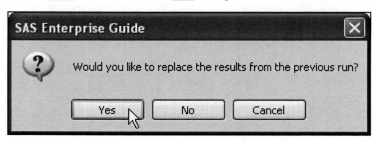

7. The updated results reflect the new title. The updated graphic looks much like the previous version, but it is a static image rather than an interactive chart.

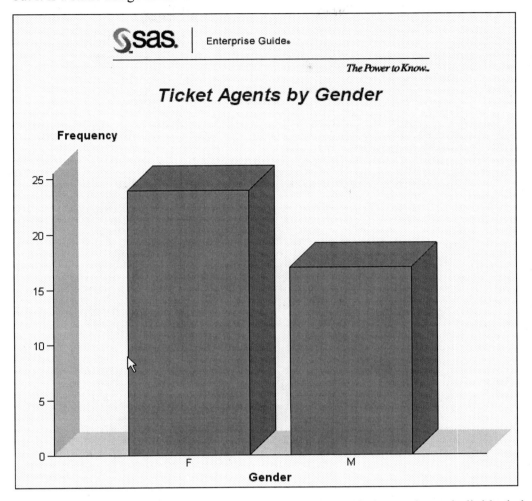

8. In the previous exercise, you saw how to modify the graphic image for an individual chart. To change the default graphic format for all images, select **Tools** ⇨ **Options...**.

9. From the list on the left side of the Options window, select **Graph**. Click the down arrow to the right of the Graph Format box to see a list of the available choices. Changing the image type here sets the default for all future graphs. The format for individual graphs can be altered by modifying the properties for the given task as shown previously.

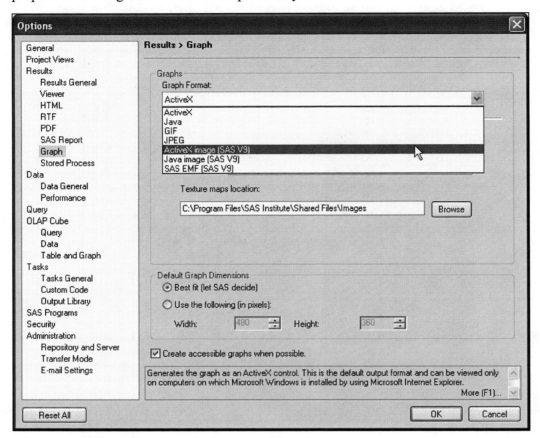

10. Select **Cancel**. Maintain ActiveX as the default image type.

B.4 Exercise 1c: Creating a Pie Chart

Before beginning this exercise, make sure that the IA library is defined as documented in Section B.1. This exercise uses the **TicketAgent** data set created in Exercise 1a. If you did not complete that exercise, you must perform the steps necessary to create the data set, prior to starting this exercise.

Create a pie chart to compare the salaries of each ticket agent job level. Each pie slice should represent the average salary for one of the three **Jobcode** values. Send the output to an HTML document containing the pie chart as a static JAVA image. Use the banker ODS style, and add an appropriate title. Explore the interactivity of the graph in the completed HTML document.

1. Highlight the **TicketAgent** data set in the Project Explorer window and select **Graph** ⇨ **Pie Chart...**.

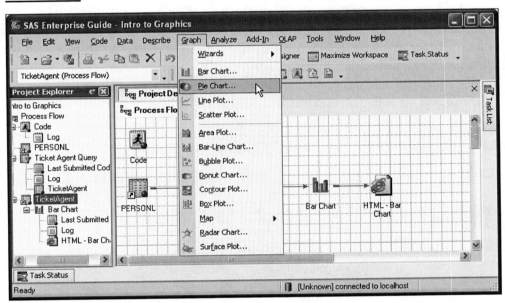

2. Select **Simple Pie** as the chart type.

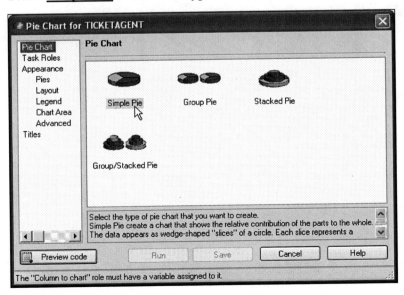

3. In the Task Roles pane, drag **JobCode** onto the Column to chart role and **Salary** onto the Sum of role.

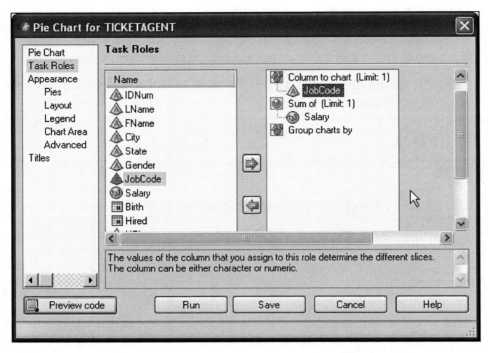

4. Select the **Advanced** pane. Click the down arrow under **Statistic used to calculate slice** and select **Average**.

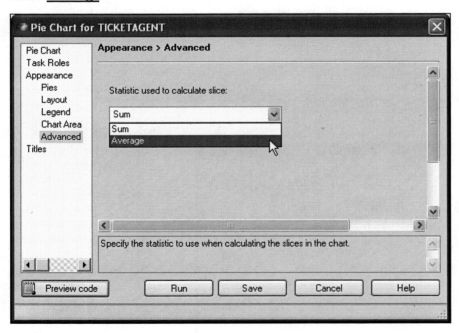

5. Select the **Titles** pane and then the **Graph** section. Deselect **Use default text**. Enter an appropriate title. Select **Save** to save the settings without running the task.

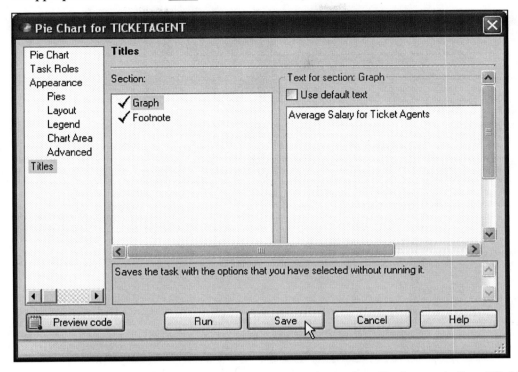

6. An icon representing the Pie Chart task appears in the Project Explorer window. Highlight the task, right-click, and select **Properties**.

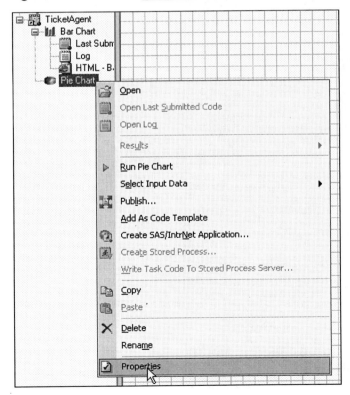

7. Select the **Results** tab, and then check the box next to **Override the preferences set in Tools →
    Options**. Click the drop-down arrow next to **HTML** to select the **Banker** ODS style.

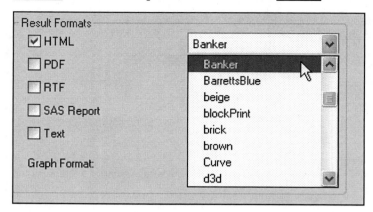

8. Click the drop-down arrow next to **Graph Format** to select **Java image (SAS V9)**.

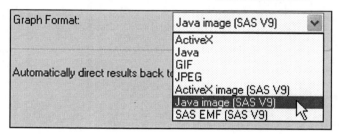

9. Select **OK**.

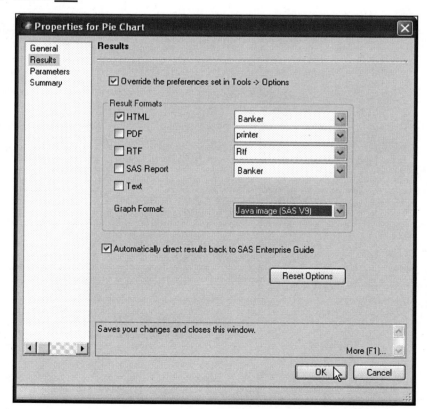

10. Highlight the icon in the Project Explorer, right-click, and select **<u>Run Pie Chart</u>**.

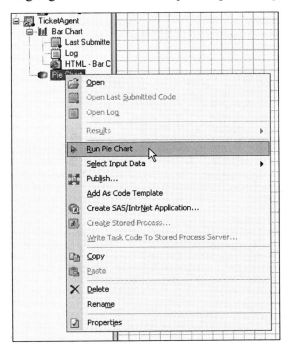

11. The HTML results appear in the workspace.

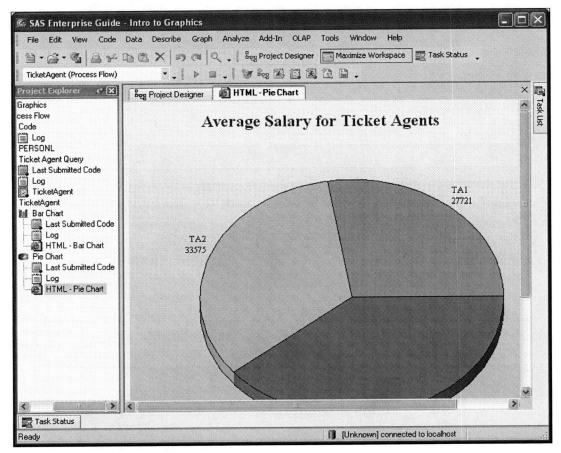

B.5 Exercise 1d: Modifying the Pie Chart

Enhance the pie chart created in Exercise 1c by exploding the slice that represents the TA3 value of **JobCode**. Change the font color for the title to red.

Some advanced options are not enabled within the SAS Enterprise Guide interface. For example, it is not possible to explode a pie slice or change the title color using the interactive menus.

1. Modify the code generated by SAS Enterprise Guide to achieve the customizations. Highlight the **Pie Chart** task in the Project Explorer window, right-click, and select **Open Last Submitted Code**.

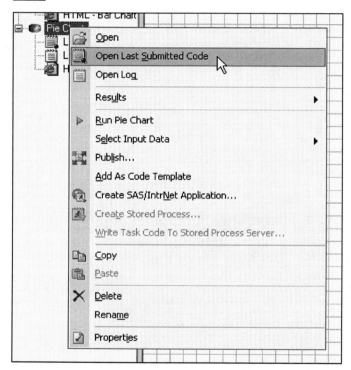

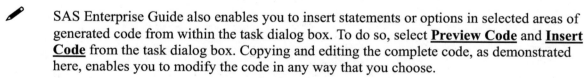   SAS Enterprise Guide also enables you to insert statements or options in selected areas of generated code from within the task dialog box. To do so, select **Preview Code** and **Insert Code** from the task dialog box. Copying and editing the complete code, as demonstrated here, enables you to modify the code in any way that you choose.

2. The code generated by SAS Enterprise Guide is opened in the workspace.

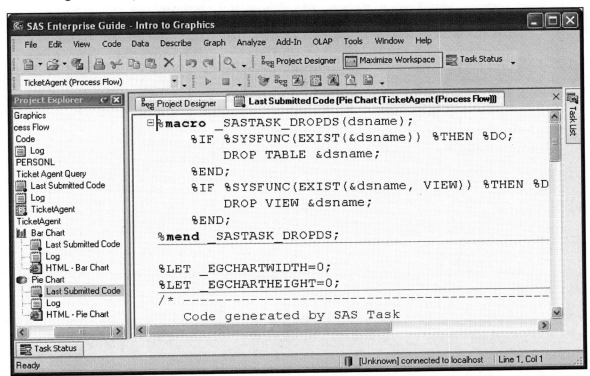

3. This version of the code cannot be edited. To create a copy that can be modified, type anywhere in the Last Submitted Code window. Select **Yes** in the dialog box.

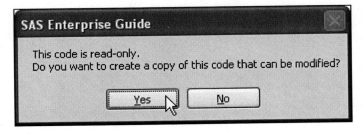

4. A new code icon appears in the Project Explorer window, and the copy opens in the workspace. The code is named **Code for Pie Chart** by default. If desired, you can rename it as shown in Appendix A. Scroll down to find the TITLE statement and add the text **c=red** before the quoted title text.

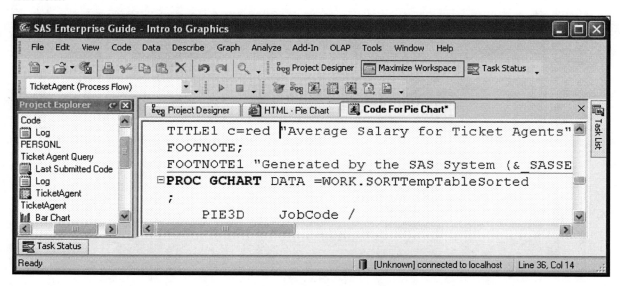

5. Scroll down to find the PIE3D statement. Add a new line after the slash (/) to specify **EXPLODE='TA3'**.

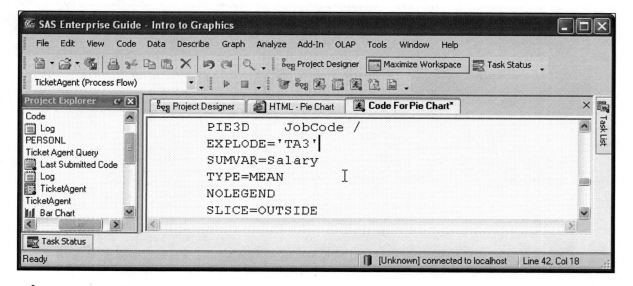

The PIE3D statement is an alternative to the PIE statement. It creates a three-dimensional pie chart.

6. To run the code, right-click on the code icon in the Project Explorer window and select **Run Code For Pie Chart On SASMain**. (Substitute the name of your server for SASMain if you are using a different server.)

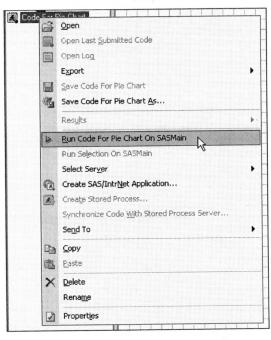

7. The HTML results are opened in the workspace. Confirm that the title appears in red and that the TA3 pie slice is exploded.

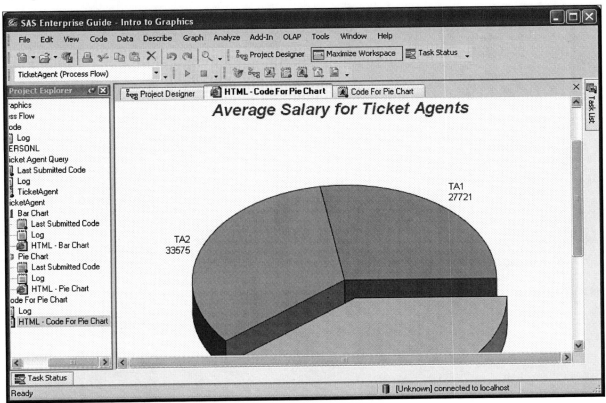

B.6 Exercise 2: Producing a Horizontal Bar Chart

Before beginning this exercise, verify that the IA library is defined as documented in Section B.1.

Use the **ia.chicago** data set to produce a horizontal bar chart that displays the total number of passengers boarded (**Boarded**) each day of the week. Create a new variable, **Day**, which contains the day of the week, where 1 represents Sunday, 2 represents Monday, and so on.

- Specify the GIF file format for the chart.
- Place an appropriate title on the chart.
- Use the label **Day of the Week** for the variable **Day** and the label **Passengers** for the variable **Boarded**.

If the chart did not generate seven bars, add the DISCRETE option to the HBAR statement and generate the chart again.

In SAS Enterprise Guide, you can use your own SAS programs in combination with the point-and-click menus to achieve the desired result.

1.   Write a program to generate the data set required for the chart. Use the point-and-click approach to create the chart.

2.   Create a new code item in the project by selecting **File** ⇨ **New** ⇨ **Code**.

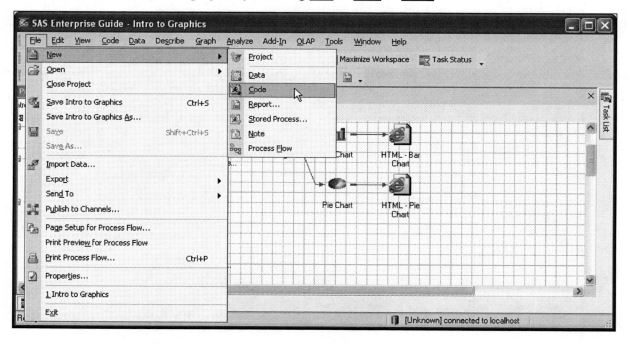

3. Type the code to create a new data set from **ia.chicago**. The new data set should contain a variable for the day of the week.

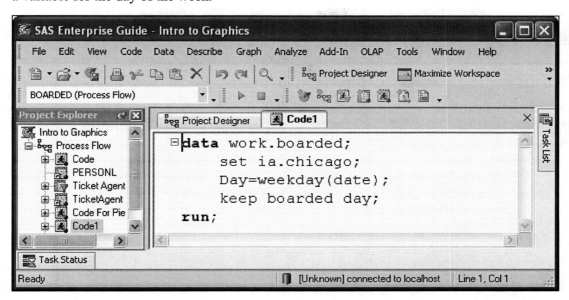

✏️ You can also create new variables within the Query Builder.

4. To submit, right-click on the **Code1** icon and select **Run Code1 On SASMain**.

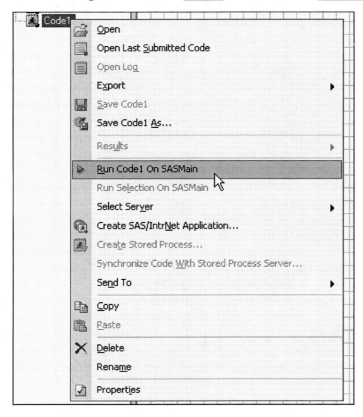

✏️ The default names for added code items are Code, Code1, Code2, and so on. You might see a different name than shown above, depending on the number of code items in your project.

5. If the code runs successfully, an icon representing the created data set appears in the Project Explorer window, and a snapshot of the data is opened in the workspace. Highlight the icon for the created data set, and then launch the Bar Chart task by selecting **Graph** ⇨ **Bar Chart...**.

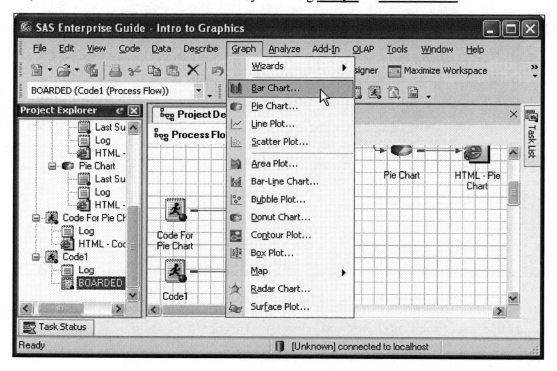

6. The Bar Chart task dialog box opens. On the Bar Chart pane, select **Simple Horizontal Bar**.

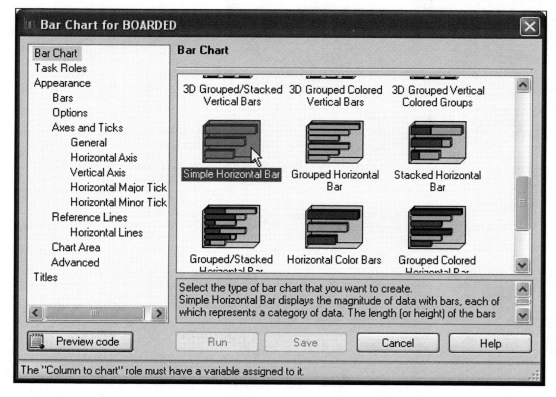

7. On the Task Roles pane, drag **Day** onto the Column to chart role and **Boarded** onto the Sum of role.

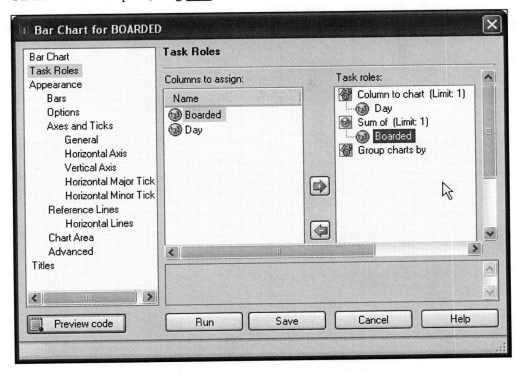

8. On the Horizontal Axis pane, specify the label **Passengers**.

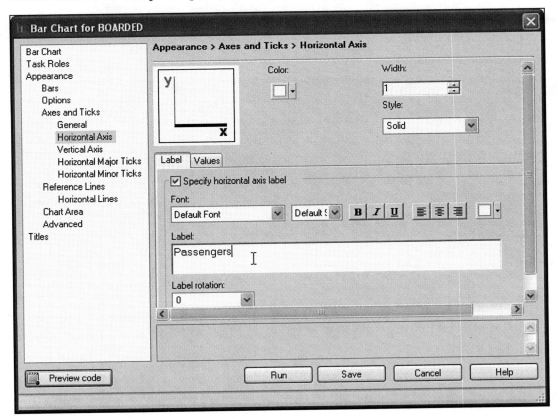

9. On the Vertical Axis pane, specify the label **Day of the Week**.

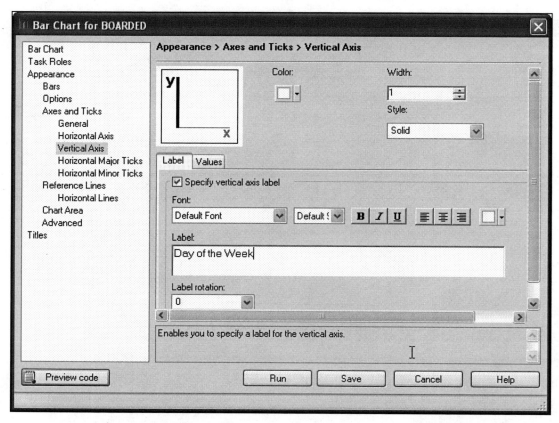

10. On the Titles pane, highlight the **Graph** section and deselect the **Use default text** check box. Enter an appropriate title and select **Save**.

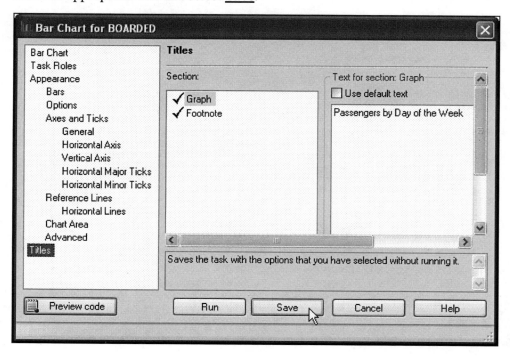

11. An icon representing the Bar Chart task appears in the Project Explorer window. Highlight it, right-click, and select **Properties** to create the graphic image as a GIF.

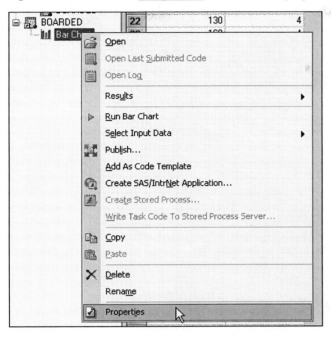

12. The Properties window opens. On the Results pane, check the box next to **Override the preferences set in Tools → Options**. In the drop-down box next to Graph Format, select **GIF**. Select **OK**.

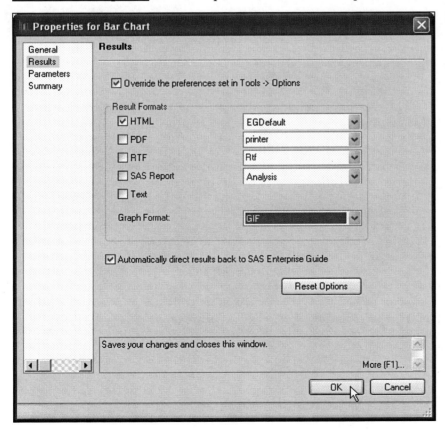

13. To run the Bar Chart task, right-click on the icon in the Project Explorer window and select **<u>Run Bar Chart</u>**. The results open in the workspace.

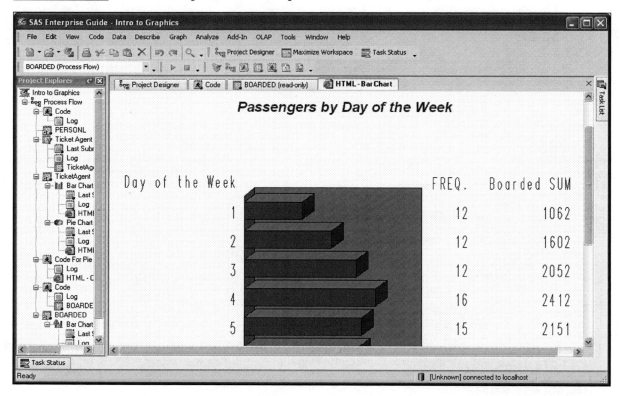

B.7   Exercise 3: Producing a Two-Dimensional Plot

Before beginning this exercise, verify that the IA library is defined as documented in Section B.1.

The data set **ia.delay** contains dates and delays in minutes for International Airlines flights. Use the data set and an appropriate WHERE statement to select flights to Copenhagen (**Dest='CPH'**) and produce the plot described below:

- Create the plot in ActiveX format within an HTML document.
- Use the ODS style named **Normal**.
- Plot the delays on the vertical axis and the dates along the horizontal axis.
- Adjust the scale on the vertical axis to start at **−15** and end at **30** with a tick mark every **15** minutes.
- Display the title **Flights to Copenhagen** in red.
- Display the points as red squares.
- Use the NEEDLE interpolation technique to connect the points to the horizontal axis.

1. Include the **IA.DELAY** data set in the project. Select **File** ⇨ **Open** ⇨ **Data**. From the menu, select **SAS Servers**. Select the **SASMain** server, and navigate to the IA library if necessary. Highlight the data set **DELAY** and select **Open**.

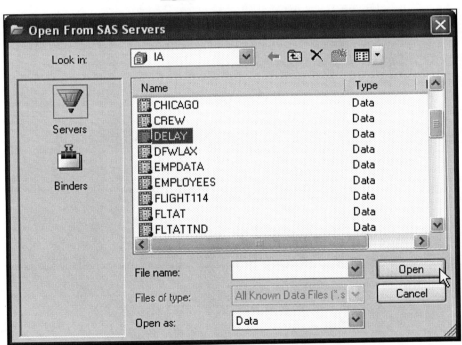

2. An icon representing the **DELAY** data set appears in the Project Explorer window. Highlight the icon, right-click, and select **<u>Filter and Query</u>**. The Query Builder opens. Name the query **Copenhagen Destination Query**. Specify that the query result be saved in the IA library with a table name of Copenhagen by selecting **<u>Change...</u>**, navigating to the IA library, and typing **Copenhagen** as the filename.

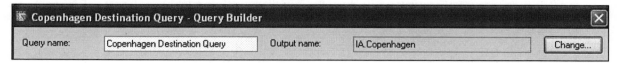

3. Specify that the columns **Date** and **Delay** be included in the query result by dragging and dropping these variables from the list of available columns onto the **<u>Select Data</u>** tab.

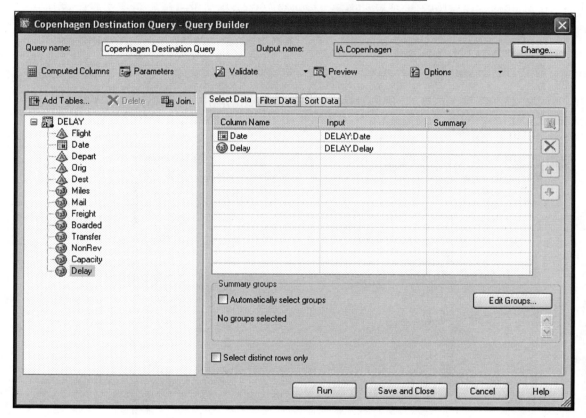

4. Limit the results to flights to Copenhagen by creating a filter. Select the **Filter Data** tab. Drag the variable **Dest** onto the window labeled Filter the Raw Data. In the Edit Filter dialog box, accept the default operator of **Equal to**. Type **CPH** in the Value box. Make sure that the box next to **Enclose values in quotes** is checked. Select **OK**.

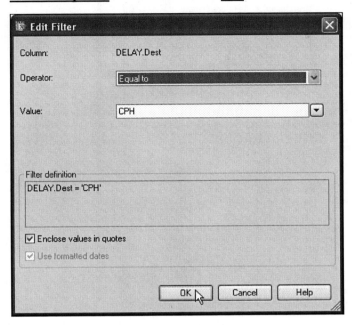

The value typed must match the desired values of the variable **Dest** exactly. If you are not sure how the values are stored in the source data set(s), you can select the down arrow next to the value box, and then select **Get Values** to choose from a list of values.

5. Select **Run** to process the query. Icons representing the query and associated code, log, and output are added to the Project Explorer window. A snapshot of the **Copenhagen** data set is opened in the workspace. Highlight the icon for the **Copenhagen** data set and select **Graph** ⇨ **Line Plot...**.

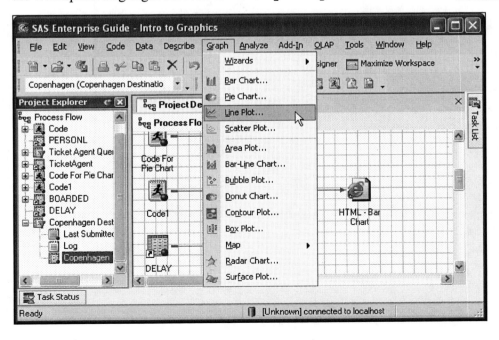

6. In the Line Plot pane, select **<u>Needle Plot</u>**.

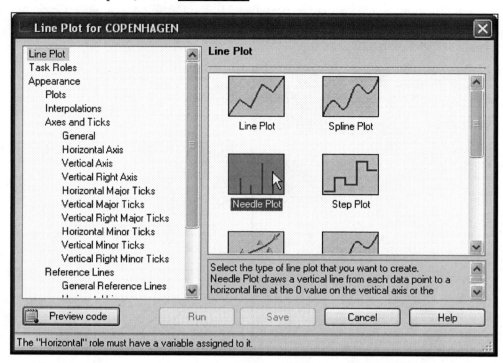

7. In the Task Roles pane, drag **<u>Date</u>** onto the Horizontal role and **<u>Delay</u>** onto the Vertical role.

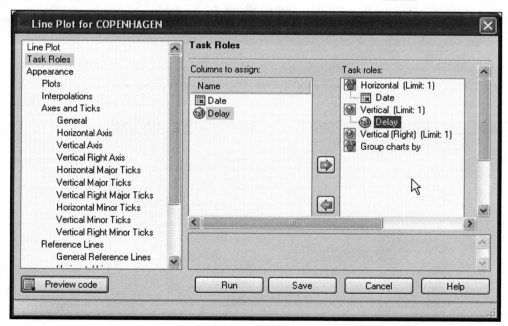

8. Navigate to the **Plots** pane in the **Appearance** section. Under Data point marker, click the down arrow under **Symbol** to select **Square**. Click the down arrow under **Color**, and then click on the red square to choose red.

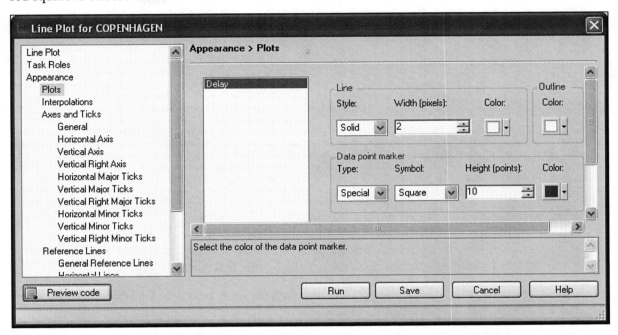

9. Select the **Vertical Major Ticks** pane. In the list of choices under **Major vertical ticks**, click the radio button labeled **Specify**. Then, type **-15 to 30 by 15** in the box next to the Add button. Select **Add**.

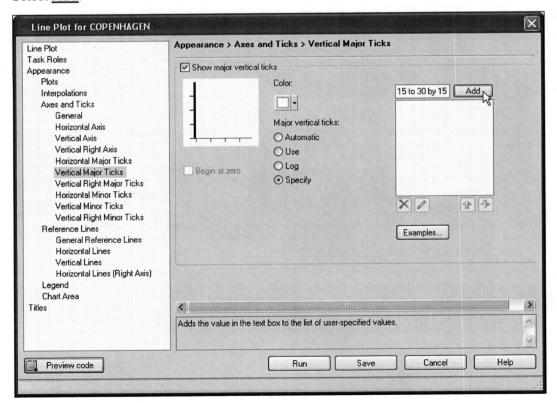

The tick mark specification is added to the window.

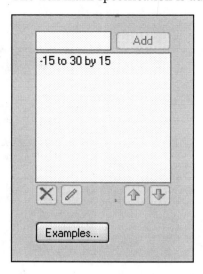

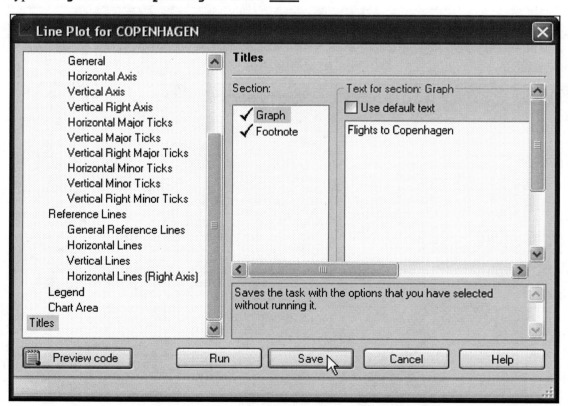

You can enter tick mark specifications as individual values or as ranges, as shown here. Select **Examples...** in the line plot task dialog box for more information.

10. In the **Titles** pane, highlight the **Graph** section. Uncheck the box next to **Use default text** and type **Flights to Copenhagen**. Select **Save**.

11. Highlight the line chart icon that is displayed in the Project Explorer window, right-click, and select **Properties**. In the Results pane, check the box next to <u>**Override the preferences set in Tools →**</u> <u>**Options**</u>. Click the down arrow next to **HTML** to select the **Normal** style. Maintain the default graph format of ActiveX.

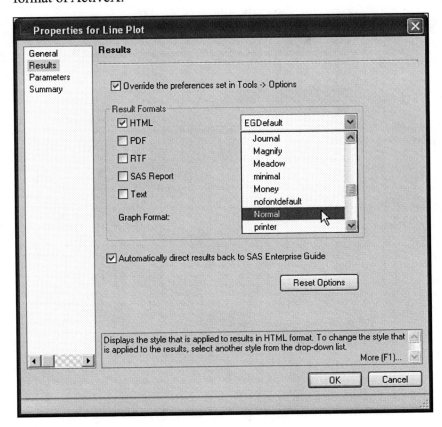

12. Select **OK** in the Line Plot Properties window. Right-click on the **Line Plot** icon and select **Run Line Plot**. The HTML results open in the workspace.

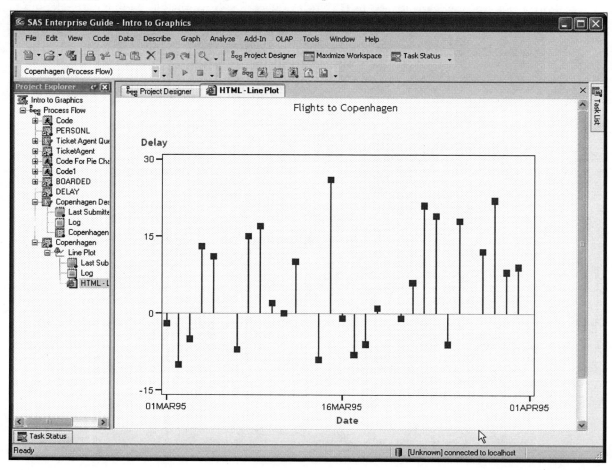

To make the title red, you could modify the code to add the C= option to the TITLE statement as shown in Exercise 1d.

Appendix C Index